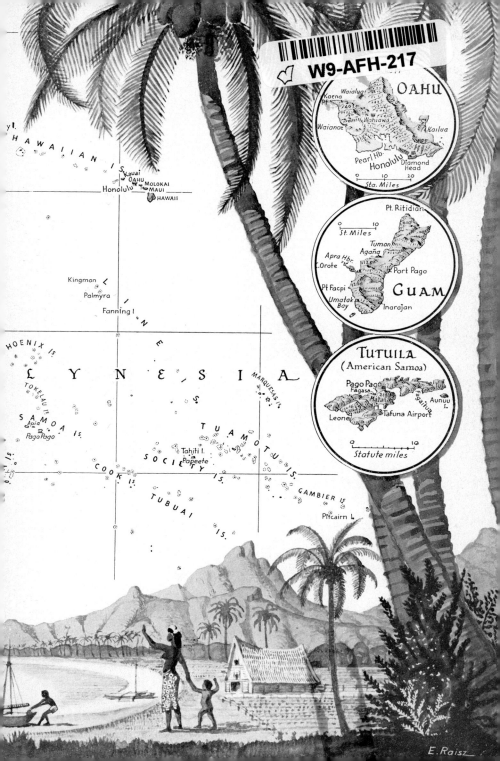

OAHU

Kaena
Pt.
AO1
Waialua
Waianae
Wahiawa
Kailua
Pearl Hb.
Honolulu
Diamond
Head
Waianae
0   10   10
Sta. Miles

GUAM

Pt. Ritidian
0   10
St. Miles
Tumon
Agaña
Apra Hbr.
C. Orote
Port Pago
Pt. Facpi
Umatak
Bay
Inarajan

TUTUILA
(American Samoa)

Pago Pago
Fagasa
Fagaitua
Aunuu
Malai
I.
Leone
Tafuna Airport
0   10
Statute miles

y I.
HAWAIIAN IS.
Kauai
OAHU
MOLOKAI
MAUI
Honolulu
HAWAII

Kingman
Palmyra
Fanning I

HOENIX IS.
POLYNESIA
TOKELAU IS.
SAMOA
Apia
Pago Pago
SAMOA IS.
MARQUESAS IS.
TUAMOTU IS.
Tahiti I.
Papeete
SOCIETY IS.
COOK IS.
TUBUAI IS.
GAMBIER IS.
Pitcairn I.

E. Raisz

THE PACIFIC DEPENDENCIES OF
THE UNITED STATES

THE MACMILLAN COMPANY
NEW YORK · CHICAGO
DALLAS · ATLANTA · SAN FRANCISCO
LONDON · MANILA

BRETT-MACMILLAN LTD.
TORONTO

The Pacific Dependencies

OF THE UNITED STATES

BY

JOHN WESLEY COULTER

PROFESSOR OF GEOGRAPHY
UNIVERSITY OF CINCINNATI

THE MACMILLAN COMPANY · NEW YORK
1957

Library of Congress catalog card number: 57-9543

To my wife, FRANCES MAVOURNEEN,
whom I met on a Pacific island,
and our children, SARAH ANNE,
MARGARET STEWART, and ALAN WESLEY,
who have not yet seen the Pacific

Preface

THIS book, the result of thirteen years of residence, research, and travel among the native peoples of the Pacific Islands, includes studies of all the indigenous populations in the Pacific administered by the United States. Shortly after I joined the staff of the University of Hawaii, in 1928, I became interested in the use of land by Polynesians in Manoa Valley, a mile away. I made a detailed survey of that area and also of other districts in the islands which were still inhabited by the indigenous people. The Hawaiians, a minority, get more space in this book than the other people in that Territory because of the significance of their history and experience in connection with the government of similar native populations still in a primitive stage in other parts of the Pacific.

In 1937 I spent four months in American Samoa under the auspices of the Navy and the University of Hawaii, with a mission there to study land utilization and problems of increase in population. I went to Fiji in that year also, to study the progress of a large-scale experiment to establish Fijians on land as peasant farmers; then to New Zealand to visit projects being carried out for the rehabilitation of the Maoris. The first four months of 1938 I spent in Australia, Netherlands East Indies (now Indonesia), Malaya, and India. In the fall of 1940 I went to Fiji again for two months with the Archbold Expedition on the junk-yacht *Cheng Ho*. In January, 1941, I stayed for a short time in Samoa on the way back to Honolulu. Results of studies of these areas have been published in some fifty research monographs, articles, and books.

In 1949 and 1950 I served for a year and a half on the staff of the United Nations as chief of the Pacific-Asia section of the Trusteeship Secretariat. In the summer of 1954 I was a little more than three months in the United States Trust Territory of the Pacific Islands, spending two weeks in Hawaii en route, and two and a half weeks in Guam.

I began with the intention of pursuing a study of land utilization, land tenure, and increase in population on Pingelap Island in the eastern Carolines where a growing pressure of numbers on the means of subsistence in a little coral atoll is causing grave concern. It was suggested that I concentrate on the problem of overpopulation there and in other islands that I would visit. When I arrived on Pingelap, I found a food shortage, for the breadfruit trees had yielded a smaller than normal crop, in part, according to the natives, because of a "blight" which was appearing on the leaves. To add to a discomfiting prospect, a hundred-pound bag of rice which I had shipped from Ponape, for my own use and to trade for other food, "disappeared" and no trace of it could be found. I therefore paid a shorter visit to Pingelap than I had planned; but, on the other hand, I had ample time to visit the three archipelagoes which comprise the United States Trust Territory and to carry on investigations on various islands during stays of from one to three weeks. Sometimes I used opportunities to attend meetings of chiefs and met some of them personally to talk about their problems. On other occasions I made the acquaintance of part-Japanese Micronesians and from them learned about Japanese government of the natives and about the Japanese colonists who settled in the islands.

On arrival on various islands I generally got in touch with the local agriculturist and in many cases accompanied him on his normal rounds; or I accepted invitations from other members of the administration to go with them about their business. The studies of the various parts of the Trust Territory are therefore not exactly parallel. Since some methods of agriculture even in regard to the same plant differ a little from one group of islands to the next, certain aspects of agriculture are associated with one island where the author noted them, and other observations are described for some other island. I have used studies of land utilization and land tenure made by others on a few islands in the Trusteeship area, with due acknowledgment in the references cited. In connection with my study of problems of overpopulation I acknowledge a small grant from the Planned Parenthood Association of New York for assistance in the field.

The success of my trip was due to the great cooperation I received from district administrators of the Trust Territory, and from members of their staffs. To all of them I am very grateful. One I mention especially is Frank E. Midkiff, High Commissioner of the Trust Territory at the time of my visit. Always interested in the natives of the Pacific Islands, Mr. Midkiff has known them and worked with them from his youth. He was largely responsible for my expedition of 1954. Others whose assistance I am glad to acknowledge here are the Honorable John C. Elliott, former Governor of American Samoa, who helped me to bring my information on that archipelago up to date; J. H. Shoemaker, who read the chapters on Hawaii and whose publications on the Territory are listed in the references; the Honorable Vicente C. Reyes, member of the Guam Congress, for reading the chapter on that island; Dr. Alexander Spoehr, of Bernice P. Bishop Museum, Honolulu, for comments on the manuscript of the Marshalls. I am grateful to the Bishop Museum for permission to use material from my monograph on American Samoa. I am very grateful to various members of the administration of the Trust Territory and of American Samoa for reading chapters on those areas. Edwin H. Bryan, Curator of the Bernice P. Bishop Museum, kindly furnished me with a complete list of references on the Trust Territory published since World War II. Only those read in connection with the various chapters are quoted at the end of each. Place names in the Trust Territory follow those of the United States Board on Geographic Names, cumulative decisions 5501, 5502, 5503, except Mortlock (Satawan), although in some cases a name locally and generally accepted is not the one adopted in those decisions. For place names not yet standardised and proper names, the author follows the spelling given in the islands. Last, but not least, I mention Miss Estelle Hunt, for her kind editorial assistance.

JOHN WESLEY COULTER
University of Cincinnati
January 1957.

Contents

xi

Tables

Maps and Climate Graphs

I

Introduction

I LAY on the beach at Waikiki one sunny afternoon watching an old Hawaiian fisherman whose tall, sinewy figure, bronzed in the sunshine, was girt only with scant trunks. His keen eyes peered out into the surf, searching beneath the surface for movement. As he gazed, he slowly lowered his lead-bordered throw net and arranged it in both hands; he crouched, turning sideways for the throw, paused a moment, then deftly pivoted to fling the net far out. It spread in a circle as it whirred through the air, struck the water and sank surrounding a fish. The brown fisherman waded out slowly, secured his struggling catch, and returned with splashing steps.

A Japanese sampan chugged past on its way to fishing grounds near Molokai. Equipped with a Diesel engine, scores of hooks and lines, and a huge icebox, it would return in a day or two loaded with *aku*. The siren of a great white ocean liner roared farewell as it edged away from Honolulu Harbor, while overhead a Pan-American clipper droned toward San Francisco. The old-time Polynesian fisherman, paying no attention to these representatives of modern civilization, silently took his place again near the water's edge to scan the inshore waves.

Few throw-net fishermen are now seen in Hawaii, and few evidences appear of any of the traditional ways of Polynesian life, for a modern American civilization has all but engulfed the brown man's primitive existence. The island of Oahu, with its great business houses, sugar mills, and canneries, is but an extension of the mainland of the United States.

It is disappointing to find one's dreams of island paradises in the

Pacific fading in an atmosphere of modern reality, for nowadays a visitor in the South Seas often searches in vain for neatly thatched native houses, only to find dilapidated huts patched with irregular sheets of galvanized iron, and empty beer bottles instead of brilliant flowers.

Some South Sea people have for so long been in contact with Western forms of civilization that they live little differently from Europeans and Americans. Indeed, modern Hawaiians and part-Hawaiians are in many ways like people in the United States. At the opposite extreme are the natives of Yap, in loincloths and long grass skirts, still considerably removed from contacts with foreigners. Throughout the various archipelagoes governed by the United States people in transitional states of advancement owe their changes to the civilizations of the Occident and the Orient which have played the major roles.

Some people from the West and the East, having lived in America's Pacific Islands for several generations, now regard themselves as old inhabitants. They speak the native languages, like native food, and understand and appreciate indigenous ways of living better than those whose contacts with primitive civilizations have been briefer and less intimate.

The Second World War focused attention upon the Pacific Islands as never before in their history. Shady palm groves were shredded by cannon fire; grassy slopes were pitted with shellholes; trysting places of erstwhile romance were the headquarters of rough-booted Army patrols. Secluded harbors are still strewn with the wrecks of cruisers and merchant vessels. For many natives who entered the armed services of the Allied nations, Army rations replaced native food-stuffs and canvas tents supplanted thatched huts. Many of those who remained at home turned from ancient agricultural patterns to commercial farming, supplying the needs of soldiers temporarily stationed in the islands. The war left sudden, deep imprints of Allied and Axis forces on islands where the influence of West and East had hitherto been little and gradual, and accelerated changes in native peoples so that some of their problems now press for solution.

Our attitudes toward primitive civilizations are changing. Polynesians and other peoples without cities are really highly civilized. They have subtle languages, ingenious arts admirably suited to their environments, well functioning social and political institutions, and

religious practices and ancient myths no better and no worse sub-
stantiated than many that prevail today among peasant communities
in Europe. Western civilization is not essential for South Sea people,
for their future does not depend on adopting it. However, representatives of Occident and Orient have come to stay in our Pacific Islands,
in many of which men of European and Asiatic races now carry on
their business, owning lands and homes and engaging in agriculture,
trade, and commerce. The way of living of the Occident, introduced
in a few islands four hundred years ago, began in others one hundred
and fifty years ago. On scores of the remainder, hitherto little affected,
it came only during World War II.

THE ISLAND HOME

The islands in the Pacific administered by the United States,
classified broadly as "high" volcanic and "low" coral islands, present
the classic contrast of the South Seas. Although islands of moderate
height have been formed in the tropical Pacific in several different
ways, the contrast is likely to be accentuated where mountainous
masses of volcanic origin jut from the ocean, their tops often obscured
in clouds. They are clothed with forests, all abound in food, and all
are remarkable for picturesque scenery.

Atolls, the *motu* or individual islets of which barely rise above the
waves, average about the height of a man above mean sea level.
Life on an atoll is a constant struggle with nature for bare existence.
In a year of drought, when the coconut crop is less than normal, the
natives, having little to fall back upon beyond the fish they catch, live
perilously near the borderline of starvation.

Our coral atolls and our volcanic islands in the Pacific, except two
very small ones, are within the tropics, where the climate is characterized by a uniformly warm temperature and considerable variation in rainfall. During the two or three very hot and occasionally
humid months of the year, the highest temperature rises to about
ninety degrees; only on rare, cool days does it fall below seventy.
Sometimes it is difficult to distinguish the hot from the cool season.
The author remembers one Christmas Day in Honolulu when the
thermometer registered the highest for that year, although December

is in the cool season in Hawaii. In general the nearer the islands are to the equator, the more uniform is the temperature.

Night is the winter of the South Seas, for there is frequently a greater variation in temperature between midday and midnight than between the hot season when the sun is directly overhead and the less hot season when the sun has moved northward or southward. The highest temperature generally occurs between one and two in the afternoon and the lowest between five and six in the morning.

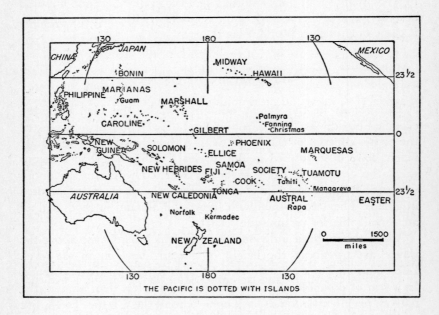

THE PACIFIC IS DOTTED WITH ISLANDS

Cloudy days without a breath of wind are succeeded by spells of fierce, equatorial sunshine; however, strong trade winds frequently temper the heat. On some sultry afternoons drenching tropical showers succeed bursts of sweltering sunshine. After the downpours on volcanic islands, the air in the forests is clammy and a miasmic odor rises from the dank, clayey ground.

The uniformity of climate at sea level on all South Sea islands is largely due to the great expanse of ocean which surrounds them and to the prevailing trade winds, which blow almost continually in the same course from a northeasterly direction in the Northern Hemisphere and southeasterly below the equator. The windward sides of the islands especially benefit from the freshness of the breezes.

Rainfall, the most variable factor in the climate of the South Seas, differs greatly not only from year to year, but from month to month and from day to day. On high volcanic islands the windward sides receive a heavy rainfall, whereas the leeward sides are comparatively dry.

On volcanic islands the heavy rainfall of the windward slopes encourages a dense vegetation, including a great variety of plants. In the well watered parts of the Hawaiian Islands, there is a luxuriant growth of trees, shrubs, ferns, and creepers—many of them flowering plants which constitute one of the charms of the islands.

Atolls receive much less rain than high, volcanic islands, for rain-bearing winds blow over them without losing much of their moisture. In a year of drought the precipitation may be only five or six inches.

Except in Hawaii the genial climate of the islands is occasionally interrupted by hurricanes. These terrific wind and rain storms, generally occurring at the season of the greatest heat, leave ruin in their wake. Usually only one island in a group is devastated; the rest experiencing a gale or a strong wind. Any one island is not likely to be hit more than once in seven to ten years. These storms, in a native phrase, "skin the land," and are often followed by famines. Natives in parts of an island group which have escaped a hurricane take food to the people of devastated areas. Many villages have bread-fruit and bananas preserved in pits against the day when their crops are ruined by the winds and the rains. Samoans frequently lower the dome-shaped roofs of their houses to the ground when threatened by a hurricane and remain under them until the storm is over.

Coral atolls suffer especially from these gales; great combers surge along the beaches, and sometimes the seas sweep entirely across the small islets. The land portion of the atoll is temporarily reduced to a fraction of its former size; the rushing waters clean out the vegetation and only a few coconut stumps remain to mark a former plantation.

The Pacific Ocean is the most important natural feature of the island home of all South Sea people. It not only tempers the climate, but also furnishes them with a slow but essential means of communication between islands and between island groups. Its wide-rolling expanse isolated the archipelagoes from the outside world for thousands of years and allowed the natives to develop their own lives and customs in their own way.

The vast extent of water has furnished South Sea people with an abundant supply of food: open-sea fish, shallow lagoon and other varieties; small ones abounding in pools in the reefs; and shellfish exposed on the rocks and hidden under ledges and blocks of coral. The great isolation which the ocean imposes is partly compensated for by the harvest the sea yields.

THE ACQUISITION OF OUR TERRITORIES

The United States began to acquire dependent peoples in the Pacific near the end of the nineteenth century. The "cession" of the port and harbor of Pago Pago to Commander R. W. Meade, of the *Narragansett*, in 1872, and the Treaty of Washington, signed six years later, constituted the port, to all intents and purposes, the first-born of America's overseas "colonies." These events, moreover, were original symptoms of a long-threatened revolution in national sentiment which was quickened by the war with Spain and which found expression in a policy of expansion.

An epitome of Samoan history during those troubled days will be found in a report, dated May 9, 1894, from Secretary Gresham to President Cleveland:*

It is in our relations to Samoa that we have made the first departure from our traditional and well-established policy of avoiding entangling alliances with foreign powers in relation to objects remote from this hemisphere. If the departure was justified, there must be some evidence of detriment suffered before its adoption or of advantage since gained, to demonstrate the fact. If no such evidence can be found, we are confronted with the serious responsibility of having, without sufficient grounds, imperilled a policy which is not only coeval with our Government, but to which may, in great measure, be ascribed the peace, the prosperity, and the moral influence of the United States.

Apart, however, from such considerations, which Mr. Gresham applied chiefly to the Act of Berlin, the treaty of 1878 claims peculiar attention as the basis on which rested for many years United States rights to Pago Pago, the earliest of America's overseas possessions.

* J. G. Leigh, "America's First and Last Colony," *Forum*, XXIX (1900), 108.

For nearly twenty years, England, Germany, and the United States had been alternately bickering and mending their disagreements over the Samoan archipelago. A tripartite condominium regarding Samoa among Germany, Britain, and the United States lasted for a decade from 1889 and, *inter alia*, proclaimed Samoa neutral territory. It was followed by German and American annexation of the two halves of the archipelago, and then, twenty years later, at the end of World War I, by the turning of the German half into the New Zealand mandate and, at the end of World War II, into a trusteeship.

The eight former German islands were mandated to New Zealand. The island of Tutuila, which had been taken over by the United States of America in 1900, at the same time as the Germans annexed their half, remained an American possession, governed as a naval station by a commandant of the American Navy. The Manua Islands, east of Tutuila, were ceded by their chiefs to the United States in 1904.

The people of the United States did not recognize the ultimate destiny of the Hawaiian Islands until, by intervention on behalf of Cuba, they had involved themselves in the Spanish-American War, which resulted in the acquisition of the Philippines. Then the holding of this remote island territory in the Pacific demanded the possession of the Hawaiian group.

The native Hawaiian government had interfered to check the influx of immigrants from Japan, believing it necessary to the preservation of the islands from Japanese control. Since Hawaii was desirable for the United States Navy as a strategic point of incalculable value to this country, to permit any foreign nation to gain control of the islands was unthinkable. The Hawaiian government had been a constitutional monarchy. The large numbers of foreigners there showed their power in 1887 by forcing a new constitution more favorable to themselves upon the crown. The queen attempted the abolition of this constitution, but drew back before the storm which her action created. Distrusting her, the American element overthrew the queen and set up a government of its own, with the avowed object of annexation to the United States. The idea of annexation was acceptable to President Harrison, and a treaty to secure that object was signed. Before it was ratified by the Senate, however, the administration was changed and the treaty recalled.

Since hope of early annexation was abandoned by the provisional government, steps were immediately taken to establish a republican form of government. A constitutional convention called to meet May 30, 1894, for the purpose of framing a constitution for the Republic of Hawaii, finished its labors on July 3rd, and on the following day the Republic of Hawaii was proclaimed, with Sanford B. Dole as its first president.

After the inauguration of President McKinley in March, 1897, negotiations for annexation of Hawaii to the United States were renewed, and on June 16, 1897, a new treaty providing for annexation was signed at Washington.

At that time the population of Hawaii consisted of 109,000, of whom 31,000 were native Polynesians, 24,000 Japanese, 22,000 Chinese, 15,000 Portuguese, a few hundred Americans, English, and Germans, and the remainder mostly mixed blood.

By the Treaty of Paris, signed December 10, 1898, Spain lost the remaining fragments of her ancient western empire, relinquishing Cuba, which the United States continued temporarily to occupy without holding the sovereignty, pending the orderly establishment of an independent government for the island. Puerto Rico, Guam, and the Philippines were ceded outright to the United States, which agreed to pay $20,000,000 to Spain, and to satisfy the claims of its citizens against that power. By the treaty Congress was to determine the civil rights and political status of the native inhabitants of the ceded territory.

The political status of Puerto Rico was recognized in 1953 as that of a self-governing commonwealth. The Philippine Islands were granted independence on July 4, 1946.

Guam passed through a period of administration under an American naval governor until the United States entered World War II after the Japanese attack on Pearl Harbor. It was occupied by the Japanese from December, 1941, to July 21, 1944, when, reoccupied by United States forces, it was administered by the Navy until 1950. Then it was made an unincorporated Territory of the United States and an organized sovereignty, governed under the Organic Act of Guam, passed by Congress and approved by President Truman on August 1st of the same year. At that time the Department of the Interior took over the administration.

The Trust Territory of the Pacific Islands includes the islands of the former League of Nations "Class C" Mandate administered by

Japan from World War I to the end of World War II. Following the cessation of hostilities, the area was designated a strategic trusteeship by the United Nations, and the United States, under the terms of the Trusteeship Agreement of 1947 with the United Nations, became administering authority. The Agreement established the area as a strategic trusteeship in recognition of those geographic considerations which render its position in the Pacific of vital strategic concern to the United States and to the other nations of the free world in the inhibiting of resurgent aggression. The United States, as administering authority, occupies a privileged strategic position in the islands of the Trust Territory, but in return for that advantage it has voluntarily accepted certain serious obligations for the present and future welfare of the inhabitants. It is with the discharge of these civil functions that the Government of the Trust Territory is concerned.

AMERICAN POLICY

The United States confronts a challenging situation in its relations with these Pacific dependencies. In Hawaii the end of the war brought a renewed and powerful demand for admission into the Union as a State, and there are a number of indications that in Congress, as well as in the executive branch of the Government, the proposal is likely to receive a far more sympathetic hearing in the near future than it has in the past. The strategic importance of Hawaii, sharply underlined during the war, and its contribution to the ultimate victory are cogent arguments in the consideration of its demands. The development of that Territory is already so far advanced that the granting of Statehood would merely be a belated recognition of the political and economic maturity of the islands. Former fears that the Japanese-descended inhabitants of Hawaii would be the main and the untrustworthy beneficiaries of such a move have been largely negated both by the demonstrations of their full loyalty during the war and by the great relative increases in people of other ethnic groups in the islands. The removal of Hawaii from the category of Territories without self-government is a step which should be taken at the earliest possible opportunity.

In the case of Samoa, a change in political status and in the responsible government department is called for. Despite the fact that those islands have been under the jurisdiction of the United States for more than half a century, they have as yet not been accorded any fixed place in the American constitutional firmament. Guam, however, is now well on the way to complete self-government.

The terms of the Trusteeship Agreement under which the United States took over the Japanese mandated islands for the first time give substance to the conception of strategic-area trusteeships which the United States was instrumental in inserting into the United Nations Charter. The extent of American control is almost unrestricted inasmuch as the United States assumes full powers of administration, legislation, and jurisdiction over the Trusteeship Territory and may establish naval, military, and air bases.

On the other hand, there is an acceptance in general terms of the standards and goals of trusteeship as laid down in the Charter and a general recognition of the right of agencies of the United Nations to request and consider reports on the Territory, and to make periodic visits of inspection. The strategic-area aspect is, however, emphasized in the further condition that these rights on the part of the United Nations are subject to the authority of the United States to close off any areas for security reasons.

It is expecting the impossible to think that the peoples of the Trusteeship islands will speedily succeed in mastering the complexities and hazards of a political system which more mature peoples manage only with difficulty. In addition, the new régime in those islands is beginning at a time of economic difficulty which will add its influence to the pressure for strongly centralized administrations.

Western government has brought unquestioned benefits to the islanders. As officials are becoming more and more familiar with native needs, institutions, and psychology, far-reaching reforms are slowly being carried out. The decline in native population has been checked, and in many islands reversed, partly as a result of an increasing natural immunity to disease, but mainly because measures of health and sanitation have introduced better regulated ways of life. The cessation of infanticide, the ending of intertribal conflicts, and the availability of medical care have reduced the death rate, and economic conditions will improve with stable government.

Obviously America has not exploited its dependent peoples in the traditional sense in which metropolitan powers have exploited colonial peoples. None the less, it has been unable wholly to avoid responsibility for the serious consequences of the impact of Western civilization upon their traditional way of life. To the extent that challenges have been brought, and brought suddenly, in terms of generations, to these islanders, challenges which their traditional institutions are incapable of meeting—to this extent they can be said to have suffered a loss in so far as many things uniquely valuable to them have been greatly reduced in value. To the same extent that Samoans, for example, have lost their ability to face confidently and traditionally their own future with the same self-respect as before, America has, in a subtle sense, unavoidably exploited them. This fact is apparent even though the United States in many ways erected barriers against foreign intrusion, because obviously such barriers could not be perfect. So, whether or not we have "robbed" the Samoans, as colonies have sometimes been robbed of material wealth, we did accept, as a solemn obligation, the protection of intangible social values and cultural resources which, in point of fact, we could not actually protect.

The wide reaction against "colonialism" involves many factors besides material exploitation, and though our government has always sought conscientiously to cushion the impact of Western civilization in Hawaii and in Samoa, and though it is still doing so there and elsewhere in the Pacific, we are only making the best of a bad bargain. It has been said that the "white man's burden" is the burden of his own culture which he has carried into alien environments. In a peculiar, philosophical sense, a considerable portion of America's burden in Samoa and perhaps elsewhere in the Pacific is a feeling of embarrassment, unexpressed and undefined, for having been compelled by the exigencies of modern times to impose Western culture upon a culture which is not only alien but in many respects felt to be superior by those of us who are most concerned about this changing, threatening, and bewildering world.

The only suitable administrators for American dependencies must have something of the patriot and missionary in their make-up, and those who lack confidence in themselves and in their own civilization should not be employed, however tender their sympathies for native peoples.

In general, Western powers regard the welfare of the natives as a trust, and their activities are directed toward the conservation of the island peoples and the promotion of their progress along the paths of modern civilization. Different administrative policies have met with varying degrees of success, but the more enlightened recognize that the necessary and inevitable adjustment of native life to modern circumstances can be made only very gradually, over a long period of time.

REFERENCES

Bates, Marston, *Where Winter Never Comes* (New York: Scribner, 1952).

Emerson, Rupert, *et al.*, "American Policy Towards Pacific Dependencies," *America's Pacific Dependencies: A Survey of American Colonial Policies and of Administration and Progress Toward Self-Rule in Alaska, Hawaii, Guam, Samoa and the Trust Territory* (Honolulu: American Institute of Pacific Relations, 1949).

Hall, H. D., *Mandates, Dependencies and Trusteeship* (Washington, D.C.: Carnegie Endowment for International Peace, 1948).

"Hawaii, The Annexation of," *Public Opinion*, Vol. 22, No. 25, pp. 771-773.

"Hawaiian Islands, First Impressions of the," *Nation*, Vol. 65, No. 1683 (1897), p. 259.

"Hawaiian Phase, The Latest," *Nation*, Vol. 66, No. 1699 (1898), p. 42.

Leigh, J. G., "America's First and Last Colony," *Forum*, XXIX (1900), 104-115.

Thomson, Basil, "The Samoa Agreement in Plain English," *Blackwood's Magazine*, CLXVI (1899), 847-851.

Woolsey, T. S., "The Law and the Policy for Hawaii," *Yale Review*, II (1894), 347-355.

Yonge, C. M., "The Form of Coral Reefs," *Endeavor* (London), Vol. X, No. 39 (July, 1951), 136-144.

১ে Part I ১ে

TERRITORIES OF
THE UNITED STATES

II

The Territory of Hawaii

MANY factors contribute to the unique character of the Hawaiian Islands: their position at the crossroads of the Pacific between Australia and California, the Orient and North America; their incomparable climate of year-round summer where people swim in the surf at Christmas and New Year's; their mountain slopes dotted with yellowish green kukui trees, the highest peaks snow capped in winter; their coral beaches, white in glistening sunshine; their gardens of colorful tropical flowers, and picturesque trees. People who have visited Honolulu think often of graceful coco palms, avenues of shower trees—golden, and pink and rainbow. The blossoming of the night-blooming cereus on Wilder Avenue is discussed in the local newspapers. Those who have seen the island of Hawaii talk of the giant tree ferns, part of the luxuriant undergrowth in the ohia-lehua and koa forests.

Among awe-inspiring sights are erupting volcanoes spewing rivers of molten lava. One of the showiest and costliest eruptions of modern times, in 1955, overran fertile fields of the island of Hawaii, the only island where that kind of activity is now seen.

Trips to the interiors of the islands among great fields of sugar cane waving in the trade winds and extensive rows of pineapples reveal the importance of Hawaiian agriculture. The cruisers and carriers offshore or in Pearl Harbor are reminders of a defense outpost of great strategic value, powerfully supported by ground, sea, and air forces.

But it is the pageant of peoples in the beautiful setting of the South Seas which commands most attention from thoughtful Americans: ethnic hues from the pale white of the *haole* through the sallow and brown of the Hawaiian and Oriental to the dark of the Negro. The most striking, perhaps, are the occasional persons who combine these varied races in themselves, challenging one to identify them. The others are easily distinguished: diligent Japanese, busy Koreans, methodical Chinese, Portuguese from the Azores, cheerful Filipinos, all mixing together in the workaday world of plantation, factory, office, and store.

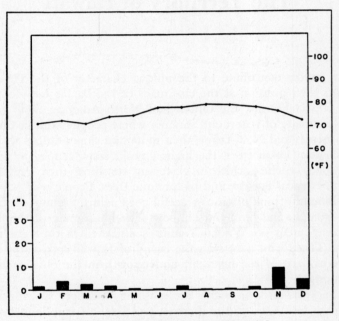

Rainfall and temperature in Honolulu

The Hawaiians themselves still occupy, for visitors, the center of the stage. But it would be more correct to say the part-Hawaiians, for there are now only about two thousand pure Polynesians in a total population of half a million. A foreign culture has all but engulfed the native way of living, a few attributes of which are now revived to please the throngs of tourists. It is too late to save the natives, even the purest of whom will soon have merged their blood as one element of a neo-Hawaiian civilization in America's far-flung

Pacific Territory. The gradual evolution of the Hawaiians from their aboriginal way of living to a modern Western society is similar to that which the Guamanians, the Samoans, and the people of the Trust Territory of the Pacific Islands are experiencing.

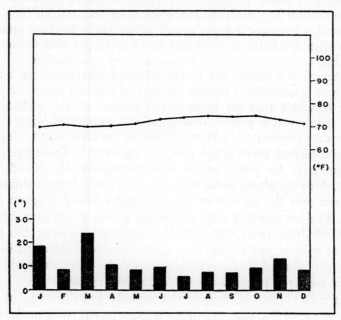

Rainfall and temperature in Hilo

THE NATURAL ENVIRONMENT

The main islands of the archipelago, Hawaii, Maui, Oahu, and Kauai, lie near latitude 20° north and between 155° and 160° west longitude. A chain of minor islands extending to the northwest, not part of the Territory, includes Midway, outside the tropics, and 1,500 miles from the main group. All the islands are really the tops of a great submarine mountain range built up from the ocean floor by active volcanoes. The major land areas are basaltic domes in various stages of dissection. Oahu and the small island of Niihau have the only sizable coastal plains.

The five large inhabited islands, Kauai, Oahu, Molokai, Maui, and Hawaii, are in general high and mountainous. The island of Hawaii, which contains two-thirds of the area of the group, consists of five volcanic mountains connected by saddles formed by overlapping lava flows. Oahu was once two immense volcanoes from which erosion has made two parallel mountain ranges. The total area of the Territory is 6,435 square miles, which is about one-third larger than the State of Connecticut. Only 10 per cent of the land is arable, and only 8 per cent is actually under cultivation.

Although the islands are at the northern margin of the tropics, they have a subtropical climate because of the vast extent of ocean water in which they are located, and because of the northeasterly trade winds which prevail throughout the year. The mean annual maximum temperature at Hilo is about 80° and the mean minimum 65°; the highest there is 91° and the lowest 51°. These figures are representative for places at sea level throughout the islands. The trades, blowing across miles of ocean, are laden with moisture. As they rise over the mountains they are cooled and precipitate heavy rains. The northeastern sides of the islands are the wettest because the winds blow from that direction. On the lee slopes, the winds become warmer, and drying, to cause arid and semiarid climates. The mean annual rainfall of 160 inches at Luakaha on one side of Oahu, and 30 inches at Honolulu on the other, are representative.

The even climate of the Territory makes it possible to plant crops at any time of the year. It is not uncommon for truck gardeners to raise five or six crops on the same land within twelve months. With a controlled water supply this warm, even climate leads to extraordinary results. Throughout the year, Hawaii enjoys what would be considered, by mainland standards, to be good summer weather. The effect of the climate permeates every aspect of island life, which in all seasons is a life of the out-of-doors. In a typical Hawaiian house, without a basement or central heating system, fuel is unnecessary except for cooking. Its light construction is like that of dwellings in summer resorts on the mainland. Many Hawaiian homes do not even have glass windows, but depend on heavy Venetian blinds to keep out the rain, since the temperature outside and inside is always the same. For similar reasons, overcoats, heavy underclothing, and seasonal changes in suits are not necessary.

The four larger Hawaiian islands, the only ones where sugar cane is raised, produce a little more than 1,000,000 tons, one-fourth of the sugar grown on American soil. On these four, Kauai, Oahu, Maui, and Hawaii, 220,000 acres used for that crop are divided among the small number of twenty-eight plantations. Each of these, because of the topography, is necessarily divided into fields of very different sizes, altitude ranges, and soil conditions.

TABLE I

TERRITORY OF HAWAII

LAND UTILIZATION, 1955

	ACRES	PER CENT
Total area	4,117,120	100
Under intensive cultivation	341,060	8
Grazing	1,510,000	37
Forest reserve	1,200,130	29
Balance—Cities, towns, waste, military installations	1,065,930	26

Hawaii's sugar industry goes back more than a century, but until the islands became American soil, in 1898, their sugar output was relatively small. Since annexation sugar production has grown considerably. It has always been the Territory's leading agricultural occupation, for the rich soil, abundant water, and subtropic sunshine have yielded heavy crops.

In Hawaii it is customary to grow from two to four crops of cane on a field before it is plowed and planted with the segments of cane stalks which are used for seed. The warm climate makes it possible to schedule plantation operations so that planting, cultivating, and harvesting are carried on throughout the greater part of the year. Seasonal unemployment is not a problem in the Hawaiian sugar industry as it is in agriculture on mainland United States.

Powerful tractor-drawn plows prepare the cane fields for planting; their subsoilers break the earth to a depth of as much as two feet on irrigated fields. In unirrigated areas, and on shallow soil, it is not cultivated so deeply. After the plowing, the fields are smoothed with disking machines. Then surveyors make certain that furrows for planting follow contours of slopes to prevent soil erosion. Surveying is especially important in laying out irrigation furrows. After the cane is planted, weeds must be kept down by spraying machines or mechanical cultivators. Weed control ceases to be a problem when the cane is waist-high. In Hawaii almost all cultivation is done by men skilled in the operation of tractors and other large mechanical

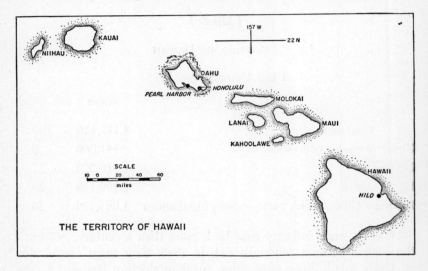

THE TERRITORY OF HAWAII

devices, for machines and skill have replaced the brawn and sweat expended there in former days.

Sugar cane in the Territory grows from eighteen to twenty-four months: since the islands are at the margin of the tropics, the long growing season is necessary to allow a maximum of sugar to form within the stalks. During all of that time scientists constantly check the progress of the crop. Soil tests are made at frequent intervals, and special fertilizers, selected to meet soil requirements, are applied as often as needed. On irrigated plantations water is allowed to flow frequently to assure steady growth.

About 57 per cent of the area in sugar cane is irrigated, producing almost two-thirds of the annual crop. Some irrigated fields yield as much as 120 tons of cane per acre. The porous nature of the soil, subsoil, and underlying basaltic rock allows much of the precipitation in Hawaii to sink into the ground, from where it is recovered to refresh the crop.

Most of the cane raised on the Big Island (Hawaii) comes from fields which depend on the abundant rainfall of that island's north-eastern Hamakua Coast. On the other hand nearly all that grown on Kauai, Oahu, and Maui gets most of its water from a complex

TABLE II

Sugar Production in Territory of Hawaii, 1950–1955

YEAR	ACREAGE HARVESTED*	TONNAGE OF 96-DEGREE RAW SUGAR	ESTIMATED VALUE OF CROP TO HAWAII
1950	109,405	960,961	$124,000,000
1951	109,494	995,759	125,000,000
1952	108,089	1,020,450	137,000,000
1953	108,337	1,099,316	148,000,000
1954	107,480	1,077,347	140,000,000
1955	106,180	1,140,112	145,000,000

* Sugar cane is a two-year crop in Hawaii, so only half the total acreage is harvested each year. The figures indicate the actual acreage harvested.

and widespread system of ditches, mountain tunnels, and deep wells. These irrigation facilities comprise one of the larger and more costly projects of their kind in the United States.

During the growing period of the crop, constant checks are made for insect pests and plant diseases, although long-range work by scientists of the Hawaiian Sugar Planters Association has obviated nearly all losses of that kind.

Cane ready for harvesting is set alight to burn off dry leaves and trash which hamper milling operations. Since the flames pass through the field quickly, no harm is done to the stalks which contain the juice. Heavy push rakes or mechanical grabs break the stalks off at ground level. In some places, on steep, rainy slopes, hand cutting is still necessary. The cut cane is loaded by cranes into trucks to be hauled to the mill.

The most conspicuous building on a Hawaiian sugar plantation is the mill or factory where the ripe cane is processed to extract the sugar. The first step is washing to remove trash and other refuse gathered in harvesting; the next, squeezing the juice out of the stalks by passing them through a series of rollers. The juice is then heated, clarified, filtered, evaporated, and finally further evaporated in large

TABLE II-a

Yield of Sugar Cane per Acre in Territory of Hawaii, 1955

ISLAND	TONS
[1] Kauai	86.39
[1] Oahu	104.40
[1] Maui	104.70
[2] Hawaii	87.36

[1] Irrigated land.
[2] Unirrigated land.

The average yield of sugar, per short ton of cane, in 1955, was 231.07 pounds.

vacuum pans to form crystals of commercial raw sugar which is about 97 per cent pure.

On Hawaii, Maui, and Kauai, the raw sugar is held in bulk storage plants without bagging at ports from where it is shipped to the "C and H" refinery on San Francisco Bay. Some is still exported in bags from Oahu. About 65,000 tons is refined at Aiea, near Honolulu, to supply granulated sugar for canned pineapples and for general public consumption.

Each of the twenty-eight sugar plantations of the Territory forms a separate community with its own schools, hospitals, stores, churches, theaters, clubs, and recreation fields. The plantations provide year-round employment to 23,000 people. Since an eight-hour day is now universal in both fields and factories, workers have leisure for gardening, swimming, and driving their cars about the islands.

There is harmony among them, although they trace their racial origins to Japan, China, Polynesia, Portugal, North America, Puerto Rico, Europe, and the Philippines. It was through the organized and systematic introduction of workers from those countries that the sugar industry of Hawaii was made a success, for, from the first settlements of people of European ancestry in the islands, it was held that their natural resources could not be developed by the Hawaiians themselves. Their resources were such that it was not necessary for them to accept plantation employment in large numbers. Their physical, psychological, and cultural traits had become nicely adjusted to the natural environment of their islands before the Europeans disrupted their whole economic and social order.

It was especially between the year 1876, when the Kingdom of Hawaii signed a Reciprocal Trade Agreement with the United States, and the annexation of Hawaii as a Territory that successive waves of immigrants were induced by plantation management and by the government to come to the islands. After annexation, the Philippine Islands supplied the major part of the immigrant labor force.

During the past fifteen years a factor of unprecedented importance has had a profound and far-reaching effect on the sugar-cane industry and on agriculture in general in the Territory; namely, the unionization of plantation labor. No change in the economy of Hawaii during the war and postwar period has been more fundamental than the basic shift in labor-management relations. This shift was not apparent until the war ended, although its causes are to be found in forces which have long been developing in the Territory. But the changes that occurred in less than two years following the lifting of war restrictions would probably have been spread over a decade had it not been for the effects of the war itself, which gave a powerful impetus to underlying tendencies.

When wartime restrictions were lifted, the sudden release of forces which had accumulated before the war, and of the resentments which military government controls had engendered, resulted in a swing from a relatively unorganized to a highly organized Hawaiian labor movement throughout the Territory.

The International Longshoremen's and Warehousemen's Union organized a wide range of island industries, but the strength of its position has derived from its domination of labor in the three most strategic economic activities in the Territory: (1) sugar production, (2) pineapple production, and (3) ship transport and stevedoring. Membership in the I.L.W.U. is estimated at 25,000 and in the American Federation of Labor and Congress of Industrial Organizations, the other important labor union, at 15,000.

Throughout the history of the sugar industry there has been a trend toward the use of machines instead of hand labor. There has been a steady decrease in the number of plantations, with a corresponding increase in the scale of plantation operations and in production per acre and per man-hour. The recent rapid rise in wages due to unionization has become a powerful impetus toward further mechanization. In order to keep going, sugar-cane and pineapple companies have developed a marvelous system of agricultural operations which has resulted in a substantial reduction of the labor force. Cane-harvesting machines now cut lanes through standing cane in fields where hundreds of human cutters toiled before the war. Weeds are now controlled by a herbicide spray rapidly applied row by row instead of, as formerly, plant after plant by men with hoes. Olaa Plantation, with a prewar employment of 1,800 people, had 865 in 1955. The total labor force on sugar-cane plantations has been cut from 50,000 before the war to about 18,000 now.

The following table shows the relation of the number of plantation employees to sugar production from 1882 to 1952:

TABLE III

PLANTATION EMPLOYEES AND HAWAIIAN SUGAR PRODUCTION, 1882–1952*

	EMPLOYEES	TONS OF SUGAR	TONS PER EMPLOYEE
1882	10,243	57,088	5.6
1892	20,536	131,308	6.4
1912	47,345	595,258	12.6
1932	51,427	1,024,354	19.9
1942	26,371	870,109	33.0
1952	18,139	1,020,450	56.1

* From A. W. Lind, *Hawaii's People* (1955).

The trend still continues to be toward larger plantation units for the following reasons:

1. In Hawaii the growing of cane and manufacturing of raw sugar are combined in a single plantation, based on a planned program to provide a continuous flow of cane into the mill. Under these conditions small-scale operations are inefficient. Where small-scale farming persists, in other sugar-producing areas, there is a sharp line of demarcation between the growing of sugar cane and its processing, for farmers sell to the processors.

2. The arid and semiarid lands, which constitute over half of the area now under cane cultivation, required the construction of large irrigation systems too costly to be undertaken except by large-scale enterprises.

3. Unlike the crop in other areas, as was already stated, cane in Hawaii takes eighteen to twenty-two months to mature. It needs a much greater quantity of fertilizer per acre. Because of the topography, it requires expensive systems of transportation between field and mill. To accomplish these ends a large capital outlay is necessary, involving risks more readily undertaken by large-scale concerns.

4. The plantations are organized in an association which was planned for the Hawaiian sugar industry as a whole and which has developed for the whole framework of economic relations necessary to their existence on an industry-wide basis, including shipping; the purchase of fertilizer, equipment, and other supplies; the development of mainland refineries and markets; the supervision of management labor policies; the maintenance of research laboratories; and the formulation of common programs of action for combating plant diseases, insect pests, and soil problems. Mass-production agriculture is the foundation on which high productivity per worker has been developed in Hawaii and which, to a large degree, determines the standard of living in the Territory as a whole. Hourly-rated employees in the sugar industry receive the world's highest year-round agricultural wages.

PINEAPPLES

The Hawaiian pineapple industry, much younger than the sugar industry, has adopted many practices borrowed from it. Its stability, however, is less sure than that of sugar, because of several factors outside the range of control of the producers, for example, competition of other fruits not raised in Hawaii. The industry did not become significant in the islands until the last quarter of the nineteenth century, for the first pineapple plantation was established only in 1885, and the first cannery in 1892.

Raising pineapples involves many practices of modern scientific agriculture. The climate is conducive to the production of good fruit, but the preparation of the soil needs special care and extra nourishment. Six to eight months before the planting, the fields are plowed and harrowed until the surface is entirely broken up, and all vegetation that has been growing on it is mixed in with the soil. The process is repeated several times, as the machines drawn by powerful tractors plow the earth to a depth of about twelve inches. The plows are followed by multiple-disc harrows drawn back and forth across the fields. Between plowings the soil is left to rest, and to let the rainfall soak in. During this period the vegetative "trash" slowly decomposes. At the time of the last plowing, the soil is fumigated by injecting a chemical, "DDT," six to eight inches deep in the topsoil.

Pineapples are started in the fall or in the spring, depending chiefly upon soil and weather conditions. Growing in a sort of continuous cycle, the plants at the same time both bear fruit and yield the material to produce a new plant.* The pineapple is grown from slips near the base of the fruit, from suckers that grow lower down on the stem, or from the crown that develops at the top. The slip, from the smooth Cayenne variety, the planting material most used, matures to bear ripe fruit in approximately twenty months; crowns take from twenty-two to twenty-four months to mature, and suckers from sixteen to eighteen months.

Before the slips are planted, strips of mulch paper are laid across the fields to form rows. Similar in appearance to tar roofing paper, it helps to prevent the growth of weeds, conserves moisture and fertilizer, and increases soil temperature.

Each planter plunges his narrow, steel trowel through the mulch paper at a spot marked, setting out the plants alternately in such a way as to allow the greatest room for growth. The regularity of the

* Very few cultivated pineapples ever have seeds. When they do appear, they are a nuisance, for they are scattered all through the flesh of the fruit, spoiling it for canning.

pattern, making it easy to divide the fields into units, helps employees to arrange sections for work. At the same time it conforms to the requirements of the various plantation machines. About 17,500 slips are planted to the acre.

When the mulch paper has disintegrated, frequent weeding is necessary, by mechanical cultivators, by chemical weed sprays, or, where necessary, by hand hoeing. Nutrient elements, taken from the soil, are replenished by the mechanical application of nitrogen, potassium, and phosphorus near the base of the plant in the form of dry commercial fertilizers. Iron, on the other hand, is applied in solution. The most serious pest, the mealy bug, is destroyed by an organic insecticide. About twenty months after planting, the ripe fruit, weighing about five pounds, is ready for harvest.

When the peak harvesttime comes, in early summer, trained pickers, some of them extra seasonal workers, walk along the rows, now three and a half to four feet tall, selecting the fully ripe fruit. They snap the pineapples from the stalks, and striking off their crowns, place them on the conveyor belt on the long, narrow boom of the mechanical harvester. When the fruit reaches the top of the machine, it rolls down into a big bin, which, when full, is detached to be hauled in a truck to the cannery.

Soon after the first crop—called the plant crop—is harvested, preparations are begun for the second or ratoon crop which will ripen in a year. All the slips are removed and all but one or two suckers from each plant, each of which produces a ripe pineapple the following year. Sometimes, however, the plants, allowed to produce a second ratoon crop, are cultivated for one more year. A four-year cycle is followed in pineapple cultivation in Hawaii—four years from the time one crop is planted until there is replanting for a new harvest.

At the cannery, the bins are lifted by tall straddle trucks to be placed on hydraulic dumping units which tilt the bins to roll the fruit onto spiral graders from where it travels on broad belts to the Ginaca machines. These remarkable machines, each coring one hundred pineapples a minute, shoot the cylinders of fruit along to trimming tables; then it passes on moving chains to slicing machines. The sliced fruit is placed in cans which slide in continuous procession down to the packing tables; next, it is trucked by hand to siruping machines. The hermetically sealed cans of fruit are pasteurized, sterilized, and packed on trays to be conveyed directly to the labeling department. Wrapped in their particular labels, the cans are placed in cartons for shipment.

Pineapple juice, extracted from any edible parts of the fruit, is also canned. The shells, ground up and dried, are "pineapple bran" for feeding livestock. Citric acid is also extracted from shells, and from ends and trimmings.

The eight pineapple companies in Hawaii, members of the Pineapple Growers Association of the Territory, operate twelve plantations on the islands of Kauai, Oahu, Molokai, Maui, and Lanai. The

TABLE IV

PINEAPPLE PRODUCTION IN HAWAII (Estimated), 1951–1955

	ACRES	CASES OF PINEAPPLES AND PINEAPPLE PRODUCTS	VALUE
1955	73,000	29,411,000	$108,000,000
1954	74,000	29,411,018	*
1953	*	29,476,494	100,000,000
1952	*	26,075,606	*
1951	*	26,076,606	100,000,000

* Figures not available, but comparable with those given.

fruit is processed in nine canneries, three each on the islands of Kauai, Oahu, and Maui. The total area used for pineapple production amounts to some 63,000 acres, of which thirty-three per cent is owned by the companies, and sixty-one per cent leased from various estates. The remainder represents Hawaiian homesteaded land leased to companies and to small, independent farmers.

The pineapple industry, a growth of this century, is still second only to sugar in importance. Unlike that product it has created its market, which, as was already stated, is not always certain. Until the restriction of Filipino immigration, pineapple planters recruited part of the necessary field labor in the Philippine Islands. In a labor shortage of 1945, almost two thousand Filipino immigrants were assigned to pineapple plantations. A larger number of laborers is required during the summer harvest, June to September, than at other times of year. As these months constitute a slack season on some sugar-cane plantations, both industries use in common a small proportion of the total labor supply. The labor for the canneries, operated at capacity only during the summer, is enlisted from housewives and daughters, schoolboys and schoolgirls, who earn pin money and school expenses during that season.

The unionization of the pineapple industry is in many respects similar to that of the sugar industry. In each the organizing drive was highly successful, resulting in written agreements covering the majority of the regular employees. Negotiations in both industries involved (1) conversion from a perquisite system, (2) the adoption of uniform job classifications and a standard wage scale, (3) special wage scales in the case of a few companies, and (4) the granting of a general wage increase.

Causes of instability in the industry are (1) repeated inroads of insect pests and plant diseases which can be controlled only by continuous scientific work and costly operations on the plantations; (2) climatic factors, particularly rainfall, which affect the quantity and quality of production; (3) the fact that pineapples are a luxury food rather than a necessity so that an economic depression causes an unusually sharp drop in sales, and (4), as was already mentioned, the competition of other canned fruits, which has a depressing effect on the pineapple market.

FOREST LANDS AND STOCK RANCHES

Approximately 30 per cent of the total area of the islands is in territorial forest reserves created primarily to prevent runoff and soil erosion. A program of planting on forest reserves is being gradually carried out year by year to increase the capacity for retarding runoff. Further protection of the watersheds includes fencing and the elimination of grazing animals. The island of Hawaii, the largest, much of it covered with lava flows, has by far the greatest extent of protected land.

Cattle are grazed on the upper slopes of the mountains of the island of Hawaii, above the areas used for sugar cane and coffee. The carrying capacities of ranges there vary widely, for some areas are very poor as pasture. Most of them, in semiarid districts, are semi-waste, covered by partly decomposed lava flows; others are in districts with excessive rainfall. Several of the better ranges in the islands, however, are on the northern slopes of Mauna Kea, the leeward slopes of the Kohala Mountains, and in Kona. Part of the great saddle between Mauna Kea and Mauna Loa is a grazing ground for sheep. On the other larger islands considerable areas are also devoted to grazing, most of it poor soil. Oahu is the only large island where less land is used for grazing than for cultivated crops. Of the small islands, almost the whole of Niihau is used for grazing cattle and sheep. Kahoolawe, at various times a pasture for cattle and for sheep, is now uninhabited, unused, and severely wind-eroded.

Notwithstanding a recent increase in local production of beef, much meat is imported from mainland United States to meet the needs of the Territory. Our military forces alone will continue to constitute a large demand.

Cattle ranches have been less directly affected by unionization than have the plantations, but the trend on those operated in connection with plantations is toward standardized work in conformity with that on the large agricultural units.

In the warm, even climate of Hawaii, little attention is given to the protection of cattle from the weather. Fence repair, weed control, and other maintenance operations are the more important activities. Many ranches maintain dairies to meet local needs, and a few raise corn and oats for feed, and fresh vegetables for use on the ranch, or for commercial sale.

Dairy farming in Hawaii ranges from that on small family units to large company-owned dairies. As on the beef cattle ranches, perquisites are generally furnished to dairy workers in the form of free housing and the opportunity to buy milk and meat at lower than market prices. Almost all the local production is consumed in the form of fresh milk or ice cream. The processing and distribution of those products, as well as the grinding and distribution of cattle feed to dairies, are regularized by operators and employers.

Milk is not a traditional food of Polynesians nor of Orientals. However, an intensive program of education, carried on by the schools, the Agricultural Extension Service, local social agencies, and the dairy industry, has greatly increased its consumption in the Territory during the last few decades. A serious problem of the industry is that of procuring enough less expensive island-grown feeds, such as pineapple bran, in place of imports from mainland United States, the freight on which is very costly.

A characteristic of hog raising in Hawaii is its great dependence on garbage collected from homes, hotels, restaurants, and schools. During the war the large amount available from Army and Navy kitchens scattered throughout the Territory was responsible for an increase in production of swine to make the islands more self-sufficient. The postwar period has witnessed a decline. Hams, bacon, lard, and sausages are all imported.

SMALL FARMS

Small farming is carried on in Hawaii partly as a result of historical antecedents, as in the case of coffee, and partly to supply both the large local market for vegetables, fruits, and nuts, and a mainland demand for products of high quality. Coffee is one of the crops grown on a family basis. Almost all of it is produced on the Kona coast of the largest island in a strip twenty-five miles long and two miles wide, in a zone from about 800 feet to 2,200 feet above sea level. The shade necessary for coffee trees of high quality is furnished by a natural cloud bank which forms almost daily during the summer. In addition, a wet period lasting from late spring until fall is favorable for blossoming and fruiting, followed by a dry late October and November when the crop is harvested.

Coffee is raised by people mostly of Japanese ancestry, many of whose parents sought in the isolated district of Kona a life free from the regimentation of the plantation; some former Filipino sugar-cane workers are also engaged in its production. Farms generally range from five to eight acres, about 20 per cent of which are owned in full or in part by their operators; the rest are leased, mainly from large landholders.

Farmers themselves prune, cultivate, fertilize, and harvest with the help of their families. Processors generally collect the "cherry" coffee (ripe fruit) to put it through pulping machines which take off the skin. The extracted beans are then placed in vats of water for about twelve hours, after which they are washed and spread out on floors to be sun-dried. The "parchment" coffee is then sold to the mill, where it is hulled, graded, sorted, and bagged.

Rice and taro may be considered as "has been" crops in Hawaii. Rice farming became an important island industry in the early 1860's, when the number of Chinese immigrants rapidly increased both in Hawaii and in California, to which it was shipped. The most important cause for its decline was competition from low-cost producers in California. Its production has been abandoned except on the island of Kauai, where about fifty farmers produce 1 per cent of the rice consumed in the Territory.

The decline of taro growing has paralleled the decline and almost disappearance of the traditional way of living of the native Polynesians. Poi made from that plant was the staff of life of the ancient Hawaiians. The cultivation of that crop by wet-land farming was their most important agricultural occupation. It was raised in patches varying in size from a few hundred to a few thousand square yards. Taro lands were generally on the flood plains of perennial streams, arranged in terraces so that water, when diverted from the streams, flowed from the higher to lower patches. The large fleshy roots or corms were pared, and pounded with a small quantity of water into the paste called "poi." After the arrival of foreigners, this paste was a favorite food not only for Polynesians but for Orientals and Caucasians who developed a taste for it. It is still served at Hawaiian *luau* or feasts. But growing taro is onerous work by native standards, and only a little is now raised, by Japanese and Chinese instead of Polynesians as earlier, for a very restricted market. A few thousand pounds are shipped to the mainland annually, chilled, frozen fresh, or canned, to be eaten by former island residents.

With the exception of pineapples, fruit production, small by mainland standards, consists primarily of bananas, papayas, avocados and mangoes. There was a considerable export of "Chinese" bananas to San Francisco before World War II, but it was interrupted by other priorities for shipping space. After the war the discovery that the fruit fly attacked these bananas placed a quarantine on that fruit. Fresh papayas are in great demand in Hawaii and on the west coast of the mainland. To avoid bruising and other injuries, the papaya must be handled with very great care during harvesting, packing, and shipping. The Territorial Board of Agriculture and Forestry has established high standards of quality for exports. Since many varieties of avocados which mature at various seasons grow in Hawaii, the Territory's opportunities to develop this product further depend principally on the relation between production and marketing costs and those of competitive areas on the mainland. Mangoes, grown for home use in the islands for a hundred years, have recently been planted on a considerable scale. A smooth-shelled variety of macadamia nuts, introduced from Australia in the 1880's, shows promise of development, for in addition to commercial shipments, large amounts are mailed by residents of the Territory and visitors as gifts to friends on the mainland.

Flowers are much more widely used in the islands than on mainland United States, for in addition to beautifying gardens and homes, they are worn as *leis* by both men and women, and by the latter as corsages and ornaments in their hair. Hawaiian women sell to visitors thousands of *leis*, made from the petals of plumerias, gardenias, carnations, *pikaki, maile,* and other flowers. The Territory has an advantage over mainland areas in the commercial production of flowers and foliage, for since they grow outdoors all year round, skilled nurserymen raise large amounts with small investments. Commercial exports are made possible by the establishment of low airfreight rates.

PRODUCTS OF THE SEA

Fish in the waters around Hawaii were sufficiently abundant to make up a fundamental part of the food supply of the ancient Polynesians. Fishing techniques, elaborate, and specific for different varieties, had many modes—by spearing, by baskets, by hook and line, and with nets. A professional class of fishermen, who had gods of their own and were hedged about with taboos and ritualistic concepts, exercised primary control of the occupation. The islanders also raised fish in ponds from less than an acre to several hundred acres in extent. There favorite varieties of fish, especially mullet, could thrive in safety from their enemies and be easily captured when needed. Now native skills in fishing have almost completely disappeared, and the competition of more energetic people in the commercial industry has ousted the natives from that form of business enterprise.

Commercial fishing began in Hawaii with the immigration of the Japanese, some of whom took it up to furnish the kind of food so important in the land of their origin. It is now fairly well developed, the best known single product being canned tuna. That industry was progressing favorably before World War II, when annual sales of canned fish were about $1,200,000, making it third among exports. But military restrictions necessitated by the war caused a temporary eclipse of the industry, and since then labor difficulties have been a drawback. Serious competition comes from tuna packers on the west coast of the mainland.

Hawaii is in a position to exploit fishing areas not readily available to mainland fishing boats, and a considerable expansion is possible in catching, processing, and marketing fish. In the field of recreation, convenient air transportation to and from the mainland might result in the expansion of fishing as a sport if more facilities were provided in the islands. *Limu,* a species of marine plant life, is still obtained for food by some Hawaiians.

TOURISTS

The rise and development of two other "industries" in Hawaii climax the economic transition from primitive times to the present day—tourism and defense spending. Hawaii's tourist industry has grown during the last half-century from an idea conceived and promoted by a group of men in Honolulu into a Territory-wide activity supported by government and business and touching on nearly all aspects of the islands' economy. Today tourism has the greatest potential for expansion of any of Hawaii's industries.

Expenditures of visitors are a basic source of income, since most of the hotels and restaurants, taxicab and car-rental enterprises, curio shops, swimming and surfboard establishments derive their revenue from this source. Tourism also furnishes a large portion of the income of clothing stores, especially those carrying beach wear, and of theaters, interisland transportation companies, and public clubs for golfing and dancing. Vendors of *leis* and hula dancers also profit largely from the visitor's purse.

Of all visitors to Hawaii, 53 per cent come from the west coast of the United States, 44 per cent from California alone. An increase in the population of that state, the most rapidly growing major area in the United States, increases the number of visitors to the islands.

Before World War II the tourist business centered in the Waikiki area of Honolulu, and relatively few tourists visited the other islands. Now, however, the Hawaiian Visitors Bureau is urging the expansion

TABLE V

INCOME AND EXPENDITURES OF HAWAII, 1954–1955*

Income (from sources outside Territory):

Exports amounted to (sugar, pineapple, coffee)	$263,000,000
Federal Government expenditures (armed forces, grants, tax refunds, etc.)	306,000,000
Services purchased in Hawaii (tourists, airlines, etc.)	80,000,000
Dividends, interest, profits	24,000,000
Remittances	10,000,000
Total	$683,000,000

Expenditures (to agencies outside Territory):

Goods bought (food, raw materials, autos, drugs, cigarettes, etc.)	$370,000,000
Payments to Federal Government (taxes, etc.)	152,000,000
Services (freight, transportation, advertising)	85,000,000
Interest, dividends	24,000,000
Remittances	5,000,000
Total	$636,000,000

An income of approximately $300 million is derived annually from the "internal" economy of the Islands, 15 per cent from locally produced commodities for sale in local markets, 7 per cent from "value added by manufacturer," and 78 per cent in the form of personal services.

* From the Annual Report of the Governor, 1955.

of hotel and transport facilities on the outlying islands to enlarge the area of tourist attraction and, to some extent, to decentralize the trade. This is not difficult, for scheduled airplanes leave Honolulu several times daily for all the principal islands, the longest flight being only about ninety minutes.

Tourist travel reached an all-time high during 1953, when nearly 80,000 visitors stayed two days or longer and spent $42,000,000 in the islands. The Territory gained in that period over $6,000,000, esti-mated in taxes on tourist dollars spent in the islands.

Climate is perhaps Hawaii's principal holiday asset, for the average island temperature makes swimming, surfing, golfing, fishing, and sailing as enjoyable in December as in July. Round-the-clock service from the mainland by major air and shipping lines and the unique cosmopolitan life of the islands have added to Hawaii's attractiveness as a nonseasonal playground.

DEFENSE SPENDING

It is not generally realized that the military personnel in Hawaii together with their dependents, plus the civilian employees of the military establishment together with their dependents, total 121,000, almost 25 per cent of the total population. They represent over a third of the people of Oahu and are only a few thousand less than the number on all the other islands combined. Local purchases of supplies and services by the military constitute the largest single source of wealth of the Territory.

During 1952 total military expenditures in Hawaii amounted to $263,695,655. Although this was a substantial increase over the figure for 1951, when the total was approximately $200,725,000, expendi-tures fell off in 1953 after the signing of the Korean truce. Develop-ment of the Kaneohe Naval Air Station as a marine base ac-counted for some of the increase. The "invisible export" formed of services to the armed forces, to tourists, and to shipping and air lines has generated nine-tenths of the income required to import necessities from the mainland to sustain a growing population.

During the last two decades the Armed Forces of the United States have played an important part in sustaining the economy of the islands, for their payrolls have added substantially to the incomes of the people. In 1935 the Navy spent $8,864,000 to maintain its defense forces and bases in Hawaii. In postwar years, the lowest annual Navy expenditure in Hawaii has been $79,000,000, nine times that of 1935. More than one person in every four in the Territory as a whole, and two in every five on Oahu alone, are directly dependent on defense activity for a living. Today, military expenditures exceed the total value of all Hawaiian exports.

All military operations in the Pacific emanate from Hawaii, headquarters of the Commander in Chief, Pacific. Here also on Oahu are the headquarters of the United States Army, Pacific; United States Pacific Fleet, and the United States Air Force, Pacific, as well as many other commands and organizations related to our defense.

Before the Japanese attack on Pearl Harbor in 1941, Hawaii was a Pacific outpost for America's security forces. Since the war, its role has changed to that of a central Pacific reserve of manpower and materials for Okinawa, Japan, Guam and other outposts. It became a center of repairs and maintenance for ships, of hangar space and mechanics for aircraft, and of training sites and rest camps for ground troops. It also developed into a hospital, supply, and communications center in the Pacific.

The possibility of an economic crisis in the islands grows out of the extreme dependence of Hawaii on defense activity. This does not imply that Hawaii will cease to be an outpost of national power, for that is Hawaii's permanent role. But if defense activity in Hawaii should decline as sharply during the next few years as it has risen since 1950, there would unquestionably be an economic crisis in the Territory.

The outlook is for the continuation of a strong defense program; but, barring new developments in international relations, the plan is to stretch out programs and reduce expenditures. A shift in international relations which would increase defense work in Hawaii—for example, further United States participation in military operations in Asia—would result in a continuing rise in the level of income, employment, and business. A defense cutback could cause a recession, ranging from mild to sharp, depending on the size of the cutback.

Tourism and defense installations are in part responsible for a high degree of urbanization on the island of Oahu. That island, representing less than one-tenth of the total area of the Territory, nevertheless contains nearly three-fourths of its total population.

Although the mechanization of plantations has also contributed to the cityward trend, there are other fundamental factors which give Honolulu such a preeminent position. Honolulu dominates the financial and industrial life of the islands for the following reasons:

1. Hawaii is separated from the markets on which it must depend by more than two thousand miles, and Honolulu is the point of contact for all of the islands with the rest of the world.

2. Our most important Hawaiian military and naval outposts are situated in and near Honolulu. They provide occupational opportunities for those enterprises which serve the military personnel and for the skilled workers who build and maintain Army and Navy installations.

3. Honolulu is the headquarters for practically all large island enterprises and is the center for the air and water transport systems which serve the islands.

4. Honolulu is the most important tourist center in the Territory. Tourists contribute to the size of the city, not only because of the tourist population, but also because of the many occupational opportunities which the presence of tourists creates in the city.

5. Honolulu is the administrative center for Territorial and Federal agencies and for educational and cultural institutions.

6. The unemployed persons in the Territory tend to concentrate in Honolulu because it is the best place to make contacts for new jobs.

In 1890, of a total population of 89,990 persons in Hawaii, 25.5 per cent was urban and 74.5 rural. By 1938, 41.2 was urban, and 58.8 rural. This trend toward urbanization reflects primarily the growth of the city of Honolulu, which in 1955 had 259,580 people, or more than half of the total population of the entire Territory. The island of Oahu had a total of 342,194. The next largest city in Hawaii is Hilo, with 29,111. Most of the population growth of the Territory during the past decade is thus represented by an increase in the size of Honolulu. At present there is no diminution in this urban trend.

The essential economic fact emerging from the adaptation of Hawaii to present-day conditions has been a transition from the primitive self-sufficient economy of the native Hawaiians to a modern specialized economy tightly geared to American markets. To obtain construction materials, clothes, shoes, automobiles, industrial equipment, and other items necessary to the maintenance of present standards, including 65 per cent of the food consumed in the Territory, Hawaii now possesses only four basic resources. These are sugar, pineapples, fish and other marine products, and services to tourists and to the Armed Forces. Barring some unexpected technical development, these, and only these, are available to maintain or increase present standards of living.

III

The People of Hawaii

THE primary factor that determines the atmosphere of Hawaii is the people who live there—their attitudes, customs, way of living, and personal qualities. These in turn determine the character of community organization and even of the streets, homes, business districts, and public buildings. This is especially true because of the insularity of the Territory.

Caucasians, the earliest migrants, show a slow, continuous growth in numbers throughout the whole period since the discovery of the islands. Maintaining the leadership in all the businesses and professions, they are largely responsible for developing the industrial, commercial, and social structure of the Territory. The "Big Five," the leading concerns, date back to a group of traders who provided whalers with supplies and often acted as agents for them. With the collapse of the whaling industry, and the expansion of the sugar industry, the agents or "factors" turned to sugar as a field of operaations. The five factors take care of all fiscal matters of the plantation, the hiring of managers, engineers, and other technicians, and arrange details of shipping and merchandising.

National groups who emigrated to Hawaii from northwestern Europe and from the United States soon bettered their economic and social status. Many of the skilled artisans, professionals, and businessmen attained prestige and affluence in the growing Hawaiian economy. The few that worked on plantations were generally employed in skilled and supervisory positions. Norwegians, Germans, and others gradually lost their identity among the Caucasian population.

Opportunities presented to the Portuguese, too, favorably affected their establishment, for unlike the Orientals they had the advantage of naturalization and of acquiring homesteads. They were advanced to skilled positions on the plantations more quickly than the Oriental groups. They came to the islands with a large proportion of women and, for that reason also, they were disposed to remain as permanent settlers. The great majority of the Spanish who emigrated to Hawaii stayed only a few years and then went to California.

Most of the Puerto Ricans, now widely scattered on the outlying islands of Hawaii, Maui, and Kauai, have continued to live in rural areas. Somewhat shiftless in disposition, they experienced difficulties in adjusting themselves economically and socially to life in the Territory.

THE HAWAIIANS

The ancient Hawaiians were farmers and fishermen. Besides taro, the native food crops were sweet potatoes, yams, bananas, sugar cane, and breadfruit. The *wauke,* or paper mulberry, was used for tapa, or bark cloth, and the fibrous olona for cords, ropes, fishlines, and nets.

Before the introduction of iron and other foreign agricultural implements, the only agricultural tool which the natives had for planting was a long digging stick made of hard wood, flattened at one end. Along with cultivation of their various types of crops, there was a continual blending of worship, prayer, and sacrifice with each advancing stage of farming.

Fish, the most important animal food of the Hawaiians, entailed much less effort to procure than a cultivated crop, so they liked to live near the sea where they could get it. The degree to which the Hawaiians formerly utilized for cultivation steep slopes, dry land, and some localities difficult of access, and the complete parceling out of the coasts in offshore fishing rights comparable to their land titles, indicate a density of population which required the development of the native resources of subsistence to a maximum.

Among house building and other native professions, canoe making was once much practiced in Hawaii, because it was this profession that provided fishing canoes, fleets of war canoes, and canoes that went from island to island. Canoe-building experts, important and honored, were favorites of the chiefs, and held a higher social rank than that of common builders.

Prior to the intrusion of foreigners, Hawaiian society was a type of primitive feudalism based on a subsistence economy. Under this society, there were generally two distinct classes of people. Highest in rank in the first class were the king and all the close relatives of the reigning family; then the governors or chiefs of individual islands appointed by the king, below whom were the subchiefs or district chiefs who were appointed either by the king or by the island chiefs. The mass of the population, who composed the second distinct class, were the commoners, generally farmers or fishermen.

The system of land tenure bore a striking resemblance to the feudal system which prevailed in Europe in former times. The hereditary chiefs or *alii*, believed to be descendants of a later group of conquering invaders, exercised functions not unlike those of the medieval feudal lord. The control of land was the measure of political supremacy, and the redistribution of land between the king and his chief retainers and favorites was the issue at stake in the frequent island and interisland wars. Theoretically, all property, including the land, belonged to the king by right of conquest. He invested most of the land among his supporting chiefs, by whom the smaller subdivisions were allocated to the commoners for cultivation. Tenure was thus at the will of the king and conditional upon the faithful fulfillment of the feudal responsibilities.

The fundamental unit in the social organization of the Hawaiians was the dispersed economic community or family, the *'ohana*: relatives by blood, marriage, and adoption, living some inland and some near the sea, but concentrated geographically in, and tied by ancestry, birth and sentiment to, a particular locality which was termed the *'aina*. Thus kinship extended far beyond the immediate biological family.

The growth of population—perhaps 300,000 at the time of the discovery of the islands by Captain Cook—was checked not so much by battle casualties as by plunder and the destruction of crops, homes, and other properties of the defeated, leaving them homeless and destitute. Famines, floods, and blights were also checks to a certain extent. Other factors included diseases, taboos, and infanticide. Infanticide was prevalent, and there were few of the older women at the time of the abolition of idolatry who had not practiced it.

It was the opinion of those well informed that two-thirds of all the children born were destroyed in infancy by their parents.

During the first quarter of the nineteenth century there was a great disruption of the primitive Hawaiian way of living. During that period Hawaii was primarily a provisioning point and a source of sandalwood for ships in the China trade. Occasionally, natives obtained passage aboard and sailors "jumped ship" to live ashore and join their blood with that of the islanders. Even the relatively slight contacts between primitive Hawaii and Western civilization in those years had a devastating effect on the aborigines. Because of their long period of isolation, the natives possessed no immunity to "civilized" diseases. Venereal disease was a most potent cause of death, but even such simple maladies as measles, whooping cough, and common colds were fatal to thousands. Other factors played a part in the decline, including liquor, firearms, the struggle of island chiefs for power, and the exploitation of natives by their own rulers to obtain sandalwood with which to buy coveted Western wares. The net result was a great decrease in the native population, a decrease which continued rapidly until the middle of the century when the total Hawaiian people numbered only about 75,000.

Toward the end of the sandalwood era, American whalers made Hawaii their provisioning and trading headquarters. This trade reached its zenith around 1850, when more than four hundred whaling vessels arrived in Honolulu annually. The trading concerns organized to service the whalers gradually became the dominant enterprises in Honolulu, and by a flexible adjustment to economic changes remained at the heart of the industrial and financial structure of Hawaii. During these early times American missionaries, establishing themselves as permanent residents, strove to guard island morals. A few of them acquired property which later proved to be of great value.

Had it not been for the increasing pressure of foreign capital seeking cheap land, a modified feudal order might have persisted for some decades after the arrival of strangers in the islands. The demands of the trading economy could not, however, be adequately met under any mere revision of the native plan of land tenure, for from the beginning of the nineteenth century individual land claims of some importance had been imposed upon the Hawaiian chiefs by foreigners.

Yielding at last to the persistent pressure of the traders and his *haole* (white) advisers, King Kamehameha III established in 1846 a Commission to Quiet Land Claims, by whose decisions fee simple title might for the first time be secured. By official proclamation in 1847, exclusive ownership of all land by the king was finally renounced; and the Great Mahele, or Division, of 1848 provided a final chapter in the collapse of the old Hawaiian land system.

The gradual displacement of the native by the foreigner, and the rise of a new order of individualized land titles, progressed concomitantly with the expanding control of the islands, chiefly by Americans and British. They and other Europeans who were early comers to Hawaii soon became owners or managers of sugar-cane plantations, administrators, or skilled laborers. A few of them held important posts in the Hawaiian Government and helped the Polynesians to shape the affairs of their kingdom. Others occupied the main business and professional positions in Honolulu. Altogether they are the ones who are largely responsible for developing the industrial, commercial, and social structure of the Territory. When the Hawaiian Church severed its connections with New England, many children of the missionaries threw in their lot with the great business expansion in the archipelago.

How did the Hawaiians fare during the great economic development of the islands? Their story is one of disappointment, frustration, and a crowding to the wall, pushed aside by hard-working Orientals and enterprising entrepreneurs of Western civilization. At first some thousands of Hawaiians were employed on newly developing sugar plantations. But the monotonous regularity of this work, so different from that of old times, and particularly the stigma that became attached to it once Chinese, Japanese, and other alien laborers were introduced, soon caused them to shun it almost entirely. Thousands of natives, accustomed to using but not to owning their little holdings, disposed of them for ready money and so became landless. This, and the attractions of the port towns and especially of the gay capital city, Honolulu, caused a shift of population from the scattered villages to these centers. Most of the Hawaiian town dwellers, being poor, settled in crowded tenements and congested areas where rents were cheapest. The Hawaiian who sold his little farm or *kuleana* to live in a crowded city regretted it afterward.

The Hawaiian character was put to a serious test as a result of being overwhelmed by an alien, almost incomprehensible, world. No wonder that some of the Polynesians showed undesirable traits. For

many there was no longer an orderly existence, and under the circumstances they became "lazy." Western standards of living and
commercial attitudes tended to replace the simpler subsistence economy of the old island environment. That so many retained a basic
cheerfulness, graciousness, and poise is greatly to their credit.

The greatest cause for concern both to the Hawaiians themselves
and to foreigners in the islands was the passing of the native *kuleanas*
into the hands of foreigners. Probably the major cause was that the
natives were unaccustomed to land titles and, living for generations
under a type of feudal land tenure system, failed to project into their
minds the value of possessing land. Attempts at resettlement and
rural rehabilitation were unsuccessful. For the most part, settlements
and gardens were deserted—given over to the foreigner's sugar cane
and cattle, or to engulfing lantana, algaroba, and other introduced
plants.

The Kingdom of Hawaii came to an abrupt end in 1893. The
islands, after being for five years a republic governed mainly by resident Americans, were annexed to the United States with the status of
a Territory. At first a large section of the Hawaiian people were
bitter over the loss of their political independence. Under the new
system, however, leading Hawaiians assumed high political posts in
local government, while those of Hawaiian blood were able to exercise
a controlling voice in the politics of the Territory, having a voting
majority.

In 1921, as a result of much planning by Hawaiian leaders and
others interested in their welfare, and on the recommendation of the
Territorial legislature, the Congress of the United States passed a
measure designed to return Hawaiians to the land. This, known as
the Hawaiian Homes Commission Act, set up a commission with the
Governor of the Territory of Hawaii as chairman, and provided land,
capital, and a basic plan with which to experiment.

At the outset the program was beset with many hurdles and pitfalls,
such as inadequate finances, marginal regions to work with, inadequate
water and other utilities, and, because of the isolated location of
most of the tracts, the lack of employment opportunities for the prospective occupants.

As the years passed, the more educated Hawaiians gravitated to
political jobs, to clerical, teaching, and police work, and to mechanical
and other skilled trades; others became stevedores, cowboys, roadmen,

flower *lei* sellers, "beachboys," and the like. On the whole, the Hawaiians have been able to find employment to their tastes in the new order, although the change has been inevitably marked by psychological and social strains and stresses.

In two economic spheres of the modern island life the Hawaiians have been conspicuously absent: business and farming. The former, with its competitive individualism and technical organization, represents perhaps the extreme of contrast to the old economic system, and as yet even the educated Hawaiians have shown little interest in it. As regards the second sphere, practically the only farmers until the rehabilitation scheme began consisted of a minority of conservative folk who continued to live on isolated coasts, growing taro and fishing to obtain their staple foods.

Under homestead laws in the early days considerable tracts of land had been allotted to Hawaiians, but a great many lost their holdings through improvidence and inability to finance farming operations. Others, after obtaining land for a nominal sum, turned about and, with no thought of the future, sold it to wealthy interests. The Hawaiians are not businessmen and have shown themselves unable to meet competitive conditions unaided.

In contrast to the unsatisfactory attempts to get Hawaiians back to farming, the successful development of residential-homestead projects has accomplished the purpose for which the Hawaiian Homes Act was intended. In many cases the Hawaiians were removed from congested areas of Honolulu and Hilo into more healthy and wholesome environments in the suburbs of those cities; they own their own homes and have, with few exceptions, fulfilled their financial obligations to the Hawaiian Homes Commission. The members of the commission maintain, and rightly, that projects such as this, allowing the Hawaiians to own their own homes in localities where there are opportunities of employment, must be developed to the fullest extent as soon as possible. The rehabilitation program carried on by the Hawaiian Homes Commission has steadily expanded since its inception in 1923. In 1952 there were 1,551 Hawaiian lessees occupying homesteads under the jurisdiction of the commission, representing a total of 10,171, men, women, and children. At that time approximately one out of every nine persons with Polynesian background in the islands was a beneficiary of the program. There are now approximately 3,000 lessees, totaling 20,000 Hawaiians and part-Hawaiians. Residential homestead owners, most of them in the city and county of Honolulu, earn a living in nearly all the ways associated with city life and with the military and naval reservations on the island of Oahu.

The Hawaiian perhaps suffered rather than benefited from the haze of romance and sentiment with which the white man surrounded him and his fellow Polynesians. The remarkable adjustments he made, and the problems he faced, tend to be obscured. Too often his character and modes of living were set critically over against some ideal standard that the white man had—but did not always attain—of industry, thrift, morality, and integrity, without regard to the fact that the Hawaiian's thought and behavior were still governed largely by values and habits of a radically different kind that came from the old Polynesian background.

THE HAWAIIANS TODAY

The Hawaiians today may be divided into two groups: a small number who live in Puna, Kau, Hana, and a few other isolated rural sections of the islands, and a very large number of Hawaiians and part-Hawaiians who live in Honolulu, Hilo, and a few smaller towns. All of them except those with little Polynesian blood still maintain as a way of life the old communal-cooperative effort rather than individualistic enterprise. The ancient 'ohana or dispersed economic community—the kinship group—is still their subconscious approach to living.

With its slow disintegration over a period of 150 years, the individuals belonging to the disarticulated 'ohana have had recourse to two means of personal and social adjustment: some, especially those who have clung to planting and fishing, in other words to the former means of subsistence, and certain families in whom, despite removal from their native milieu, the instinct of loyalty to their Hawaiian progenitors has remained very strong, have stayed in their 'ohana with its inclusive obligations and privileges. Others, particularly those most affected by intermarriage and by American education, or by city life, have chosen to try wholeheartedly to adhere to the American system. Most Hawaiians nowadays have in some degree both the old Hawaiian attitude and the American. Oriental-Hawaiians generally combine, with the Hawaiian-American, many habits and conventions derived from Chinese or Japanese life as a result of social and personal ties with Oriental relatives, and transference of habits and conventions.

A large proportion of the Hawaiian people still have their roots in the country, even those who reside in the city; and attachment to the soil and the sea that nourished them is a profound feeling met with amongst all Hawaiians and other Polynesians everywhere in the Pacific. Equally, attachment to blood relatives is with most Hawaiians a deep and unchanging sentiment. One has to know intimately country Hawaiians, or city Hawaiians who remain Hawaiian at heart, to realize the inner depth and strength, and the outer importance in current living, that blood relationship has today.

Since the time of the *mahele*, Hawaiians have repeatedly attempted corporate enterprise in what are termed *hui* or groups. These have for the most part had to do with cooperative agricultural and fishing enterprises, and practically without exception they have been failures because those responsible for them were completely lacking both in the business acumen and experience necessary for dealing with Caucasians and Orientals, and in the sense of personal responsibility. The last Hawaiian (nearly pure blood) who owned and operated a small store in Honolulu closed its doors about 1935. "Why did you give up?" his friends asked him. "Well, you see," he said, "some of my poor relatives were always borrowing cans off my shelves, and they never paid me." From a Hawaiian point of view to store up wealth, rather than lavish it on one's fellows, brands a person not as successful but as stingy; to work when one has money or feels like fishing is foolish.

Many part-Hawaiians, on the other hand, have, in their childhood, enjoyed the advantage of a different cultural tradition, they have benefited more from school attendance, they have been favored by employers and, in general, they can adjust more easily to the requirements of the situation. Economically they are in a better position, their social status is higher, and their record as law-abiding citizens is superior.

Today nearly all Hawaiians speak English and most of the younger ones do not know the Hawaiian language. However, the sentimental interest in that language continues. Food, clothing, and shelter of the Hawaiians is little different from that of the other peoples in the Territory. They probably eat more poi than non-Hawaiians but they also eat much rice. The flowing *holoku* and loose-fitting *muumuu* had become the badge only of the elderly Hawaiian woman, until a few years ago when it became fashionable for women of other groups as well. There is now nothing very distinctive about Hawaiian housing.

By religion many are Congregationalist, but Mormons, Catholics, and revivalistic sects have drawn large numbers into their respective churches. The Hawaiians have also started their own sects, for instance the *Hoomana Naaoao,* which has several churches in Honolulu and on the island of Hawaii, and which is popularly known as "Hawaiian Christian Science." Kawaiahao Church, built in 1841, is the Westminster Abbey of Hawaii. In this historic old structure, which is in constant use today by Hawaiian Congregationalists, services are conducted each Sunday in the Hawaiian language.

The falling death rate among the Hawaiians is a testimonial not only to the increasing efficiency of the social health agencies of the Territory, but to a fundamental change in the beliefs and mental attitudes of the people so that they can cooperate more satisfactorily with those agencies. What is true of the Hawaiians is also, in a measure, true of most of the immigrant groups.

An exceptionally important factor working in the interest of the Hawaiians is the activity of the local tourist bureau, aided by the government. The tens of thousands of visitors from the mainland come not only to enjoy the liquid sunshine and coral sand, but also to see Hawaiians, hear them play their ukuleles, sing their own songs, dance their hulas and chant their ancient legends, and ride the waves on their surfboards. The tourist bureau realized there was money in it. So, aided and abetted by hotel corporations, sea and land transportation companies, and sellers of beachwear, curios, and "grass shack" gifts, tourism in Hawaii has promoted a renaissance of Hawaiian culture. Hula dancing teams entertain at hotels and beach resorts afternoons and evenings the year round. Every hotel has a Hawaiian orchestra to play old-time Hawaiian music, and singers to charm the transient guests. Good native chanters now make small fortunes.

The Hawaiians have seized with avidity the opportunity to revive traditional aspects of their old civilization, for they regard them as factors contributing further to their unification at a time when they are losing their grip on things because of competition with other racial groups, especially the Japanese. Furthermore, they are still proud of their lineage and restrict membership in their civic clubs and other organizations exclusively to people of Polynesian blood.

Many of them have been indifferent toward or even opposed to statehood for Hawaii, for they have a general fear of any change which suggests to them a further lessening of control in politics. They are inclined to regard it as a further threat to their security.

The village of Papakolea, a suburb of Honolulu, exclusively Hawaiian, furnishes a picture of the modernization of the present-day Polynesian. The site of the settlement, Territory-owned land, is a ridge of Tantalus Mountain, where the native forest was cleared to make way for small plots which were leased to the natives for ninety-nine years at a dollar a year. The government lent them each $3,000 on a prewar home to be paid back in rent. Four rows of one-story frame houses are perched, one behind the other, above Tantalus Road. "They are cliff dwellers," a Hawaiian said. "They just climb up." Some of them hoist heavy packages by pulleys from garages on Tantalus Road up the ridges to their homes. Two main streets, Kaululaau and Moreira, run northward up each side of the crest of the ridge to end in the forest. Kalamaku, Keaupua, and other side streets, each a block long, project to the edge of the steep slope of Pauoa Valley on the west and to a precipitous ravine on the east. Each home has a tiny garden where *ti* plants flourish; in some of the gardens an occasional mango tree and coconut palm furnish shade. Although the homes have a very modest appearance, almost every one of them has a television mast. Along the longer roads and single blocks, lines of automobiles bespeak a high standard of living. Diminutive mongrels trot about, yapping incessantly; occasionally one of them, bolder than the rest, darts in to snap at a visitor's ankles. They are good guards in Hawaiian sections where the Polynesian system of "borrowing" still lingers.

Papakoleans live very much like their Anglo-Saxon contemporaries in Honolulu or continental United States. They are off in their cars in the mornings to work on military or naval reservations or to hustle cargoes as stevedores on the docks; some are electricians and mechanics, earning high wages. A considerable number of women sell *leis* at the passenger wharf to incoming and outgoing visitors. The flowers are purchased from Japanese gardeners. The big difference between the residents of Papakolea and other Americans is the old-time native spirit brought to fruition in the community house at the south end of the ridge where the Hawaiians meet once a month. By means of it the natives govern themselves in a considerable way through committees appointed on health, recreation, native festivals, and various aspects of government. A respected homesteader is chosen to arbitrate committee disputes and settle quarrels between members of the community. In the community center, and at home, the Hawaiians learn the old Polynesian dances, and listen to old native chants, for Papakoleans can earn money by relearning their culture. Their hula teams regularly furnish entertainment for tourists, and a young chanter from the area is recognized as one of the more accomplished in the islands.

The essence of Hawaiian sentiment, of the islands' old-time pageantry, of the revival of past hopes, of the Polynesians' attempt to keep their place in the sun is the annual celebration in memory of Kamehameha the Great, who united the islands under his rule. The day is a legal holiday.

A Hawaiian in the Homes Commission Office maintained to the author that the young Hawaiian people in the islands are changing their attitudes to try to face the new and more difficult economic situation confronting them, and that they are, for example, taking more interest in getting an education. "Education is their only salvation," a former Hawaiian member of the Territorial legislature stated. "We have to educate them if we want them to hold their own." Then she added thoughtfully, "Now some of them are going to the University."

Unfortunately for the Hawaiians, however, they are less desirous of taking advantage of the educational facilities available in the Territory than are the Japanese and the Chinese. This fact alone relegates them to a position of economic disadvantage, and secures for the Orientals preferential consideration in business and government. The Hawaiians then feel resentment toward the children of the immigrants for winning out in the civil service examinations. In prewar days, when governmental appointments were made by a commissioner, the Hawaiians got preferment.

Today many Hawaiians are still showing the strains of a difficult adjustment. Occupationally they are not well represented among the vocations at the higher levels. Many are leading lives of usefulness and happiness. A few are among the recognized leaders of the community: in politics, in education and social welfare, in labor councils. They continue to welcome others into the family circle, as their out-marriage rate continues high. Their influence and that of their ancestors will not soon be lost.

THE ORIENTALS

The most prominent people now in the modern scene because of their background, their number, their willingness to work hard, their aggressiveness, and their record in World War II are the Americans of Japanese ancestry. Their fathers, brought over as contract laborers for sugar-cane plantations, held down by rigorous discipline and small wages, have helped the children, gradually and persistently, to pull themselves out of their subservient status to become in some ways the more important racial group. Their number, 200,000, gives them

TABLE VI

ESTIMATED CIVILIAN POPULATION OF TERRITORY OF HAWAII BY RACE

As of January 1, 1956

RACE	NUMBER	PER CENT
All Races	516,878	100.0
* Hawaiian	10,608	2.1
Part Hawaiian	88,327	17.1
Puerto Rican	9,838	1.9
Caucasian	109,607	21.2
Chinese	33,162	6.4
Japanese	190,831	36.9
Korean	6,743	1.3
Filipino	63,398	12.3
Other	4,364	0.8

* The author regards this figure as much too high. Many with a little foreign blood claim to be pure Polynesians in view of benefits to be obtained.

superiority over any other group at the polls; and their desire for an education and their industry give them the edge on any other group in filling civil service positions in the Government. Members of the 442nd Combat Regiment and the 100th Infantry Battalion, made up of American citizens of Japanese ancestry from the Territory of Hawaii, were the most decorated units in World War II, and naturally claim all the privileges, perquisites and benefits which accrue to distinguished veterans. In general the effect of the war on the Japanese in the Territory was to hasten among them the process of assimilation. In rural districts the Japanese have acquired land in fee simple from the Caucasians, and farm it successfully by hardworking family units where the former owners could scarcely make a living. They have excelled in the coffee industry, tempted by the soaring prices of that commodity in continental United States. Always the most important coffee farmers, these indefatigable people are largely responsible for the flourishing condition of the Kona coffee district. With a racial majority of votes on Kauai, Maui, and Hawaii, they have many political opportunities.

A survey of the ethnic distribution of workers in various industries shows the dominance of the Japanese. They are the next to largest racial group in the sugar industry, and account for one-third of the labor force. In clerical jobs they are nearly five times as many as Filipinos. Japanese also outnumber Filipinos by more than two to one in maintenance work on the sugar-cane plantations.

The Japanese hold second place numerically among men employed on pineapple plantations. In the pineapple canneries a summary shows that about 50 per cent of the men and 62 per cent of the women are Japanese. In the group of regular employees, 60 per cent of the men and 70 per cent of the women are Japanese.

Japanese outnumber all other racial groups combined in office positions in the Territory. On the island of Oahu they hold Federal jobs in the post offices, customs service, veterans' bureau and local branches of the Department of the Interior. Mr. Tsukiyama, a past president of the senate in the legislature of Hawaii, is of Japanese ancestry. The only major field of office work in which Japanese do not hold a dominant position is in the public utilities, where Americans of Chinese ancestry are the most numerous men employees, and Caucasians the largest racial group among women.

Although the "Big Five" and other *haole* commercial groups are still the business entrepreneurs in Honolulu with their associated managers of plantations, and representatives in other offices on the various islands, they are largely dependent on the Japanese in securing foremen, clerical help, clerks in their stores, and other personnel in their business enterprise. No Japanese, however, has as yet been appointed manager of a sugar-cane plantation.

Old-time Japanese customs are celebrated more to add color to island life than because of continued attachment to the land of their origin. Bon Dances are held during July and August. Although the dance is a religious affair, the present-day performances have become an amalgamation of religious and folk-dance festivals. The dances came from Iwakuni, Fukushima, Niigata, and other parts of Japan and Okinawa. Music is provided, and it is the custom for all dancers to be dressed in the cool summer cotton kimono called "yukata." Part of their costume is a cotton towel which dancers drape around the neck.

THE CHINESE

The first large groups of immigrants to Hawaii were Chinese, who have since achieved the economic and social advantages which accrue to the descendants of early settlers. Thrifty and hard working, many of them, as soon as their period of indenture on sugar-cane plantations was terminated, became wealthy rice farmers—and rice at one time was second in importance in the islands to sugar cane. Some of them married Hawaiian women, to bring up energetic and attractive families.

The Chinese in Hawaii have become a wealthy class, among other things owning much more property than they did before the war. Eighty per cent of them live in Honolulu, where on "Mandarin Heights" a group of homes belong chiefly to well-off Chinese. Immediately after "Pearl Harbor" hundreds of Caucasians sold their homes as quickly as they could, and therefore cheaply, to depart to mainland United States. The Chinese bought most of these houses "on a shoestring," and then, good businessmen and shrewd gamblers that they were, finally acquired the property outright. They are now organized into little business groups or *hui* to buy large lots and subdivide them into little plots for Oriental or other homes. In some instances, four or five such houses stand in a space used by one Caucasian before the war. Both Japanese and Chinese live in every residential area in the city of Honolulu. The Chinese have been very successful in medicine, law, and other professions in the Territory, and many of them are leaders in the political and general life of the community. They still carry on some of their traditional customs to add color to the local scene. Their Narcissus Festival includes a parade of lion, unicorn, and dragon dancers, floral and fireworks displays, a mandarin banquet, a Chinese play in English dialogue, and the coronation of a Chinese-American beauty queen.

KOREANS

The Koreans, like the Chinese and Japanese of peasant origin, have placed a high value on hard work and education. A large proportion of them are engaged in various businesses and professions in Honolulu. For many years they kept an active interest in freeing their homeland from Japanese rule. This was largely stimulated by Syngman Rhee, now President of the Republic of Korea, who was for a long time a resident of Honolulu.

FILIPINOS

The Filipinos have climbed more slowly up the economic scale in Hawaii than have the members of the other Oriental groups. That slowness, however, is not any reflection on their ability, but rather an indication of the progressively changing situation in the islands, where the economic opportunities for betterment have become less and less as the Territory has approached its full development. They make up about one-half of the male workers on sugar-cane plantations, where they far outnumber the Japanese in manual labor. Many of the Filipino workers in the sugar industry have been brought in since the war and, lacking previous experience, are generally employed in field or mill jobs requiring little training.

Filipinos as a group account for a larger proportion of the labor force on pineapple plantations than they do on sugar plantations, for three-fourths of the adult men employed on the former are

Filipinos. The comparatively small number of Filipino women employed on both sugar-cane and pineapple plantations is explained by the fact that the great majority of the Filipino immigrants are single men.

Concentrated for the most part in plantation settlements, Filipinos are hard working and ambitious, seizing any opportunities that arise for bettering their economic status. They carried over from their homeland colorful folk dancing, quaint marriage customs, and attractive dress. Since few of them brought wives, the small number of Filipino women has led to keen competition for them on the part of the men. A considerable number of Filipinos have left sugar-cane and pineapple fields to operate barbershops, restaurants, clothes-cleaning establishments, laundries, and other small concerns. They are represented, although only in a small way, in the professions. A few children of early comers are now students at the University of Hawaii. Many workers on plantations save a substantial part of their high wages to buy little farms in the Philippines, and hope to return there permanently.

NEO-HAWAIIANS

For over half a century there has been a gradual trend from various Oriental modes toward an American pattern. This trend was sharply accelerated by the war, because of the desire of all groups to show their loyalty to the United States by being "as American as possible," and because of the large number of returned veterans. There has never been a period in the history of Hawaii when the cultural gap between the older and the younger generation of Orientals was greater, the shift in standards of living more pronounced, and inter-racial marriages more frequent than at present. Thus a complex mixture of standards ranges from one extreme to the other, and embraces every conceivable combination of Chinese, Japanese, Filipino, Korean, native Hawaiian, and American ways of living.

The Hawaiians and part-Hawaiians have played the leading role in the racial amalgamation which has been going on for a century in the islands. The Koreans, Puerto Ricans, Chinese, and other smaller ethnic groups have also contributed to the people of mixed ancestry.

The net effect of the social processes within Hawaii is to produce

slowly but irresistibly a unified organization of life appropriate to
the local setting. Happy relations with the government of the islands,
and with Uncle Sam, in general, have brought not only loyalty but a
thorough appreciation of American citizenship. Marriage of a Caucasian with a person of Hawaiian descent is not regarded with disapproval. Indeed, to have Hawaiian blood in one's veins is something

TABLE VII

POPULATION, TERRITORY OF HAWAII, 1850–1950

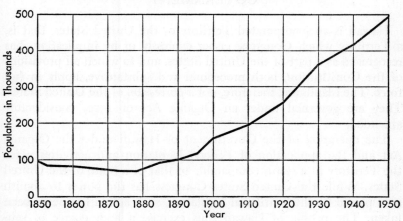

Source: Bureau of the Census Reports for 1950.

of which to be proud. There is a prospect that the Hawaiian ideal
of a real unity of peoples in this group of islands will be attained
in the course of a generation or two. The happy mixing of the
youth of the various races in the schools and university is a good
augury for the future, as is the religious tolerance among Buddhist,
Shinto, and various Christian denominations.

It is probable that the cosmopolitan cast of Hawaii's emerging culture will continue to impress the visitor for many years to come.
Oriental, Polynesian, and European cultures, in attenuated and
modified forms, will persist alongside the neo-American pattern of
life and will add color and interest to the island scene. But out of
the mingling of peoples are growing up new conceptions of life, a

local tradition, and indigenous forms of literature and art. Local pageantry and music, expressive of the common experience of all races in the island setting, are contributing to a growing neo-Hawaiian consciousness and local solidarity and pride.

Although destined by its economic and geographic position to share in the changing fortunes of a Pacific archipelago, Hawaii is gradually achieving a mode and a conception of life appropriate to itself. An island commonwealth has come into being.

GOVERNMENT

Hawaii is an incorporated Territory of the United States, that is, a Territory which Congress, either expressly or by implication, has recognized as a part of the United States, and to which all provisions of the Constitution, both procedural and substantive, apply in full force. The islands are, therefore, not a *possession* of the United States. They are governed under an Organic Act of 1900, considerably amended.

The operation of the Government of Hawaii under the Organic Act and the application of Federal legislation and activities place the Territory in a status comparable to that of a State of the United States. While the United States Congress has the power to abolish laws passed by the Territorial legislature, such action has never been taken. The people of Hawaii thus exercise a high degree of self-government and assume the basic responsibility for the adoption of economic, social, and educational programs through their elected representatives in the legislature.

Federal activities for the promotion of Hawaii's economic, social, and educational advancement are carried out under general Federal legislation and through the programs of grants-in-aid applicable to the states of the United States. Assistance is thus given in education, agriculture, housing, Social Security, public health, and other fields.

Hawaii's government has the familiar division of powers: a governor, a bicameral legislature elected by districts, and an independent court system. The governor and the secretary of Hawaii, the second ranking executive, are appointed by the President of the United States, with the advice and consent of the United States Senate, for four-year terms. The principal administrative officers are appointed by the governor. At the time of their appointment, all Territorial officials must be citizens of the Territory, that is, must have been in residence for at least one year; the governor and his appointive department heads must have resided in Hawaii for three years next preceding their appointment. Among the Federal officers are a delegate to Congress, elected for two years, who may introduce bills and debate, but not vote.

For more than a century Hawaii has had constitutional government. The first constitution, established during the monarchy, was granted by Kamehameha III in 1840. Although as early as 1854 Kamehameha III took steps looking toward annexation, it was not achieved until after many years of negotiations. Hawaii and Texas are the only two portions of the United States that have ever come in by voluntary annexation. According to the Northwest Ordinance of 1787, Territorial status is a transition form or prelude to full Statehood, variously defined in American juridical literature as an "inchoate state" or a state of "pupilage" preparatory to full Statehood.

Six congressional committees (1935, 1937, 1946, 1947, 1948, and 1950) which investigated Hawaii's readiness for Statehood returned favorable reports. The last four recommended immediate action on Statehood for Hawaii. In June, 1947, the House of Representatives enacted legislation approving Statehood for Hawaii. The vote was 196 to 133. This was the first time either house of the Congress had acted on the measure. Although President Truman indicated that he would sign the bill, the Senate Committee decided on further investigation. In March, 1950, once again the Hawaii Statehood bill passed the House of Representatives, this time by the overwhelming majority of 262 to 110. The bill then moved a step ahead when on June 29, 1950, the Senate Committee on Interior and Insular Affairs reported favorably on the measure. The time element and impending legislation involving matters of international concern kept the bill from reaching the floor of the Senate before Congress adjourned. On March 10, 1953, the House of Representatives for the third time passed the bill to enable Hawaii to become a State.

In April, 1954, the United States Senate for the first time passed a Statehood bill, which, however, differed from that passed by the House because the Senate version combined Statehood for both Hawaii and Alaska in one bill. The bill went back to the House but was not sent to conference before the close of the Eighty-third Congress. Republicans have generally supported Statehood for Hawaii in the belief that both senators from there would be Republicans. Democrats believe both senators from Alaska would be Democrats. On an issue as grave as this, neither party should be for or against Statehood for any Territory merely or mainly because it seems to offer some temporary advantage in the number of members the party may have in the Senate. Both parties should recognize the request from the Territory of Hawaii for Statehood on its own merits. Incidentally, the uncertainty of this course from a practical political standpoint was illustrated in the elections in Hawaii in November, 1954, when both branches of the island legislature were won, for the first time, by Democrats.

The granting of Statehood would enable the people of Hawaii to select their own governor and local judges, to elect national congressmen, and to participate in the election of the President of the United States. Statehood would replace the present Organic Act with a constitution already drawn up by popularly elected delegates and approved by the electorate.

American citizens living in the Territory of Hawaii assume all of the responsibilities but are denied some important rights of their citizenship. Only the change from Territorial status to Statehood would rectify the inequalities. It is an action that has been taken twenty-nine times previously in American history—an action implied in Hawaii's acceptance as a Territory, but so far denied. The politically inferior status of a Territory for a progressive, populous American area which pays into the Federal Treasury more than do ten of the present States, and has a population greater than four of them, is a contradiction in our position of moral and spiritual, as well as material, leadership in the world.

THE FUTURE

It has been pointed out that in spite of the small percentage of arable land, Hawaii has developed a significant agricultural economy, for the land available can be farmed with extraordinary intensity. Under such conditions, the economic life of the Territory has been channeled toward a specialization in sugar and pineapples, toward a unification of plantation policies in order to obtain the advantages of agricultural mass production, and toward those economic and political relations with other parts of the United States which would provide the basis for stability and the sound growth of Hawaiian industry.

The soil is Hawaii's chief economic resource. Other important natural resources are its forests—which take up more than one-fourth of the total land area of the Territory, but, as was already indicated, are primarily valuable as cover for watersheds. Like the other islands of the central Pacific area, Hawaii lacks mineral resources. These facts place strict limits upon the industrial possibilities of the Territory.

A few minor developments in agriculture are possible. Hawaii is the only place where the macadamia nut has been grown on a commercial basis. Because of its unusual flavor, it may supply a restricted export market on a luxury level, but few people can earn a living in this field. Repeated, but only partially successful, efforts have been made to establish and expand export markets for bananas, guavas, papayas, and mangoes. The limitation in the quantity of land which is favorably situated for cultivation of fruit restricts future expansion.

Although other possible developments are not of primary importance, taken in the aggregate they are additions to island industry. Among them are nurseries supplying orchids and other flowers by air to a rapidly expanding market on the mainland, and handicrafts and manufactures that turn out distinctly Hawaiian products, such as (a) *lauhala* ware; (b) perfumes specializing in the more exotic island flowers; (c) woodenware and wood carving, based on types of wood which are uniquely Hawaiian; and (d) garments typical of Hawaii, such as *aloha* shirts and beachwear. Because of the tourist trade, there is a larger volume of local business and of exports to the mainland in these items than would otherwise obtain.

Hawaii is in a position to exploit fishing areas not readily available to other fishing fleets of the United States. It is probable that a gradual expansion in this field will eventually offer more occupational opportunities in the catching, processing, and marketing of fish. As yet it represents less than 1 per cent of the total employment in the Territory.

The tourist business in Hawaii can be expanded considerably, but because of the necessity of building new local facilities its growth will perforce be gradual. Everything considered, the expansion of

tourism is the most promising basis for the development of occupational opportunities in Hawaii during the next few years. It is the
tourist Hawaii that native Hawaiians have done the best job of
selling, its center the white sand crescent of Waikiki beach rimmed
by big hotels.

However, the projection of past trends of the tourist industry into
future years cannot be considered as a "prediction." A war of serious
proportions in the Far East, or a World War III, would in all probability cause a cessation of tourism in Hawaii as it did during World
War II. A national or world-wide depression would inevitably cause a
sharp decline in the volume of tourist trade there, as it did in the
early thirties. Another strike in either surface or air transportation
between Hawaii and the mainland would cause a temporary setback as it did during the long waterfront strike of 1949. On the
other hand the visitor industry is the most rapidly growing part of
the economy of the Territory, reaching into and affecting economic
life on all the main islands. Unless unexpected developments interfere, it will be the most important field of expansion in Hawaii during the next ten years.*

An increasing dependence on tourists, however, will add to the
complexity of employment and welfare problems in the Territory.
Unlike the sugar industry, the tourist trade is a luxury trade and is
highly sensitive to basic economic conditions on mainland United
States. For this reason the greater the dependence on it, the greater
will be the ups and downs of prosperity and depression in Hawaii.

Important among economic factors is the rapidly increasing population of the Territory. In the past three-quarters of a century, the
population of Hawaii has grown nearly tenfold, from a low of 56,897
in 1872 to 500,976 in 1955. The excess of births over deaths is now
12,000 yearly. Yet even if the population were stable, the age distribution in Hawaii is such that the number of persons of working age
will grow rapidly during the next few years, for the Territory is an
unusually youthful community, where over half the population is less
than twenty-five years of age. Those who will be growing up and
entering the labor force are already born and their numbers are
known. To meet this addition alone will require more than a 50
per cent increase in the number of jobs in Hawaii during the next
twenty years.

* J. H. Shoemaker, . . . Hawaii's Visitor Industry 1955–1965.

TABLE VIII

NATURAL INCREASE IN POPULATION, TERRITORY OF HAWAII,

1941–1954

Bureau of Health Statistics

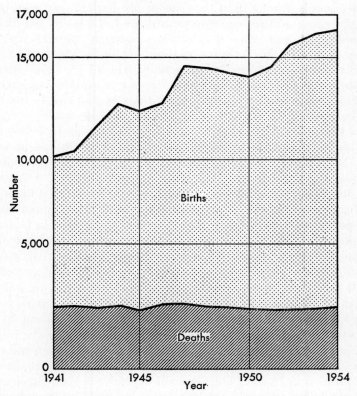

With a relatively high birth rate and a low death rate, the population of the Territory is growing by natural increase. In the last ten years the excess of births over deaths amounted to 111,000. However, during that period, gains from natural increases were reduced through movements of population out of the Territory.

Unemployment in the Territory varies from year to year within wide limits: in 1951, 9,700; 1952, 10,200; 1953, 9,200; 1954, 30,000. In 1954 a public works program instituted to relieve the situation resulted in 1955 in a decrease of approximately 2 per cent. In 1955 insurance benefits paid to jobless persons totaled $3,255,514.

It is now generally recognized throughout the islands that economic expansion is imperative to create jobs for the increasing stream of young people flowing from the schools into business life, to support rising living standards and government services, and to provide the stability that will carry the Territory through setbacks that are likely to develop in the future as they have in the past.

The ups and downs in defense activity, which have vitally affected business life; repeated disruptions in shipping; and the rising intensity of competition in the principal export markets, all point to the need for broadening and strengthening the economic position.

In efforts to create better living conditions, Hawaii faces two hard realities. As population expands, there will be a decline in living standards unless there is an increase in employment and production to take care of the increase in numbers. If wages and living standards are to rise, there must be an additional increase, an increase in per capita productivity. The per capita level of living cannot exceed the per capita level of production. The greatest problem in Hawaii is economic, for the whole brown and white mosaic rests on a semi-colonial economy that is founded upon agriculture, and agriculture is restricted by the extent of the available land. The total area of the eight islands is about a third larger than Connecticut, but the workable lands are mere fringes running from the sea steeply to the rugged, volcanic mountains. Thus, from an agricultural standpoint, Hawaii is about the size of a county in Ohio.

The development of an integrated island economy which will most effectively utilize local resources is basic to every other type of stabilization in Hawaii. The degree of dependence upon the fluctuating conditions of world markets leaves a considerable element of uncertainty, but the accumulated experience in dealing with economic crises in the islands in the past is perhaps some assurance for the future.

REFERENCES

Adams, Romanzo, *The Peoples of Hawaii* (Honolulu: American Council, Instit. Pac. Rel., 1933).

Alexander, W. D., *A Brief History of the Hawaiian People* (1899).

Chun, P. M. P., Sequent Occupance in Waihee Valley, Oahu, M.A. thesis, Univ. Hawaii, 1954.

Coulter, J. W., "The Territory of Hawaii," in *The American Empire*, W. H. Haas, ed. (Chicago: Univ. Chicago Press, 1940; 5th impression, 1948), pp. 216-295.

———, *Land Utilization in the Hawaiian Islands*, Univ. Hawaii Research Publications No. 8, 1933.

———, *Population and Utilization of Land and Sea in Hawaii, 1853*, Bernice P. Bishop Museum Bull. 88, 1931.

———, and C. K. Chun, *Chinese Rice Farmers in Hawaii*, Univ. Hawaii Research Publications No. 16, 1937.

Handy, E. S. C., "The Hawaiian Family System," *Jour. Polynes. Soc.*, Vol. 59, No. 2, June, 1950, Wellington, N.Z.

Keesing, F. M., *Hawaiian Homesteading on Molokai*, Univ. Hawaii Research Publications No. 12, 1936.

Lind, A. W., *Hawaii's People* (Univ. Hawaii Press, 1955).

———, *An Island Community: Ecological Succession in Hawaii* (Univ. Chicago Press, 1938).

Lowrie, S. G., "A Constitution for Hawaii," *Amer. Pol. Sci. Rev.*, Vol. 45, No. 3, Sept., 1951, pp. 770-774.

Philipp, P. F., *Diversified Agriculture of Hawaii* (Univ. Hawaii Press, 1953).

Shoemaker, J. H., *The Economy of Hawaii in 1947, with Special Reference to Wages, Working Conditions, and Industrial Relations*, U.S. Dept. Labor Bull. No. 926, Washington, 1948.

———, reports of the Department of Business Research, Bank of Hawaii, Honolulu: *The Economy of Hawaii Today* (1950); *People, Jobs and Mainland Dollars* (1950); *Opportunities for Hawaii to Produce More* (1950); *Earning, Spending and Saving* (1951); *Men, Land and Jobs in Hawaii* (1952); *Working Dollars in Hawaii* (1953); *Islands at Work* (1954); *Hawaii: Growing Islands* (1955); *Moving Forward in Balance: A Preliminary Report on Essential Programs of Action for the Development of Hawaii's Visitor Industry 1955–1965* (1955).

United States Department of the Interior, annual reports of the Governor of Hawaii.

United States Territory of Hawaii, annual reports of various Departments.

Watson, "Hawaii's Water Resources, All About Hawaii," *Thrum's Annual*, pp. 42-47 (Honolulu, 1954).

IV

American Samoa

On the mainland of the United States, many people either have never heard of American Samoa or could not locate it more precisely than "somewhere in the Pacific." People in Hawaii, however, do know about it, for they see Samoans in the islands and read about them occasionally in newspapers.

The Samoan archipelago extends from latitude 13° 26' south to 14° 32' south and from longitude 168° 10' west to 172° 46' west. American Samoa comprises the island of Tutuila and all other Samoan islands east of longitude 171° west of Greenwich; they extend from 14° 10' south to 14° 32' south. From west to east they are Tutuila, Aunuu, Ofu, Olosega, Tau, and Rose Island. The last mentioned is an uninhabited coral atoll. Swains Island, 11° 04' south and 171° 06' west, also a coral atoll, is administratively part of the Samoan group. Aunuu is part of Saole County of Tutuila; Ofu, Olosega, and Tau are called the Manua group. The total area of all the American islands, mostly mountains, is about 75 square miles, and its population 21,500 (1955). American Samoa is to be distinguished from Western Samoa, the western islands of the archipelago, a trusteeship of the United Nations administered by New Zealand.

The climate of Samoa is one of high temperature with small daily range, and little variation from day to day, the thermometer usually hovering about 85° Fahrenheit. Precipitation is very heavy. The average annual rainfall at Government headquarters on Tutuila is approximately 160 inches. The year may be divided into a wet season, November to March, and a less wet season, April to October, although in some years there is little difference between them. There is great variation in the rainfall from year to year, from month to month, and from day to day.

The trade winds of the Southern Hemisphere affect Samoa from April to September; the prevailing direction during those months is southeast. From October to March the winds are variable, but much of that time the direction is northwest. The relative humidity ranges from 70 to 90 per cent during the wet season, and from 40 to 60 per cent during the less wet season. The absolute humidity is always high; articles stored away from the wind and sun are covered with mold in a few days. All of Samoa suffers hurricanes at irregular intervals during the hotter season. American Samoa experienced seven such storms between 1903 and 1936, the last of which, very violent, caused a serious food shortage. Since then there have been several smaller ones.

THE TERRITORY OF SAMOA

Not merely the climate of American Samoa is unfavorable. Its topography is such that a farmer in the United States, with his methods of tillage, would consider it entirely unworkable. Eighty per cent of the terrain is mountainous; not more than 20 per cent can be used for agriculture; and agriculture is almost the only resource of the islands.

The island of Tutuila has a general trend from slightly north of east to south of west; it is 19.7 miles long, 6 miles wide at its widest extent, and 1,400 yards wide at the narrowest place, where Pago Pago Harbor on the south and Fagasa Bay on the north almost cut it in two; its area is about 40 square miles. The island is traversed from one end to the other by a continuous ridge of varying elevations extending in places into peaks and descending to the ocean steeply or precipitously. Outstanding from west to east are Lealafaalava, 1,104 feet; Olotele, 1,639; Taumate, 1,415; Matafao in the center is the highest peak, 2,141 feet. Pioa, or "The Rain Maker," is a steep ridge varying in height from 1,717 feet to 1,616 feet; it rises almost vertically from the eastern shore of Pago Pago Bay, and constitutes, with Matafao, one of the two principal landmarks of the island. Rain

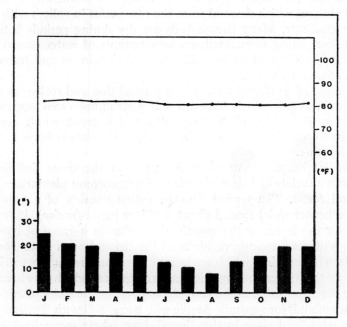

Rainfall and temperature in Pago Pago

Maker is literally what its name implies, for the moisture-laden, prevailing trade winds striking its southeast face are deflected upward into cooler air zones, causing frequent and heavy precipitation in the Pago Pago Bay area, particularly in the Pago Pago Valley, which lies directly in the "rain shadow."

The volcanic activity which produced Tutuila began in the east and proceeded toward the west; thus the highest and most recent peaks are in the western half. Pago Pago Bay resembles a drowned crater, the vertical slopes of which give it its fiord-like appearance.

In the west where the volcanic activity was most recent, flows of lava, unfringed by coral reefs, project into the sea in the Vaitogi ("water-throwing") area. There the prevailing swells, driven by the southeast trades, strike its abrupt face in a series of spectacular blowholes ("*pupu*"), which are the landmarks of that area, and may be seen from far out at sea.

The volcanic islands of American Samoa are drained by scores of short streams which descend from the mountains in valleys with very steep gradients. Many stream beds are dry during periods between rains, but during frequent downpours torrents of water course over falls and rapids evolved by differential erosion in *aa* and *pahoehoe* lava, ash, and cinders.

The soil of American Samoa is in general thin and rocky; on some mountain slopes which have no soil agricultural crops apparently thrive in the rocks. High temperatures and strong winds dry the surface to some extent, but a dense natural vegetation helps to hold the moisture.

The landscape of American Samoa from the shore line inland presents a variety of scenes of native villages, coconut plantations, and natural forest. The typical Samoan village consists of a group of native houses (*fale*) spaced about a village green (*malae*). It is situated on the beach at the mouth of a valley in a grove of coconut trees. Villages are easily visible from the sea and open to its cooling winds. The buildings which are nearest the shore are, in most villages, those of the higher ranking chiefs, an arrangement which may have had some defensive value in the early days. They are healthier places than farther inland, for generally people who became ill with filariasis were those who lived close to the "bush" from where mosquitoes could easily reach them.

The shore places are used for the reception of visitors, and it is very pleasant to be able to see the wide stretch of coastline and ocean from nearly every principal home in the village, and to feel the cool sea breeze which blows at all hours. Curtains made of woven coconut fronds, much like our Venetian blinds, are suspended around the eaves of all houses, and may be lowered for protection against strong winds and rain, or for privacy. The most conspicuous features of all of the structures are heavily thatched, domed roofs supported on stout posts.

Two or three long, low, thatched boat sheds project from among the dwellings; fishing boats, with decorations fore and aft, and dug-out canoes (*paopao*) are drawn up on the beach. Boat sheds are usually between the village *malae* and the shore at points at which canoe channels are found running through the reef. These channels, created where the outpouring of fresh stream water from the mountain valleys prevents the growth of coral, are, in some cases, not adjacent to the *malae*, which is usually on high ground. Some of them have been deepened by blasting.

In most villages small concrete copra sheds with corrugated iron roofs stand near the edge of high water. A large, whitewashed, concrete church, also with an iron roof, provides a remarkable contrast to the native houses. In some villages there are churches in various stages of construction, partly covered with grass and weeds; in others there are only solitary, dilapidated walls of those now abandoned.

At the backs of the villages, on the land side, are ovens (*umu*), little thatched structures over piles of small stones, one for each group of three or four houses. Near the ovens are small irregular patches of important Samoan food crops, mostly bananas and breadfruit. The patches range in area from a few square feet to one hundred square yards; towering above them are more coconut trees.

THE PEOPLE

The Samoans are a brown-skinned people very similar to the Hawaiians. Formerly confining themselves largely to the seashore, they never cultivated the soil inland to any high degree. An element in the Samoan cultural heritage, perhaps leading to proclivity for marine rather than horticultural life, combined with ideal coastal dwelling grounds, may offer the reason why Samoans took small interest in their inland areas. The terrain and climate of their islands may have in part accounted for it, since the Samoan Islands are both smaller and more rugged, and also warmer and more humid, than those of Hawaii. The traditional democracy of the Samoans, in contrast with the Hawaiians, may also be a factor, or may be, in part, the result of this. The family unit, doing its own work and governing itself, would not be likely to engage in large-scale undertakings with other families because of the lack of central leadership with authority to plan and direct coordinated labor for extended periods. The pressure of population has changed their habits in this respect, for now they farm wherever it is practicable.

The great majority of the natives still live in beehive-shaped houses with floors of coral rubble, no walls except the perishable woven *pola* (blinds) which are lowered in bad weather, and a roof of sugar-cane or pandanus thatch over which it is necessary to bind palm branches in every storm.

Variations from native architecture include the "palagi-style" (American) houses and bungalows which are found not only in the Pago Pago Bay area, but elsewhere, especially wherever there has been a road or other means of direct contact with Europeans over a considerable period of time. This usually indicates both an opportunity to make enough money to acquire the necessary foreign materials, and their availability through purchase, theft, or political influence. In almost every way the foreign construction is distinctly inferior to the traditional Samoan style, the sole exception being that a metal roof lasts longer than even the best thatch, which is only good for from five to seven years. Of course, ostentation is also a factor, of particular importance in the peculiar psychological make-up of the part-Samoan who seems to prefer a poor approximation of a European bungalow, even in slumlike conditions, to the healthier atmosphere of a traditional Samoan *fale* in a well arranged location.

Samoa is like Hawaii in historic background and in natural environment, although decidedly more tropical. The Samoans live in well established villages ruled by hereditary chiefs, villages that are aggregations of domiciles housing strongly cohesive families. There are from thirty to forty families in a village, fifty-two organized villages in American Samoa, and a few smaller ones.

Each of the thirty to forty households is presided over by a headman called a *matai*. These headmen are either chiefs or "talking chiefs," that is, the official orators, spokesmen and ambassadors of chiefs. In a formal village assembly, each *matai* has his place, and represents and is responsible for the members of his household, which includes all the persons who live under his authority. Their composition varies from the biological family consisting of parents and children only, to households of fifteen to twenty people, the *aiga*, who are all related to the *matai* or his wife by blood, marriage, or adoption. The adopted members of a household are usually but not necessarily distant relatives.

Within the household, age rather than relationship gives disciplinary authority. The *matai* exercises nominal and usually real authority over every individual under his protection, even over his father and mother. As "father" of his family, he directs and controls all family affairs, including the lands, which are owned communally. Earnings of family members should be given to their *matai*, who sees to it that they are distributed evenly among his *aiga*, or family members. This traditional responsibility of the *matai* is being gradually weakened by the impact of Western customs.

The word *aiga* is used roughly to cover all relationships by blood, marriage, and adoption. A relative, as is the case among the Hawaiians, is regarded as one upon whom a person has a multitude of claims or to whom he owes a multitude of obligations. From a relative anyone may demand food, clothing, and shelter, or assistance in a feud. Refusal of such a demand brands a man as stingy and lacking in human kindness, the virtue most esteemed among the Samoans. No definite repayment is made at the time such services are given, except in the case of the distribution of food to all those who share in a family enterprise. But careful count is kept of the value of the property given and of the service rendered, and a return gift is demanded at the earliest opportunity.

A family chief generally ensures that his family raises more food crops than it needs, as his prestige requires the giving away of food on ceremonial occasions, for in Samoa a man's social status is measured not by what he has but by what he gives.

All social occasions require the presence of a talking chief, a *manaia*, and a *taupo*; and if persons actually holding these titles are not present someone else has to play the role. The *manaia* is the head of the young men of a village and the *taupo* the head of the young girls.

Rank not of birth but of title is very important in Samoa. The status of a village depends upon the rank of its high chief; the prestige of a household depends upon the title of its *matai*. As for the titles of chiefs and talking chiefs, each carries many other duties and prerogatives besides the headship of a household. The Samoans, with rank a never failing source of interest, have invented an elaborate courtesy language which must be used in talking to people of high social status. A complicated etiquette surrounds each rank in society.

Chiefs are not necessarily hereditary, and sons do not succeed their fathers except when the family chooses. Chiefs are elected by the *aiga,* and their choice has sometimes come outside the immediate family of a dead chief. There have been occasions when the *aiga* has selected its leader, not from its own customary ranks, but from men or even women rather far afield. This conspicuous feature of Samoan life helps explain a number of the differences between these people and other Polynesians. Chiefs may also, of course, be deposed in the same manner as they are elected.

Matai meet in village discussion groups *(fono)* where most matters of interfamily and village concern are discussed and decided, including land boundaries and other land matters. The *fono* is a directive for much cooperative economic effort, and has wide social and political powers. It generally takes place in the house of the leading chief, where each titleholder in a special position in the group must be addressed with certain ceremonial phrases, and given a fixed place in the order of precedence in the serving of the kava, a native ceremonial drink. The house has certain fixed divisions; in the right sector sit the high chief and his special assistant chiefs; in the front of the house sit the talking chiefs whose business it is to make the speeches, welcome strangers, accept gifts, preside over the distribution of food, and make all plans and arrangements for group activities. Against the posts at the back of the house sit the *matai* of low rank, and between the posts and at the center sit those of so little importance that no place is reserved for them.

In the Samoans' very simple style of living, clothing is scant, in adjustment to the hot climate. A man wears a long kilt *(lavalava)* folded about the waist; the upper part of his body is bare. Women wear kilts and blouses, or long dresses. Children run about their homes naked. Shoes are occasionally worn on Tutuila, seldom in Manua. Cotton has replaced bark cloth, which is now used only for ceremonial occasions. Both sexes go barefoot, and hats are worn by women only to church, on which occasions the men don white shirts and collars. A chief and any aspirants to that rank wear a coat to church also. Sleeping mats, generally the only "furniture" in a house, are rolled up during the day. All the cooking is done in the outside oven.

Work in American Samoa consists only of those necessary tasks which keep life going: planting and harvesting and preparation of food, fishing, house building, mat making, care of children, and the arrangement of feasts to validate marriages and births and succession to titles and to entertain strangers. These are the necessary activities of life, activities in which every member of the community, down to the smallest child, has a part. Every household produces its own food and clothes and furniture: there is no large amount of fixed capital, and households of high rank are simply characterized by greater industry in the discharge of greater social obligations. In this setting the American picture of saving, of investment, of deferred enjoyment is completely absent.

The part played in Samoan life by leisure has to be understood before one can grasp the real nature of Samoa. The importance of time-consuming activities such as ceremony and oratory can only be appreciated in the light of the great amount of free time which the Samoan considers necessary to his happiness.

In matters of work the village makes few precise demands. It is the women's part to cultivate the sugar cane and sew the thatch for the roof of the guest house, to weave the palm-leaf blinds, and bring the coral rubble for the floor. The women catch fish on the reefs— eels, mullet, and shellfish. The men go out in canoes beyond the reef to catch tuna, bonita, barracuda, and swordfish. Women do not enter into house-building or boat-building activities, nor go out in fishing canoes, nor may men enter the formal weaving house or the house where women are making tapa in a group.

There is no daily routine, for each day has its own schedule, which is not known until the morning or perhaps the evening before. Samoans rise before daylight and do their hard work before the sun is high. After their labors they return to the village and have a light meal; during the afternoon they rest—stretched on mats in their homes. The main meal of the day is eaten about sundown.

The *matai*, or family chief, designates the work for the members of his group. He delegates one man to clear land for a new taro patch, another to fish, a third to cook; he tells the women when to weave mats or to make thatch. Or he may decide that all the working members of his family will go to the taro lands on one day, or that all will fish on the reef. Deep-sea fishing frequently depends on the appearance of a school of fish offshore, when fishing takes precedence.

In Samoa the young men mostly do the cooking, but sometimes both men and women. The food is wrapped in leaves and baked from two to four hours between two layers of hot rocks in a ground oven, with coconut leaf mats placed over the whole. A more modern method, faster and easier, consists of boiling it in pots or empty kerosene cans. Yams, taro, sweet potatoes, breadfruit, bananas, are now often boiled, although in general food tastes much better when baked in the ground oven.

The lands owned and operated by a family under a *matai* are called plantations, of which a family generally owns from five to ten of various sizes from about a twentieth of an acre to three or four acres. They are in scattered locations, most of them near the village in which the family lives. Many of the larger landholdings are controlled by family heads with titles of high chiefs and high talking chiefs.

After more than fifty years under American government, all forms of the social make-up of the ancient Samoans, and to some extent their political life, have been modified by the impact of Western customs. Their economic life has been little changed. They must still raise their own food in their mountainous islands. But, with a population phenomenally increased during the half-century of foreign administration, their serious problem is how to get enough food, and this struggle for existence has affected all phases of their traditional way of living.

The population of American Samoa increased from 5,679 in 1900 to 20,500 in 1955. The following table shows the increase by intervals:

TABLE IX
POPULATION OF AMERICAN SAMOA, 1900–1955

		PER CENT INCREASE OVER PRECEDING CENSUS
1900[1]	5,679	
1912[1]	7,251	27.7
1920[1]	8,056	11.1
1930	10,055	24.8[2]
1940	12,908	28.4
1950	18,937	46.7
1955	20,500	8.3

[1] Population of area as then constituted.
[2] Rate of increase, exclusive of population (99 in 1930) of Swains Island, annexed in 1925, 23.6 per cent.

The density per square mile, of an agricultural population, was 273 in 1955. On these small islands 20,500 people are now living where approximately 5,679 lived in 1900.

AGRICULTURE

The land used for agriculture—almost all that is arable even by native standards—is widely scattered on the various islands, in valleys, on small coastal plains, in saddles between peaks, on slopes, some quite steep, and in pockets. Trails lead from a village up the valley and mountain slopes where, under heavy stands of coconut trees, bananas and scattered breadfruit trees grow luxuriantly. Between the trees there is a rank growth of shrubs, ferns, and weeds.

Above the coconut plantations is a dense natural forest, where taro is planted in clearings—the *ma'umaga*, or main taro lands of the village. In the clearings dead trees are still standing, killed by girdling or by lighting fires around the bases of the trunks; stumps two feet high show where some have fallen, and rotting trunks and thick branches lie everywhere on the ground. Among these forest remains, taro grows in various stages of development from plants a few weeks old to mature plants seven or eight months old.

Taro is also raised along streams and in swampy areas near the coast where the water courses spread out. On the island of Aunuu there is a marsh on the north and west sides, amounting to nearly one hundred acres, which is elaborately diked and ditched into dozens of small islets where taro is produced in great abundance. The rich soil of the swamp is dug from the water channels and heaped onto these islets, the sides of which are made of retaining walls built of posts and woven coconut fronds. Water levels are controlled by sluice gates. This particular area, farmed in this way since the earliest times, shows considerable agricultural skill.

There is no systematic planting of breadfruit (*'ulu*), which has been growing here for many years—Samoans do not know exactly how many—and which is seen everywhere. Besides furnishing one of the staple foods, it provides timber extensively used in building native houses. There are many varieties named by the Samoans, some of them not considered very good to eat, but good for house posts. *Mase*, or breadfruit stored in pits in the ancient Polynesian way, is still important for food in northern Tutuila and other parts of American Samoa. This odorous substance, however, is not popular with most younger Samoans, who now obtain an appreciable part of their food from stores. Since breadfruit comes in great abundance at certain seasons and much of it is wasted, a way might be found, now that *mase* pits are going out of fashion, to conserve this food supply. For example, a suitable small-scale dryer might be developed for village or family use. In some atolls to the north, breadfruit is cooked and dried, and stored in baskets under the eaves of houses. Driers might be made out of oil drums, of which the Samoans have a considerable supply.

Yams *(ufi)*, not particularly favored by the Samoans, although liked by the Fijians and some Micronesians, are raised because of their usefulness in times of food shortage. Once planted, they will continue for years without further care, and a prudent *matai* always requires his *aiga* to keep a number of such plantings. In Samoan legend the eating of wild yams is always associated with times of famine.

Yams grow with taro in some clearings, their vines clinging to short poles or trailing on the ground. Near many of them are older clearings, formerly used for taro, but now used for bananas, where giant taro, a wild plant, is also found. A number of old taro lands have reverted to second-growth forest.

Each village group generally owns the plantations in its vicinity, but people from another village may have lands there too—by permission, through marriage relationships or by grants of plantations which have come down by heredity and which were originally given to a family chief as a reward for valor in battle.

Each plantation, of whatever kind, has a specific name by which it is identified, and its limits are shown generally by certain marked trees, by large rocks, or by other natural features. The ownership of trees growing near the imaginary boundary lines is exclusive, and should a member of one family take a coconut from a tree belonging to another there is trouble.

Nearly every Samoan village has patches of paper mulberry *(u'a)*, the inner bark of which is used to make tapa cloth *(siapo)*. Among several other trees grown in the islands, pandanus *(fala)* is important, but trees occupy a very small part of the total area devoted to crops.

Pandanus is common, growing alone or in small patches near villages. The leaves of the varieties *fala* and *paongo* are woven by the Samoans into floor mats and sleeping mats; another and distinct variety, *laui'e,* is chosen for fine mats. An export of mats, developed in recent years, has stimulated the propagation of these varieties, and young trees are seen here and there.

Kava, a small shrub, is cultivated, and its large dried roots are used in preparing the important ceremonial drink already referred to. The shrub is commonly planted in places where there is some deep soil in which the large roots may develop fully.

In recent years experiments in raising cacao beans have been carried on by some Samoans, and small shipments of dried cocoa have been made to Western Samoa.

Of the non-tree crops in American Samoa, taro is the most important; it is second only to bananas as a food crop and is preferred to bananas when the supply is large. Taro is acceptable as a ceremonial gift on important occasions. The higher plantations in Samoa are almost exclusively taro, many of them at elevations of from 700 to 1,000 feet. The lands used are clearings in the forest where the soil is not yet worn out, or where sufficient time has elapsed since the last planting to let the forest grow up and provide the soil with food. Taro plantations, farthest from the villages, are generally grouped together, identified with the families which own and operate them.

Cassava is commonly cultivated in little patches, mostly near the houses. Two forms are distinguished by the Samoans: *maniota,* which is made into starch, and *tapioka,* which is made into pudding.

Sugar cane, raised in patches near all the villages, is grown in part for house thatch. The variety commonly propagated is called *tolo fua lau. Tolo ula* and *tolo fiti* are sweeter varieties, chewed by children.

Samoan methods of agriculture are much the same as they were when the islands were discovered by Jacob Roggeveen in 1722. The digging stick *('oso)* is still used for planting. Of hardwood, generally *filofiloa,* about 5 feet long and 2.5 inches in diameter and pointed at one end, it is pushed into the ground to make a hole in which the seed or young plant is placed. Since much of the ground is rocky, a sharp iron or steel implement would soon become dulled.

A bush knife, as a tool for felling trees, has replaced the adz of prediscovery years. With a steel blade, about two feet long and three inches wide, curved outward at the end, it is also used for weeding, swung with a rhythmic movement backward and forward close to the ground.

On new coconut plantations bananas are raised so that there will be a return from the land for the six or seven years before the coconut trees bear. After the fruit is taken from a banana tree, it is cut down, but a shoot is allowed to grow from the root to bear a new bunch which is ready to eat in from seven to nine months. The Samoan swings his knife a few times about the base of the shoot to destroy the weeds. As for breadfruit, new trees spring from the roots of the old. Occasionally, however, Samoans set out a few young trees of a variety they especially like.

The traditional Samoan method is to obtain three crops of taro from a forest clearing, each requiring seven or eight months to mature. As a crop is dug out of the ground, the tops are cut and placed about a foot away from the old ones. In former times, at the end of two years, taro lands were usually abandoned and new clearings made. Samoans rotated their taro lands instead of their crops. But now, because of the pressure of population, they cannot afford to do that, and, since they do not use fertilizer, the yields are small. Only patches where young plants are growing are weeded, for if an area were always kept clear of weeds, whatever soil is there would soon be washed away by the rains, especially on slopes, which now are frequently utilized. Weeds also help to keep the thin soil moist. Taro on high sloping lands can be left in the ground several months after it is ripe, but that on low flat lands, where the soil is generally swampy, must be harvested and used soon after it has matured.

Yams are raised by building little hillocks about them as they get larger. After six months they may be harvested; but if they are left in the ground the tubers keep on developing for a year, some of them becoming as much as two feet long and eight inches in diameter.

Little work is necessary for other crops. Sugar cane is planted by slips, and the leaves are big enough to use for thatch in three or four months. Pandanus is started mostly from seed, though sometimes from shoots. At the end of a year, leaves may be cut to make mats. The plants develop into trees, and grow for many years. Similarly, when the stems of paper mulberry are cut, new ones develop, and the same patch continues to produce. Cassava slips are merely stuck in the ground. Kava slips grow best in dry soil. The few kava shrubs of a family are generally distributed among several of the family lands.

By the native method of taro growing, only a small part of the total area of forested land is used in any one year. In a thinly populated area, as American Samoa was formerly, the system of rotation of the land was in harmony with conditions generally. The cultivated plots were widely scattered. Soon after they were abandoned they were covered with young forest, which, in due course, grew to be indistinguishable from the surrounding primeval forest. This system, practiced from time immemorial, is a form of primitive economy in which a large amount of land is available for a small group of people. The pressure now for every square yard of possible land is so great that many slopes far too steep for use are nevertheless cultivated. A plantation on Olosega in Manua is on a slope so precipitous that the Samoan who works it has to let himself down by ropes, and has to keep himself, his implements, and his baskets all tied from above to prevent falling a hundred feet to the rocks below.

In the mountainous country of Samoa an outstanding result of the repeated use of forest clearings for agriculture is soil erosion, which is increased in some places by clean weeding, a practice which has been discontinued in other rainy tropical climates.

The forest in Samoa affords several products without requiring any replenishment. Some of them are important as emergency foods. Wild taro and yams are edible. The fruit of the Tahitian chestnut (ifi) and the heart of the tree fern (olioli) are relished. Arrowroot (masoa), established in the forest, is used to make a pudding and to make paste for gluing bark cloth.

As to livestock industries in American Samoa, the natives are most interested in the production of pigs and poultry. Pigs enable a family to make a good showing at various ceremonial functions demanding pork. They are generally kept near the villages in enclosures, the animals marked to show to which family they belong. The meat of the coconut is their principal food; those being fattened are also fed the waste of nearly every kind of food that the people eat. Carelessly looked after, they frequently escape from their enclosures to damage taro and other crops. Poultry are raised primarily for meat rather than for eggs, the production of which is small. In the past a considerable number of cattle furnished milk and beef. The Government maintains a dairy farm at Tafuna where the herd eats mostly imported hay and other feed. A considerable item of import from New Zealand is canned corned beef, of which the Samoans are very fond.

An experimental farm operated by the Government to produce fresh vegetables and fruits for the hospital and for outside sale serves primarily as a plant-introduction station. There a considerable number of fruit trees and of Temperate Zone vegetables have been established, including several varieties of avocado, oranges, grapefruit, and other citrus fruits, and green beans, cabbage, and peppers. Although the culture of these is demonstrated as practicable, the natives have evidenced little interest in the work of the farm or in its products and it has therefore little influence in introducing new food crops. People's tastes in food change very slowly, and new food plants introduced to Samoa will not become popular for many years unless famine forces their use.

The area of American Samoa available for agriculture is now nearly all in use. Perhaps a little more ground could be cleared, especially on a small plateau on top of the ridge at the western end of Tutuila Island. Existing land could be more intensively cultivated. Yet even if such clearing and more intense cultivation were accomplished, the rapidly increasing population would still press more and more on the restricted food supply. The agriculture of American Samoa is merely one of bare subsistence. Commercial agriculture is at present out of the question, except for coconuts for copra.

The soils of the island are variable, the most fertile lying along the coastal fringe of the southwestern plateau and in the small valley areas where alluvial deposits have been built up. On the steep mountainous slopes there is little chance to accumulate a layer of earth because of the heavy rainfall, which, as was already stated, averages one hundred and sixty inches a year, concentrated mostly in the more rainy season from December to March. It is astonishing, however, what a plant cover these slopes maintain. But all of the soils of the island, although varying in fertility, are uniformly low in needed food elements because of their excessive leaching by the tremendous growth of tropical vegetation.

Several tracts of land formerly cultivated have returned to bush as a result of disputes over ownership which have as yet not reached the courts, or which have not been adjudicated. This unfortunate situation arises in part from the reluctance of Samoans to permit boundary surveys of their lands, and in part from the inability of the Government to obtain a suitable staff of surveyors familiar with the area and the people. Thefts of produce, which are common, are at present a very troublesome crime. Young men sincerely devoted to improving the productivity of their land are often discouraged by the thievery of others, even members of their own *aiga*, or family group.

When the United States acquired American Samoa, all the land was owned by family groups except for a few small tracts owned by foreigners whose titles thereto had been established between 1890 and 1899. The Government, realizing that the chief basis of the Samoans' prosperity, health, and happiness is their continued ownership and cultivation of their soil, has pursued a policy of "Samoan land for Samoans." The laws of American Samoa accordingly provide that there shall be no alienation to a non-Samoan of tracts by Samoans. These tracts, however, may be leased to non-Samoans, with the sanction of the governor, for a term not to exceed thirty years, for any purpose except for the extraction of minerals and the cutting of timber. Approximately five hundred acres are owned by the Government, much of it built up by dredging and filling on the fringing reefs, where part is occupied by Government buildings and quarters for personnel. Small amounts are owned by missions and churches, and by traders—some of it by a few individuals in fee simple, but no records are available to show the areas.

With the slow but consistent trend toward greater individualism among the Samoans owing to contacts with Americans, the *matai* has tended to lose some of his old authority over family lands. Young men often in one way or another obtain from him an allocation of specific portions for their own use. Once they have these in production they are not always inclined to cooperate with the traditional family leaders in sharing all the produce, and some of the ensuing disputes have even reached the governor's office and the courts. There have been a few instances of violence and a number of threats. Occasionally a young man able to earn a sufficient sum of money, say five hundred dollars or so, has persuaded a chief to let him use some tracts as his own. There are a number of privately worked areas of that kind in Samoa, not strictly "freehold," since it was not so recorded at the time of cession, but still alienated from communal or family property though not from Samoan ownership. This legal problem apparently has never been fully understood by anyone but the chief judge, who somehow sees to it that no rights to such sections are granted to a non-Samoan.

American staff members in the Department of Agriculture give informal encouragement to their native students and former students trying to better themselves as farmers, and to resist what may seem to some members of the administration to be the asserted and parasitical rights of chiefs. Tufele, possessor of one of the higher titles in Manua, recently appointed Assistant Director of Agriculture, will probably encourage the development of a sense of self-sufficiency among the young Samoans, but it is not likely he will do so at the expense of destroying the family tradition of loyalty and obedience to the *matai*. Tufele's concern is great over the decline in family organization, and he hopes, by developing initiative on the part of young men, to improve the next generation's capacities for family leadership. Ownership of land in fee simple will someday come to American Samoa, as it came in Hawaii, and in Guam. The responsibility of the American agriculturists and the Government in general is to see that the transition occurs as painlessly as possible for all concerned.

LAND TENURE

Land tenure in American Samoa is intimately bound up with the organization of Samoan society. As has been pointed out, the control of land is vested in the *matai*, or head of the Samoan family. Certain tracts belong to the chiefs. The uncultivated bush is claimed by those who own the grounds at its borders. The lagoon, also, as far as the reef, is the property of those off whose village it is situated. Although the power of selling land, and doing other things of importance affecting all the family, is vested in the titled head of the family, yet he dare not do anything without formally consulting all concerned. Were he to persist in attempting to do otherwise, the *aiga* would take his title from him, and give it to another. The members of a family can thus take the title from their head, and heads of families can unite to take the title from their chief, and give it to his brother, or uncle, or some other member of the chief's family, who they think will act more in accordance with their wishes.

Certain traditional rights go with the high titles. A man may obtain rights of use over some land by marrying the daughter of a chief or of a *matai* who has control of it. If his wife dies and he marries a woman from another family, by Samoan custom he obtains the usage of certain tracts of her family. But by reason of his former marriage, he still has a certain kind of control or *pule* over what he had used by reason of his marriage to his first wife, and can collect products from it. On the other hand, the sons and daughters of a chief, on his death, have no rights by Samoan custom in the areas which he governed because of his chiefly rank.

A woman divorced from a member of a family retains a claim upon the lands of the family to which she belonged before her marriage. She may return to her family with her children and share with all her *aiga* the products of their areas. A widow also may return to the communal bond of her own family.

A rich Samoan may become poor in this way: Suppose a member of a family is a very high chief; he is thereby entitled by Samoan custom to food and other support from the village for himself and his immediate relatives, and this easy living may continue for many years. If he is lazy and a poor manager he may have neglected the family land, and a large portion of it, through intermarriage rights, may be used by other families. When he dies, any married sons and daughters living with him have no title to further support by the village and perhaps they will have no title to any lands which may have been yielding them a living. So from occupying a high position in the village they may drop to having very little. The *pule* or right which some *matai* have over the produce of land not in their families is difficult for an American to comprehend. The cohesiveness of the Samoan social organization and native Samoan public opinion have resulted in the persistence of intermarriage rights and other traditional land-use customs *fa'a Samoa.**

The Samoans have almost no written records of their own land-ownership or land tenure. On the other hand the methods of the West put much emphasis on records, and since the American Government of Samoa was established, some records have been kept.

The titles which give the holders certain rights in land are as significant to Samoans as titles of peers were to the English in feudal England. Samoans know the prestige of titles and talk them over in their family *fonos* and in their village *fonos*. It is the duty of the young men of a family to listen to these family discussions and become especially well acquainted with the order of precedence of titles and the prestige and rights associated with them.

Titled names and claims thereunto have been more fruitful of wars, either for the actual ownership of lands or merely for the title,

* *Fa'a Samoa* is a term commonly used in Samoa for "according to Samoan custom" as compared with *papalagi*, or "white man's custom."

than any other factors in all periods of Samoan history. High titles, now being more and more decided in the American Court at Pago Pago, are very important, since only those who hold them are eligible to be chosen as native government officials with salaries.

The advantages of a name are counterbalanced by the duties and responsibilities connected with it, the least of which is the feeding and housing of relatives, however remote, whenever they may demand it. It also entails the principal expenditure in entertaining visitors.

The *fono* of a village retains jurisdiction over all the land within its titular limits, which may far exceed the limits of cultivation. Any one holding land within these limits is subject to a village levy upon his crops or upon his labor. Although he be a *matai* in some other village, he will meet the *fono* of the village where he plants and harvests, and the young men of his household will work in the *'aumage* (taro land) of that village.

The land on Tutuila, once held by chiefs in the Atua District of East Upolu in Western Samoa, made Tutuila, as far as land tenure is concerned, an appanage of Upolu. Because subchiefs held the land of Tutuila in fief for their overlords on Upolu, when the government of Samoa was divided between Germany and the United States in 1900 the subchiefs on Tutuila were glad, for that meant they would probably be freed from their overlords on Upolu.

Many titles of *matai* on Tutuila also came originally from Atua District on Upolu. Because of the political separation of the two when the United States occupied the eastern islands, the chiefs on Tutuila have been able to attach more significance to their rank than when the islands were politically united. However, as late as 1920 a chief from Upolu who had certain rights over land in Leone came over there and collected one hundred baskets of coconuts. No objection was offered by those who held the land, since they knew of the *pule*, or traditional right. It is not likely that a chief would be allowed to exercise that right today.

The establishment of an American court has changed the old circumstances of control over land, for the chief justice of the American court has supreme power in making a decision. He is assisted by native judges who act, however, in an advisory capacity. Many high chiefs now do not control any more land in American Samoa than many *matai* who have much lower titles. In the old days, according to Samoan customs, they did control more land. They had *matai* under them, and if the *matai* was not loyal to his chief and did not serve him well, the chief, with the approval of the village *fono*, could remove him and appoint another in his place.

American law, however, does not allow this. A *matai* whose title is registered with the Government can be removed by his family only for just cause, and the removal must be approved by the administration. The power of the chief is thus annulled, for if the *matai* does not donate appreciable food and service to the chief, the chief has no recourse in American law.

Some decisions in the American court according to Western law weaken the purely Samoan attitude toward land and land tenure. Land itself to a Samoan is not valuable: it is only use which makes it so. Thousands of acres of forested land in American Samoa, unused and apparently not claimed, are nevertheless owned according to Samoan tradition, and the ownership is well known to Samoans through their family histories.

There is, however, no written evidence of the ownership of forest lands, and the court bases its decisions of the ownership of such lands largely on their use. That is to say, if a piece of forest land has been cleared and used for four or five years and is then surveyed and registered, the registration is likely to be uncontested. If it is contested, the asserted historical circumstances of family ownership will count for something, but actual use of the land by another family is a weightier consideration.

Yet more significance is attached to the use of land for some crops than for others. A Samoan may plant taro on strips which, by Samoan right, do not belong to him, without objection by the *matai* of that area, and similarly he may plant bananas. But should he try to plant coconuts or breadfruit, there is likely to be a quarrel, for that looks like permanent ownership. In the court in Western Samoa, the fact that taro has been planted on land even by a *matai* for two years is not necessarily considered a good indication of ownership. Such peculiar Samoan rights complicate very much the settlement of disputes regarding tenure. For example: A young man may be adopted into a Samoan family, and, having served it well for many years, may be rewarded with a *matai* title. He immediately takes on the government of the family lands. Naturally he wishes his wife and biological family to have some property when he dies, so he may exchange a pig for a strip. There is no written record, and when he dies the *aiga* may maintain that this strip is part of the communal land of the Samoan family. The distinction between privately owned property and communal property brings very complicated cases before the court.

Disputes regarding land tenure in American Samoa come before the court in several ways. A usual procedure at present is for a Samoan *matai* to appear at the court and say that he wishes to sue another for trespass. The court asks if the area in question has been surveyed. If not, the Samoan, provided the family can afford it, has the disputed spot mapped by a registered surveyor. If notice of the survey is posted at the court for sixty days without objectors, the land is registered in the name of the *matai* who brought the suit.

If others claim title to the land, they must appear before the court to voice their objections. The *matai* who sued for trespass is the proponent. In some cases both the proponent and the objectors seek to establish ownership by swearing that their fathers and grandfathers picked breadfruit from the trees on that land. Another important argument at court is the presence, on the disputed territory, of the grave of a member of one of the contending families, for usually only members of a family who hold land may according to Samoan custom be buried on it.

During a recent inter-Government meeting between Western Samoan officials and American Samoan Government officers, Chief Tamasese of Western Samoa broached hopes that chiefs from his part of the archipelago might come to courts in Tutuila in connection with landownership cases and the settlement of claims to high titles. Local chiefs were very strongly opposed to this, and always will be.

Land tenure in American Samoa is made still more complicated by the scattered nature of holdings. The land of the people of Amanave, for example, comprises most of that in the watersheds of the two valleys which converge on the village, some on the watersheds of neighboring valleys, and some far away on the top of the ridge. People of nearby Poloa use by permission of Amanave some pieces in the watersheds of the two valleys.

If Amanave people should have a quarrel with the Poloa people, a not infrequent occurrence in Samoa, they will try to prohibit the Poloa population from using their land. But the right of the Poloa people would probably be upheld by the American court since they are in actual occupation.

The litigious nature of Samoans adds another difficulty to a just settlement of disputes over land: the Samoans love to argue. It is a spirit which has developed from time immemorial in their *fono*. Some Samoans who have little to gain in a legal case encourage one or other of the participants in the dispute not to withdraw his claims. If the case is held off for a while, it sometimes becomes apparent who these people are and influence to desist can be brought to bear on them. Samoan problems over land are likely to be settled most satisfactorily by letting them drag on a bit in the old-fashioned Samoan way. A local surveyor stated that in twenty-odd years of land surveying in American Samoa, he had almost never worked on any cases in which boundaries and ownership were not disputed by many factions.* That is especially the situation today.

There are *matai* in the village of Fitiuta on Tau in Manua District who are afraid to build new *fale* (houses), for they know that by Samoan tradition they don't own the land in the village on which their present houses stand and, if they tried to put up new ones, the rightful owners might become active objectors.

In the Manua District, however, there is less friction over land tenure than on the island of Tutuila, since the Manua District is isolated, and has no permanent white residents. The people therefore lack examples of the acquisitive Western nature which may be seen on Tutuila, where the less steep land is nearly all being used and where Samoans have noted that some of the permanent residents among the whites have bought control of a considerable amount of good land registered in the names of their Samoan wives.

A number of white residents argue that it would be wise to hasten a change from the Samoan custom of land tenure to the Western system, maintaining that natives should be encouraged to register lands and hold title in fee simple. They believe that the greatest drawback to agricultural prosperity and production is the *matai* system and communal ownership of property. The almost universal opinion seems to be that the *matai* institution will die of itself, but in the distant future. Almost all *matais* report that the younger men of their families will neither work willingly nor obey their orders as in the "old days." Members of the administration, agreeing that this is the case, feel that nothing can be done or should be done at this

* B. F. Kneubuhl, letter to G. B. Landenberger, Governor of American Samoa, Aug. 18, 1932.

time to interfere with the *matai* system, for to do so would work too great a hardship on the older people who know little or nothing of the new order and individual ownership of property. The younger members of the present generation are in a position to live either within or without the *matai* plan. Many of them endeavor to earn for themselves, and ignore the traditional family arrangement altogether.

Be that as it may, we have to concede the Samoans the liberty to establish their own property rights; they do not of necessity, at present at any rate, have to adopt the system of Americans or any other people.

In a change from family (communal) ownership to individual or freehold ownership, a division of family lands would be exceedingly complicated and difficult, whether or not an individual should have or could have all of his property in one unit. If all of it were in one unit, he would not know how to prolong the use of his taro patches, for he is unacquainted with fertilizer.

Some young Samoans think that freehold ownership should be encouraged. But they have no appreciation of the change in their society which that would involve; especially they do not realize the insurance for the individual which must be provided for under the Western arrangement. Under the present native plan no member of a family is in want unless all are in want.

There are great differences in the mental and moral caliber of *matai*. Some diligent persons carry out their duties conscientiously. Others, who are negligent, merely assign work to be done by various members of their families. Some *matai* spend a good deal of time away from their lands, visiting other *matai*, hatching "political pull" for young men in their groups or wasting their time in idle gossip.

Yet, whatever its faults, the *matai* system is a cohesive social organization, and if the Samoans were to take over suddenly another social structure which they do not understand they would bring upon themselves social and economic chaos. They have an efficient social organization except in economic production. Within certain limits they have moral obligations as rigid as those of people in the United States, but their horizon is much narrower and scarcely goes beyond their family and their village. The reasons of one who argues against the *matai* system are implicit, not explicit. To insist that the natives take over moral, social, and legal systems strange to their traditions, and to put upon them economic burdens under which they become very restive, would entail so drastic a reorganization that it would destroy the patterns of living still essential for the circumstances of today. Abolishing the *matai* system in Samoan society would be as significant to the Samoans as establishing a *matai* system in villages of comparable size in the United States would be to Americans. If such a plan were established in America, the whole social order would have to change, since instead of individual production and ownership, in the cooperative output of a system of group loyalty, people would have to recognize social obligations to cousins and uncles and aunts.

Contacts with Western civilization are slowly changing the attitude of Samoans toward their own customs and traditions of land tenure as well as their attitude toward other aspects of their society. In the recent past many older chiefs holding the highest titles in American Samoa have passed away—Mauga, Tuitele, Leiato, Tufele, Misa, two Sateles, two Letulis, Fuimaonos, Leosos, and others.

Successors to the titles of *Satele, Leoso,* and *Letuli* have not yet been chosen. The *Misa* title was awarded after a bitter court fight. No doubt the others will also be fought out in court. The Fagatogo title of *Tiumalu* has always been settled by the *matai* themselves. For the first time in Samoan history, it will be settled in court in the near future with a woman claimant among the contestants.

Most of the men who have taken the places of the deceased are of the newer order, and have had the advantage of closer contact with the kind of civilization brought to their islands by the United States and its representatives.

Teachers in the public schools are enjoined by the Department of Education to instill in their pupils respect for the *matai*—a bolstering of his position which may be taken as a sign of his weakening authority. In the old days his authority was so unquestioned that it was unnecessary to try to inculcate respect.

Making English the compulsory medium of instruction in public schools seems likely to lessen the interest of Samoans in their cultural heritage. Soon their interest in their status in their own society will wane. Their familiar departmentalized system of chief, talking chief, *matai*, and *manaia* will be replaced by a cultural mélange which may produce serious social unrest. In short, a drastic change is coming too rapidly for the best interests of Samoa, for this sudden impact from the West on a highly complex organization is not likely to bring beneficial results.

In land tenure in American Samoa, there is no indication of great change for the immediate future. Some Samoans, however, are beginning, under wise leadership, to look far ahead. The Government should be prepared to supervise any spontaneous evolution from traditional Samoan organization to patterns fashioned in the Western World, a change which should come gradually. It must plan to help the people bridge the gulf between their primitive culture and the requirements of modern days, to ensure their social stability, economic welfare, and future progress.

Since the boundaries between many lands are not well defined, the Government should be prepared to supervise a just settlement of boundary disputes. With the growth of population and consequent use of new forest land, quarrels are increasing and settlements are being demanded in the American court.

Young Samoans of today will play an important role through the difficult times ahead. They can best lead their fellows through the transition period from their old ways and traditions to the new. More of the best qualified young people should receive part of their education according to Western methods in a Western country so that they may serve as "go-betweens" for their own people and customs and American ways. They can then help to settle land questions more intelligently.

Tuitele, the young district governor with a Western education, is giving much attention to training young chiefs who will have to face the coming changes. The old chiefs, set in their habits of thought, are not easily persuaded to look at a problem from various points of view. It is likely that someday, perhaps not far off, a commission to decide land cases would give the most satisfaction to all concerned. It might be composed of chiefs from British Samoa as well as chiefs from American Samoa and American Samoan Government officials. It would be a great advantage if some of the Samoans on it had received part of their education, including a little legal training, in the United States or in a British country. Decisions of such a commission would be accepted with greater confidence by the Samoan people.

The real problem in appointing such a commission lies in a serious shortage of non-Samoans who can speak the native language and yet who could not be suspected of bias. A working majority of non-Samoans would be essential for securing impartiality. The Samoans are not slow to admit that even the most judicious and fair-minded of their own leaders are often subject to unbearable pressures from within their family groups. If non-Samoans had to depend upon interpreters, their work would be impeded and, quite probably, their judgments influenced unfairly by translators. Most of the *palagis* (Americans) who can speak Samoan either are related by marriage to some island family (and therefore questionable on this ground), or are missionaries (and therefore questionable by all who are not of the same faith). As for American officials, because of the shortness of their tenure hardly any one of them, either active or retired, knows the Samoan language.

THE COPRA INDUSTRY

The copra industry is the mainstay of the economy of American Samoa. Ripe coconuts for copra generally lie under the trees for a month or two, until there are enough to make a cutting worth while. Nuts from plantations near the villages are gathered from time to time and strung around poles in villages where they remain until it is decided to cut copra. Storing them thus *(feti'i)* keeps them from rats and thieves. The Government prohibits harvesting green nuts for copra because of the inferior quality of the product.

The nuts are husked, split open with the backs of bush knives, and the meat is cut out in strips with a copra knife. The fresh meat is dried on mats near the houses and is "raked" by hand at intervals to dry it evenly. In sunny weather the meat dries in four days, but the average drying period is seven days. When showers come, the mats are hurriedly dragged inside.

The copra is carried in baskets to the village weighing station, where a receipt or copra chit, negotiable at face value anywhere in American Samoa, is issued, generally in the name of the family chief. The product is then stored in a copra shed to await transportation to Pago Pago. The Government buys and markets the copra and thereby saves the Samoan from trading with people whose ways he does not understand. Moreover, if it is sold on contract, it brings a better average price over a period of years than could be gained by individuals.

With the money the Samoans buy cloth, thread, kerosene, soap, matches, knives, belts, and tobacco, pay their taxes, levied on every man over eighteen years of age, and support the church.

Copra, the only agricultural cash crop of American Samoa, is the island's main economic resource. Although the total production has never been large, it will always be an important item in the native economy. For the year ending July, 1945, the return for the copra was $39,167 at $67.34 per ton. In 1946, at $105 per ton, the crop returned $80,000. With the current price at $215 per ton, it is expected that there will be an even greater increase in the copra output.

Because of the importance of the copra industry, the island Government is trying to take special steps to ensure proper planting, cultivation, sanitation, and insect control within the groves. These measures have been incorporated into the Samoan Code and provide for the control of the rhinoceros beetle, or coconut beetle, which was introduced to the island more than thirty years ago.

The rhinoceros beetle attacks the growing heart of the treetop, burrowing into the tender undeveloped fronds and destroying or deforming them, thus reducing the vitality of the tree, and sometimes even killing it. The grubs of the beetle develop in rotten wood, usually coconut trunks. They feed on this until they pupate. The stick insect also attacks the treetops, but to a lesser degree.

Notches cut in coconut trees near a house or a village aid natives in climbing these trees in order to take nuts in various stages of growth short of ripening. The Samoan, like all Polynesians, is very fond of the various kinds of green nuts, and has many different names for them. The *palagi* knows them only as "green," and cares very little about them as a rule because they are useless for copra and cannot be grated or desiccated. However, they contain important food elements not found in ripe coconuts, particularly vitamins in the "B-1" group which are valuable to the Samoan diet, and particularly helpful in converting starches into proteins.

The difficulties of the Government in trying to improve the copra output are shown by the following incident. In an effort to control the increasing ravages of the coconut beetle, a law was enacted which required each *pulenu'u*, or village chief, to organize and conduct weekly a search in his particular area for beetles and their grubs. These were collected at a central point where inspection was made by Government officials, and the insects were then burned. Chiefs who were found to be assembling small catches of the bugs were rebuked, and in some instances the villages were fined small amounts for not having made a good showing. However, it was discovered that many villages were maintaining "farms" where beetles were raised so that there would always be plenty for the inspectors! Similarly, during a plague of rats before World War II, shortly preceding the author's first study, when the Government offered a bounty on the tails of the pests, it was found that some natives were breeding them.

Many of the coconut trees in the islands are about eighty years old, past the age of most productive bearing. Thousands of trees are deeply notched to enable climbers to obtain nuts and leaves for their own use. These notches form openings where rot begins, and mosquitoes breed.

The inroads of the beetle have seriously affected copra production, for no adequate control measures have as yet been developed, although there are several promising leads. A wasp, a small predatory beetle, and a mold have been discovered, but American Samoa does not have the funds with which to develop and experiment, and thus must wait for research agencies of other countries to do so.

Until recently, the Government was procuring selected high-yield seed nuts from the Crown Estates in Western Samoa and distributing these at cost, or below. In recent years the Agriculture Department has been active in sponsoring replanting of selected seed from local sources.

The Department of Agriculture employs a dozen Samoans under Chief Tufele as agriculture extension employees or agents who make regular visits to all villages to advise natives on replanting new trees and to give them general information in regard to other agricultural problems.

There is, however, much inertia on the part of the natives, and the tendency to rely on over-age plantations is great. It seems to the Samoans that it takes a long time for a nut to become a bearing tree, and the need for cash is much more urgent. They do not like to cut down over-age trees for the sake of giving space to new plantings. Chief Tufele of Tau is making some headway, and at last the old growths are beginning to be replaced. The native legislature has requested the Government to establish a copra processing plant in the Pago Pago area, hoping that other Territories in the adjacent Pacific will ship their copra there and augment the production of

Samoa, which is by no means large enough to justify local processing. This, however, is a questionable economy, in view of local sun drying which gives the people more to occupy their time.

The Government recently began a schedule of motor launches to the north side of Tutuila with a copra clerk, who weighs the copra on the beach and pays for it at the rate of five cents a pound. The market price in March, 1956 was from $155 to $160 a ton.

The Samoan rate of copra production is closely connected with the price of copra, although other factors have an effect on it. In the Manua Islands where the family tradition is somewhat stronger than in the rest of the Territory, its amount has remained fairly steady, accounting for between 50 per cent and 75 per cent of the total output of the islands each year. Competitive fund-raising activities, particularly for the construction of churches, tend to increase the output in various places at various times.

Rapid rises and falls in the market have had elevating and depressing effects on production. The total amount of copra in Samoa is so small that by the time the necessary four hundred tons are available to bring a north-bound freighter, the market in San Francisco may have risen or fallen several times, and when the freighter arrives perhaps the entire shipment may be sold at a low figure, whereupon within a month or two the price will rise again. The demand for copra in the United States is closely connected with the price of cattle feed, and with Government stockpiling for the manufacture of napalm. Philippine copra dominates the San Francisco market anyway, and a large Philippine shipment depresses prices. Under the Navy, the base at Cavite Bay near Manila used to keep an eye on outgoing Philippine copra shipments, in order to advise the Government of American Samoa of the best marketing time. But that service is not available now.

The necessity for a greatly increased copra production has developed since World War II. During the war years a significant change occurred not only in the economy of the islands, but also in the habits, customs, and tastes of the Samoans. Prior to the war less than 10 per cent of the adult males were in the service of the Navy, but during the war years almost every able-bodied adult male was employed by the Navy on the naval station, in the Marine Reserve, or in the Fita Fita Guard. This employment brought a different mode of living to most of the families. The only way to satisfy their newly formed tastes is by selling copra.

TABLE X

COPRA OUTPUT OF AMERICAN SAMOA, 1954, 1955
(in tons)

YEAR	WESTERN DISTRICT	EASTERN DISTRICT	MANUA	SWAINS ISLAND	TOTAL (TONS)
1954	794	327	716	58	1,895
1955	495	61	814	189	1,559

FISHING

Fish, plentiful in the islands, are the most important flesh diet of the Samoan people. The pools on the coral reef, where, as we have noted, women fish, are a source of abundant supply; from them fish are taken with rods and lines, spears, nets, and traps: mullet, sea eels, octopuses, and a host of others.

The Samoans enjoy reef fishing and many spend hours at it every day, combing the reefs at low tide for crabs and other shellfish. Wearing goggles and using short metal spears, both young and old may be seen wading in pools and peering into holes in the rocks. A diligent reef fisher catches in a day from five to twenty-five eels and assorted fish up to twelve inches long. Net throwing, as among the Hawaiians, is also popular. Offshore subsistence fishing, however, has seen a serious decline recently. There are two main reasons: the high incomes during the war enable the natives to buy canned fish; and the chiefs have lost authority until it is no longer possible for them to organize fishing expeditions efficiently and to apportion the catches. For a number of years most of the fish consumed in the Pago Pago area have been supplied by Niue Islanders resident in that vicinity who have little access to Samoan lands and who ventured far out to sea in small one- and two-man canoes, usually at night. With the advent of a Japanese fishing fleet now serving the cannery in Anua near Pago Pago, there has been an abundance of fresh fish available to most of the population in the areas within easy reach of the Government station. The Samoans in that area have done virtually no offshore fishing in the last two years. Unless the Government is able to provide leadership and retrain the Samoans in modern techniques, and give them an incentive to use them, fishing seems likely to become a lost art in most of American Samoa.

One method of reef fishing is by poisoning or stunning the fish at low tide with the pounded seed of the *futu* tree and other native poison which is scattered in pools. The pressure of population has caused inshore waters, particularly in Tutuila, to be seriously over-fished with derris root, stolen dynamite, and native poisons. Portions of the fringing reefs have virtually lost their capacity to support marine life, and recovery will be very slow, if indeed it is possible.

The open sea furnishes mainly bonito, mackerel, sharks, swordfish, tuna, ulua, and barracuda. Bonito are caught by trolling with special canoes. Wormlike marine animals (*palolo*) are scooped out of the water near shore during their breeding season in October and November.

The most important recent development with regard to food has been the opening of the tuna cannery at Anua. Japanese sampans employing the long-line technique have, since February, 1955, been bringing remarkably large and excellent catches of tuna and sword-fish from nearby waters. The cannery has already reached better than one-half of its productive capacity, and, provided seasonal factors do not affect the fishing, it is to be expected that a major source of income and low-cost food has finally been found. The probability of cheap fish meal for fertilizer is also good. While Samoans appear to work more or less satisfactorily in the cannery, it is not likely that they will be able to replace the Japanese when it comes to catching, although it is possible that other Polynesian people of nearby islands may in time become proficient fishermen with the long-line system.

EXPORTS AND IMPORTS

There is a very striking increase in exports from American Samoa owing to the operation of the cannery. Nearly a million dollars' worth of fish products were shipped in the fiscal year 1954-1955. Of course, the production of the cannery is limited by refrigerator and cold-storage space, which is very inadequate. It is estimated that if about $300,000 could be obtained, adequate facilities could be built

TABLE XI

EXPORTS AND IMPORTS OF AMERICAN SAMOA, 1954, 1955

EXPORT ITEMS			1954	1955
Copra, sun-dried			$293,975.00	$243,065.00
Laufala floor mats			38,288.15	38,363.23
All other mats			16,535.79	4,854.23
Woodcraft			914.50	532.92
Tapas			1,337.25	1,655.07
All other curios			2,131.00	2,389.69
	1954	1955		
Tuna fish, canned	8,178 cases	66,160 cases	107,700.10	959,673.90
Fish meal	456 bags	3,319 bags	1,586.88	30,015.06
		Total	$462,468.67	$1,270,548.10

IMPORTS		1954	1955
United States		$389,503.60	$603,056.14
Australia and New Zealand		277,335.51	302,440.20
Apia and Suva		36,317.21	59,331.18
Great Britain		4,753.74	9,255.09
Japan		11,247.80	11,275.03
Tonga		12.00	574.13
Hong Kong			1,115.56
Holland			920.98
	Total	$719,169.86	$987,968.31

which would permit full-time year-around operation of the cannery on an eight-hour basis, since fish can be taken all year in commercial quantities within a radius of one thousand miles of Samoa by use of the current fishing methods. It is unfortunate that there seem to be impediments preventing this full utilization of about the only undeveloped resource.

The Government of the United States could perhaps establish for its Pacific dependencies a Territorial fund out of which projects of this kind could be financed, the loans to be repaid out of increased Government revenues thus generated. If the Congress of the United States and the Administration felt it desirable, such a fund could be set up on the basis of a bond issue, and could be offered with tax-free interest through the usual channels for public subscription.

V

Government of American Samoa

THE President of the United States, by Executive order dated June 29, 1951, directed that the administration of American Samoa be transferred from the Navy Department to the Department of the Interior, effective on July 1, 1951, when all positions held by naval personnel were taken over by civilian personnel. The first civilian governor took office on February 23, 1951. No change in nationality status of the inhabitants took place, and the Samoans are still classified as American nationals.

The Government of American Samoa today is, in practice, by indirect rule, a type which has been successful in dealing with native peoples elsewhere, and is in line with the more recent developments in native administrations. The administrative body uses in part the native political structure to carry out the routine of government, taking natives with high titles and giving them governmental responsibility and salary. It recognizes village, county, and district gatherings for discussion—the traditional way of Samoan native government.

American Samoa is divided into three administrative districts, each with a native district governor appointed by the governor of American Samoa. The districts are divided into counties, and the native chiefs of these subdivisions are also appointed by the governor. Unless there is good personal reason against it, the highest chief in the county is appointed county chief. Village chiefs are elected annually by village councils composed of family heads, but the chiefs selected must be approved by the governor.

The Government comprises the customary three branches: the

executive, the legislative (or Fono), and the judicial. The Fono of American Samoa consists of two houses. Without full legislative authority, its enactments are resolutions addressed to the governor in the form of advice and recommendation.

The Fono, reorganized to its present form in 1952, had its first regular session in 1953, when it enacted laws providing for the registration of all adults over the age of eighteen as voters, and set up procedures for nominations and for the conduct of elections by secret ballot, the first ever held in Samoa.

The reorganized legislative branch of the Government became sharply differentiated from the executive as both had been from the judicial. The Fono was divided into two houses, with membership of both based on the counties, the Lower House attempting to afford proportional representation. The total number of members was reduced from that of the previous House in an effort to improve the caliber and develop greater efficiency. A permanent staff was organized and an anthropologist employed to give advice. The Senate is comprised of fifteen titled members elected in accordance with Samoan customs. The House of Representatives consists of eighteen members who are elected by universal suffrage in secret ballot. Members of the Senate must be *matais*, but the Representatives need not be. The Senate thus embodies the *matai* system without the rigid aristocracy of the House of Alii, or chiefs who formerly comprised the Upper House. This was felt to be more in accord with both Samoan and American democratic traditions. The Alii fought it, for the most part, but the old Fono went into joint session and outvoted them. The Alii had been informed that, regardless of the outcome of the vote, there could be no more dual membership in both legislative and executive branches. Because the executive branch paid better, their choice between the two was made easy. The suggestions for this whole revision and for the tactics with which it was accomplished came from the members of the old Fono. The House of Alii, as a council of paramount chiefs, has now almost passed into oblivion.

The present attorney, a part-Samoan and graduate of a law school in the United States, has been of considerable help to the Fono, clarifying points of procedure and helping the members to frame their resolutions for presentation to the governor. He has had to meet difficult problems in supervising the police and fire departments, which are under his jurisdiction. A lawyer from the United

States, expected in Samoa in the near future to assist him, will take over those departments, and will also help him to make the final compilation of the Code of American Samoa. The police of the Territory need more training and discipline.

There is as yet no Organic Act of American Samoa, as that term is generally used; the Territory is unorganized and unincorporated. An unincorporated Territory is a Territory or possession of the United States whose inhabitants, under the doctrine of insular cases, can claim only substantive rights of the Constitution, and not such procedural rights as a common-law jury trial, or indictment by a grand jury before being held for trial.

Notwithstanding the awareness of a native culture, the logic used by Americans in analyzing actual situations in American Samoa reflects Western conceptions of human nature. In personal relationships, administrators there look for emotional responses equivalent to their own and, when they are not forthcoming, are amused, annoyed, or angered.

A district governor and high chief of American Samoa, together with another high chief who held an important public office, asked a recent governor if they might escort him as far as Western Samoa when he was leaving the Territory, saying that it was the custom in ancient times for very important persons to be accompanied in their travels by others of only slightly lesser status—a flattering reference to themselves and to the governor—whenever they set out upon considerable journeys. The governor understood that while this was undoubtedly so, their real motivation lay in their desire to go to Western Samoa where they might enjoy the status of privileged visitors, and receive suitable customary gifts, not the least of which would be a good-sized roast pig or two, or a few bottles of precious whisky forbidden them by law at home. It had been the governor's custom, following a naval practice, to allow such official travelers between the Territories to pass through Customs inspections without a particularly careful search of their effects—much in the same way that officials of the American Government and Congress are courteously treated on coming back from abroad. He was dismayed to learn later that upon the return of his escorts to Pago Pago, the largest of their roasted pigs was opened by an overzealous Customs official, who found several bottles of whisky inside. As a result the district governor, whose title rather than personal ability was responsible for his office, was summarily dismissed, and threatened with imprisonment. His family, a very large one, greatly humiliated, offered public atonement en masse in front of the governor's offices, covering themselves with fine mats, and prostrating themselves with lamentations on the ground. There is no more completely Samoan custom than this, nor one held in deeper respect by the people themselves. Yet the new governor was not moved in any way. It was left to the chief judge during the governor's absence to find a legal flaw in the indictment, and to dismiss the charges. Both the high chiefs were out of office for a while, a fact which in itself was no great hardship to them.

Over the past thirty years undue emphasis has been placed on the subject of organic legislation for Samoa. No one knows exactly what "organic legislation" really means as it applies to Samoa, because the form which such an Act would take, if and when passed by the Congress of the United States, would be the outcome of much planning, legal research, discussion, and compromise. This fact has been lost sight of, for long periods of time, and particularly by the Samoans, because to them the process of getting legislation enacted in Washington is completely beyond the present range of their understanding and experience. But because so many Americans have placed such emphasis on the Organic Act, many Samoans quickly began to attach their own kind of importance to it and began employing it not as a concept but as a weapon. The fact that Samoa did not have an Organic Act became in the minds of many islanders the key element of a legend, the substance of which was that great benefits and privileges and even rights were being withheld from the Samoan people by "Washington," who in some malevolent way desired to keep them in a condition of subjection and poverty. No one knew or even cared about the exact nature of any benefits which might flow from the passage of such an act, but the natives freely supposed that whatever they particularly desired would be provided in it. Many Samoan Government employees maintained that if only Washington would give Samoa an Organic Act, the salaries and wages of all local employees of the Government would immediately be raised to equal those paid to civil service employees in Hawaii, the stateside rates, plus a large overseas bonus. Also, those who had lost cases before the court—and nearly everyone in Samoa has been involved on a losing side at some time or other—were convinced that the courts would be changed and previous opinions against them reversed. It was never assumed that opinions in their favor might suffer the same fate! Those who had claims against the Government and who were not satisfied with their compensations believed that these would be set right. Those who yearned for the return of the Navy believed this also would occur, even as those who in years past yearned for its expulsion believed that an Organic Act would accomplish it. In short, the Organic Act would create a paradise for all, and it was only after some very hard talking on the part of the governor and other members of the administration that this legend which had grown up over the years began to be taken apart and deliberately examined by Samoan leaders. It was suggested that an Organic Act which contained provisions for the protection of Samoan-owned land against alienation might be held unconstitutional in view of Supreme Court decisions setting aside racial barriers to land ownership. It was further suggested that Territorial laws requiring young men and women living under the *matai* system to render obedience to and perform labor for their chief might be held to constitute a kind of peonage or involuntary servitude and so, also, be unconstitutional. When the *matai* began to see how their very status was involved in organic legislation, the legend of the all-bountiful Organic Act began to fade away. They have now decided, and wisely, to approach the matter very carefully by devising a Territorial constitution for approval by the governor and the Department of the Interior to be followed by its final submission to Congress for enactment.

Democratic processes are an inherent part of Polynesian society, but the means of expressing the collective will and the relationship of leaders to followers do not resemble Western ways. In accord with American standards of judgment, governors employ an instrumental test in evaluating native institutions. The measure of government in mainland America is the extent to which it obtains good results. If tested by that criterion, government in American Samoa does not stand very high. Governors view any social situation as controllable, and because of our skill in handling material things we feel equally confident of our ability to order social relationships.

The issue of the adequacy of American administration in Samoa is not that of a colonial power which has exploited its dependent peoples, nor is it one of cultural imperialism. Rather is it a question of the kind of administrators who serve as governors of native peoples.

The American Government in Samoa serves honestly, faithfully, and energetically, but is uncertain as to the means and the ends.

Since the Navy pulled out of American Samoa in mid-1951, economic conditions in the Territory have been bad. For almost fifty years the Samoans had relied on a Navy economy, and when this prop was suddenly withdrawn it was found that the small amount of land in the Territory could no longer support the much increased population. Many of the Samoans who had served in the Fita Fita, or local guard, and in Navy jobs had been so long away from village life that it was difficult for them to adjust themselves to altered conditions. The present unhappy situation in American Samoa is largely caused by the pressure of population.

One of the wiser actions of the early naval authorities in Samoa was the establishment of the Fita Fita guard and band as an élite Territorial service for particularly qualified young men of high family connections. Over the years this institution gained great prestige in the Territory and afforded, among other benefits, a source of loyal and well trained material for selection to *matai* rank. Much of the strength of the *matai* system today derives from the fact that many of the better *matai* were formerly Fita Fita. When the fact of transfer from the Navy to the civilian administration was firmly determined, the Navy disestablished the organization, stopping all recruiting, and transferring all members short of retirement age to Honolulu. This not only left the Territory without any organized police or militia, but also deprived the American Government of an important agency for the training of future leaders and offered no replacement.

The Navy was the source of income for the people in general. When the United States Department of the Interior assumed charge, conditions became worse. It was the people of Leone who were largely involved in having the Navy ousted, for they were jealous of the people of Pago Pago because they got so much income from the naval station there. The people of Tau established a village on Tutuila on the opposite side of the island from Pago Pago, where their naval employees lived.

A contributing factor to American Samoa's troubles has been lack of communications, for there is no regular shipping between the Territory and other American possessions or mainland United States, and there is no regular airplane service.

Maritime communication in Samoa has improved considerably since the opening of the fish cannery. Northbound space is much more frequent now that cannery tonnages are added to the Territory's copra output. Two new Norwegian freighters ply between the South Seas and the West coast, and four Oceanic freighters will soon be augmented by two 500-passenger vessels carrying, also, refrigerated cargo and freight in both directions. These will stop regularly at Pago Pago, providing considerable hope for a modest tourist industry which could be developed when the larger passenger lines begin calling at that port, and particularly if the program for airfield improvement is carried out. The South Seas, for all its fascination, has had far less than its proper share of the boom of tourism in the world today. All that is needed is the improved transportation which appears to be definitely in prospect.

Native handicrafts can be stimulated now that northbound shipping is becoming more regular. Because reasonably quick delivery has always been impossible to guarantee, demand has been small. The Government should stimulate the local native cooperative; and because prospects are brighter it should employ one or more competent people from outside the Territory to assist the Samoans in problems of marketing, styling, and design, and possibly even production.

At present there is one "first-class" road on Tutuila, on the southern coast of the island running east and west from Pago Pago, for a total distance of forty miles. Only about thirteen miles of this road is paved, and this is in the area immediately adjacent to the Government Station. The remainder of the system is graded and rolled with crushed rock and coral, which is subject to considerable deterioration during heavy rains. Costs of asphalt and paving equipment are too high for the modest budgets to provide more good surfacing, even though maintenance cost of unsurfaced road is abnormally expensive. It is hoped that money can be obtained for the improvement of the Tafuna Airfield, and that equipment bought for this purpose will also be useful for paving roads.

It must be mentioned that at present things look brighter for Tutuila than at any time since the Navy left. A local dock-improvement project has, for the last two years, been employing ninety Samoans; the new fish cannery employs three hundred; and it is estimated that a new airport project will give temporary employment to three hundred natives.

The program of clearing small-boat channels and turning-basins in the reef opposite each village and arable valley should be continued. In a number of cases small docks could be built rather cheaply of local materials, and a daily launch service might run out of Fagasa Bay, where a suitable dock foundation is already partly completed, and the channel opened. From Fagasa a passable road for trucks and buses has been built over the narrow backbone of the island to Pago Pago. This road is badly eroded and it should be paved, but until there is money to develop a small-boat system for the north shore this would not be too pressing.

The permanent basing of a cargo-passenger launch at the new dock in Faleasau not only will have a good economic effect, but will facilitate the treatment of the sick at the centralized small-scale hospital on Tau. Perhaps it may even be possible to transport students daily to a junior high school on Tau rather than require them, as at present, to reside continuously there if they come from distant points.

Since the termination of the war, water and air transportation between American Samoa and Hawaii and the United States has been confined almost entirely to that of the United States Government.* Every effort should be made to induce commercial transport lines by water and air to list Pago Pago as a port of call. It must be acknowledged that the chances of this are small without a heavy subsidy. The total inadequacy of transportation facilities, however, is a serious handicap to good government.

SOCIAL PROBLEMS

Overpopulation, the most serious and continuing problem of American Samoa, is being relieved chiefly by emigration. Thousands of Samoans, finding the natural resources of their islands inadequate, go to Hawaii or the mainland of the United States, where a wage economy offers better opportunities than in their overcrowded and underdeveloped home islands. Among those who have already gone are many of the more experienced and skilled employees of the Government.

* Pan American Airways now makes a flight about once every twenty days between Tafuna Airport on Tutuila and Nandi, Fiji, with DC-4's.

Young men desirous of obtaining wages and of freeing themselves from burdensome family restrictions continually seek work in Pago Pago, either for the Government or for any other agency that will pay them in cash. The war period, and the years immediately preceding it, greatly accelerated this tendency, and while large numbers of the men were forced to return to the land in the lean years that followed, the majority did so with considerable reluctance and have seized eagerly any opportunity to obtain employment in Pago Pago or, better still, in Honolulu or the United States. There was great agitation for the establishment of enlistment facilities in the Territory so that Samoan boys could join the Marines, the Navy, the Air Force and the Army, and after years of effort a naval recruiting team recently visited Pago. Tests were given, and out of three or four hundred applications eighty were chosen and flown to Honolulu to begin naval training. Others, it is said, will be given a similar opportunity in the future if all goes well. Relatives of Samoans already living in Honolulu, particularly young people, eagerly took advantage of low-cost or free naval transportation afforded by the visit of two transports in 1951 and 1952. Nearly a thousand people traveled to Hawaii in this way, causing considerable comment in that Territory, where Samoans, as a group, are not always readily assimilated. Two airplane loads of Samoans under contract to West Coast farmers were flown direct to California during the years of 1951 and 1952, and other young men have traveled northward whenever they were able to do so, often at considerable personal expense, since it was usually necessary to travel by air most of the way. Even passing yachts have hauled their share, and the annual visit of the United States Coast Guard vessel has given opportunity for emigration to a restricted number. Very few, however, have gone to New Zealand from American Samoa, although there has been a considerable amount of emigration from Western Samoa in that direction. A few Samoans having attained retirement age in the services, or disillusioned with the prospects elsewhere, have returned home, but their accounts of life abroad have apparently not tarnished the bright vision the young people have of life away from their islands.

During the year 1954 more than 1,500 young Samoans offered themselves for enlistment in the armed services and asked that recruiting facilities be established in the Territory. Enlistment in the armed services is now possible, but on a restricted scale. Numbers of young Samoans, having succeeded in making the trip to Honolulu previous to 1954, are today serving in the Armed Forces. Allotment checks from these volunteer servicemen are one of the few sources of cash income of the Territory's families. Some men achieved distinguished combat records in the Korean campaign and several were killed or are missing. The Fourth Fono, in 1955, requested by resolution that a Navy recruiting station be set up in American Samoa.

Problems of government are made more difficult by the necessity for providing increased accommodation for school children, by tropical diseases with which Americans are unfamiliar, and by tuberculosis, to which the natives are very susceptible, and by problems of sex among a people whose codes of behavior are very different from those of Americans.

Admissions to the first year of school continue to rise, reflecting the rapid increase in population growth and foreshadowing shortages for the near future in elementary teachers and school facilities.

A new opportunity for prospective teachers will be known as the Feleti Memorial Teacher-Training School in memory of Frederick Duclos Barstow, in whose name a foundation was established for the education of Samoan children. The Feleti institution will offer a one-year program in teacher training, but it is hoped that soon this will be extended to two years.

Although English is encouraged, Samoan is still the predominant language of the first four grades in school. A local weekly newspaper, Le Aso, staffed by Samoans, appears in about four hundred copies which are distributed among natives on all the islands. The editor and a staff of other Samoans operate the local radio station which broadcasts mornings and evenings five days a week. The subjects are news and general educational items, about 85 per cent of which are broadcast in Samoan. The radio men visit villages in various parts of Tutuila to hold discussions concerning general politics and world events, and have even tried to tell the people what communism is. They also show moving pictures borrowed from the South Pacific Commission.

Almost all Samoans are infected with intestinal parasites, a condition chiefly traceable to the lack of adequately purified water supplies in the various valleys. The parasites are rarely fatal, except in infancy. The weaning period and immediately thereafter is a time of great danger for the average Samoan baby. In a people for whom adequate nutrition is becoming an increasingly difficult problem, this widespread infection by parasites is a serious matter. As a rule, each village has its own water supply, or perhaps two or three villages may share what remains of an old wartime system built for the Armed Forces. All these systems have a way of breaking down because of silting of the reservoirs and deterioration of the equipment. As a rule the Government maintains the equipment, and the villages are expected to keep the reservoirs clean. But of course even the best of them cannot prevent contamination by wild pigs, and there is no procedure for chlorination or filtration. Only in the Pago Pago area where the Government maintains and operates a substantial system is anything like modern water sanitation found. In the village water systems the bacteria count is exceedingly high. The problem of pure water for native settlements in the tropics is often virtually unsolvable because of the prohibitive cost involved in construction, maintenance, and operation of reservoirs.

The climate of Samoa makes it a great hotbed for bacteria. Skin diseases are rife, wounds heal slowly, and respiratory infections are common. The expectation of life of a healthy Samoan is considerably shorter than the expectation of life of a healthy citizen of mainland United States.

In Samoa problems of sex relations have to be viewed differently from those on mainland United States. Among Samoans sex is regarded as a natural, pleasurable thing; freedom of indulgence is restricted only by social status. Chiefs' daughters and chiefs' wives, for example, should abstain from extramarital relationships, but native opinion considers them all right for the rank and file. The only dissenters are the missionaries, who object so vainly that their protests are unimportant. Missionary authorities, sorely vexed to reconcile Samoan sex ethics with a Western code, see the great disadvantages of permitting unmarried girls to become church members unless they are segregated in church boarding schools. The native pastor does not encourage an adolescent female to contemplate her eternal salvation, but advises her to wait until she is older, which she is glad to do. The religious setting in Samoa, as in most Pacific islands, is one of formalism, compromise, and acceptance of half-measures. Because of the great number of native pastors trained in their own seminaries and holding peculiar interpretations of Christian teaching, missionaries have found it impossible to establish the

rigor of Western religion which condemns sex offenses as sinful.
Young Samoans upon whom the religious setting makes no demands
follow their traditional code.

Marriage is an uncertain relationship. If a wife tires of her husband, or a husband of his wife, divorce is an informal matter, one
or the other simply going home to his or her family. The conjugal
relationship is a very brittle monogamy, often trespassed and more
often broken entirely. The adulteries which occur even among church
members from time to time are mildly rebuked. The claim that a
woman has on her family's land renders her as independent as her
husband, and so there are no marriages of long duration in which
either person is very unhappy. After a small flare-up a woman goes
home to her own people; if her husband does not care to conciliate
her each seeks another mate.

THE FUTURE

The future of the economy of American Samoa is dependent upon
several cash-income factors: (1) the quantity and the world price of
copra; (2) the production and future off-island demand for native
handicraft; (3) employment in the cannery, and in a prospective
coconut-button factory, and any other small businesses that may be
established.

There is no apparent source in Samoa for an appreciable additional
revenue even should the price of copra remain high, a supposition
which is not warranted in view of the price fluctuations of past
years. As was already emphasized, the islands of the Territory are
mountainous and only about one-third of the land is considered
arable even in terms of the rudest types of hand cultivation. On the
main island, Tutuila, where most of the people are wage earners, little
attention has been given to enlarging or even maintaining, through
replanting, the coconut groves. Nearly all producing trees on that
island are now over age and should have been replaced years ago. A
thoroughgoing, systematic plan might be drawn up to develop this,
by far the main resource of the island. The Government could proceed by the methods businessmen know well: first, size up the problem;
second, devise ways and means of solving it; third, accomplish what

can be done immediately and make preparations to accomplish the remainder in the future.

Approximately one thousand Samoans, nearly all on Tutuila, or 4.7 per cent of the population, have regular employment for wages which run from $20 to $200 a month. The remainder of the people rely on farming and fishing, sharing their products with the wage earners or selling to them.

The people of the remote Manua Island group, where little outside employment has ever been available, have continued to depend on their copra export for cash earnings and have, therefore, replanted and kept their trees at a fair productive level. These Manua Islands, as was already mentioned, account for a very large part of the copra produced in the Territory, although they contain less than 30 per cent of the arable land and only 17 per cent of the population.

In the past, artificial drying of copra has been practiced on a small scale in American Samoa. In Western Samoa and elsewhere, of course, the process is widely used and of great value when correctly done. It would help the people if the Government were to promote the efficient use of copra dryers of smoke-free design. Particular emphasis might be placed on small units suitable for operation on a family or village basis in order to avoid the necessity of shipping wet copra considerable distances under adverse conditions.

In view of the very restricted income from copra sales, the cost of living for the natives should be kept down by ensuring a steady supply of kerosene, cloth, and some food products as cheaply as possible. Uneconomical procurement and costly distribution are factors that call for intense and serious study. For example, kerosene is an essential item, but the quantities consumed are not sufficient to warrant the use of a private tanker for transportation to Pago Pago and thence to private tank storage, or to warrant maintaining private tank storage facilities at Pago Pago. In consequence, the price of kerosene is exorbitant. The Government might perhaps make this particular item available for sale at cost to wholesale or retail outlets.

To achieve a reasonable cost of living, the Government should consider placing on the free list of imports such staples as are determined to be "necessities of life." It should study the practicability of the establishment of consumer cooperatives at wholesale and retail levels. Meanwhile, it should maintain strict enforcement of a price control code.

As was already mentioned, there are only a few areas on the island of Tutuila of moderately level land which could be utilized for other crops. These parcels lie for the most part high in the hills of western and eastern districts, and the problem of their accessibility by villagers living on the seacoast has prevented, so far, their satisfactory development. One village, Aolau, formerly located in a steep valley on the northern shore, successfully removed itself to a point atop a plateau in the Western District where a road was constructed to connect the settlement with the main highway. The villagers, in a courageous and unprecedented response to a bad situation, have founded New Aolau in what looks to be a promising agricultural area. A very energetic young chief is the driving force of this relocation movement. Breadfruit and coconut, traditional Samoan crops, do not do well at high altitudes. Moreover, the people have to carry their drinking water a mile uphill. However, bananas and taro are grown in abundance, and the young chief has ideas that perhaps cacao, coffee, and tea might be suitable crops. Several of the leaders of the Fono have asked the Government to begin the development of unused lands as a Government project similar to the Crown Estates of Western Samoa, but as yet no direct action has been taken perhaps because of the problem of surveys and ownership, and certainly because of the problem of thievery and lack of funds. If other roads could be built—they would be very expensive both to build and to maintain—several other villages might be relocated if leadership were available.

A barge arrived at Pago Pago from Honolulu in 1954 which will make possible the construction of a small deep-water dock on Tau Island in Manua. When this dock has been built, road equipment can be landed there and some of the better interior lands of that island can be brought under cultivation. There are three hundred to four hundred acres of good land in this area which the hard-working people of Manua may be able to bring into use in about ten years. Efficient low-priced transportation, essential to the soundness of any economy, will result in a less expensive handling of freight to and from all the islands.

Until recently no consistent and coordinated effort was made in American Samoa to encourage the growing of cacao, an important cash crop. As long as thirty or forty years ago several enterprising *matai* planted trees, but no systematic development of plantations followed until the last few years. There are now two to three hundred acres planted to cacao in the islands. New plantings are being made from time to time. Pressure for immediate production of foodstuffs is, however, an inhibiting factor. The Tufele cacao plantation on Tau Island is already in production for seed in Manua. The Tuiasosopo plantation in the Western District of Tutuila, planted four or five years ago, has now begun to bear seed. In the latter plantation cacao and bananas are planted together. No local facilities for processing have been set up as yet. There should be few difficulties in doing so when a sufficient crop is available, since there is plenty of expert advice and assistance to be had in Western Samoa.

The introduction of cacao to the Western Samoan Islands, successfully begun by the Germans before World War I, has been carried forward with brilliant results by the New Zealand administrators of the Crown Estates in Western Samoa. In recent years, because of the blight in other regions, Samoan cacao has been receiving top prices in world markets.

A consistent demand in New Zealand for bananas suggests the possibility that this traditional food crop might become a source of cash for some Samoan farmers. However, many factors appear to discourage this development, among them the poor shipping and holding facilities, high cost of boxes, and heavy demand on the crop for local consumption. The possibility of marketing all agricultural crops through Western Samoa should be thoroughly explored. The amount of produce exported from American Samoa will never be sufficiently large to attract commercial transportation to the islands. But it is a very short distance to Apia, through which exports from Western Samoa are shipped. Export is, of course, tied up with markets, but there again arrangements for the small amount to be shipped and marketed do not offer any serious problem. It may be mentioned here that a cause of discontent in American Samoa is the barrier between American and British Samoa. The average native in his frequent exasperation does not reason beyond the fact that someone ought to correct a perplexing and irritating situation that divides people of a common heritage from one another, makes complicated and difficult family relationships, and renders contacts among friends subject to red tape and official complications. He does not know that there are other situations in the world no less embarrassing for the people concerned—the boundary between Northern Ireland and

Ireland, for example; the armistice line between Israel and her neighbors; not to speak of the artificial trace between Pakistan and India. Much of the discontent about inter-Samoan Island barriers comes from natives of Western Samoa who would like to get over to Tutuila by the easiest method, generally to sponge off relatives, get better jobs and higher wages than they can on Upolu.

A source of continued hope for economic development lies in the handicraft export trade based principally on floor matting and other items woven of pandanus (*laufala*) and articles such as bowls and trays carved from local hardwoods. Under the naval administration, considerable encouragement was given in this field through establishment of a producers' cooperative. Over the years, exports, mainly in naval vessels, increased, and a modest cash income was thereby enjoyed by many families. Despite the present serious limitations on outbound shipping space, exports have remained substantially the same. The handicraft industry offers promise for considerable growth if visits of northbound vessels can be scheduled more frequently. However, from a strictly business standpoint they have little incentive to call. The Department of Native Industry should be maintained and expanded, and no less important, native artifacts should be advertised on the mainland, so that Americans there would be encouraged to buy from distant cousins who have special abilities in attractive goods.

There are a considerable number of native trees the wood of which is used by Samoans, but there are no large stands of timber trees as such. Several varieties of introduced hardwoods—broad-leaf mahogany and teak—are thriving in the small areas at present given over to them, and there is hope that marginal lands may be devoted to this purpose, if ever there should prove to be any "marginal" lands. Two varieties of softwood suitable for making crates and boxes have been introduced, and it appears that these would grow well and quickly if any further effort were made in this field, and a local demand for shook were to develop such as might follow the expansion of banana shipments. The scarcity of land and the ruggedness of terrain make an increase in plantings difficult. However, it is believed that a specialist in tropical vegetation could render substantial help to the Samoans in the reproduction, planting, and handling of their native timber trees and increase the output. A tropical forester could be secured from the Territorial Government of Hawaii or the United

States Forest Service on the mainland to make a study and recommend the best practices for maximum timber production.

There are very few cattle in American Samoa because of the absence of suitable pasture, and other factors. The Government maintains a small dairy herd principally for hospital use, and inspects and tubercular-tests a few other head which are kept by Mormon and Catholic missionaries for their own dairy purposes. The success with which Aberdeen Angus have been raised on coconut land by Capital Estates in Western Samoa indicates that beef production could be increased substantially in American Samoa. One trouble would be to keep the cattle from being eaten for feasts a week or so after they were put out to pasture. The Government recently imported several choice sows and a boar from New Zealand to improve the island breed of pigs. Blooded piglets were given to some twenty or thirty of the best agricultural students for breeding, and local sows bred to the imported boar were also distributed. All were eaten within a few days of the distribution, even the sows before they had time to produce litters. The students had for the most part nothing to do with this. Their *matai* ordered them to provide the pigs for feasts!

The experimental farm should serve as a center for distribution of better animals and poultry. This can probably be a self-sustaining activity. A livestock specialist could be obtained for the staff of this farm in accordance with the governor's recommendation. Dairy farming is not likely to be successful, for advances in the manufacture of powdered whole milk and canned cream make it possible to use these in the tropics in place of fresh milk. The maintenance of a dairy in the tropics is very expensive, among other things because of the necessity of importing feed for the cows and furnishing refrigeration facilities for the milk.

Despite the seeming lack of interest on the part of Samoans in its work to date, the experimental farm fulfills a definite need. The steadily mounting pressure of population with a present annual gain of at least five hundred will require the best possible use of all agricultural land and the selection of the highest-yielding crops. In addition to the introduction and testing of desirable new foods, the farm should gather for testing and propagation from the widely different varieties now grown the highest-yielding and best-quality strains of the present native foods, especially coconuts, bananas, breadfruit, and taro.

The farm should also serve as a testing laboratory for fertilizer. At present the ground is worn out by constant cropping and is in no condition to be used for demonstration until built up through effective soil management. Fruit trees should be thinned out, as they are now too crowded. They should also be pruned, sprayed for pest and disease control, and given adequate fertilization, if they are to demonstrate their productiveness and value in Samoan life.

The farm also should serve as a training institution in cooperation with the schools, and should ultimately conduct demonstrations and short courses on crop production, farm practice, pest and disease control, and simple farm mechanics adapted to Samoan agriculture.

As the population increases, questions of land use and landownership become more pressing for solution in the courts. Land-use and landownership surveys are needed, but the Government has been unable to undertake them because of the lack of sufficient skilled surveyors and proper land records. An aerial survey was completed in 1955, as a preliminary step toward a ground survey of land usage. Records of all land held in fee simple should be obtained and recorded immediately. The holding of land in fee simple should not be pushed by the Government, but when the proper time comes, as was already suggested, the Government should be prepared to stand back of such a change. Since the hold of the *matai* is seriously weakening, the old communal system is in a state of transition, and sooner or later this question will come to the fore.

With regard to government, the great volume of legal research directed toward the revision of the antiquated Code of American Samoa and the preparation and study touching on organic legislation and applicability of Federal laws is being pushed. An experiment in encouraging the Samoans to develop their own constitution may have some value. Such an experiment has, as yet, little importance because of their ignorance of such basic articles of government in general. There are strong indications that the traditional Samoan system of *matai* leadership has retained much of its original capacity for self-government despite the unsettling intrusion of Western civilization. With patience, an increasing amount of self-government can be developed in traditional ways, particularly as the effects of an ever widening school system make possible the selection of better educated *matai*.

The citizens of American Samoa are treated on a basis of equality with all others living there, except that certain regulations, principally with respect to land, give the Samoans special protection.

The few white people who own land in American Samoa have not benefited from it financially. One of them has about thirty acres near Taputimu on which Samoan relatives reside as caretakers, but they make almost no effort to improve the land or even to clear it of brush. In return for supplying them food and other necessaries, he gets from four hundred to five hundred ripe coconuts a year, which are sold in his store. His expenses are higher than his income. Constant stealing of products makes farming for Caucasians in general a very poor investment.

Much in the Samoan way of life is good in itself and is admirably adapted to the people of these islands, but Samoa is undergoing change, especially through the influence of Western civilization. In view of this change, which is likely to become greater continually, the main objective of education should be to conserve the best in Samoan culture and at the same time give Samoans acquaintance with the intellectual tools, the social concepts, and the institutions of the West, so that they may maintain respect for their native heritage and skill in their traditional arts and crafts as well as learn to cope with the problems of the modern world.

Western civilization has made an impact upon the Samoan people and their culture. This was accentuated by World War II and the presence there of many thousands of American troops. Increased opportunities for education are also having an effect. However, Western ideas and institutions are frequently not welcomed. Since the Samoan is independent and proud, he wants to take his own time to make up his own mind in his own way with respect to them. But, whether or not he likes the new ideas, his country is in a period of transition.

The more outstanding results of population pressure in American Samoa are the clearing of inferior land which therefore is susceptible to dangerous erosion, the mounting count of land disputes, and the high incidence of thievery. Stealing, in the legal sense of the word, was not known in Samoa until after the white people began to arrive in the islands. Because of the Samoan unwritten concept of "What's mine is yours; what's yours is mine," a person could take something belonging to another either with or without the latter's knowledge. The person who removed the property for his own use almost always notified the owner, who usually agreed to it because he himself might sometime later take something belonging to that person.

Another result is the strong desire of young Samoans to emigrate or to work locally for cash wages if emigration is not possible. Examples of congestion are the Pago Pago Bay villages of Utulei, Fagatogo, and Pago Pago, where an indescribable litter of shacks and lean-tos crowds the slopes behind the Government reservation. A very large proportion of the readily communicable diseases such as tuberculosis, chicken pox, and scarlet fever are traceable to these settlements.

Representative of population pressure are statistics for the month of September, 1953, when nine people died, and twelve times that number of children were born. During the same month $122,000 worth of goods were imported into the Territory and less than $1,000 worth exported; a total of 937 employees was working for the Government out of a population of a little more than 18,000.

With a current annual increase in population of over five hundred a year, it is difficult to conceive of any local solution for alleviating population pressures and at the same time developing a higher standard of living, much less continuing the general level of Government services. There seem to be only two possible courses to follow, both involving emigration, since it does not appear likely that the Samoans will willingly reduce their birth rate. Incidentally, four chiefs on Tutuila in their forties are fathers of a total of sixty children and are by no means beyond the age of fatherhood!

The two forms of emigration depend entirely on the future political status of the Territory. If Western Samoa, as is quite likely, develops a substantial measure of self-government within the next ten years, it is possible that a desire for union of both Samoas may arise, although there are no indications of it at present. It will certainly be a long time before American Samoa will have any measure of self-government to compare with what Western Samoa will probably receive soon, for since American Samoa will for years to come be dependent upon grants from Congress, it is not likely that Congress will relinquish its authority over the Territory while continuing to foot what is bound to be an increasingly large bill every year. In Western Samoa the population pressure at present is not nearly so great as in the American islands of the archipelago, and there are large tracts suitable for cultivation in the islands administered by New Zealand, especially on the island of Savai'i. The population of Western Samoa is concentrated mainly on the north shore of Upolu and is approximately five times that of American Samoa, while the total land area is slightly less than twenty times as great. Moreover, Western Samoan land is less mountainous and rocky. Thus it would seem that if the people of both Samoas desired and effected a political union, the population pressure in American Samoa would, for a time at least, be alleviated. So many political factors are involved, however, that the other form of emigration must also be considered. If American Samoa remains under the American flag, increasing numbers of people must emigrate to other American areas, probably to Hawaii and to the West Coast. In Hawaii, however, the Samoan is not particularly welcome, although it is indisputably the place to which nearly all the Samoans would go if they were given the chance, and possibly the place in which their immediate problems of adjustment to new ways of life would be less difficult than elsewhere. If Samoans were to emigrate in large numbers to the West Coast, they would probably find employment in those fields of work where the Spanish-speaking Mexican is now employed, principally as field hands, and also in unskilled manual labor and perhaps domestic service in urban areas. Their numbers would in no way result in the difficulties to the community that would probably be caused by their arriving in similar numbers in Hawaii. The social welfare, however, of these island people and their families in strange countries with alien customs would constitute a serious problem. It is possible that some Samoans might be temporarily employed at Guam in the place of the Filipinos there, but whether or not they could permanently settle and support themselves in that small island is doubtful. There appears to be no room for them, or no reason to speculate about their introduction into the United States Trust Territory, except perhaps in very restricted numbers. As Government workers there, they might be of some value in dealing with people of a similar but somewhat less advanced cultural level.

It has been informally suggested that some Samoans and other inhabitants of densely crowded Pacific islands might be settled in New Guinea, but the idea is impractical, for New Guinea is a high, mountainous island where the climate is much too cold, and where Asiatic diseases to which island peoples are easily susceptible are rife.

What are the main problems of administering American Samoa? America, an anticolonial nation, has not a tradition of administering other people alien to her own civilization, or of developing in them a mutually satisfying blending of the American and the native way of life. The simple fact that our Territories are administered by a department known as "Interior" is indicative of this. These are general difficulties, and there are others which apply particularly to Samoa. The Samoans, a proud and stubborn people, even though bewildered, refuse to abandon many of the traditional values of their past.

On the American side the largest single problem in Samoa has been lack of stability caused by rapid changes in key Government officials. There have been five governors since the Department of the Interior assumed charge in 1951. As none of them got to know intimately the problems of the administration, the result has been great unrest among the Samoans.

Within the limits of their islands the natives developed a way of living, including a government well suited to the circumstances of their environment. Throughout 150 years of contact and influence by Westerners, Samoa has survived as a stronghold of Polynesian culture. Status within Samoan society is dependent, in large measure, on political knowledge and ability, for the native leader is schooled within his village council, and in his district and Territorial *fono*. Almost every phase of his life is oriented toward political awareness. To some extent the lifeblood of the Samoan leader is politics. The unsettled nature of the executive branch has, therefore, caused him great concern and uncertainty. In Samoan eyes the stability of the entire Government is dependent upon the tenure of office of the governor.

There is a very great distance between Washington, where the critical decisions must be made, and Pago Pago. This, coupled with poor and infrequent transportation and circuitous and expensive routes of travel, virtually isolates the Territory. People outside Samoa who for one reason or another wish to influence affairs there, find it far easier to reach Washington's ears than do the inhabitants of the islands or their local government.

There is also a persistent and apparently indestructible bit of folklore to the effect that Samoa is a paradise where nobody takes anything seriously. Consequently, few people outside take Samoa seriously. People have to have a map to locate the Territory. Many confuse it with Guam, others with the United States Trust Territory. Everyone appears surprised to learn that Samoa has been under our flag for more than fifty years. Rulings and procedures are often laid down in Washington that have little or no relationship to actual problems in Samoa, but are, no doubt, the product of an instinctive desire to bring about administrative tidiness and uniformity. Insofar as this amounts to belief that form, rather than spirit, is the important element of government, such policies can and do cause considerable difficulty in Samoa. Yet, getting these policies changed is almost an impossible job, involving spending of far too much time in Washington and the use of immense amounts of tact. The maintenance of a Samoan commissioner in the Capital would eliminate a lot of this waste and confusion.

The administration of all of our dependent peoples in the Pacific and their Territories should be taken out of the Department of the Interior where it is now lodged in the Division of Territories and Island Possessions. An independent agency under the executive could be created, perhaps a commission. Each Territory, except for Alaska and Hawaii, would have a commissioner, and Hawaii's and Alaska's delegate would be seated ex officio. The chairman might be of no Territory, and appointed by the President. There should also be an advisory board of members of pertinent congressional committees and Cabinet representatives, such as State, Defense, Commerce, Health, Education and Welfare. A permanent secretariat for the commission would not need to number more than the present staff in the Office of Territories, and a Territorial Service would embrace these, and those who worked in the field.*

Commercially, Samoa is at a disadvantage in that it is far closer to nondollar areas than to its parent country and yet cannot always supply its needs from these nearby sources, particularly in most items required by the Government. Since it must by law requisition through United States agencies, an undue amount of the money appropriated for Samoa goes into freight costs, helping steamship companies and others more than the Samoans. As a processing point within the dollar area, outside United States Customs barriers, but close to

* This suggestion for a commission or small "Department of Dependent Territories" was made by the Honorable John C. Elliott, recently Governor of American Samoa. The author of this book heartily endorses it.

sterling sources of production, and yet having duty-free privileges of export to the United States, Samoa could find this circumstance a benefit, but so far it has been only a handicap. At present fresh and canned meats are purchased from New Zealand because there is no freezer space available on American freighters operating to and from American Samoa. This results in a considerable saving to the Government since prices for these commodities in New Zealand are considerably lower than in the United States. If greater latitude were permitted in regard to purchasing supplies, there would be ways to reduce expenses, not only in freight costs but also by buying in dollars foreign items available much nearer at hand and more readily replaceable, thus obviating the necessity of heavy stockpiling.

With intelligent planning and genuine interest it would be possible to develop the Territory into a more productive area with industrial and trading activities that would augment the small land area's capacity to support a growing population. But, as was already stated, the Samoans are stubborn, and they and the people in Washington are very ignorant of each other—a circumstance which is not surprising, in view of the very great distance that lies between them.

Part of the governor's time in Samoa is taken up with the difficulties and troubles of his United States staff, their wives, and their children. This is also true in the United States Trust Territory. The government of our Pacific dependencies is no haven for people who want to get away from something that is probably within themselves, no place for the prejudiced, or for those who hunger for power or money. It calls for—and in a few cases actually gets—a peculiar blend of the good civil servant and the tolerant missionary. This combination of attributes is ideal for American Samoa and the islands comprising the United States Trust Territory.

When the drafts of organic legislation for Guam and American Samoa, prepared by the Department of the Interior, received the approval of the President, the Department of the Interior was designated as the governing civilian agency "without prejudice to future consideration based upon further study of long-range plans for administration of United States territories and possessions."* It is time now for that "future consideration."

Special training is necessary for members of the administrative

* Letter to the Secretary of the Interior from the President, dated May 14, 1949. Mimeographed for general distribution.

staff of dependent peoples. For a college graduate with no previous experience in such work a minimum course of one year is necessary to enable him to perform his duties satisfactorily. The curriculum should include social anthropology, languages, and administrative procedures and tropical agriculture. Holland trains its young citizens who go out to govern its dependencies and so does Belgium. England and France require preparation for their services abroad. Australia and New Zealand educate their Government representatives for service in New Guinea and Western Samoa. Witness the successful régime of Western Samoa. But untrained Americans have no special intuition for dealing with native peoples in the Pacific. Indeed, the confusion arising from lack of preparation and aptitude is cumulative until someday—not far distant for American Samoa—the situation will be drastically forced upon our attention. If this tide in the affairs of that Territory is not taken at the present flood, the ebb may be long and harrowing.

But the preparation of the fit must be more than mere exposure to classroom lectures. It calls for an educational program which takes into account the American structure of character and seeks to reorient it for the role of administrator of native peoples. It entails a type of administration at the Federal level which recruits, trains, and retains the kind of staff required. Such a program is not at all utopian, but entirely feasible; it is used by other nations engaged in similar enterprises and even in some areas of American life. As a nation we can afford to invest in this enterprise the kind of effort which would enable us not only to declare, but also to achieve, our goals.

REFERENCES

Churchward, W. B., *My Consulate in Samoa* (1887).

Coulter, J. W., *Land Utilization in American Samoa*, Bernice P. Bishop Museum Bull. 170, Honolulu, 1941.

Elliott, John C., Notes on American Samoa, 1955 (in the files of J. W. Coulter).

Mead, Margaret, *Coming of Age in Samoa* (New York: William Morrow, 1928).

O Le Fa'atonu, Pago Pago, American Samoa, various volumes and numbers.

Sachet, M. H., *A Summary of Information on Rose Atoll*, Pacific Science Board, Atoll Research Bull. No. 29, 1954 (National Research Council, Washington, D.C.).

Sady, E. J., "The Department of the Interior and Pacific Island Administration," *Pub. Admin. Rev.*, Vol. 10, 1950, p. 17.

United States, Committee to Study the Naval Administration of Guam and American Samoa (E. M. Hopkins, Chairman), *Report on the Civil Governments of Guam and American Samoa.* Washington, 1947.

————, annual reports of the Governor of American Samoa.

————, Samoan Land Records, files of the Administration of American Samoa.

VI

The Territory of Guam

GUAM, the farthest-flung Territory of the United States in the Pacific, is decidedly in a transition stage, economically, socially, and politically. An island of peasant farmers is emerging from an old, traditional way of living to rub shoulders with the modern world. Civil government took charge on August 1, 1951, when, after 230 years of Spanish rule and fifty-two years of rule by the United States Navy—interrupted by two and a half years of Japanese occupation— the island was made by Congress an unincorporated Territory of the United States.

Beginning steps in the process of self-government can be measured annually. The First Guam Legislature, among other Acts, codified the laws of the island, for the first time, in 1952. The Second Guam Legislature, in 1953, enacted a military code to establish a National Guard. Among the laws passed by the same legislature in 1954 were those regulating the operations of savings and loan associations and compensation of public employees. The more important enactments of 1955 included laws providing for juries and trial by jury, and for funds to continue construction of the Guam Memorial Hospital. Significant in the general program for an increasing measure of self-government for the people of Guam has been the modernization of the judicial system and the appointment of a number of heads of departments in the Territorial Government from among the resident population instead of from the United States.

Agriculture, normally the mainstay of the people of the island, is trying to adapt itself to a new market for which some degree of mechanization would help. This effort is being made, although the

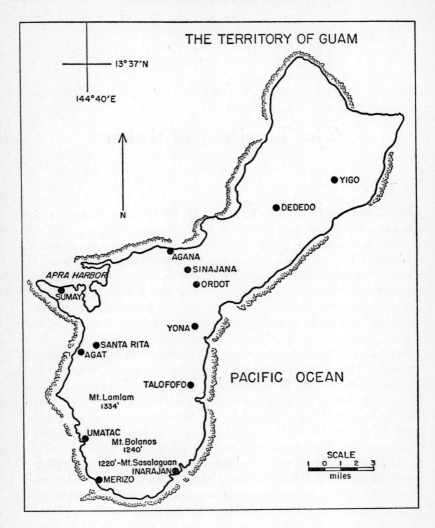

weather is frequently not propitious for good crops. Over everything is still the shadow of World War II, for Guam is the only part of the United States which felt the full, devastating effect of that conflict.

NATURAL ENVIRONMENT

World War II marked the end of an epoch for Guam economically and socially, as it did for the Territory of Hawaii. But in order to understand the present situation, we have to review briefly the earlier history of the island. We must think of a small, remote piece of the world, 1,500 miles east of the Philippines, with nothing larger east of it until we cross 3,300 miles to Hawaii. It is 5,200 miles from San Francisco. The only regular prewar transportation to Guam by water was by two United States Navy transports and one United States Army transport, each of which called at Guam on its semiannual trip to and from the Orient; an American President Line freighter which stopped at Guam to pick up cargo about once every six months; and the United States Navy Government supply ship stationed at Guam, which made three or four trips to Manila and the Orient annually.

In this very isolated island, the only way of living was by subsistence agriculture. Coconut trees yielded the money crop, for copra was in demand in world markets then as now. Natives hauled their produce from their fields to their homes in wooden, springless carts, pulled slowly along by water buffaloes. One of them told the author it took him four hours to go twelve miles from Yigo to Agana with his carabao, now an old animal which is grazing in one of his fields.

Guam, 13° 26' north latitude, 144° 39' east longtitude, the largest and southernmost of the Mariana Islands, is shaped like a boot with the instep bent down facing east; Orote Point, the heel, juts out toward the west. From Ritidian Point in the northwest corner of the island to Aga Point in the southeast is thirty miles. Across its narrowest line, in the ankle, it is four and a half miles, broadening out above to nearly eight miles, and below, across the instep, to a little more than nine miles. The total area is about 225 square miles.

The island is sharply divided, just below the ankle, into a northern limestone plateau with a general elevation of about 500 feet and an area of volcanic hills to the south. The northern limestone plateau, with a maximum elevation of 674 feet above sea level, is covered with a thick growth of jungle. The volcanic hills, supporting mainly sword grass, rise to a height of 1,240 feet above sea level, and their lower slopes to the east and, in part, to the west are blanketed with an apron of younger limestones generally similar to those of the northern limestone plateau. The higher hills are found in the west central part of the island, where Mount Lamlam rises to an elevation of 1,334 feet; Mount Jumullong Manglo is 1,260 feet, Mount Bolanos, 1,240 feet; and Mount Sasalaguan, 1,220 feet. The ridge from Mount Lamlam at the south to Mount Alifan, 869 feet, at the north, is capped by some of the older, if not the oldest, postvolcanic limestones on the island. Like the younger limestones, the older

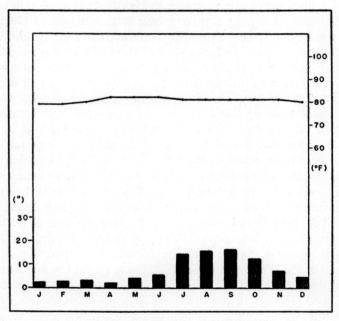

Rainfall and temperature in Sumay, Guam

limestones of the crest support a dense jungle vegetation that prominently defines their general distribution by contrast with the sword-grass cover of the volcanic terrain.

In the northern half of the island, coconut palms grow abundantly on the coast and in the interior; in the south they are mostly near the ocean. The interior of the southern half, uninhabited, is a rough, hilly country of coarse grass, bamboo, various other species of tropical vegetation, and jungle where in prewar days there was plenty of deer and other game. Guam has a pleasant tropical climate.

Temperatures range from 70 to 90 degrees, and are fairly even throughout the year. Average annual rainfall is about 95 inches, three-fourths of which falls during the wet season, which generally starts in May or June and lasts through November. The equable climate is punctuated by destructive typhoons which occur at irregular intervals.

POPULATION

The native Guamanians, ethnically called Chamorros, are basically of Indonesian stock with a considerable admixture of Spanish, Filipino (Tagalog), and other blood. Their vernacular is called the Chamorro language. It is not a Micronesian dialect, but a distinct language having its own vocabulary and grammar. The word Chamorro is derived from *chamorri*, or *chanioli*, the ancient name for "chief." Pure-blooded Chamorros are no longer found on the island, but in every native family the Chamorro language is still the medium of communication. Some of the older people do not speak English, but all the younger people do. Though the men were decimated under the early régime of the Spaniards, many women became wives of the Spanish, Mexican, and Philippine soldiers brought to Guam to "reduce" the natives. There has been a thorough amalgamation, including the descendants of Englishmen and Scotsmen who lived on Guam. The Chamorros live in villages from which they go out to cultivate their farms.

There has been a steady increase in the native population of Guam since the beginning of this century, when it became a part of the United States. No pressure, however, has been felt on the means of subsistence, except, of course, during the period of Japanese occupation. With the continuing increase in population, and the appropriation of a considerable area of farming land for defense installations of the United States, some concern is being felt for the future. Nevertheless, as long as defense spending continues at its present rate, there will be plenty of wage-money available for Guamanians who want to work.

The greatest factor in the postwar population of Guam is the introduction of thousands of men in the Armed Forces of the United States, many of them with their wives and families. Other thousands include civil-defense workers from the United States and between ten and fifteen thousand Filipinos from the Orient who work for contractors on Government jobs. The rapid economic and social changes which are occurring on the island are due to the influx of the large foreign population. The following table shows the increase in native population from 1901 to the present:

TABLE XII

GUAMANIAN POPULATION OF GUAM, 1901–1955

YEAR	POPULATION	INCREASE OVER PRECEDING CENSUS	
		NUMBER	PER CENT
(1) 1901	9,676		
(1) 1910	11,806	2,130	22.0
1920	(2) 13,275	1,469	12.4
1930	(3) 18,509	5,234	39.4
1940	(4) 22,290	3,781	20.4
1950	(5) 27,958	5,668	25.4
1951	28,170	212	0.8
1952	31,055	2,885	10.2
1953	32,822	1,767	5.7
1954	34,889	2,067	6.3
1955	35,844	955	2.7

Population of Agana City (6)

1920	7,432		
1930	8,690	1,258	16.9
1940	10,004	1,314	15.1
1950	1,330	−8,674	−86.7

(1) Census taken by naval governor.
(2) Includes native men enlisted in the U.S. Navy, but excludes U.S. naval station personnel, who numbered 319.
(3) Includes 1,118 reported on U.S. naval reservations and on U.S. naval vessels stationed at Guam.
(4) Includes 213 reported on U.S. naval vessels in Apra Harbor.
(5) The total civilian population was 59,498.
(6) No data available for years prior to 1920.

AGRICULTURE

The traditional economy of the Chamorros is for the most part that practiced today. The representative farm is still much like that of prewar days, with more attention given to vegetables in areas near the new and growing market. By far the larger area of farmed land is near the coast in the southern, volcanic part of the island. Only three or four acres on a farm are generally cultivated, five or six times that amount being coconut forest, scrub, sword grass and waste land. Corn is still the most important crop, one or two acres to a farm. There is a similar area of pasture, an acre or so in bananas, bread-fruit, papayas, tapioca, melons, pineapples, sweet potatoes, and other vegetables. Farmers raise a few scrub cattle for meat, oxen for draft animals, and each generally has a carabao. Swine are native scrub stock, fed for the most part on swill, bananas, and coconut pulp. Both cattle and swine are generally tethered from place to place. Poultry are also predominantly native mongrel stock. Farm equipment includes a two-wheeled cart, a couple of machetes or bush knives, and a *fosino*, or scuffle hoe. Fertilizers are not used, not even barnyard manure, which is not available, for livestock are rarely concentrated in one place. In accordance with long-established practice, new land is cleared when the soil of the cultivated areas becomes depleted. That can still be done at the present stage of population growth, but signs are that the number of people to feed may one day make that method impracticable.

Nearly all farmers own the land they operate, also the sites of their homes in the village. Sometimes the owners of neighboring farms cooperate to work together on each of them successively.

Many farmers have two houses, one in the village and a hut or shack out in the jungle on their land, where they farm for a few days a week; but they always make sure to return to their village homes on Saturday to be ready to go to mass on Sunday, for their priests, Capuchin missionaries formerly from Spain, now from the United States, insist on church attendance. Ninety-eight per cent of the Guamanians are Roman Catholic.

Umatac, the most isolated village on Guam, still represents something of the prewar era. The Catholic chapel is the most conspicuous building, standing out amidst the rows of houses strung along both sides of the road which borders the bay. Spanish days are recalled by the remains of the Spanish Chapel and of the thick, slowly crumbling walls of two old forts on the heights commanding the approach to Umatac Bay. On an obelisk in the village an inscription reads, "Near this place Ferdinand Magellan landed, March 6, 1521." Though Guam was discovered in 1521, no settlement was made upon it by Europeans for nearly 150 years, when, on June 16, 1668, a mission was established by Padre Diego Luis de Sanvitores, a Spanish Jesuit, in obedience to an order of Philip IV of Spain. The Spaniards continued in possession of the island until June 21, 1898, when it was seized by the United States.

The peasants of Umatac have most of their farms up in the neighboring valley where a few are in the midst of coconut trees on the slopes of the hills. One sees a woman balancing a long-handled *fosino* to dart it into the ground like a javelin, preparing the soil to plant beans; near her may be a small patch of sweet potatoes. Before the war a sailboat came down from Agana to take copra, the dried meat of the coconut, in exchange for sugar and coffee. There was only one store then in Umatac, for people had no money with which to buy except when they sold a little copra. In those days, when the roofs of houses were generally of coconut thatch, and the sides of some were constructed entirely of the same material, a thatching party was a happy break in the family routine. Relatives and friends of the house owner gathered to prepare and erect the roof. Now roofs and sides are of galvanized iron; the buildings are set on posts two or three feet above the ground, and each has a little veranda where people love to sit and chat. In the rainy season the dirt road through the village is almost impassable even by carabao carts.

Agricultural activities on Guam are largely governed by the seasons of rain and drought which are so characteristic of the cycle of weather on the island. The dry season is one of preparation—burning the *tangan-tangan* and other brush and weeds which grow so luxuriantly in the rainy tropics. Guamanians, like many natives of other equatorial areas, burn and plant. To them, lacking knowledge of scientific agriculture, the advantages are much greater than the disadvantages. Although burning destroys the humus in the soil, it saves much manual labor in the hot sun for one thing; furthermore it kills insects and other pests, especially the African snail and the rat. Some farmers clear their fields in part at least with machetes, slashing the tall weeds, for the Island Department of Agriculture has made a little progress in helping the people to improve their methods. However, the Guamanian is still unaware of the necessity for conservation.

When fields have been cleared, the soil is plowed and harrowed in preparation for a crop. A farmer generally plants two crops of corn a year, the first in May, depending on when the rains begin, and the second in October near the end of the rainy season when the soil is still moist. The author watched a farmer drive his slow-moving carabao in an old-fashioned one-handle plow to turn up six inches of rich loam, while his little son followed, dropping corn at intervals into the furrow, grain by grain, then pushing soil from the side over each one with his bare toes to keep birds from getting it. A crop takes about three months to mature.

High humidity and attacks of insect pests must be reckoned with during the maturing of the grain and after it is picked. The first step is to break over the stalk beneath the ear soon after the grain has filled out. This practice presumably prevents some grain decay, since it permits the water from frequent rains to drain off. The second step is to gather the ears when the grain is nearly hard. The corn is then shelled as soon as possible, generally by hand, for mechanical shellers of the types available are unsatisfactory for removing from the cob grains which are still relatively soft. The last step is spreading the grain on mats to dry in the sun for several days, a process which also gets rid of weevils. When the grain is quite dry, it is placed in tight containers to protect it from moisture and subsequent decay and to preserve it from destructive attacks by insects.

Sweet potatoes, yams, beans, eggplant, and rice are also planted at the beginning of the rainy season. Rice is now restricted to a few acres, for nearly all the land formerly in that crop is used by the defense forces. It is raised in seed beds and transplanted laboriously by hand in paddies, the time-honored method of the Orient. Well cured in the field on the stalk, it is cut by sickle, and threshed by flails or by beating the heads on the edge of a gasoline drum.

Some farmers plant wet-land taro, also in the rainy season. Other crops have no regular planting time, for, if the coastal lowlands are wet in the rains, there is higher, drier land inland where peppers, squash, dry-land taro, and other vegetables are raised. Every farmer has a clump of bananas in his back yard. Breadfruit can be had for the picking; in the hills and jungle wild yams can be found almost any time.

Although the land of a villager is often seven or eight miles away from his home, its ownership is well known by everyone in the village. Its limits are shown by the location of coconut trees, breadfruit trees, rocks, or other boundary marks.

Land tenure in Guam is traditionally based on inheritance and individual ownership. A farmer leaves his land to his son or divides it among his children to take effect at his death. If he is still active at the time of a son's marriage, he generally gives the young man a tract on which to start farming. Since most families still have relatively much acreage, the divisions of a family holding are large enough to support the children, especially now that some of them are generally wage earners away from the farm.

CHANGES IN LAND UTILIZATION

As a result of World War II, great changes have occurred in the surface pattern. Prior to that war, the military establishment on Guam was small, consisting almost entirely of the naval station, which was staffed by less than one hundred transient personnel, and so only a relatively small amount of land was required for military purposes. After the reoccupation of the island by United States forces in July, 1944, the military establishment rapidly increased many fold. As the island was turned into a major military base for the final prosecution of the war in the Pacific, a large part of the land area in the northern half was taken over for defense. The larger proportion of that part of Guam is nonagricultural. Few farms were ever developed there because of the thinness of the soil and especially the lack of water during the dry season. Some prewar villages were relocated because of the need of their sites for military purposes: Agat, Santa Rita, Asan, Piti, Sinajana, Barrigada, Dededo, Yona, and Talofofo. The south portion of the island remained virtually unchanged, but the land-utilization pattern in the northern half has been much altered. Some of the problems of the use of land and most of the problems of its ownership are attributable directly or indirectly to the war. An appreciable area of the agricultural region near the waist of the island has been taken for military use, and most of it will remain within military preserves. The loss of this agricultural section has necessitated the use by some farmers of poorer ground in its stead, or has forced the former operators to abandon farming—not always unwillingly—to accept wage employment. Many farmers, however, who have become truck farmers and market gardeners, have, according to their old standards, grown rich. The following table shows land use on the island in 1950:

TABLE XIII

Guam: Land Utilization, 1950 (Estimated)*

LAND USED BY THE ARMED FORCES	ACRES	TOTAL	PER CENT
Permanent	43,341		
Temporary	5,787	49,128	34
USED BY THE GOVERNMENT OF GUAM			
Sites for schools, police stations, roads, etc. (leasehold)	815		
Public land	29,603	30,418	21
PRIVATELY OWNED			
Urban	2,600		
Rural	61,854	64,454	45
		144,000	100

* Robert Coote, "Land-Use Conditions and Land Problems of Guam."

AGRICULTURAL PROGRESS

During the war, agriculture on Guam, like everything else, suffered severely. The Guamanians produced as little as they could for the benefit of the Japanese, themselves subsisting on a bare minimum. They refused under the lash to work for the Orientals, believing that some day the Americans would return.

Since the end of the conflict agriculture has made a slow, steady, and substantial recovery. More and more acres have been planted by full-time and part-time farmers. Considerable increases have been achieved in the numbers of poultry and livestock. The replacement of fruit trees destroyed during the war and during a hurricane of November, 1949, has progressed. Table XIV shows the trend in production of the major agricultural enterprises from 1947 to 1952:

TABLE XIV

GUAM: PRODUCTION TREND OF MAJOR AGRICULTURAL ENTERPRISES,
BASE YEAR: 1947

	1947	1948	1949	1950	1951	1952
Fruits and vegetables (pounds)	1,350,000	1,999,942	2,375,000	1,514,736	2,343,175	2,271,485
Poultry (birds)	35,506	48,945	71,675	87,550	101,432	130,437
Cattle (heads)	2,546	2,855	3,243	3,513	4,042	4,796
Hogs (heads)	3,888	4,218	5,596	8,891	10,359	11,558
Fish (pounds)	336,242	469,087	1,150,000	232,185	691,140	559,620

Table XV shows the total pounds of crops harvested during 1952:

TABLE XV

CROPS HARVESTED IN GUAM, 1952

CROPS	POUNDS
Banana	453,070
Cassava	149,630
Corn	137,250
Muskmelon	17,375
Papaya	154,680
Pepino	16,450
Pineapple	21,980
Sugar Cane	51,040
Sweet Potato	143,630
Taro	328,600
Yam	70,040
Watermelon	34,590
Vegetables	354,175
Others	338,975
Total	2,271,485

During the fiscal year 1952, a great surge in postwar agricultural economy took place with an increase in production of 37 per cent over 1951. Fruits and vegetables were planted on 3,759.25 acres in 1952, an increase of 1,399.25 acres over 1951.

Some of the major problems confronting attempts to secure for the new market larger crops, especially of vegetables, relate to the natural environment of the island. The more difficult farming area is in the north where observable surface runoff is essentially non-existent on the northern limestone plateau. This part of the island is a virtual sieve, for, except where depressions are floored and plugged up with a soil deposit, most of the rainfall soon sinks into the ground. Even temporary and minor natural surface water courses are almost absent. Nearly all down drainage occurs through pipelike vertical solution channels, caves, crevasses, and the generally pervious body of the detrital and coralliferous limestones themselves. Subsurface caverns and many other sinks are scattered over that area. A large number of caverns of various sizes and shapes exist in the limestone, which owes the particular details of its present expression almost entirely to the effects of solution. It is everywhere pitted, pinnacled, and crevassed from the action of solvent waters, aided by the physical and chemical processes that accompany jungle vegetation. In that area there are surviving *ifil* trees (*Intsia*) and other tropical hardwoods, and dense tangles of second-growth jungle. Much of the limestone is still forested with coconuts and other trees, and some of it is covered with brush, part of which is cleared for vegetables. The soil is generally so shallow and stony that it must be cultivated with a *fosino*, or other hand tools.

In this part of the island the author visited a demonstration farm operated by the Department of Agriculture where, by dint of hard and regular effort with hoe and mattock, carrots, onions, eggplant, and other vegetables were made to grow healthily. But the Guamanians are loath to struggle with that type of land, preferring to work for the armed services as unskilled laborers and to buy their food and clothing at one of the local stores which have sprung into existence since the war.

Agriculture is carried on much more successfully in the southern part of the island, where the volcanic hills have weathered to conventional patterns and where a normal drainage system seems to have developed. Accordance of summit levels in some areas of volcanic rocks suggests dissected older surfaces of broadly benchlike nature, the most conspicuous of which is a wide, tilted, and dissected terrace that dips eastward from the island crest and that has experienced many relative changes of land and sea. Continued burning until modern times has reduced the humus, soil fertility, and depth to such a degree that little else but sword grass can live. In areas cleared of forest and brush, however, the soil is rich. At lower elevations above the coasts and inland are stretches of mixed brush with a variety of trees, mostly small hardwoods; or of *tangtan tanga* (*Leucaena glauca*), an acacia-like small tree or tall shrub, in virtually pure stands or interspersed with occasional breadfruit, coconut palms, and casuarina or Polynesian ironwood; in some places patches of bamboo thickets have little else between. Near the tops of the ridges are thin stands of pandanus, and along the coast, in north and south, occasional mangrove clumps grow in protected swampy locations.

The difficulty of raising vegetables with unvarying success is in large part due to the irregularity of the rainfall, for, in the tropical climate, droughts soon wilt green growths. There are periods of a week or two when no rain falls at all. Rainfall records from January, 1919, through July, 1948, show that monthly rainfall ranges from 44.5 inches (October 1924) to less than an inch in each month from February to May. During this period many months had much less than one-half inch, although no rainless month is recorded. There is much erosion on the volcanic hills during short torrential rains, between which the tropical heat soon evaporates the water from the shallow soil. Minimum temperatures from December through February occasionally fall to a low of 68°F, but in other months rarely go below 74°. Mean maximum temperatures vary from about 86°F to 89°F, with occasionally a maximum of about 95°. Vegetables are raised more successfully during the cooler months of the year, if the distribution of rainfall is at all favorable.

Droughts are more severe on vegetables because of the general thinness of the soil in all parts of the islands. The soils of Guam are mostly of two general types: the heavy clay soil of the valleys and coastal plains, and the porous limestone kind of the northern plateau. Much of the clay variety is only six or seven inches deep. The limestone soil, even more shallow, is underlaid with coral, some of which is disintegrated. In many places coral rock outcrops at the surface. Mechanical cultivation can be practiced in the lowland volcanic soils, but in the limestone area only after surface rock has been removed. Only frequent rains in the latter area can produce a profitable crop. Yet, because the tropical weather permits a farmer to raise two or three crops of vegetables a year, the failure of one is not as serious as it is for the truck farmer in continental United States.

Steady progress in agriculture since 1945 in spite of the difficult natural conditions is due to the low level to which production sank during the war, and, after it, to the almost unlimited market which has arisen, and the assistance which agriculture has received.

Soon after hostilities ceased and a Department of Agriculture was set up, extension agents helped to establish better farming methods, a factor which contributed to an increase in the total yield per acre of farm land. An entomologist and a veterinarian were employed to give skilled professional assistance to farmers. Plant quarantine work received an impetus with the assignment of a Federal plant inspector to Guam to help enforce existing plant quarantine regulations. The great market was created by the huge increase in the population of the island, which includes military personnel, Federal civil service employees, and workers for civilian firms which are under Federal contracts.

Agriculture will continue to increase in importance, in large part because of the ready market for everything produced. The "pineapple king" of Guam, a retired Navy enlisted man, has a twelve-acre farm at Yigo in the northern half of the island. He delivers a ton of fresh pineapples a week to the Armed Forces "as long as they last."

Guamanian farmers dispose of their products in different ways. Some who have large quantities of vegetables to sell haul them directly to a military commissary or to a civil employees' mess hall like that at Asan which serves a large number of people. Others earn money from their back yards by selling bananas to retail stores at twenty-five cents a pound. Farmers also sell fruit and vegetables from booths along the roadside to the many foreign residents who drive about the island on sight-seeing tours.

The public market in Agana, another postwar factor in Guamanian economy, is a lively center of trade every Friday. Cucumbers and watermelons are displayed on rows of wooden trays; avocados, taro, yams, and several varieties of bananas are laid out, together with little piles of betel nuts and cherry tomatoes, eggplants, coconuts, and *calabaza*, a species of squash. Farmers take their produce there

themselves, many in jeeps. Those arriving from the country before
dawn try to sell their vegetables as quickly as possible, and return to
do chores on their farms.

The personnel of the sellers continually changes throughout the
day, those who have sold going home, and fresh ones from the
country taking their places. In the afternoon and evening, the market
place is crowded with Aganans, Filipinos, military personnel, and
others. A good many Guamanians doing business in Agana or employed by the armed services now purchase much of their own food.

Unfortunately, the great boom in agriculture has been accompanied by a plague of insect pests. The establishing of Guam as a
Pacific crossroads for airplanes has enabled tiny winged passengers
to get in from Japan, Korea, Hong Kong, southeast Asia, and India.
It is held to be impracticable at present to fumigate all planes on
their arrival, although the Government-subsidized Pacific Micronesian Lines in the Trust Territory set a good example in this regard.
The most objectionable of the new pests, which does not fly, but
crawls—the African snail—was probably introduced on machinery
brought in from the former Japanese mandated islands, now United
States Trust Territory. The Japanese introduced it there for food,
but now it eats everything. A large one has a head the size of a baby's
fist. In the evenings the sidewalks in Agana are alive with these
crawlers. However, two assistant entomologists, a well-equipped
laboratory, and several projects under way are all beginning to make
their presence felt in pest-control work.

FISHING

Guamanians, on an island in the middle of the Pacific, are still
really landsmen. True, they fish on the reefs with spears, nets, and
weirs, but in all make little use of the great natural resources of the
surrounding ocean.

The fishing industry has scarcely changed from its prewar status.
Guamanians catch squirrel fish and small sturgeon in pools on the
reef; in weirs or traps they take young mackerel and mullet. Large
lagoons are found only in the vicinity of Sumay and Merizo, where
fishing has been important since ancient times. Most of the fish
caught, however, are taken by pole fishing and spearing. Schools of

tuna and barracuda are seen from time to time outside the reef, but they attract merely a few fishermen from Umatac, and servicemen who fish for sport. A school of *atulai* or "mackerel" offshore creates excitement in a village and is the signal for communal fishing parties. There is almost no commercial fishing in Guam, despite the present large market which exists especially among the Filipino population.

Guamanians prefer the small reef fish to which they have grown accustomed rather than the deep-sea varieties. Various species of *siganas*, small fish caught in the lagoons inside the reef, are considered very good eating. Large quantities of shellfish were taken and eaten in prewar days, in Apra Harbor and its vicinity. But that area, dredged for Navy use, is now restricted.

After hearing the statement many times, "The Guamanians don't know how to fish in the open sea, for they have neither the experience nor the equipment," the author elicited an alleged explanation from an old-time Guamanian in Agana. He told the following story: "Some hundreds of years ago, when the Spaniards were trying to convert the Guamanians to the Christian religion, there was much opposition, especially on the part of the men. The Spanish, finally exasperated, imported a large contingent of soldiers from Mexico and the Philippines who decimated the male population of Guam. The soldiers intermarried with the Guamanian women. Because they knew nothing of fishing, the art of fishing in deep water ceased entirely and has never been recovered since."

There is no doubt that the Chamorros suffered terribly under Spanish rule. The following brief account of the situation in early times is taken from a longer one: "This island . . . has no trade or communication of any kind with the rest of the world, except when the wind permits the galleons to put in there two or three days to land a few articles of merchandise. . . . In that unhappy country one can find nothing to wear . . . the people are slowly dying out. The natives . . . are unwilling to reproduce their species. The reason . . . is the frightful despotism exercised by those in authority. As there are no courts of justice, the laws of the kingdom are not enforced."*

Even the relatively small amount of fishing carried on suffers from

* M. Le Gentil, "Misrule in Guam One Hundred Sixty Years Ago," translated from the original French by the Hon. Fred C. Fisher, *Philippine Magazine*, Vol. XXVI, No. 11, p. 717; republished in the *Guam Recorder*, Vol. VIII, 1931–1932, p. 459.

the destructive typhoons, a factor in Guam's uncertain weather. Typhoon "Hester," which struck the island on December 31, 1952, completely destroyed or severely damaged the greater portion of the fish weirs of the island, the replacement and repair of which were slowed by a shortage of materials. The disaster accounted for a 33 per cent decrease in the total catch from that of the previous year.

SOCIAL INSTITUTIONS

The great changes which have come to Guam since prewar days have considerably affected the traditional social institutions of the island. Prior to World War II, the village was the social and economic unit, preserving conservatively the customs and traditions of nineteenth century Europe. A family worked for a year, for example, preparing for a wedding, which was a very expensive affair. Food was regularly saved, and a poor family was economically embarrassed. The young man courted the girl of his choice only in her home. Indeed, marriages were largely arranged by the parents. Relatives and other friends came to the fandango, or wedding party, bringing gifts of pigs, chickens, rice, and corn to be cooked for the feast. They came two or three days before it to build temporary houses of coconut leaves and boughs and to help cook breadfruit, taro, and fish. After the wedding a special kind of rice pudding was always part of the feast. The young bride and groom made a tour of the relatives, each of whom contributed something—a pig, a pair of chickens, a young carabao or a cow—to help set them up in farming; pots and pans for housekeeping were, of course, also among the gifts. The young man had already secured title to a small piece of land.

The fiesta held in memory of a patron saint was the great social and religious event of the year in the village, for it was one of very few occasions when people traveled from one village to another. It is carried on today in much the same way as of old. The author had the pleasant and interesting experience of attending one afternoon, with a Guamanian friend, the fiesta of San Juan Bautista at Ordot. A long procession of villagers, some six hundred of them—men, women, and children—filed very slowly and quietly in a column of twos and threes from the church to march solemnly the entire length of the village. Small children were at the head of the line, followed by young girls and then the older women. The women wore heavily starched, wide-sleeved blouses, lace shawls, and long, full skirts. All the girls wore kerchiefs on their heads.

Boys and men followed the women. Older men and women, with wrinkled faces, cast their eyes on the ground or looked steadfastly and thoughtfully in front of them. At the end of the column, half a dozen young women chanting a hymn were followed by eight young men carrying a statue of St. John on a litter, a dark-robed priest and his acolytes bringing up the rear.

The procession broke up in the village square close to the chapel, where, from a stage, the priest recounted the main events in the life of St. John the Baptist, and encouraged the people of Ordot to live like him. After the sermon the people lined up to the entrance of the social hall where a feast was spread, the like of which is seldom seen in a rural community. At one end of a long table dishes were heaped with slices of corn pie and Spanish rice. Then followed platters of pork—boiled, fried, roasted, and stewed. Next on the festal board were trays of chicken and beef similarly cooked. There were dishes of fried fish and of fish cooked with vegetables, of salads and various kinds of Guamanian cakes. A side table was heaped with bananas. Iced fruit juice was the main drink. The villagers took their food outside on paper plates and ate it sitting about chatting; then they moved away in small groups to their homes, where they entertained friends who had come from other villages. In the evening a program for boys and girls included games, singing, and dancing. The following Sunday morning, a high mass in honor of St. John was held in the chapel.

A touching feature of the afternoon festivities was the respect children paid to older people. As the social part of the fiesta proceeded, a boy or girl would approach an older person, generally a friend or relative, curtsy, kiss his or her hand, and say a word of greeting.

The fiestas are an economic drain on the villages, for the modern era of transportation brings more and more visitors for these great annual celebrations. In the old days these were often the only occasions of a visit from distant friends and relatives, who arrived after hours of travel in their carabao carts. Now the jeep brings them in twenty-five minutes. The number of people attending the feast is estimated in advance, and families volunteer to prepare shares of the food. Nine days before the fiesta, prayers to the patron saint begin, and during the interval meetings are held to make final preparations and delegate relays of young women to serve the dishes. The day after the festival is over, a family decides what pig it will raise for the next year's celebration, or what chickens it will have, or what other meat it may be able to provide. The Bishop of Guam has made an official pronouncement against fiestas, stating that the feasting and merrymaking should be given up and that only the purely religious part should be continued. Notwithstanding his objections, they are still the outstanding events of the year in a Guamanian village. The women, more religious, and liking the social aspects of the fiestas especially, want to continue them more than do the men.

In Chamorro life women, traditionally holding a prominent place socially, also take an important part economically: in child and household care, in fishing with hand nets, in making coconut oil and earthenware pots for cooking. The ancient Chamorros were organized into kinship groups in which descent was reckoned through the female line. Respect for the authority of women is still accentuated by the doctrine of the Catholic Church, which plays a dominant role in Guam, for they are considered the guardians of religion in the home.

Rapid changes in the social activities and institutions of Guamanians have come concurrently with the economic improvement of the people and with their closer contacts with Western civilization, including that of the Philippines. For almost three centuries in Guam, a pattern of life based on absolute values had been imposed on the individual by the family, the church, and the state. In his moral standards, and to a considerable extent in his social and political affairs, the individual had little or no choice. Now, however, since American democratic ideas, ideals, and institutions have disturbed the traditional ways, serious conflicts are arising in home life, religion, economics, and politics.

Guam has employment for everyone. It was the general shortage of professional skilled and unskilled workers that necessitated the importation of thousands of Filipinos. During the fiscal year ending June 30, 1952, about ten thousand contract laborers were imported by the armed services, nearly all of them Filipinos, among whom were high-school graduates, mechanics, electricians, and clerks in offices and stores. They come with fares paid on an agreement to work for at least a year, after which they may go home again on a free ticket. At the end of three years in Guam, they have to return unless they can renew their contracts.

In physical appearance Filipinos cannot be distinguished from Guamanians. The author asked members of each ethnic group several times how the other could be distinguished. In every case the answer was: "We don't know until we hear them speak English. They have a different accent from us." Almost all Guamanians and many Filipinos speak English fluently.

The Filipinos have stimulated the Guamanians to put forth more effort than their easygoing attitude prompts. "If not today, perhaps tomorrow or the next day" is the approach of South Sea people to doing anything which is not part of their traditional way of living. The Guamanians, on their part, regard the Filipinos as unwelcome visitors who pocket very high wages that they, as yet, have not qualified themselves to earn.

Other elements of the population, small, but interesting, are 150 Palauans, mostly young people going to school, and a few from Yap, Tinian, Saipan, and other islands. A Palauan high-school boy, when asked why there were so many from Palau, replied, "We have a hospital in Palau, and schools, and an administration run by Americans from the States, and we would like to learn how to take them over." He said that Yapese and other children want to go home after finishing elementary school.

The other nonresident population, estimated at sixty thousand, comprises American military personnel and dependents, civilian contract laborers, civil servants, and a few Chinese and Japanese.

The changing attitudes of the younger generation are of considerable concern to the older folk. Instead of courting his girl friend in the home of her parents, a young man now takes her to the movies and for a ride in a jeep. The villages hold beauty contests annually in which one candidate from each of the eleven villages enters the final round for honors. In the meantime, the eleven are the "pin-up girls" of the unmarried men on the island. A former Guamanian judge said to the author: "The changes that have come in the last ten years are revolutionary without the shooting. If we could have had those changes come over a period of fifty years, we would feel better about it."

The older generation also looks askance at the great influx of

American illustrated magazines of various sizes and varying literary and pictorial moral standards. In nice Guamanian homes attractive children from eight to fifteen pore over "Tubby" and "The New Funnies." "When we were children we did not read them," parents say, "but now all the children do."

In view of the rapid increase in the Guamanian population, one of the pressing problems is the education of the children. The indigenous population of the island, growing at a phenomenal rate, is made up mostly of youths under twenty-one. A large percentage, 46.4, is under fifteen years of age, while the average Guamanian age is only sixteen. Among the aspects of the increase are shortages of qualified teachers, school buildings, and equipment.

With jobs plentiful and wages high, young Guamanians are reluctant to return to agriculture as the sole source of livelihood. There are now about six hundred part-time farmers, and only four hundred full-time agriculturists. The majority of Guamanians want to change from a self-supporting basis or subsistence economy to a dollar economy, dependent on cash received from sale of goods or from services, primarily to the Armed Forces.

A great many young men work at unskilled jobs for contractors who are erecting buildings of various kinds. Some work on their farms in the evenings and on Saturdays. Hundreds of them drive jeeps or good-looking cars. On a trip from Agana to Umatac one meets a score of jeeps driven by happy young Guamanians who look as if they are riding on the world. Those in Agana, Asan, Piti, and other war-damaged areas, after receiving thousands of dollars for war damages, spend their money for automobiles as soon as they are available. It is not uncommon to see a frame building patched with galvanized iron and a new car parked in the yard.

Houses in general have changed little since prewar times, except that there is more use of galvanized iron. Almost every home now has an unpainted galvanized iron roof, and some have walls of that material; many show signs of dilapidation in the heat and rain of the tropical climate. For the island in general, the farther away one goes from Agana, the less well kept are the houses. The people with the better houses and the more flourishing farms are those nearer the market furnished by American military personnel and their dependents.

Improvements in health and sanitation are lagging somewhat behind the general advance in social and economic welfare. The mortality and morbidity rates of tuberculosis are still high compared with those in the United States. A recent survey with a mobile X-ray unit revealed that out of 10,000 people screened, 4.9 per cent had tuberculosis in various forms. Mortality due to that disease is between 7 and 8 per cent of all deaths. One reason for the high rate of t.b. is that the problem of finding cases lacks the leadership and close cooperation of the Guamanians. Improvements in the situation, however, are in sight. An educational program is under way and the tuberculosis section of the Health Department is being reorganized. But the recruiting of competent additional personnel from the United States is difficult because of the isolation of Guam and the lack of funds to attract qualified medical practitioners. A general island-wide sanitation program includes efforts to keep flies and mosquitoes out of homes and to eliminate rat-breeding places. More attention is being given to the disposal of village dumps and other debris near dwellings. It is anticipated that better health and sanitation will contribute signally to the welfare of the island population.

Perhaps it is in the field of health and sanitation that the Navy rule is missed most. Older people in Guam sometimes wish for the Navy days again, for they remember that after a typhoon Navy trucks scurried here and there carrying relief to sick and injured. Now they have to depend on their own resources, which, in medical help and supplies, are meager.

When the Navy first took over the Government, the local native police of Spanish times were replaced by American marines called "patrolmen," one stationed in each village, who assisted in enforcing sanitary regulations besides performing normal patrol duty. Now when something is stolen from a house or yard, a Guamanian sometimes hurries in vain to find a policeman. One of them remarked to the author, "There was always a policeman when the Navy was here!"

POLITICAL LIFE

The political consciousness of Guam has developed with its economic and social betterment but especially with its new status of independence or semi-independence in the American commonwealth. As was already mentioned, a significant forward step of the Government has been the completion of the codification of the laws of Guam. All Acts of previous Guam congresses, and all executive orders, memoranda, and letters having the force and effect of law were brought together in a systematic arrangement. After being edited they were presented to the legislature, which repealed old statutes and enacted the new code into law.

The Organic Act of 1950, passed by the Eighty-first Congress of the United States, provided for a unicameral legislature for the Territory of Guam whose members, elected biennially, shall not exceed twenty-one in number. Guam is unique among the States and Territories of the United States in that it has only one political party, the Popular Party, and that party has no identity with either of the national parties of the United States. All candidates not members of the Popular Party, grouped under the heading of Independents, run for office as such. The present legislature, which often ignores party lines on crucial issues, consists of nineteen Popular and two Independent members.

Before the war, under naval administration, there were two legislative houses, an upper and a lower, whose powers, however, were merely advisory to the governor. The unicameral legislature now enacts the laws of the island, provided they are signed by the chief executive. If he vetoes a law, and it is repassed, it is then referred to Washington for approval or disapproval.

The legislature has adopted a Judiciary Act which revised and modernized the judicial system of the Territory in order to provide prompt justice and enforcement of the law. Another basic measure has been the adoption of a ten-year capital improvement program for the construction of schools, roads, bridges, hospitals, community buildings, and power, water, and telephone facilities. With the authorization of this program, the Territory undertook to complete the rehabilitation of the public facilities of the island which were destroyed by the United States Armed Forces when the island was recaptured from the Japanese in the summer of 1944.

The author was a visitor at a session of the Second Guam Legislature when the governor vetoed a bill to establish a censorship board on films. The Congress came to order at five-thirty in the afternoon. The Stars and Stripes were on the right of the speaker and the Guam colors on the left. When the roll was called, the pastor prayed for "temperance" for everyone. Sixteen members were present and the gallery was half full of visitors. Two little boys carried microphones to the members speaking, one for each side of the room, for the proceedings were broadcast. The members listened in stony-faced silence to the governor's message accompanying his second veto of the censorship bill. Later the former mayor of Yigo village explained: "You see, we got our citizenship so recently, only in 1950, that we are not yet ready for all kinds of movies. Some of them upset our young people. Anyway, it was nice that the governor signed the bill against taxi dancing."

A Juvenile Court Act became law in 1952. As the young people in the process of becoming "Americanized" break away from the restraints imposed upon them by their parents and the Church, the amount of juvenile delinquency tends to increase and the problem of treatment and prevention becomes more acute. One of the admonitions which the priest gave at the Ordot festival particularly applied to modern Guam. "When John the Baptist went to a party," he said, "it was not like some of the parties Guamanians are giving now, with lots of whisky." At this remark the older people maintained their serious demeanor, but many of the younger crowd tittered. When Guamanians were granted United States citizenship it included the right to buy and sell liquor.

Eighteen-year-olds balloted for the first time in the November election of 1954, representing an additional 2,400 new voters to the electorate. The law extending suffrage to all citizens of Guam eighteen years of age or over places Guam on a par with the foremost States of the Union in its program of social and political advancement, and in this respect makes it unique among the Territories of the United States. The older people felt that giving the youngsters a vote would add a great deal to their sense of responsibility. Since many of them have received a better education than their elders, the latter think the young people will vote more intelligently and will scrutinize the character and abilities of candidates more carefully.

It was apparently a surprise to large numbers of the Guamanians that as citizens* of the United States their new privileges included payment of Federal income taxes. Their resentment was appeased when they found that all of the Federal income taxes collected on

* Although the Guamanians are citizens of the United States, they cannot vote in national elections, nor do they have representation in the Congress of the United States.

the island—about $7,000,000 a year—are remitted by Washington to the Guam Government. Local taxes amount to about $3,000,000. After operating expenses, the Guamanians have a surplus of about $2,000,000 for public works every year—a sizable sum for a small island where most of the roads and public utilities are maintained by the Navy at no cost to the local government.

A disadvantage of the administration is the short term of office of the governor, two years. Entering upon his duties without any background in regard to the Guamanians and their problems, he has just become acquainted with the local situation when his term of office has expired. As was already suggested in an earlier chapter, serious consideration should be given to the establishment of a separate Federal agency chargeable with the administration of and general supervision over all the Pacific Islands areas under the sovereignty or jurisdiction and control of the United States. Since one of the main factors involved in all three Territories of the United States in the Pacific is national defense, a separate Department of the Federal Government is the best place to lodge general supervision over all of them.

THE FUTURE

At the end of the war the Guamanians were faced with the tremendous task of reconstructing the parts of their island which were leveled, of discovering and developing profitable home industries, and of doing their share in fulfilling Guam's potential position as an important new hub of Pacific activity. Agana, the seat of Guam's government, formerly a city of 12,000 inhabitants, was completely destroyed in the bombardment.

One of the more complex problems of the island is the land situation in Agana. In its prewar days the city was a maze of streets crisscrossing each other as in old Spanish towns. The naval administration decided that a new city should be laid out with straight streets and good public utilities. A city planner was hired who did a masterly job of designing what was assumed to be a new and beautiful metropolis, but unfortunately after the work was completed it was found that the new thoroughfares chopped up private property to such an extent that to this date ownership of most lots has never been established. Rarely in the city is one sizable piece of property owned by one man. In some places three people own a lot, one owning one corner, another the middle, and still a third the other corner. No one wants to sell, for there is a strong Guamanian feeling against the outright sale of property which has been in the family for decades. Further to complicate the situation, many real-estate records were lost during the Japanese occupation. Much land in Agana, therefore, cannot be leased to construct new buildings, and as a result of the confused property situation and the difficulty of obtaining a clear title of possession to an entire lot, relatively few structures have been erected in the new city. Entire blocks have no buildings at all. Guam's Planning Commission has made some progress in clearing up many land disputes in the capital by bringing the owners of controversial strips together for conferences toward a settlement.

Manufacturing and processing for the Guamanian market in Agana, and elsewhere, are largely dependent on locally produced agricultural crops. Coconut oil, soap, ice, soft drinks, woodwork, furniture, jewelry, cement and tile, leatherwork and bakery goods are the only manufactured or processed items worthy of note. A number of Guamanians in Agana and vicinity are employed as mechanics, repairmen, electricians, plumbers, and carpenters. Construction work, shipbuilding, and repair work on the island are conducted by the Army and Navy. The Guamanians are still clever at some of their old-time occupations—shell and bead work, weaving pandanus mats, wood carving, and metalworking.

To keep pace with the increase in population and the size of payrolls, there has been an expansion of retail business and of the various service industries. Before the war almost all important business was centered in Agana, for a trend toward a money economy, instead of a subsistence way of living, began there early in the period of American occupation. Since reconstruction, the commercial growth of the island has lagged; many new businesses have been located elsewhere. Just north of Agana, in the town of Tamuning, a development is taking place on both sides of the new marine highway, where an important trading center has been established. South of Agana, between it and Apra Harbor, there is considerable new construction along the Marine Drive, particularly in the town of Piti.

Self-government opened the door of the island to American businessmen with a background and tradition which is still entirely new to Guamanians. In Agana now, the names of Jones, Smith, Wilson and others are already well known in drygoods. This influx of Americans who have started business of various kinds in Agana and who take the lion's share makes Guamanians in business very uneasy. Some of them say boldly that they fared better under Navy government. Prior to civil administration, the United States Navy had established a policy of granting business licenses to persons of Guamanian ancestry only. In 1950, when the practice was discontinued, there was a rush of applications for business licenses by American citizens. During 1952 some 1,600 new licenses were issued.

Guam's economic future from the point of view of a favorable balance of trade will be dependent almost entirely upon the wages of Guamanians working for the United States Government in various capacities and on wages of Guamanians rendering personal service to the military and civilian personnel. Agricultural exports will be so small as to be almost inconsequential in any consideration of the island's economic problems.

For the immediate future in Guam the problems of agriculture are largely those of production, since the present output falls far short of meeting local demands for fresh fruits and vegetables, for poultry and other meat. Several factors have a bearing on future agricultural land use. Prior to the war, poultry and livestock were adequate. Now, however, the supply could be increased several fold and still not exceed the demand. Yet this does not necessarily mean that much additional acreage would be required. With proper machinery, larger-scale enterprises and better techniques, production could be considerably advanced without using additional acreage. Furthermore, there are some thousands of acres that could be brought into profitable use and many thousands that could be developed into fair pasture land. In order to facilitate the movement of agriculture from the producers to the consumers, it will be necessary to provide much better facilities for processing, storing, and distributing produce than now exist. The control of insect pests, snails, and rats will further encourage Guamanian farmers to put forth new efforts in agriculture, the mainstay of their way of living.

The future of farming depends in part not only on controlling insect pests, but on producing more and better crops by the use of fertilizer and modern agricultural equipment. The demonstration farms with agricultural extension agents will be of further help. The legislature has made possible long-term loans for farmers to improve their methods by purchasing better equipment and improved breeds of stock.

Grazing lands are far below maximum carrying capacity. In general, whether they are rolling or rough, they have suffered greatly from soil erosion. Sword grass and other native grasses, very low in forage value, could be replaced by good pasture.

During the war much of what remained of Guam's forests was destroyed. While never extensive during modern times, the forests were of economic importance as a source of lumber and firewood, and of even greater value for the protection of the watersheds. Their disappearance is an important factor in erosion. A conservation program looking to protection of watersheds, range rehabilitation, and reforestation should be instituted in the near future.

A commercial fishing industry awaits development, for about 1,500,000 pounds of frozen fish are imported annually. The market for Guam's agricultural products will hold indefinitely into the future as Guam continues to be a defense outpost in the Pacific. As the strategic importance of the island grows, the military requirements, increasing proportionately, will bring more officers, men, civilians, and their dependents.

Agricultural education will play an important role in the future of the island. Younger Guamanians earning good wages on defense projects are losing interest in farming and someday may resent having to go back to agricultural work. Those in school want to look forward to serving customers in a store or doing office routine. However, it is obvious that the throngs of youngsters coming along cannot all find in those activities a means of earning a living. Furthermore, plans must be made which will provide a continued era of well-being on the island when the lucrative days of defense spending have passed.

Guam has taken on importance as a main way station on the sea and air routes of the entire Pacific area. A modern harbor now allows dockside transfer of freight and passengers in contrast to the old system of lightering from ships anchored offshore. Modern airfields are used by commercial airlines providing regular and frequent service.

Guam is now a port of call for two major shipping lines: the

Pacific Far East Line, and the American President Lines. Ships of the Pacific Far East Line call at Guam on the average of four times a month, carrying freight and passengers between the West Coast ports of the United States, Guam, and the Orient. The ships of American President Lines call at Guam once a month, and additional ships carrying refrigerated cargo will be added in the future. Guam is the home port of the Pacific Micronesian Lines, a wholly owned subsidiary of the Pacific Far East Line, under contract to the Trust Territory of the Pacific Islands. These ships provide logistic support to the various administrative districts of the Trust Territory. To keep pace with increased business, the commercial port of Guam has constructed fourteen new warehouses and has acquired considerable additional dock space.

It is possible that industrial and commercial enterprises will find Guam attractive as a stable area from which to conduct business. Preliminary investigations have been under way concerning the question of establishing hotels, beverage plants, coconut desiccating establishments, fish processing, furniture manufacturing, and auto assembly lines. These prospective undertakings will require relatively small amounts of land.

Considerations for the future of Guam do not at present contemplate an export market, for that has not, as yet, crept over her horizon. "Even if there is no export market," one Guamanian said, "our people will always be self-supporting; every Guamanian has a farm, so he won't starve. Even if labor for the Armed Forces is laid off, he will have something to lean back on. He will have chickens and cattle. And," he added, "there are always the wild crops—taro, and breadfruit and yams—if any enemy invades the island again."

Since the war Guamanians feel a much stronger sentimental attachment toward the United States than they had before. They are hesitant to talk about the days of Japanese occupation. From December, 1941, to July, 1944, they worked from dawn to dusk in the fields and on Japanese military emplacements. The cruelties and privations they endured, the ruthless murders, the courage and belief of the people in the return of American forces, however, will remain symbols of their struggle for the right to be American citizens. Remembering the hardships of the Japanese régime, they are pleased to live happily under the Stars and Stripes. Boys drafted into the Army feel proud they have been called on to serve. Appreciating the relationship of

THE TERRITORY OF GUAM 157

Uncle Sam and nephew, they hope that the Uncle feels obligations toward them, too.

Guam will need continued guidance from the United States, not only through the governor, but through cooperation and help in agriculture, and through further opportunities for Guamanians to study in Hawaii and on the mainland of the United States to equip themselves mentally for leadership in the development of their island, which is becoming the western metropolis of the Pacific.

REFERENCES

Cloud, P. E., "Reconnaissance Geology of Guam and Problems of Water Supply and Fuel Storage," Military Geology Branch of U.S. Geological Survey, April, 1951, 50 pp.

Coote, Robert, "A Report on the Land-Use Conditions and Land Problems of Guam," U.S. Dept. Interior, Bureau of Land Management, 1951, 30 pp., mimeographed.

Dyer, G. L., "The Present Condition of Guam," *Independent, LVIII* (1905), 883-889.

Guam Recorder, Vol. 8, 1931–1932.

Johnston, Lucius W., "Guam Before December, 1941," *U.S. Naval Institute Proceedings,* 68 (472): 991-1002, July 1942.

Reed, Erik K., *General Report on the Archaeology and History of Guam* (Washington, D.C.: National Park Service, 1952), 133 pp., 3 maps, 22 pp. illustrations.

Safford, W. E., "The Chamorro Language of Guam," *American Anthropologist,* 5: 289-311, 508-529; 6: 501-534 (1903–1904).

Taylor, John L., "Guam: Focus of the Western Pacific," *Jour. Geog.,* 48 (1): 27-38, 3 figs., map, Jan., 1949.

Thompson, L. M., *Guam and Its People,* rev. 3rd ed. (Princeton University Press, 1947), 367 pp.

———, "Guam's Bombed-Out Capital," *Far Eastern Survey,* Vol. 16, No. 6, pp. 66-69, March 26, 1947.

———, "The Women of Guam," *Asia and the Americas,* 44 (9): 412-415, Sept., 1944.

United States, Committee to Study the Naval Administration of Guam and American Samoa (E. M. Hopkins, Chairman), *Report on the Civil Governments of Guam and American Samoa.* Washington, 1947.

United States Department of the Interior, annual reports of the Governor of Guam.

ཉ Part II ཉ

THE TRUST TERRITORY
OF
THE PACIFIC ISLANDS

VII

Introduction to the Trust Territory

At the end of the war of 1914–1918, the United States Government took the position that none of the dependent Territories which were detached from Germany and Turkey should be annexed by any of the Allied and Associated Powers. In order to avoid that contingency and to give effect to the two fundamental principles of native welfare and equal economic opportunity, the mandates system was devised. This placed upon the League of Nations responsibility for supervision over the administration of the dependent Territories taken from Germany and Turkey. In this way the welfare of the dependent peoples involved in the mandates system, and the actions of the mandatory powers specifically entrusted with responsibilities of administration over them, became matters of continuing international concern.

The United States, although not a member of the League or a party to the Treaty of Versailles, had interests in the mandated Territories resulting from its membership in the Allied and Associated Powers. To safeguard these interests, it made with the mandatory powers a series of treaties which protected its national rights and its international position.

Early in 1942 when the United States Government began to develop its policies with respect to a new international organization, the need for the establishment of some international mechanism to replace the mandates system of the League of Nations was clearly recognized.

The projected new international machinery to deal with these Territories came to be described as Trusteeships, a description which differentiated it from the League of Nations mandates system. It was designed to be not only a substitute for the old mandates system, but also a definite improvement.

On November 6, 1946, President Truman announced that the United States was prepared to place under trusteeship, with the United States as Administering Authority, the Japanese Mandated Islands which had been taken at great cost by our Armed Forces. On the same date copies of a draft Trusteeship Agreement were transmitted for information to other members of the Security Council of the United Nations and to New Zealand and to the Republic of the Philippines. The draft Trusteeship Agreement was formally submitted to the Security Council on February 17, 1947, and, after slight modification, was unanimously approved by it on April 2, 1947. This agreement came into being on July 18, 1947, when, pursuant to authorization by the Congress, the President approved it on behalf of the United States. The agreement designated the Territory of these islands as "a strategic area," and the United States as the Administering Authority of the Territory Under Article 83 of the Charter of the United Nations. The functions of the United Nations relating to strategic areas, including the approval of the terms of the Trusteeship Agreements and of their alteration or amendment, are exercised by the Security Council.

NATURAL SETTING

The islands of three archipelagoes, the Marshalls, the Carolines, and the Marianas with the exception of Guam, lying north of the equator and considerably west of the Hawaiian Islands, comprise the Trust Territory of the Pacific Islands. There are 2,137 separate islands in all, ranging in size from volcanic masses of 153 square miles to mere sandspits. These are grouped into 96 clusters or single islands scattered through a vast expanse of ocean roughly equaling the area of the United States. Generally, the islands are fragmental bodies of land; the great majority are less than 1 square mile in area, giving rise thereby to the name Micronesia (small islands), by which that part of Oceania is commonly known. The name Micronesia for one of the great divisions of the Pacific was proposed by Domeny de Rienzi to the Société de Géographie of Paris on December 16, 1831.

It distinguishes this area from Malaysia or Indonesia further west, Melanesia (black islands) to the south, and Polynesia (many islands) to the east. These distinctions are based not only on geography, but also on racial, linguistic, and ethnological factors. The islands of the Trust Territory, constituting the major portion of Micronesia, fall into three main categories: atolls, single low islands, and high volcanic islands.

TABLE XVI

TOTAL NUMBER OF ISLANDS IN THE TRUST TERRITORY

GROUP	NO. OF ATOLLS	SINGLE LOW ISLANDS	HIGH VOLCANIC ISLANDS	COMPLEX ASSEM-BLAGES	NO. OF ISLETS	TOTAL LAND AREA IN SQ. MILES
Marshalls	29	5	—	—	1156	70
Carolines	30	12	1	4	952	461.4
Marianas	—	—	15	—	29	380.6 (inc. Guam)
	59	17	16	4	2137	912

This island world, recently brought under the administration of the United States, stretches from latitude 1° to 20° north and from longitude 130° to 170° east, covering some 3,000,000 square miles. The distance from Tobi Island in the extreme west of the Carolines to Mili Island in the extreme east of the Marshalls is approximately 2,400 nautical miles or 2,727 statute miles. At its greatest width the area extends 1,300 nautical miles or 1,477 statute miles north and south. The total land area which makes up the Trust Territory—the Marshall Islands, the Caroline Islands, and the Marianas excepting Guam—is only 687 square miles.

Most of the volcanic islands, in the western part of the Trust Territory, are the exposed peaks of a submerged volcanic ridge which stretches from Japan southward through the Bonin Islands, the Marianas, Yap, and the Palaus in the Western Carolines to New Guinea. On many of these islands, the igneous rock of which they are composed is overlaid with limestone. Eastward of this ridge lies a series of submarine elevations which form the rest of the Carolines and the Marshalls. With the exception of the volcanic outcroppings at

Truk, Ponape, and Kusaie in the Caroline group, the islands to the east are of coral formation, mostly in the form of atolls.

The atolls are, in the main, typical coral atolls, ordinarily consisting of an oval or irregular ring of small islets surrounding a lagoon. They include the two largest atolls in the world, Kwajalein and Namonuito. Until other conclusions are drawn from the current extensive atoll research in the Pacific, it may be assumed that most of the atolls owe their existence primarily to coral growth on slowly subsiding or stationary peaks of a great submarine plateau. Those in the Western Carolines may be associated with peaks of the folds along the edge of the ancient shelf of continental Asia. Presumably the islands that preceded these atolls were eroded to shoals or sank beneath the surface, and coral growth continued close to the surface, keeping pace with the sinking; or the coral grew from submarine peaks which never were islands. Continuous change is going on, with islets of atolls being added to or divided or eliminated by regular weathering and severe storms. In 1907 an islet of Woleai Atoll in the Western Carolines was completely eliminated by a typhoon.

High islands and low islands are surrounded by coral reefs both living and dead. Living coral reefs are associations of marine animals and plants found only within shallow tropical seas where temperatures seldom fall much below 68° F. They are thus largely confined to the tropics, although extending beyond these limits where there are outflowing warm currents, as in the Atlantic around Bermuda. The most conspicuous organisms on most reefs are the stony corals, or Madreporaria, animals essentially similar to sea anemones, but with a calcareous skeleton, from the surface of which they expand, and with protective cups or calices into which they are able to withdraw. Massive, branching, foliaceous, or encrusting colonies are formed according to the species, modified sometimes by environmental conditions. These are reef-building corals, to be distinguished from related species that inhabit cold or deep seas.

The climate and weather of the islands are, in general, tropical and rainy, characterized by small seasonal changes of the various climatic factors. Both the temperature and barometric pressure are remarkably uniform throughout the year, the maximum temperature seldom rising above 90° or falling below 70°. The relative humidity varies from 85 per cent to 75 per cent. Over 100 inches of rain per year is not uncommon.

Weather conditions are subject to great local variation and to rapid change, especially on the high islands. Rainfall is heaviest in the belt between 1° 30′ and 8° 30′ north latitude, where the average annual precipitation is over 120 inches. On the high islands within this zone the precipitation is considerably greater, being augmented by orographic rain. There is considerable local irregularity in the rainfall from month to month and year to year.

Only two islands in the Trust Territory are outside the tropics, both uninhabited, and both in the Marianas. They are Maug, which is one minute north of the Tropic of Cancer, and Farallon de Pajaros, a volcanic cone a few miles north of Maug.

The wind systems of the islands are influenced by three major factors: the interplay of the trade-wind systems of the Northern and Southern Hemispheres, the equatorial low-pressure belt, and the monsoon system of the Asia-Australia area. Although local squalls and thunderstorms are frequent during the summer months, the most serious storms to which the area is subject are typhoons or tropical cyclones. These moving storms, with intense cyclonic circulation and winds of hurricane force, are particularly destructive on the low islands, where the ensuing high waves can work more harm. Typhoons develop in any month but they occur with greatest frequency between July and November. The islands in the southern and western portions of the Territory are most subject to destructive typhoons; Truk and the islands to the eastward are relatively free from these disturbances.

Two major ocean currents flow through Micronesia. The first is the Equatorial Countercurrent, south of the islands, and just above the equator, moving from west to east. Part of it veers northward in the center of Micronesia, past the Mortlocks and Truk, and turns westward past the Western Caroline atolls. The second major flow is the North Equatorial Current, which moves westward from the area of the Marshall and Gilbert Islands to meet the arm of the Countercurrent in the Western Carolines. After this union, the water approaches the Philippines, where it turns northwestward as the Japan Current.

The soils of the islands, not very complex, fall into several simple groups. First of all, they may be divided into the soils of high islands and of low islands. The former are more complex, having volcanic or coralline or mixed volcanic and coralline origin. Those of the low

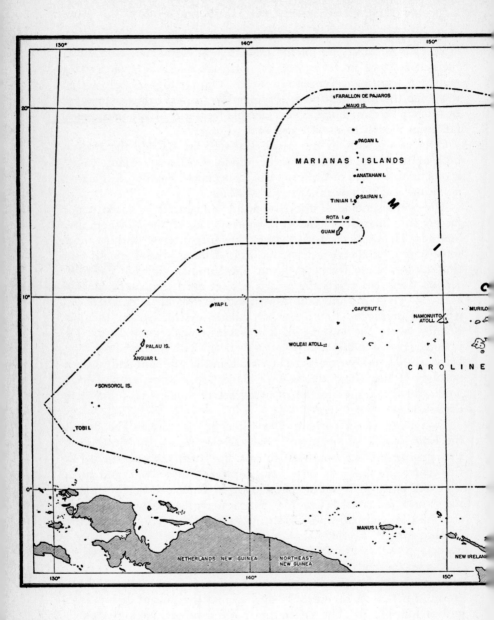

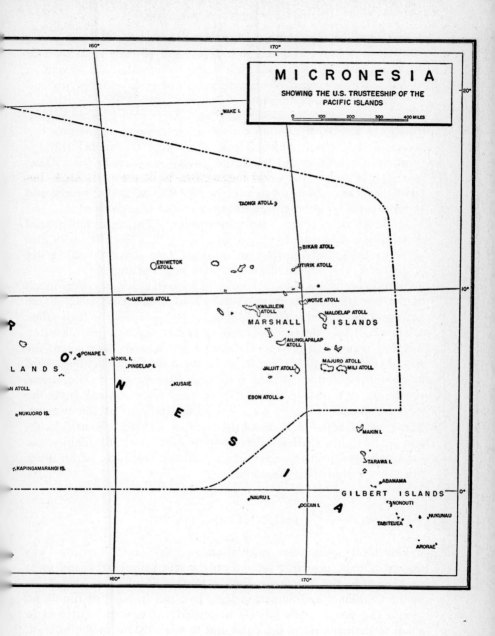

islands have an almost purely limestone derivation. On the young volcanic and young coral islands, actual soil or even sand may be extremely rare. The principal high island soils are lateritic in nature; that is, they developed by decomposition of rock under warm and humid, or tropical, conditions.

The original materials on an atoll are loose, or rarely consolidated, consisting mainly of calcium carbonate, with some magnesium carbonate and a little pumice. There is constant weathering through solution by rainwater and the flushing away of solutes by tides. However, plants and animals add humus. Sea birds are particularly important, as they add nitrogen and phosphorus; and crabs, insects, and legumes are also important, and possibly also blue-green algae.

Atoll soils do not retain moisture very well. The water table varies in salinity and is usually only slightly above sea level. It varies also with the tides, and the fresh or brackish layer above the salt water is thicker in the middle of an islet than near the shores.

Strand vegetation lines the shores of high islands and covers much of the low islands. On many raised islands, the strand zone is very narrow. This vegetation is halophytic, or characterized by high saline tolerance. It tolerates not only salt spray but brackish ground water. The first plants that get a foothold on a new low island represent the strand vegetation which persists and only rarely tends slightly toward a mesophytic forest. Where mangrove swamps occur, the strand vegetation is found on some narrow sand spits seaward from the swamps, or where the land starts to rise landward of the swamps. Mangrove swamps line much of the low shores of the volcanic islands, and are found in shallow inlets of some coral atolls. Ordinarily, the mangrove grows on mudflats, in bays and in riverbeds, or on other low areas within the tidal zone.

THE NATIVE PEOPLE

The total indigenous population of the Trust Territory was 63,992 in 1955, primarily located on the seven principal island units of Majuro in the Marshalls, Kusaie, Ponape, Truk, Yap, and Palau in the Carolines, and Saipan in the Marianas. In most of the island groups the people are relatively nongregarious, and are scattered in small settlements along the coast and to some extent in the interior.

Many of the isolated islands and atolls are inhabited by only a few dozen people and many more are entirely uninhabited. Population density is greatest on the low islands. The natives are broadly classified as Micronesians, a term which carries no implication of a homogeneous population, for regional and local groups exhibit marked variations in physical characteristics, languages, and customs. Nine major languages with multiple dialects are the more direct manifestation of distinctive ethnic entities within the Trust Territory. As is to be expected under conditions of disparate cultures separated by great expanses of water, discrete interests and feelings of exclusiveness work against efforts of the Territorial administration to encourage national or even regional unity in the political and economic fields.

Physically the average Micronesian is of medium stature—five feet four inches to five feet five inches for the males—with brown skin, straight to wavy hair, relatively little face and body hair, and rather high cheekbones. People in the western and central districts—Palau, Ponape, and Truk—tend to have slight Mongoloid characteristics. By contrast, those in the Marshalls to the east resemble somewhat their Polynesian neighbors, with longer and narrower hands and faces and narrower noses and lips. Of these various combinations, which characterize the island groups, there are many examples of intermediate mixtures.

The population is believed to be descended from canoe-voyaging immigrants who came from marginal islands in Malaysia, possibly before the Christian era. Some may have made purposeful voyages of exploration, others were probably carried eastward by westerly winds and storms, or by the Equatorial Countercurrent eastward throughout southern Micronesia.

Some maintain that man first entered Micronesia along the Equatorial Countercurrent. From New Guinea the migrants moved from Tobi to the Mortlocks, Truk, and finally westward into Yap and its neighborhood. These first arrivals were Negroids of rather short stature, with small heads and strongly curved hair. Many students of Oceanic racial history consider them fundamentally Negritoid.

The second wave of migrants were of medium stature, with long heads and faces. They may have come from northern New Guinea to the outliers in Melanesia where Polynesian is now spoken, through the Bismarcks and Solomons, and thence into Micronesia. They occupied all of Micronesia and mingled with the first wave. They resembled most closely the modern natives of Ponape, the Mortlocks, Truk, and the Western Caroline atolls.

The third wave of immigrants into Micronesia were Polynesians— tall, with large heads and faces. They may have come along the Equatorial Countercurrent, but hardly reached the Marshalls at all. Most authorities believe that at least some of the Polynesians crossed Micronesia on their way from Indonesia eastward to their present homes. Nukuoro and Greenwich (Kapingamarangi) are two Polynesian islands in the Trust Territory where the people belong to the same ethnic groups as the Samoans.

After the Polynesians came the Indonesian Mongoloids, with shorter stature and shorter heads, who not only occupied Palau, Yap, and the Marianas, but to a lesser extent followed the Equatorial countercurrent to Kusaie and the Western Marshalls. As was pointed out earlier the Chamorros of the Mariana Islands are a distinct group, with many customs derived from the Philippines. The early comers to Micronesia were skillful navigators whose voyages undoubtedly led to the spread of cultural ideas across the entire area.

The greatest disparity among the Micronesians exists in language, for although all the island languages are Malayo-Polynesian, nine individual types are spoken within the Territory, subdivided into distinctive local dialects. At present Japanese is the nearest approach to a lingua franca, but in the areas immediately adjacent to civil administration units English is now an accepted medium. English, introduced and used widely in the Marshalls and Carolines in the nineteenth century, came from two sources: traders' and whalers' lingo—mostly pidgin—and the teaching of missionaries.

HISTORY

Islands in the group now known as the Marshalls were discovered by the Spanish in 1529, and by subsequent Spanish explorations during the century. No serious efforts were put forth in these early times by Spain or other European powers to assume effective control of Pacific Islands. Spain, however, in 1565 made the port of Agana on Guam a regular food-and-water stop for vessels plying between Mexico and the Philippines, and she continued to claim sovereignty over the Marianas, the Carolines, and the Marshalls.

By the middle of the nineteenth century the islands had become involved in European colonial rivalries. German traders especially were active, and when Spain attempted to control their trade the Germans moved toward seizure of political control. In the Marshalls, where the Spanish claim of sovereignty was least substantial, the Germans assumed a protectorate in 1885. This action precipitated disputes both with Spain and with Great Britain, but by 1886 both nations had formally conceded the Marshalls to Germany.

Spain, however, was able to keep control of the Carolines. In 1885, the same year in which she seized the Marshalls, Germany had sent a gunboat to various spots in the Carolines and had claimed formal possession of these islands as well. But Spanish reaction was violent, and serious international complications were avoided only when the issue was referred to Pope Leo XIII for adjudication. The Pope confirmed the claim of Spain to sovereignty over the Carolines on condition that she maintain an orderly government there, although he awarded Germany the right to trade, to fish, and to establish settlements and coaling stations.

No further change in the political administration of Micronesia occurred until 1898, when the United States, during the course of its war with Spain, seized Guam. The next year Spain decided to withdraw from the Pacific and sold the Marianas, except Guam, and the Carolines to Germany for 25,000,000 pesetas.

The Germans took considerable interest in Micronesia, sending missionaries and doing a little colonization and exploitation, the principal form of which consisted of using native labor and enforced quotas to plant large numbers of coconut palms. The German administration operated from New Guinea, with local administrative centers in Ponape, Yap, Saipan, and the Marshalls. German trade was principally between Samoa and Saipan and between New Guinea and Ponape and Yap. More economic development was accomplished by the Germans in the areas under their control during the fifteen years of their possession than by the Spanish during more than three centuries.

Spanish colonial policy in the Pacific was autocratic and restricted to the pacification and Christianization of the Marianas and maintenance of control over them. At no time did the Spanish make more than halfhearted attempts to exploit the islands in an economic sense. German administration, although autocratic, was moderate and efficient, every encouragement being given to the development of trade and the expansion of production. Emphasis was placed on economic exploitation for the benefit of Germany, but it was tempered by a policy of enlightened self-interest, as far as treatment of the natives was concerned.

German control of Micronesia was abruptly terminated by the outbreak of World War I. In October, 1914, Japanese naval squadrons took military possession of the undefended Marshalls, Carolines, and Northern Marianas. At the conclusion of the war, Japan became the mandatory power for these islands under the mandates system of the League of Nations. The mandate was confirmed by the Council of the League of Nations on December 17, 1920. The United States gave its consent to this arrangement in a treaty with Japan signed on February 11, 1922.

In 1922 Japan substituted civil rule by the South Seas Government (*Nanyo-Cho*) for the previous military rule of the area, and began at once to develop the islands economically, to prepare them for Japanese emigration, and to indoctrinate the indigenous inhabitants through education, propaganda, and cultural changes.

Japanese rule of the Pacific Islands was complete and direct, and permitted little use of the inhabitants in government. The basic laws of Japan were extended to the mandate, and only the necessary modifications were made to meet local conditions. Formal educational facilities for the indigenes were restricted, emphasis being placed upon the teaching of the Japanese language, but considerable attention was paid to the health of the people. Although German exploitation had reduced the islands so far below a subsistence level that, when the war began, many of the inhabitants were dependent upon imported consumer goods, Japan took over practically all aspects of the economic life and in an unprecedented fashion made the area more productive than is possible in a free government.

When Japan became a belligerent in World War II, the Japanese used the Pacific Islands, which by then were fortified, as bases for Japanese aggression to the south and the east. In turn they served as a great barrier to the liberation of the Philippines and Wake and Guam. Not until November, 1943, when the Gilberts were invaded, did United States forces begin to break through the barrier. In January and February of 1944 the Marshalls were seized; in June and July the Marianas were invaded; by August the Eastern and Central Carolines were neutralized; in September Angaur and Peleliu in the

Western Carolines were captured. Many of the individual islands were bypassed, and with most of these communication was not established until the war was over.

Except on the question of sovereignty, the Japanese colonial policy was officially identical with that of the League of Nations. Actually, however, it was very different. The colonial policy of the Japanese Government with respect to her mandated islands can be summarized under four headings: (1) to develop the islands in an economic sense; (2) to prepare them as a place to which Japanese nationals could migrate as colonists, thus relieving population pressure in Japan itself; (3) to Japanize the natives as rapidly as possible through education and propaganda, through interracial marriages and by promoting cultural change; and (4) to establish offensive and defensive military, naval, and air bases in the islands in preparation for a war of aggrandizement in the Pacific.

Japan developed the islands much more than did the Germans, colonizing them extensively. More diversification in agriculture was achieved, and sugar cane, in particular, was extensively planted in the Marianas. The islands thus supplied to Japan large quantities of sugar and copra, in addition to phosphate, bauxite, dried bonito, and alcohol. Extensive trade was carried on between Japan and Micronesia, especially through Saipan and Palau. There was also trade directly with Okinawa and the Bonin Islands, primarily to Saipan. The Japanese administrative center was at Koror in Palau, with branch stations at Saipan, Yap, Truk, Ponape, and Jaluit.

THE UNITED STATES TAKES OVER

At the end of the war, having driven the Japanese out of the Pacific Islands at a fearful cost, Americans found themselves in military occupation of the Marshalls, the Carolines, and the Marianas. We could not repeat the inexplicable blunder of 1898, when we took Guam and the Philippines and left for sale on the open market these strategic islands lying directly athwart our lines of communication to the Philippines. For this blunder we had paid dearly in blood. Never again could we afford to permit these Pacific bastions to be held or fortified by any militaristic state.

After the war, which caused widespread destruction, the seventy thousand Japanese who had managed and administered the government, and had operated farms and many other businesses and the educational programs of the islands, were repatriated, leaving the entire territory without a vestige of the former administrative organization.

Catapulted into this archipelago of problems came American naval officials to fill the vacuum and take up the administrative tasks left by the Japanese who had been killed or who were sent home. Military government policies and activities were based on the assumption that the indigenous inhabitants should be treated as liberated people, the immediate problem being to furnish them with food, water, clothing, shelter, and medical attention.

The Commander in Chief of the Pacific and the United States Pacific Fleet continued to hold the office of High Commissioner of the Trust Territory until January 8, 1951, when he was succeeded in that office by the first civilian high commissioner. The latter's appointment by the President was an initial step in the transfer of the administration of the Trust Territory to a civilian agency of the Government.

The executive authority of the Government of the Trust Territory and the primary responsibility for conducting it now rest with the High Commissioner of the Trust Territory, an officer of the Department of the Interior whose headquarters are in Guam. Earlier, because rapid demobilization of the Armed Forces had reduced the number of available military government officers, the United States Navy had arranged with Stanford University to establish a school for the training of naval officers for the tasks of administration. The first class was graduated on August 28, 1946, and these officers and those of following classes took posts in the islands. When a civil government succeeded the naval that school, unfortunately, was discontinued.

The Trust Territory, the tenth largest Trusteeship in population and land area, is the only strategic Trusteeship in the United Nations' Trusteeship system. This means that the United States may seal off certain areas for security reasons, as was done at Bikini and Eniwetok in the Marshalls for the atomic bomb tests there.

On January 1, 1953, the President, for special security purposes, by Executive order transferred administrative responsibility for Saipan and Tinian islands in the Marianas to the Navy Department. Subsequently, the President, by later Executive order, included in the transfer to naval jurisdiction those outlying islands of the Northern Marianas that are linked directly to the economy and social institutions of Saipan by traditional bonds. Reasons of efficiency lead to maintaining this natural unit under the care of a single administrative agency. The island of Rota, not far north of Guam, is in a more isolated position, geographically and economically, and therefore responsibility for its administration continues to rest with the Department of the Interior.

The Trust Territory is divided into five administrative districts: Saipan in the Northern Marianas, the Marshall Islands, Ponape and Truk in the Eastern Carolines, Palau in the Western Carolines. Yap is a subdivision of Palau. Each district except Saipan is headed by a civil administrator appointed by the high commissioner and responsible to him for the administration of the district. District headquarters are located at Majuro, Ponape, Truk, Koror, and Saipan. The problems involved in administering the Trust Territory are not easily solved, for the islands are hundreds of miles apart in dangerous coral seas; few have good harbors suitable for large vessels, and many can be reached only in small boats manned by natives who can negotiate the often treacherous surf. The elementary business of transportation, therefore, becomes a paramount and costly problem. The Japanese solved it only through heavy government subsidies, and it was among the more serious problems of the United States Navy in the postwar period when crews were vanishing through demobilization.

In brief, it may be said that the big problem of agriculture is to develop a better subsistence economy. Agriculture in these tropical islands differs greatly from that in temperate climates. The number of crops cultivated is small, and domestic animals are few. The most important and most widespread crop is the coconut palm. Coconut groves fringe the high islands and cover large areas of most of the low islands.

The fullest possible development of land resources in the Trust Territory is dependent upon the settlement of landownership problems. These problems, which existed in the days before World War II as a result of the impact of alien contacts upon the aboriginal landownership system, have been further complicated by the destruction of land records and survey markers during the war years. In general, the policy is to permit the Micronesians to assert their own wishes concerning their land, and, insofar as is consonant with group welfare, to attempt to implement these wishes. The traditional types of land-tenure and inheritance laws do not appreciably impede the development of improved methods of agriculture for subsistence farming. Very few areas are suitable for large-scale farming methods.

Indigenous inhabitants hold about 250 square miles of the Trust Territory land, nearly all of which is held under the collective system of clan or lineage ownership, in which individuals have certain rights of possession and use. The system varies in detail in different parts of the Territory. In turn, these rights are subject to other successive underlying rights vested in the head of the family lineage or clan or, in some instances, in a high chief. Ownership of trees and buildings is often separate from that of the land. Individual private ownership in fee simple exists only in a few small localities.

The goal of the administering authority to create a self-sustaining economy is far from fulfillment. Economic betterment has been due mainly to the increased production of copra, the main export of the Territory, and the high prices which this commodity has brought in the world market. However, under the most favorable circumstances the islands can never be rich because the meagerness of their natural resources precludes any economy higher than a subsistence level. The total cost to the United States of administering the Territory for the fiscal year ending June 30, 1955, was $6,180,534.

The people themselves lack the initiative, training, and capital necessary to develop additional sources of revenue and methods of diversifying their economy. The outstanding problem in the economic field has been the difficult and delicate one of developing a sense of individual initiative and responsibility within a framework of established customs and traditions which, except in the Saipan administrative district, tend toward a basically communal society.

On the other hand, there is sound basis for the concern expressed in the Security Council of the United Nations regarding the risk involved in setting up a more expensive economic structure than the people of the Territory themselves can support.

Public health has received major attention from the administration. One of the more important achievements in that field has been the control of yaws, which now, except in a few communities, is no longer a major problem. A remaining social problem—a subject of great emphasis in the educational program—is the control and treatment of tuberculosis, to which the natives are very susceptible. Sanitation is still a challenging issue in spite of appreciable improvement. Scientific data have been collected on local culture, traditions, and food, in order to guide a policy and procedure in keeping with the lack of native capacity for understanding the ideas and accomplishments of Western civilizations.

Language barriers in the islands continue to be a major social problem, but progress is being made through the teaching of English at all civil administration centers and through study of local languages by a few administration personnel. Unfortunately, there is no incentive to study languages because of the short length of time Government officials stay in the Territory.

Despite a density of population on some of the low islands, population at present creates few critical economic problems. As population growth causes economic stress in the future, especially in places like Pingelap where continuing subdivision of family land results in too small individual plots, the problem will have to be met by resettlement on Government lands. However, the long-range plan of the administration to accommodate population growth is the expansion of local production rather than compulsory relocation of the inhabitants.

The attitude of the native people themselves is a serious barrier to their improvement. Through decades of subjugation to their own rulers and to supervisors placed over them by four successive foreign governments, the islanders have become most reluctant to express any views other than those which they feel the persons talking with them wish to hear.

At the end of a decade of American administration, it has become very apparent that time alone will be the vital agent in the process of a very slow evolutionary change in the indigenous population both socially and in the domain of government and economics.

REFERENCES

Burrows, E. G., and M. E. Spiro, *An Atoll Culture: Ethnography of Ifaluk in the Central Carolines* (New Haven: Human Relations Area Files, 1953).

Coulter, J. W., "Impact of the War on South Sea Islands," *Geog. Rev.*, Vol. 36, No. 3, July, 1946, pp. 409-419.

———, "Environment, Race and Government in South Sea Islands," *Scott. Geog. Mag.*, Vol. 63, No. 2, 1947, pp. 49-56.

———, "The United States Trust Territory of the Pacific Islands," *Jour. Geog.*, Vol. 47, No. 7, Oct., 1948, pp. 253-267.

Freeman, O. W. (Edit.), *Geography of the Pacific* (New York: Wiley, 1951), Chaps. IX and X.

Goodenough, W. H., "Native Astronomy in Micronesia: A Rudimentary Science," *Scientific Monthly*, 73 (2): 105-110, map, figs., August, 1951.

Gressitt, J. L., *Insects of Micronesia*, Vol. 1, "Introduction" (Honolulu: Bernice P. Bishop Museum, 1954).

Hunt, E. E., Jr., "A View of Somatology and Serology in Micronesia," *Amer. Jour. Phys. Anthropology*, New Ser. 8 (1950), pp. 157-184.

Keesing, F. M., "Administration in Pacific Islands," *Far Eastern Survey*, 17 (9): 105-108 (1948).

Murphy, R. E., " 'High' and 'Low' Islands in the Eastern Carolines," *Geog. Rev.*, Vol. 39, No. 3 (1949), pp. 425-439.

United Nations, "Trusteeship Council Session: Report on Pacific Islands Trust Territory," *UN Bull.*, Vol. 7, No. 3, Aug. 1, 1949, pp. 108-110.

United States Board on Geographic Names, *Decisions on Names in the Trust Territory of the Pacific Islands and Guam*, Part I, "Caroline Islands," Cumulative Decision List No. 5501; Part II, "Marshall Islands," Cumulative Decision List No. 5502; Part III, "Mariana Islands and Guam," Cumulative Decision List No. 5503 (Washington, D.C., 1955).

United States Civil Affairs Guide, "Agriculture in the Japanese Mandated Islands," OPNAV 13-17.

United States Navy Civil Affairs Handbook, Studies 2, "The Languages of the Japanese Mandated Islands," OPNAV 50E-15, 47 pp., June 20, 1944.

United States Report on Trust Territory, Dept. State Bull., Aug. 1, 1949, Vol. 21, No. 526.

United States Trust Territory of the Pacific Islands, U.S. Navy Report, July, 1950–June, 1951.

Yonge, C. M., "The Form of Coral Reefs," *Endeavour* (London), 10 (39): 136-144, 14 figs., July, 1951.

VIII

The Mariana Islands

THE Trusteeship Mariana Islands, north of Guam, were colonized by thousands of Japanese, mostly Okinawans, before the outbreak of World War II. Agriculture was dominated by the production of sugar cane, and a high prewar standard of living among the Chamorros there was the indirect result of Japanese industry. Because all of the Orientals have been removed, the native population cannot develop the area to the extent necessary to attain their former level.

All the Mariana Islands are the peaks of a submarine mountain chain strung out at intervals from Guam north for approximately five hundred miles. There are fifteen islands altogether, the northern-most of which, although small, include several of the higher summits in Micronesia. These northern islands are entirely volcanic, and some of them constitute the only active volcanoes in that part of the Pacific. The southern group, comprising Farallon de Medinilla, Saipan, Tinian, Aguijan, and, as was already discussed, Guam, are large, and in part raised coral limestone. With Guam, they have a tropical marine climate, tempered by the trade winds. Typhoons occur at all seasons of the year, but especially in the fall.

The Chamorros of the Trusteeship Marianas are ethnically similar to those of Guam, with the exception that in the decades preceding the end of World War II they added an intermixture of Japanese blood to all the other strains. Their language, the same as that of the Guamanians, has also persisted, and is the lingua franca of the islands today. Indeed, in most ways they are like their relatives on the big island at the south, now a Territory of the United States. The main difference between these islands and Guam is that, with the exception of Rota, they are of such strategic value that they must be governed by the United States Navy. Rota is administered from the Headquarters of the Trusteeship Territory in Guam.

Guam was the focus of the Spanish colonization of the Marianas. After the northern islands had been conquered by the Spaniards, their populations were removed to Guam, except a few persons who escaped to remain on Rota. In the latter part of the nineteenth century, a colony of natives of the Caroline Islands settled on Tinian, but some years later they moved to Saipan. Chamorros came back to the latter island at the end of the nineteenth century. At various times since then some have settled on other islands.

The Marianas north of Guam were neglected by the Spanish after the removal of their populations, though hunters used to go there occasionally. The Germans, interested mainly in copra, were represented by only a few of their nationals who maintained the law and order necessary for best exploitation and who also bettered public health. The Japanese realized that various aspects of commercial agriculture could be developed, especially sugar cane on Saipan.

The invasion of the islands by American forces in the summer of 1944 left devastation in its wake and caused havoc on Saipan, in the battle for which the American casualties were high and those of the Japanese tremendous. Civilian loss of life among the Orientals and natives was also high.

The rehabilitation of agriculture was made very difficult not only because of the destruction in the islands but for other reasons as well. Large areas of arable land have had to be taken for military purposes. Since landownership records were destroyed in the war, revocable permits were issued to the natives, not guaranteeing them, therefore, permanent possession; this has not been an encouragement to the best use of the land.

The Chamorros of the Trusteeship Marianas who are now carrying on agriculture like that of the Guamanians are not as competent farmers as those on the big island. The majority of the Tinian Chamorros were moved there by the American administration from the island of Yap in the Western Carolines: some of the Chamorros from Yap went to Saipan. During the Japanese régime the natives of the Marianas rented their lands to the Okinawans and lived on an easy income from that or from wage labor. The Chamorros transferred from Yap by the American administration had lost some of their ability to farm, for they had been middlemen between the Yapese and the Orientals on that island, collecting copra, keeping small stores, supervising labor, and performing other tasks. The Carolinians on Saipan lost some of their original skill also because of the opportunities afforded them by colonizers who rented part of their lands. Both groups on Saipan developed a deprecatory attitude toward farming as an occupation, for, having lived among a great foreign population, they considered other ways of earning a living easier.

The older Chamorros and Carolinians do remember the techniques of their former agriculture and they and younger men are trying to make out as best they can. Their cultivated tracts are irregular plots with adjoining fallow land. Corn, the staple, is planted at the same seasons as on Guam and harvested by similar methods. The other Guamanian crops are represented, and manioc (tapioca) also.

Social activities and institutions among all the Chamorros are similar to those described for Guam. Catholicism is the mainstay of native village life, with its fiestas, fandangos, and Church holidays. The Church is an important factor in law and order, especially since there are many fewer temptations to deviate from the strait and narrow way in those small, still isolated islands than there are in the American Territory.

Medical care and public health, important responsibilities of the administration, are looked after with the high degree of efficiency characteristic of naval government. The district hospital, serving all the Marianas north of Guam, is on Saipan, where there is a medical staff of naval officers and enlisted men; nurses and technicians are Chamorros and Carolinians. A leprosarium for the Trust Territory is on Tinian island.*

ROTA

Each of the larger islands north of Guam has environmental characteristics and an economic development which differentiate it from the others. More of the Chamorro racial and cultural heritage

* Construction of a hospital on Rota was begun in 1955, since this was written, and new leprosarium wards and mental wards were completed in Truk, Yap, and Ponape to accommodate leper and mental cases which are no longer taken care of by the Navy on Saipan and Tinian.

survived on Rota than in any other part of the Marianas. During the few years before the war, however, the raising of sugar cane and other products was promoted commercially by the Japanese, whose associations with the Rotans changed the latter to some extent.

The island, about eleven miles long, northeast to southwest, and some four miles wide, comprises an area of about 48 square miles. It has a volcanic nucleus, covered in part with limestone. A peak in the southwest portion, with an elevation of 1,168 feet, just northeast of Rota village, is a long-extinct volcano; another peak in the northwest is 1,612 feet high. Near the latter there is a rapid drop to a plateau 350 feet in elevation which extends to the northeast end of the island. The interior of Rota includes terraces whose level surfaces are covered with reddish clay scattered with loose rock. The usual Chamorro crops are raised, and in the same way as on Guam. During the author's visit the most conspicuous features of the island were the great extent of volunteer growth of sugar cane and the wreckage of a bombed sugar mill and plantation machinery.

TINIAN

Tinian offers an opportunity for considerable agricultural development on land not required for airplane fields. The Chamorros there try to provide for most of their own requirements by subsistence agriculture and fishing, and in addition to raise something extra to ship to Guam. The island, about ten miles long north to south and four and a half miles wide, has an area of about thirty-nine square miles. One hundred miles north of Guam, it is separated from Saipan only by a narrow channel. Its small land mass consists of a series of raised limestone terraces on a volcanic base.

During the Japanese régime the island was also used intensively by the Japanese and Okinawan population for growing and processing sugar cane. The Spanish, however, used Tinian for grazing wild cattle which were hunted for meat. The naval base there now operates a cattle ranch where under the administration of the United States an attempt is being made to develop a strain suitable to the islands of Micronesia.

SAIPAN

Saipan, the largest and most important of the Marianas in the Trust Territory, about 13 miles long by 5½ miles wide, has an area of 71 square miles. Topographically, it is more diverse than the other Mariana Islands, and its geology is more complex. The outline of the island is irregular, with bays on both sides. There is an extensive coral reef on the west side but very little on the east. A chain of mountains traverses the middle in a north-south direction. The east side of the range is steep and rocky; the west and south sides slope gradually to level, cultivated land. The highest peak is Mount Tapotchau, 1,554 feet, just south of the center; the lesser peaks— Mount Atchugau, and others—are in the northern third. Much of the higher land consists of irregularly raised coral limestone pushed up by volcanic action, but there is also a considerable area of volcanic land distributed irregularly. Coconut trees, once plentiful on this island, have almost disappeared. An infestation of coconut beetles during the period of the Japanese occupation destroyed all but a few isolated groves, much to the detriment of Saipan's appearance as well as her resources.

The tremendous increase in population on Saipan by Japanese colonization was accompanied by a complete change in the island economy. The Japanese early instituted the production of sugar on a large scale. The island was transformed into a vast sugar-cane plantation, and large sugar refineries and factories for by-products were constructed. The natives, considered unsuitable for factory work and inefficient as farmers, were seldom employed, and Japanese laborers were imported.

The natives, however, remained essentially a farming people, while modern Japanese towns with shops, movies, theatres, restaurants, and geisha houses grew up around them. Automobiles and bicycles filled the streets, and railroads traversed the island. In spite of the fact that most of them were concentrated in their own quarter of the former village of Garapan and were excluded from much of the Japanese life, the islanders were inevitably influenced by these changes, and experienced consequent alterations in their outlook and standard of living.

The Chamorros of Saipan, as elsewhere in the Marianas, preserve the custom, developed under Spanish rule, of living in villages and going out daily to their fields. Some of them practice skills in carpentry, mechanics, and other vocations acquired under the Japanese; others are small storekeepers selling a variety of goods.

The Carolinians on Saipan maintain their identity apart from the Chamorros, preserving their own language and customs, for they are conscious of a different ethnic origin. Their forebears migrated to the island from atolls to the west and north of Truk. They preserve kinship ties similar to those at present in the islands from which their ancestors came. Their houses, much like Chamorro dwellings, generally have Western furniture, for their long association with the civilization of the natives of the Marianas has influenced them. They subsist by working their small farms; during the Japanese occupation they sometimes earned wages from the Japanese or leased to them their holdings of land.

The Saipan Chamorros, like the Guamanians, are neither sailors nor fishermen except along the shore and on the reefs. They rely for fish on the Carolinians, with whom fishing is routine, and who fish with nets, spears, weirs, traps, and from boats. However, there is no commercial fishing on Saipan for an export market like that developed by the Japanese. The Carolinians lack both the proficiency necessary to maintain the equipment essential for deep-sea fishing and the managerial ability to organize the export of fish. One attempt of this kind since the war ended in failure.

The people of the inhabited islands north of Saipan—Alamagan, Pagan, and Agrihan—make their living by subsistence farming, and by selling copra through the naval government.

THE FUTURE

The economy of the Trusteeship Marianas, unstable for several years after the war, is not yet a going concern. It is still in the aftermath of the devastation caused by the conflict. In view of the fact that a satisfactory settlement of land titles and questions of ownership will necessarily precede stability, natives must be guaranteed permanent titles to the lands they farm. The solution of all problems associated with resettlement should be pushed as rapidly as possible. As in the case of Micronesia in general, the maintenance of acceptable standards of living and public welfare must be considered in terms of the strategic value of these islands to the United States.

The great market on Guam for fresh vegetables will further stimulate their production in the islands north of it. The demand for fish in that Territory has already been mentioned. As for Tinian, its economy may be assisted through the further development of cattle raising for export to other islands in the Trust Territory.

The future of the Trusteeship Marianas depends, in part, on the character of the relationship between administration and community. There were cordial relationships between the Samoans in general and the naval administration of those islands when the author visited them before World War II. At that time the Samoans felt that the Navy was giving them the thing they needed most, namely, a régime of improved health and sanitation. The physical proximity of the administration to the people of the Marianas warrants an acquaintance with any special problems and difficulties which confront the natives there. The effective communication within the administrative area—a close, informal relationship—will go far to solving difficulties as they arise.

REFERENCES

Bowers, N. M., "Problems of Resettlement on Saipan, Tinian and Rota, Mariana Islands," *Microfilm Abstracts*, Vol. 11, No. 1 (Ann Arbor, 1951), pp. 314-315.

Embree, J. F., "Military Government in Saipan and Tinian," *Applied Anthropology*, 5 (1): 1–39, Winter, 1946.

Joseph, Alice and V. F. Murray, *Chamorros and Carolinians of Saipan: Personality Studies* (Cambridge: Harvard University Press, 1951), 381 pp.

Spoehr, Alexander, "The Tinian Chamorros," *Human Organization*, 10 (4): 16–20 (1951).

———, *Saipan: The Ethnology of a War-Devastated Island* (Chicago Natural History Museum, Fieldiana, Anthropology Series, Vol. 41, 1954), 383 pp.

Thompson, Laura, *The Native Culture of the Marianas Islands*, Bernice P. Bishop Museum Bull. 185 (1945).

United States Navy, "Military Government on Saipan: A Photographic Record, June, 1944, to Dec., 1945," compiled by Military Government Section, Navy, No. 3245, FPO San Francisco.

———, "A Climatic Summary of the Marianas Islands," NAVAER 50-IT-11 (1944).

Williams, J. Z., "Administration of the Natives of Saipan," *Amer. For. Service Jour.*, 23 (4), April, 1946.

Worden, W. L., "Notes on a Saipan Farm," *Harper's Magazine*, Dec., 1944.

IX

Palau

THE Carolines, stretching over a great expanse of ocean east and west from Palau about five hundred miles from the Philippines all the way to the Marshalls, extend in a broad belt from 131° east longitude to 163°, and between the first and tenth degrees north latitude. They were named in 1686 after King Charles II of Spain. Most of the inhabited islands each support only a few hundred people.

The archipelago includes three assemblages of high islands, Palau, Yap, and Truk; two single high islands, Ponape and Kusaie; thirty-one atolls; and eleven isolated low islands. In addition, there are coral islands associated with the high islands, for example, the islands of raised coral rock in Palau; low islands of the Palau and Truk barrier reefs, and of fringing reefs on Ponape and Kusaie. The mountains of Truk and Ponape break the monotony of a great open ocean and occasional coral islets, the latter so low that they are invisible from more than a few miles away. Because of their meager resources, inhabitants of the low islands have always been forced to go to the few larger, higher ones to trade. For several centuries Carolinians from the western islands sailed annually to Guam in thirty-foot outrigger canoes to purchase iron tools and tobacco from the Spaniards, their voyages covering four hundred miles of open sea. Some of their native navigators went as far away as the Marshall Islands, New Guinea, and the Philippines.

PALAU

"This civilization that Westerners brought did not do anything for us women." The speaker, using excellent English, was Princess

187

Emaimelai, daughter of Aibedul, the highest chief in the Palau Islands. She went on to say, "In pre-civilization times when the women wore only grass skirts, the men loincloths and the children nothing, there was no washing nor sewing for the women to do. But now with all the clothes in a family, we have to spend a great deal of time at laundry work." Another thing Emaimelai complained of

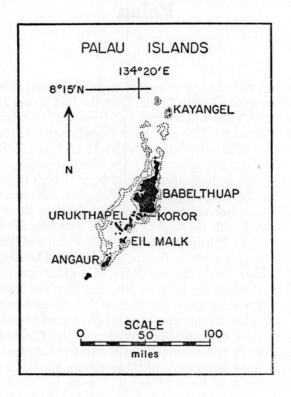

was the great variety of pots and pans and cups and saucers which civilization had brought, and which caused women much more work to keep clean. Formerly the people ate with their fingers out of a common bowl. Now Emaimelai has to dust tables and even make a bed, appurtenances to a home never dreamed of in the old days. She stated that it was traditionally part of women's work to keep taro lands and small gardens cleanly weeded, and that to maintain a good social status women vied with each other to have the neatest looking garden. She said, "We still carry on this custom as much as we can between washings."

Other women also complained that they have to do all the cooking, weeding about their houses, and clearing trails while men merely dig a little, build houses, and—if they are not too tired—go fishing. While women may exaggerate the tasks which fall to their lot, the traditional division of labor between the sexes on Palau is much the same as in the rest of the Caroline Islands.

The Palauans, the most sophisticated people of the Trust Territory, owe this sophistication in large part to years of close contact with thousands of Japanese. On Koror, the most densely populated island of the archipelago, the skeleton remains of the headquarters of the Japanese South Seas Bureau, *Nanyo-Cho*. It was the most impressive building on that island, and parts of its tiled floors which withstood the bombing are still intact. There the Japanese governor had his secretariat and five sections or departments.

Palauans wear Western clothes, and many of their houses are much like those in villages in the United States. Ngiwal village on Babelthuap island is representative. It has a dock, surrounded by carefully built walls of coral boulders. The houses, larger than those found in general in the Trust Territory, have running water piped from the hills at the back; many of them are constructed of galvanized iron except for a hardwood or a bamboo floor. A few have tables and chairs, and the author noted that at least one had an iron cot on which a small baby was sprawling. When the author visited the village, the natives were filling in areas bordering the ocean with clay and boulders dug from the slope at the backs of the houses. Withered and scrawny fronds of the coconut trees in the village and vicinity showed the ravages of the rhinoceros beetle, introduced from Asia.

NATURAL ENVIRONMENT AND POPULATION

Palau, the largest group of islands in the Carolines, consists of a chain of coral atolls and volcanic islands stretching about a hundred statute miles from north to south; the 180 square miles of land are concentrated primarily in one large island, Babelthuap, which is about

150 square miles of rolling volcanic hills whose highest elevation does not exceed 700 feet. All of the islands are narrow, the widest one at its maximum only eighteen statute miles across. In addition to Babelthuap, there are eight other sizable islands, a dozen smaller ones, and numerous tiny islets. The main inhabited islands are five: Kayangel, an atoll at the northern end of the group; Babelthuap and Koror in the central sector; and, at the southern end, Peleliu and Angaur.

The location of the islands in the far west of Micronesia lends itself to introductions from the Orient. The archipelago, about 500 miles east of the largest island in the Philippines, is approximately the same distance north of Berau Peninsula in New Guinea; the islands are about 800 miles southwest of Guam, and nearly 6,000 miles west of the United States. The larger and more important lie between 7° and 8° north latitude and 134° and 135° east longitude.

The rocks generally found in the archipelago are of volcanic and coral origin. Volcanic areas include almost all of Babelthuap, the western half of Koror, and most of Arakabesan and Malakal. Angaur, the southernmost island, is a raised atoll with extensive phosphate deposits.

The Palau group, both coral atolls and volcanic islands, share the natural attributes of the other sections of Micronesia. Their tropical marine climate with heavy rainfall encourages a dense vegetation. The volcanic islands, hilly and heavily wooded, are, like the atolls, surrounded by coral reefs.

The Palauans are ethnically related to the people in the islands all about them, sharing certain physical traits with Indonesia and Melanesia. The origin of the indigenous people is not fully known; they seem to derive not only from Malaya but in part from waves of successive migrations from islands east of them. Since there is an admixture of Japanese blood and probably of Filipino also, there is a wide range of features and other physical characteristics. They are of medium stature, and usually have medium-brown skin and black hair.

The language of Palau, like the population, has also evolved, and is a mixture of irregular forms related to the languages of their neighbors, but not readily understood by them. The dialect of the north is easily distinguished by Palauans from the slow speech of the south.

The total population of the archipelago amounted to 7,726 in 1954, of which half lived on Babelthuap in villages scattered along the western coast. Koror, next in importance in point of population, had 2,230. Because of its location between Babelthuap in the north and the important island of Angaur to the south, Koror, the base for trade and government by foreigners and for the development of all the islands, is now the pivotal island in Palau.

The Palauans like to cultivate associations with foreigners for what they can learn from them. People in general do not hark back to the old days in spite of the alleged grievances of the women. Incidentally, these are frequently the women who don the best clothes and jewelry they or their husbands can afford. Differences of opinion exist as to what old customs should be changed or abandoned and how far reforms should be pushed, but there is unanimity of opinion that the way foreigners live is good for them. However, like many natives of the Trust Territory, they do not realize that raising their standard of living will depend on their own efforts.

CHANGES BY THE JAPANESE

Like most people of the Pacific Islands, the Palauans traditionally had a subsistence-handicraft type of economy. A livelihood was easily extracted from the abundant local supply of coconuts, taro, and fish. Every clan had its artisans who were experts in weaving, thatching, and wood carving. Specialists in native crafts erected the long, palm-thatched huts each occupied by a family, built canoes, and designed the utensils required by everyone. The greatest creative efforts were concentrated on elaborate interior decorations of the *abai*, or community house—inlaid carvings portraying the community's pornographic stories, moral lessons, sagas, and folk tales.

Spanish administration was almost entirely in the hands of the Capuchin order of monks, whose efforts were directed to converting the natives and preserving order. Although the first missionaries, in 1886, were received with indifference, continuous efforts eventually resulted in the conversion of most of the people to Catholicism.

The Germans, with characteristic thoroughness, set about exploiting the copra industry of the islands. They forced the Palauans to plant large groves of coconuts, establishing an industry which was the mainstay of native economy for many years. They took an interest in the economic and social welfare of the people, trying to inculcate a measure of initiative and responsibility.

The short period of Spanish and German influence, with Spanish officials absent and with only a small number of Germans in residence, resulted in little permanent change in the native way of living. The face of the islands, however, was completely changed by Japanese colonists to fit a new industrial and commercial economy. Japanese administration passed through four phases: the Navy period of control, 1914–1918; a mixed Navy and civil-service organization, 1918–1922; the South Seas Bureau, 1922-1940; and in the end a mixed Army-Navy rule, 1940–1945.

The Japanese interfered directly in the internal affairs of native society and government, stripping chiefs and their councils of much of their authority. They brought carpenters to the islands to build houses and to train natives, who began to build similar structures for themselves. Japanese colonists raised pineapples on a large scale to sell for canning. Cassava (tapioca) became an important commercial crop, used as a staple in the diet of natives and Japanese alike. Considerable research was done on cassava, and commercial factories for production of cassava flour were established in Palau and also on Saipan and Ponape. Cassava was the raw material for a successful distilling industry. The emphasis which the Japanese put on raising that plant accounts in large part for its present popularity in the islands. Easily cultivated, not requiring great care, it produces more food by weight per unit of area than any of the other food crops of the Palauans. Its greatest use is as a coarse meal or flour ("farine" or "farinha") for bread or cakes. They eat it prepared in different ways: boiled, baked, boiled and fried in coconut oil, boiled and pounded and then baked in flat cakes coated with sugar.

The Japanese developed the Palau archipelago, as they did other islands, entirely for themselves, bringing in capital and cheap Okinawan labor. The laborers raised radishes, cabbage, eggplant, and other vegetables, but imported rice, for there is little flat land in the island suitable for its production. On the other hand, the natives benefited economically from the foreign occupation and acquired a taste for Japanese foods and ways of doing things.

The established Christian churches in the archipelago were tolerated temporarily by the Japanese until the time when they thought the natives would become reconciled to the new order. They made attempts to convince the islanders that Christ was the God of Europe and America and Buddha the god of the Far East. At the start of World War II Christian services were outlawed. On Shinto holidays the people were required to pay homage at the shrines. The Palauans, however, have remained loyal to the Christian faith, but many of the economic and social effects of the Japanese régime are carried over into the islands of today.

NATIVE ECONOMY

Palauans produce the crops necessary for their food: taro, breadfruit, cassava, coconuts, yams and sweet potatoes. Bananas, papayas, and several others are of less importance; only a few pineapples are grown now. Attempts to introduce beans, carrots, tomatoes, and corn have met with little success, for it takes a long time to establish new tastes in food among any people unless they are faced with hunger. Fish, of course, constitute the main animal food.

The native economy has suffered a serious setback by the ravages of the rhinoceros or coconut beetle, which has ruined the copra industry. It is believed to have been introduced into Koror during 1942 by Japanese ships coming from the Orient. However, some natives maintain that they noticed its destructive work as early as 1936. It spread rapidly during the war and by 1945 had reached more than halfway to the northern end of Babelthuap; by 1950 it had spread throughout the entire archipelago.

The insect, the size of a cockroach, dark chocolate in color, has a small head armed with a stout horn. It forces its way down between the bases of the younger fronds of a palm to gouge an entrance into the tissue of the midribs. It then bores downward until the growing point is killed and no more young fronds are produced. The ruined trees are most conspicuous from an airplane, hundreds of them standing gaunt like huge stringy, inverted mops. In its native, Asiatic home the beetle is controlled by predatory insects and various other factors, but when introduced for the first time into isolated islands like Palau it spreads unhindered. Beetles are conspicuously abundant in and around villages and other places which were bombed during the war, for the dead palms provided abundant breeding sites for the larvae.

The natives, seriously concerned about the loss of their money crop, are trying out various others under the direction of the American administration. A Government cacao plantation on Babelthuap is one of the new ventures. On that island there is a large area of Government land where successful production is achieved because of partial shade and protection from the wind. Furthermore, the first processing procedures for the beans, the raw material for chocolate and cocoa, are not difficult.

Another possibility for a commercial crop is hardwood timber. Hundreds of seedlings of mahogany and teakwood have been planted, also on Babelthuap, in an area formerly farmed by the Japanese. A market could be cultivated in the United States.

Something might be made of various tropical crops introduced on an experimental scale by the Japanese. There is a large grove of rambutan trees on Babelthuap. A native of Java, it produces delicious fruit something like that of litchi. There are also plantings of mangoes, mangosteens, cherimoya, cashew nuts, lemons, limes, and coffee trees.

Each of the main islands in the Palau group has aspects of development which differentiate it from others. Kayangel atoll, the northernmost land area of Palau, very rainy, is largely covered with trees, mostly coconut palms. On the broadest part of the largest islet, cyrtosperma, or giant taro, is conspicuous in a swamp. The poor soil of the island, sand and coral gravel, does not permit any other crop in place of coconuts, which have suffered very much from the borer. Selling trochus shells brings a meager income to the natives, now numbering about 150.

The people of Babelthuap are entirely subsistence farmers and fishermen who sell a little copra now and then, as one of them said, "to buy clothes and shoes." They even make their own sugar, boiling sugar-cane stalks to a sirup. Food is sent from time to time to relatives working on Koror. Fish, an important part of their diet, are taken in traps, throw nets, and by line fishing in the lagoon from canoes. Because of the efforts of the Japanese, they have better breeds of pigs and chickens than on many islands in Micronesia. They appreciate these improved strains and apparently take good care of them, feeding them on boiled pickings of taro and tapioca and tops of sweet potatoes.

Babelthuap has thousands of acres of good land awaiting exploitation. It is rolling to hilly, the highest point 713 feet. In the north-western part the Japanese mined bauxite, and a considerable deposit of that ore still remains. Babelthuap has a large river, Ngardok, the haunt of estuarine crocodiles hunted by the natives, who shot one from the boat in which the author was visiting their island.

The use of the land on Koror is affected by social traditions, economic activities other than agriculture, and foreign populations. That island has traditionally obtained some of its food supply from Babelthuap by an established trade. This trade was increased when the high rentals paid by the Japanese to the natives of Koror for land afforded them money. Although there is a high density of population, there is no pressure on the means of subsistence because of the access to food resources from other high-production areas and from stores which sell rice and other imported goods. Some natives, working for the Government, commute to Koror from southern Babelthuap, and there is a regular flow of visitors from other parts of the archipelago.

The two southern islands, Peleliu and Angaur, benefited economically from the mining operations carried on there by the Japanese, who exploited in a large way the phosphate deposits. The natives, however, suffered heavily during the latter part of the war, for those islands formed the perimeter of Palau's defense installations. Mining on Peleliu has ceased, but Angaur's high-grade deposits were until recently exploited by the Japanese through an arrangement with the American administration. The phosphate was taken by open-pit mining from between blocks of coral. A large scoop shovel dug it out; some ordinary picks and shovels were also used. The Angaurans benefited from the income of a Trust Fund into which the profits were put. About four hundred Japanese were engaged in digging, but the Palauans, like the Micronesians in general, cannot be depended on for regular onerous manual labor. Phosphate mining on Angaur was discontinued in 1955. The Japanese have departed, and no further mining there is contemplated.

The phosphate industry inculcated Palauans with ideas of Western trade and commerce. In native times trading on Palau was done in part through money, most of which was held in the families of chiefs and the possession of which today is still an indication of wealth and social prestige. This money consisted of small pieces of polished minerals, polished bits of pottery, and other objects which Palauan women now wear like jewelry, on chains around their necks. There are various traditions as to how these "coins" came to Palau; one is that an angel brought them down from heaven, another that they were brought from islands in the southwest Pacific in a big ship.

Palauan money played an important part in native warfare. Although wars were finally given up during Spanish times, several families of chiefs today owe their wealth and social position to the fact that their ancestors waged successful fights against enemy clans from which they demanded money indemnities. Chiefs occasionally lured allies for attack or defense by payments of native money.

There is a reluctance today to accept native money or American dollars for anything done by one Palauan for another—that is, if payment can be made through the old system of exchange and reciprocal obligation. However, the idea of direct payment for value received is gradually being accepted. Individual ownership of certain things is also gaining approval. Young men uphold the idea that property acquired by a married couple should be theirs alone. Most of them insist on this and resist demands upon such acquisitions by clan relatives. Nowadays young men are gaining more money as a result of their work, for they are refusing to give any of their earnings to family heads. They have taken the attitude of individual ownership of land in contrast to clan-owned land as formerly.

A goodly number of Palauans are employed by the Government or by private employers. Women and girls work as domestics in Koror, and men and boys find odd jobs as gardeners or helpers in one way or another. Some have established themselves in business in a modest way, selling rice and other groceries and drygoods. A few are capable mechanics. Others have learned to sew, repair boats, bake, and drive automobiles. There is a taxi service on Koror!

Since the end of World War II, the subsistence economy of the islands has been restored more fully than a commercial way of living. Although economic rehabilitation is progressing, no substitute has been found for the copra trade. The trochus-shell industry, an important prewar source of income, has been revived; the export goes to Japan for the making of buttons. Although every household raises most of its own food, few are entirely self-sufficient and all must purchase cotton, kerosene, and other commodities.

The following table shows the exports of Palau for 1954, which are representative:

TABLE XVII

Exports of Palau District, 1954

COMMODITY	UNIT	QUANTITY	COUNTRY OF DESTINATION	VALUE
Copra	Short Ton	655.8	Japan and U.S.A.	$ 60,698.88
Phosphate	Long Ton	105,702	Japan	2,049,900.00
Trochus	Pound	190,843	Japan	28,626.45
Handicraft	Each	1,059	U.S.A.	730.60
Total				$2,139,955.93

The exports of the islands indicate the sources of wealth important in foreign trade. They go out from two harbors, one on Angaur, and the other, Malakal Harbor on Koror.

Preparations have been completed for homesteading Government land in Palau, so that the natives will have an early opportunity to plant various crops. The administration is almost ready for applications for homesteads and entry on the land. The code of regulations for the Trust Territory Government specifies that there shall be homesteading, and an amendment effective July, 1954, specifies that clans, families, villages, and other groups, in addition to individuals, may homestead lands in the Trust Territory. Individuals who are citizens of the Territory, over eighteen years old, and who do not own more land than that allowed by the homestead law—seven hectares, or about seventeen acres—are eligible. The amount of land to be homesteaded and the requirements are to be decided by a land board in each district. In Koror it consists of the district Administrator as chairman, the island affairs officer as vice chairman, and the land titles officer as executive secretary, and five Palauans who were chosen by the natives from a panel of some thirty-five leading citizens. After several meetings they recommended that only individuals and families in Palau get homesteads, for the clans and villages had lost their cohesiveness and would not want to take up land as groups.

To prove a homestead, the land must be cleared in five years in accordance with recommended practices. Valuable trees or shrubs may remain on it. Seventy per cent of the homesteaded area must be planted in any of their native crops or introduced crops within the five-year period, and at least 10 per cent must be cleared and planted each year in accordance with specifications. If coconuts are planted, for example, they must be set thirty feet apart, in holes three feet by three feet and three feet deep, about fifty-five trees to an acre. Cacao must be planted with shade trees. Coffee and pepper are among other crops being considered. The area to be first opened for homesteading is the best agricultural land on Babelthuap, land cultivated by the Japanese around and near the margin of that island. Babelthuap was chosen in part because of the press of population to Koror, with the idea of keeping the people more widely distributed. The Palauans themselves have drawn up an evaluation schedule, so that they will have some way to compare land on the various islands. For example, land on a main or secondary road is classified as "A," on other roads "B," and the remainder of the land is classified as "C."

The following table shows the distribution of Government land and native land in the islands:

TABLE XVIII

DISTRIBUTION OF LAND ON PALAU, 1954
(sq. mi.)

ISLAND	GOVERNMENT	NATIVE	TOTAL
Koror	2.1	1.7	3.8
Babelthuap	113.3	44.7	158.0
Peleliu	6.2	4.8	11.0
Angaur	3.3	0.0	3.3
All other islands	20.0	0.0	20.0
Total	144.9	51.2	196.1

SOCIAL LIFE AND INSTITUTIONS

The social attributes of Palauans are in a transition stage favorable to innovation. Some of the changes which have taken place have modified their traditional institutions without undermining social morale. In many respects the time-honored principles of ordering human relationships remain relatively intact, especially as exemplified in the great deference still paid to chiefs.

The adoption of foreign ways by the élite of Palau took place about the middle of the Japanese era of government when the two more powerful chiefs, those of Koror and Babelthuap, led modernization movements. The Japanese sponsored tours of chiefs and other important people to Japan to impress them with Japanese civilization and increase the willingness of the natives to accept it. Chief Aibedul of Koror became an enthusiastic supporter of the Japanese way of life. Other aspects of the Japanese effort to induce the Palauans to receive and naturalize the foreign program included an extensive educational setup and even the subsidization and encouragement of both Catholic and Protestant missions. For the Orientals believed that the promotion of any factors contributing to change was a move in the proper direction.

Notwithstanding Japanese efforts to change the social setup, each locality in Palau, as in the old days, has its own determinants of social status. An individual's social rank is imputed through the village and district to which he belongs. For example, the social prestige of a chief's family on Koror is above that of a similar family on Kayangel. Villages are ranked in social position within each district. The confines of the native's world are still those of his village, and loyalty to it is considered second only to that of the family, even if it is less intense than before the Japanese came. Younger Palauans feel the burden of traditional obligations in their home villages where they no longer reside or work. A man now living permanently on Koror who did not pay his share to build a new school in his former village on Babelthuap feels he cannot visit that village because of the social condemnation of his old friends and relatives. The fact that he contributes to the school on Koror where his children attend makes no difference.

Because of a high degree of population movement in present-day Palau, the village to which a native "belongs" is in many cases not that where he works. Every day land and sea conveyances transport hundreds of people in various directions. Native hospitality still requires a near relative or a member of the same clan to provide food and shelter for the traveler.

Distinguished visitors to an island or district are frequently honored by a dance and feast, usual diversions for Palauans as they are for the natives of the Trust Territory in general. To promote community spirit and friendly rivalry, dance programs are given monthly in the community house of Koror in turn by teams from each of the fourteen villages on that island and Babelthuap. A dozen girls do a *matematong* dance, rhythmically marking time with their feet. Perhaps this is followed by a stick dance with twice that number of girls participating. Songs accompanying the dances relate incidents in village life. The author was present at a song and dance prepared for an occasion in honor of the magistrate of Koror, who is both capable and popular. On the same program a group of young men acted an Okinawan comedy learned during the Japanese régime, an interesting feature of which was the music of the Japanese samisen mimicked on a guitar.

Villagers and visitors attend dances and other celebrations dressed in their Sunday best. Much of the money earned by Palauans is spent to improve their personal appearance and their homes. Some of it purchases betel nuts and the lime and pepper leaves that go with chewing them, and of course all men and boys want to buy American cigarettes. Indeed, there is considerable social pressure on an individual to dress well in Western style and to have money to contribute to social affairs.

Feasts are held for house raising, for dedications of churches, hospitals, and community houses. They pay for themselves, for those who come contribute food or money for their share. At a feast of dedication of a new hospital in Koror, the average Palauan family donation was ten dollars.

Palauans are bent on improving themselves in part through education. Parents urge their children to be educated so that they may be qualified for a role of leadership in their villages, and chiefs believe that education will solve the problems of Palau and help people to abandon old customs no longer useful. The practice of permitting only members of formerly powerful clans to use main roads and trails has been given up, and all routes are now open to everyone. Among customs which they plan to keep is that of hospitality to visitors, especially to older people. Chiefs of districts are always courteous hosts to those from other communities and islands. Another old custom to be preserved is the meeting of the older men of a village or district in the *abai,* or men's clubhouse, to discuss plans for the general welfare of the people. Young men also customarily meet there to decide what they can do.

The community house, a native structure, built with traditional Palauan materials, is the outstanding building in a village. It has a ridgepole roof, thatched with leaves of the nipa palm, set high on posts. The hardwood crossbeams which reinforce the structure are decorated with figures of natives, canoes, fish, crocodiles, and other designs representing legends and traditions in Palauan history. Bamboo curtains, like Venetian blinds, are raised or lowered according to the weather.

During the author's visit to Palau, the dedication of a new public elementary school in Koror was an event which aroused considerable interest and enthusiasm among the local people. The hereditary chiefs and the second chiefs—some fifteen of them—came in twos and threes and took the places of honor in the first two rows. Chief Aibedul, the highest chief on Koror, sat at one end of the front row, and next to him Chief Reklai of Melekeiok District on Babelthuap. The former belongs to the Idid clan, and the latter to the Udes clan, traditionally the two most powerful clans in Palau. The members of the Congress of Palau, elected by the people, took their seats behind the hereditary chiefs, respectfully leaving a vacant row in between. Behind the congressmen, leaving another vacant space, the commoners gathered, men, women, and children. This voluntary arrangement in seating is representative of social feeling and prestige in Palau. The crowd listened to Chief Aibedul's speech with close attention and gave him hearty applause when he said that the building of the school was the greatest achievement he had seen on Koror during his lifetime.

Although the chiefs promote learning, one of its effects is to decrease their own prestige, for young men better educated in a Western way than their chiefs sometimes maintain that, because of their conservatism, needed reforms are delayed. On the other hand, paramount chiefs are anxious about the gradual rise of the influence of commoners. The accumulation of American money in the hands of commoners who earn it in various ways threatens to disturb the customary concentration of wealth which differentiated the several levels of society. While chiefs are pleased to have access to additional money, they are loath to have it lessen—and perhaps someday bring to an end their own prestige growing out of its greater possession. Palauans have retail stores, so many that none of them seems to be doing a big business. However, the operators are accumulating profits, something new for natives of the South Seas. A native sawmill on Babelthuap not only provides that island with part of its lumber, but also sells some of its product to other islands. A good many people in the islands add to income by collecting scrap metal—old war materials—to sell to the Micro Metals Company.

The important new way for many Palauans to earn money is through civil service for the Government, which employs about five hundred natives. The more important positions are those of interpreters, administrative assistants, policemen, judges, and native advisers. Some who have made Government service their lifetime occupation have continued in office through successive changes in the foreign administrations. Because they are specialists in affairs necessary for the good conduct of the administration, their help is indispensable. Drawn largely from the élite of certain districts in Palau, they have considerable influence and prestige in their own right.

Unfortunately, nearly all the ambitions of young Palauans run to white-collar jobs rather than to farm work and thus to improving their islands' economic position, which depends almost entirely on agriculture. Boys and girls who are graduates of the intermediate school in Koror, for example, do not want to have anything to do with the copra industry. First in order of priority is working for the Government, not only for the money, but for the social prestige which it brings. All departments of the administration have native assistants in various capacities. Various other professions have their own attractions for the tastes and aptitudes of Palauans. Saburo Ramarui in Enkassar village has a son at Suva Medical School, another a student of medicine at the University of Washington, and a third at the University of Hawaii; a daughter is teaching at the Catholic mission school in Koror.

Mission schools play an important role in education as they try to do in spiritual uplift. As was already stated, Roman Catholic missionaries have been in Palau for a long time. The first Protestant missionary, a German, arrived in Koror in 1930 to establish the Liebenzeller Mission. It includes a vocational school where boys bake bread, milk cows, and look after cattle and pigs. They learn to take the responsibility of making regular deliveries of bread and fresh milk to Americans who want them. They also do practical work in mechanics with trucks and jeeps. Their studies include arithmetic, reading and writing both in the Palauan language and in English. The graduates, with a good reputation for work and dependability, have no difficulty in finding jobs. Five of them are doing excellent work on the cacao plantation.

Christian missions have not been able to dispel the native belief in ghosts. Most families burn a light in the house all night, for they are afraid to sleep in the dark. Certain trails in the islands are notorious for the spirits which may be encountered on them. Before the coming of foreigners, belief in evil spirits was inculcated by priests and medicine men as a means of keeping commoners subservient economically, politically, and socially.

Missions have also had slight influence in curbing the sexual freedom which has always existed among young people. It is an old pattern that has changed very little since the coming of foreigners in general, perhaps because many of them have not found it objectionable. Courtship is conducted in pretended secrecy, and trial marriages are a usual procedure, preliminaries to which are often carried on in school where boys and girls write notes to each other signifying their intentions of love and courtship. Divorce, a matter of economic arrangement between the two families concerned, is frequent, a payment going to the wife's family. In some villages most of the adult population have been married more than once.

Natives of the Palauan archipelago appear to be in tolerably good health. The common physical ailments found are similar to those throughout the Trust Territory: tuberculosis, influenza, intestinal parasites, and various digestive disturbances. Education in health and sanitation is playing an important role in lessening their incidence.

The continued contacts with people from the outside world have resulted, from the Palauans' point of view, in an advance in their standard of living. But, as was pointed out, there is considerable rivalry between the old entrenched social hierarchy of the chiefs and a new social order in which commoners can rise to affluence and influential positions. Regardless of position, however, there is acceptance by everyone of the concept of progress for Palau, predicated, however, on an economic development which it is doubtful the Palauans themselves can accomplish.

GOVERNMENT AND THE FUTURE

In view of the fact that the management of affairs in Palau has been concentrated in the past almost exclusively in an élite class, considerable progress has been made toward the evolution of democratic methods, but the main thing for the administration is not to push new ideas too hard, but to let the situation develop under close supervision. In the old days authority was symbolized in titles of public office which designated certain people as senior-ranking members of society. They were not only superior in secular matters but also holy in sacred ones. In the modern era, the chiefs are still generally thought of as the real rulers of Palau. However, the American introduction of election to office will probably bring about sometime in the future a redistribution of power within the ruling class. Most of the people favor the selection of future paramount chiefs from senior-ranking chiefs.

The four islands of Kayangel, Koror, Peleliu, and Angaur each constitute an administrative unit, while Babelthuap is subdivided into ten small areas. Native officials fall into three categories: chiefs who hold office through their hereditary titles, members of the Palau Congress who are elected, and judges and departmental officials who are appointed by the administration. The roles of elected magistrates and hereditary chiefs have led to some irreconcilable situations from a Western point of view, but the good sense of the Palauans and their desire to cooperate have helped to resolve some of the difficulties. There are a few districts in which the elected magistrate is merely a symbol of the American occupation because of the insistence of the administration that the people be democratic. In some districts the hereditary chief is the elected magistrate who wields the same power that he had before. In others an elected district magistrate looks after taxes and similar matters of direct concern to the administration, while the hereditary chief attends to all customs, traditions, and native institutions of the indigenous population. The latter official never lacks cigarettes, tobacco, and betel nuts, though commoners may often find these things hard to obtain.

Clan feeling is still strong in Palau, and hereditary chiefs of clans are jealous of their power. A chief deprived of power would feel as a father in the United States might feel if he left a son a big manufacturing business and someone else had arbitrarily taken over the management. An old chief in Palau is about to retire and his hereditary title will go to his sister's eldest son, the oldest child in the matrilineal line. However, the heir apparent is not very popular with the majority of the people, for they have lost confidence in him because of some of his business dealings, and would like the succession to go to another relative. Yet there is no way according to traditional custom to deprive him of his hereditary title and influence. In Micronesia a hereditary chief can still generally get what he wants. When a native goes off to another island and earns money, he must, on his return, give the chief a share of his earnings if the latter requests it. Chief Aibedul on Koror often calls a native taxi, but never pays for it.

There is considerable political factionalism in Palau, for the people of the whole archipelago are divided into two political entities which might be referred to as confederations, the highest two chiefs of which—Aibedul of Koror and Reklai of Babelthuap—wield the greatest political power in the islands. However, within each confederation there is a struggle between lesser district chiefs to achieve the higher places in the hierarchical ranking.

Each of the two highest chiefs tries in various ways to preserve and extend his authority, a purpose which he can achieve only at the expense of the other. However, they pull together in facing foreigners and district chiefs who might question their position. Neither fully trusts his neighbor, and each watches the other's overtures to check any political adventures which might change the balance of power. Chief Aibedul is eager to push modern innovations economically, socially, and politically, while Reklai is conservative and wishes to retain as many native customs as he can.

The American administration largely governs in fact by the system of indirect rule practiced by British and French and other colonial governments, where European members of the administration, very few in number, are little familiar with the institutions and ways of living of the people they govern. By it the native officials, ruling as far as they can by the traditional code, are held responsible by the administration for law and order. The more the foreign heads of departments know and appreciate the native institutions, the more successful is the government by this method. In the Trust Territory the term of office is so short, and the offices are manned by people with so little background for their positions, that small progress is likely to be made in this way. The situation is also rendered more difficult by the stated American policy of democratic indirect rule within the framework of Palauan traditional customs. The United States program for Palau, as for the Trust Territory as a whole, is predicated on economic self-sufficiency, a goal which will be achieved largely by subsistence agriculture. The amount of money coming into the Territory will be restricted to that received from a few exports, copra, trochus shell, and native crafts, and to wages received from the administration. A native conception in Palau of rapid economic development is not likely to be achieved.

The Palauans, refusing to believe that the United States does not intend to carry on the industrial development that the Japanese initiated, are awaiting the day when American businessmen and colonists will arrive. They themselves, aware that they cannot develop the agricultural, mineral, and marine products of the islands to the extent that the Germans and Japanese did, also know that if the potentialities of their islands are not exploited they will not be able to obtain the goods from outside which they had begun to regard as necessary for the new Palauan way of living.

The Palauans expect more help from the American administration than do the people of other districts in the Trust Territory because they have suffered losses from the coconut beetle, and because they have a large area of land suitable for other tropical crops. They must still be persuaded that the beetle can be kept under control, as has been the case in other parts of the world where copra is an important product. They are inclined, perhaps, to lean too heavily on the administration, for they regard all Americans as being very wealthy. One of the subjects discussed at a recent meeting of chiefs was how they could wangle a loan from the Government!

Copra is likely to continue to be an important export from Palau, despite the borer and the broad fluctuations of price in the world market. The Palauans are more discouraged than need be over the depredations of the coconut beetle, since it is the first time in their history that anything like the failure of their only marketable crop has befallen them. However, other tree crops should be encouraged, especially now that the natives are in the mood to try them. An important point is whether or not they will have the patience and perseverance to keep on trying, for economic improvement in their way of living will come slowly over periods measured by decades.

REFERENCES

Barnett, H. G., *Palauan Society: A Study of Contemporary Native Life in the Palau Islands* (Univ. of Oregon, 1949), 223 pp., mimeographed; CIMA Report No. 20.

Bridge, Josiah, and G. G. Goldich, "Bauxite Deposits on Babelthuap Island, Palau Group" (abstract), *Geological Society of America Bull.* 59:1313 (No. 12, Pt. 2, Dec., 1948).

Gressitt, J. L., *Description of Kayangel Atoll, Palau Islands,* Pacific Science Board Atoll Research Bull. 14, Washington, D.C., 1952.

Mayo, H. M., *Report on the Plant Relocation Survey and Agricultural History of the Palau Islands* (1954), 62 pp., mimeographed.

Nugent, I. B., Jr., "Elevated Phosphate Islands in Micronesia," *Geol. Soc. Amer. Bull.* 59:977-994 (No. 10, Oct., 1948).

Ritzenthaler, R. E., *Native Money on Palau,* Milwaukee Public Museum Publications in Anthropology, No. 1, 1954.

Rodgers, John, "Phosphate Deposits of the Former Japanese Islands in the Pacific: A Reconnaissance Survey," *Econ. Geol.* 43 (5): 400-407, Aug., 1948.

United States Department of Commerce, Weather Bureau, "Local Climatological Data, Koror Island, Pacific, 1953."

United States Department of the Interior, "Trust Territory of the Pacific Islands, Palau District Statistical Report—Fiscal year 1954," mimeographed.

Useem, John, *Report on Palau* (CIMA Report No. 21, 1949), 135 pp.
———, "The Changing Structure of Micronesian Society (Angaur, Palau)," *Amer. Anthropol.,* Vol. 47, No. 4, Oct.-Dec., 1945, pp. 567-588.

Vidich, Arthur J., *Political Factionalism in Palau: Its Rise and Development* (CIMA Report No. 23, 1949), 128 pp., mimeographed.

X

Yap

THE Yapese, in contrast to the Palauans, are the old conservatives of Micronesia, for they still maintain that their native way of living is best for them. They are self-reliant and self-sufficient, with an attitude toward the American administration much the same as toward the Japanese: "You have nothing to offer us."

Unlike other Micronesians, they do not greet you on the road unless they know you. Occasionally some of them get off the road when strangers are approaching, and hide in the bushes until they pass—men as well as women. They are condescending to a visitor, saying to themselves: "Here is someone who wants to know something. It won't do us any harm to tell him, so we shall be courteous."

They bear an independent attitude, for if something new in the way of bettering their welfare is offered, they say, "We'll think it over and discuss it." That takes several months! About two years ago, one of their chiefs who does cooperate with the administration tried to make a rule that the natives must wear clothes when they came on any business to the offices of the Government. The matter became a popular issue, but it failed for lack of support. "I am a good Catholic, but what has that got to do with wearing clothes?" a Yapese said to a missionary who wanted him to wear shorts to mass instead of a loincloth. Men in Yap wear only loincloths, women nothing but grass skirts.

Balabat village, only a mile from Colonia (or Yaptown), the largest settlement in Yap, and headquarters of the Trust Territory administration for that archipelago, is one of the more conservative villages in the islands where the traditional chief still has a powerful hold on the people. Considering himself also the director of public works, he has made the people repair the old stone house-platforms and other ancient monuments in the vicinity. The author watched the women of Balabat practice their traditional dances, not for any public performance, but so that the people would keep alive one of their old and important customs. There also one can examine the most ancient type of canoe in the islands, with the bow and stern shaped like a bird's head.

The administrative problem on Yap is one of reconciling the indigenous population, some three thousand people, to change in their own best interests. Living in ill-lighted, unsanitary huts, they have immediate need for improved health and sanitation, a field in which some advancement has been made.

Since there is an abundance of land, and consequently abundant food in the islands for the relatively small population, landownership problems are not pressing. Changes in native government, introduced slowly by the administration, will aid in the improvement of social conditions. The raising of the level of education, which in itself creates immediate problems of acculturation, will eventually help the Yapese to solve some of their own difficulties.

Included in the administration of Yap are the people of a scattered group of coral atolls to the west where, at this time, changes seem less important to the welfare of the natives than in the larger, Yapese islands.

NATURAL ENVIRONMENT

Yap, in the western Carolines, consists of four main islands, 450 miles southeast of Guam and 326 miles northeast of Palau; like those of many archipelagoes in Micronesia, they are separated by narrow passages and surrounded by a fringing reef. Their total area is approximately 85 square miles. On Yap, the largest island, a series of hills, of which the highest is about 600 feet, divides the east coast from the west. The southern end is a fertile coastal plain. A central plateau-like area, tapering off to the coastal plain, is grassy and contains scattered pandanus trees. Burned over during the dry season by the natives, it is pockmarked with shell holes distinctly visible from an airplane. Roads extend from the north to the south of the main island, but ruts and mud render them impassable for wheeled vehicles a good part of the year. Trails, winding through the hills across the island, can always be negotiated by the barefoot natives. The soil, derived from basalt, is fertile compared with that of coral atolls.

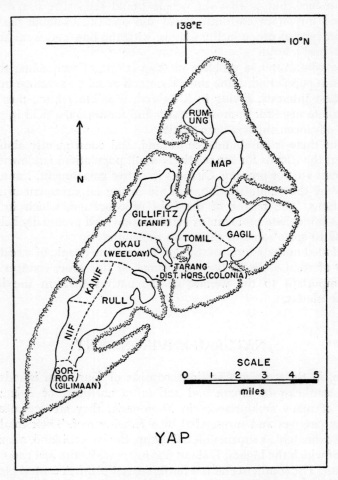

The hot, damp climate which prevails most of the year is difficult for Americans. The mean monthly temperature, about 81 degrees, varies only two or three degrees during the twelve months. The rainfall, which averages annually 122 inches, is less in the early months of the year when trade winds blow regularly. One of the more characteristic features of Yap weather is the alternation of five minutes of rain, then an hour of clear weather. Looking over the ocean, one can see the next squall, but in a few minutes it is over. Yap and the islands to the east are visited by typhoons which sweep through this part of the Pacific almost annually. Some typhoons have their genesis in the vicinity of Yap. Others originate in the Ponape area to the east, from which they generally travel westward or northwestward, toward the Philippines and Japan. Occasionally one of them makes a loop covering the same area twice. Sometimes Ulithi, Ngulu, or other atolls in the vicinity of Yap are hit by a storm when Yap escapes. Then the people of Yap send food to the stricken islands. These devastating storms destroy native houses, copra sheds, and any other buildings in their way. The Japanese built many houses of reinforced concrete which are proof against the hurricane winds that accompany typhoons. Although the storms in the outlying islands in recent years have not been as severe as one in 1907, which necessitated mass evacuation of natives to Yap, each destroys food crops, sometimes to the extent that relief supplies must be provided by the administration. From time to time islanders in canoes lose their lives in these sudden storms.

The fauna of the islands is restricted. Of mammals there are the huge fruit bats which hang in clusters from trees all day. Almost the sole use of the natives' very simple blowgun is to kill these bats; many people eat them. There are no poisonous snakes, and the large green lizard (Hydrosaurus marmoratus) is important principally in certain magical rites. It grows to be four feet long, but is rarely found more than three feet. Geckos, the little lizards so common to the tropics, abound. Flies are everywhere, for rotting vegetation and damp brush make ideal breeding grounds.

The Yapese have coffee-colored skins and good-looking bodily structure and development. Their origin is unknown, but affinities of their language with some of the Indonesian languages suggest that they came from Malaya to their present home in Micronesia. The people of the archipelago are all alike, the only difference being slight dialectical changes in their language. Men are liberally tattooed. Even in cumbersome grass skirts the women are pretty, but when they smile they reveal blackened teeth, acquired by staining with herbs and by the constant chewing of betel.

DEPOPULATION

The conservative attitude of the Yapese is in part due to their isolation and to the history of their contacts with other civilizations. However, it was the introduction of diseases by foreigners which chiefly caused the great and continuing decrease in population in the archipelago that went on during the Spanish, German, and Japanese régimes. The tradition of those harassing contacts is one of the factors that cause them to shun all people of foreign origin.

It is thought that Yap was first made known to Westerners in 1526 through the crew of a ship sent out from the Moluccas by De Menezes. The islands remained under a nominal but wholly dormant discovery title of Spain until 1885, when the German flag was raised at Tomil, signifying annexation to that empire. From 1886 to 1899, however, Spain maintained a garrison in the islands and a government administrative agent. The principal effect was some missionary activity, with sporadic conversions of natives by priests and monks of the Capuchin order. After prolonged negotiation Yap passed to German ownership in 1899 through Germany's purchase of the Caroline Islands.

America's interests in Yap centered, in the early part of this century, about cable and radio rights. Yap was a cable station on the direct line from the United States to the Dutch East Indies by way of Guam; another cable ran from Yap to Shanghai. A controversy with Japan over rights in the island when she received the mandate for the former German possessions in the Pacific was settled at the Washington Conference in 1921. In that year, when Japanese armed forces were withdrawn from the islands in general, the South Seas Bureau, a civilian administration, was put in charge.

Japanese policy, the primary ends of which were political and military, contemplated a substantial emigration from the homeland to Yap as well as to other islands. Native authority was restricted and foreign trade quietly discouraged. When Yap was thoroughly drawn into the war machine, the people were forced to work on farms, on ships, and building military installations and air fields. During the actual fighting, Yap was bombed by American planes which destroyed most of Colonia. A full-scale invasion, however, was not necessary, for the garrison capitulated with those of other islands at the end of the war.

The aftermath of disease on Yap left by early traders and explorers, continuing unchecked, reduced the population considerably. The Germans tackled the problem of health and sanitation with energy and insight, setting about to control the further importation of venereal diseases and serious epidemics. At the same time they began a program of treatment of chronic illnesses and an educational plan which eventually would have been an important step toward betterment. The depopulation, however, during their régime, was particularly severe during epidemics of influenza and typhoid.

The Japanese were no more successful than the Germans in checking the downward trend of population. Three epidemics which occurred during their occupancy seem to have been influenza, diphtheria, and amoebic dysentery. They reduced still further the dwindling numbers of the Yapese.

Indeed, with the coming of the Japanese, all the undesirable aspects of foreign life seemed to descend on the natives and tended to make them shun more and more all associations with foreigners. They became so uncooperative that Chamorros from the Marianas were imported to work. Their aloofness from foreigners was so great that during this period there were very few inter-racial mixtures. However, under German administration, and particularly under that of the Japanese, great numbers of Yapese men were impelled to participate in various commercial enterprises in other parts of Micronesia. Many were used in the phosphate development of Angaur in the Palau group.

Evidences of a much larger population in earlier times are seen everywhere in the islands in the form of stone platforms, each of which was associated with a dwelling. A considerable number of them, very old and broken, are moss-covered. Trees and shrubs growing between some of the flags have pried them apart. Others, apparently abandoned in relatively recent times, are still in good repair. These old paved surfaces are to be seen along the coast, in the valleys, and far inland at the summits of divides. Near many of them, old as well as recent, great pieces of Yapese stone money lie about.

Traditionally, Yapese regularly rebuild their homes on ancestral sites to remain close to the family spirits resident in the stone foundations. Consequently any additional construction of house platforms would indicate population increase instead of a possible shift of residence, and abandoned foundations are eloquent of decrease. Many villages have completely disappeared and some of those still existing are only ghost settlements with three or four houses. There are approximately 485 stone platforms in Kanif District. Conservatively estimating at the rate of four individuals per dwelling, one arrives at a maximum population of 1,940, or nearly ten times the number of people there now. Some believe that in the middle of the last century the islands of Yap had a total population of 15,000.

Among other causes believed to be responsible for the great decrease in numbers of the Yapese are unnatural sexual practices, female sterility, and infant mortality, and perhaps, also, a kind of psychological despair or delusional melancholia. The native, faced with new ideas, with his old religion, clan, and tribe all gone, is left only with the feeling that he, too, must pass on. Having made up his mind to die, he forces his body to follow in a dramatic protest against "civilization." No doubt pride in his own race also makes him want to shun the foreigner. His ceremonial dances recount the exploits of his early history. His legends extol the prowess of his people who ruled the islands before the foreigners came. Why should he bend his knee to an alien?

Fanechoor, judge of a district court and an elected magistrate, told the author proudly that his clan, the Weeloay, was in old times the strongest and the highest caste clan in Yap. The Fanif ranked next. There are only a few members of the Weeloay left, for in great wars between the clans in the days before the Spanish came, according to him, sometimes as many as one hundred men were killed in a battle. The Weeloay, after suffering heavy losses, allied itself with the Fanif clan.

The reign of "His Majesty O'Keefe" in Yap may also have contributed to the aloofness of the native population. O'Keefe, an American sea captain born in Ireland, achieved an affluent and influential position in the islands, where he lived from 1872 to 1901. He dealt in copra for the famous "stone money" which his vessels brought from Babelthuap in Palau. Wishing to keep the lion's share of Yapese trade, he persuaded the people to do little business with the Germans who came in the latter part of the nineteenth century. Perhaps he convinced the natives to distrust all foreigners. Tarang, a little island in Tomil harbor where O'Keefe's "palace" stood, is still a showplace for visitors.

SUBSISTENCE AGRICULTURE

The native economy of selling copra to O'Keefe for stone money gave way to disposing of it for German marks, Japanese yen, and now for American dollars. Yapese economy is a subsistence agriculture in an archipelago where food is overabundant for the small population. Products of field agriculture and small gardens, wild plants and fish—all contribute to the food supply. Taro, yams, sweet potatoes, bananas, Polynesian chestnuts, breadfruit, papayas, oranges and pineapples grow in abundance. Chickens and pigs, raised on all the islands, are usually eaten only at special feasts.

Giant swamp taro, botanically named *Cyrtosperma chamissonis*, and called *lak* by the Yapese, is a highly esteemed food. It is widely cultivated in hundreds of patches in the islands. The municipality of Weeloay, where, according to a legend, it originated, is famous for the quality of its product, not only in Yap but in other parts of Micronesia also. Many Yapese eat it two or three times a day the year round. It is also offered ceremonially to couples at weddings, sometimes with copra and stone and shell money. The preferred variety is *bulugumau*, but at least five other kinds are commonly raised.

Methods of propagating this plant are similar to those practiced elsewhere in Micronesia. Cormlets—offshoots arising from the parent corm or root—or pieces of the mature plant itself are used as seed.

Although planting and harvesting taro is carried out in Yap without ceremony, the Yapese have superstitious beliefs about the conduct of people in taro patches. During the preparation of an area for planting, workers are forbidden to eat cooked food the night before. That usually taken is the water of a coconut and raw fruit. If the taboo on cooked food is violated, the Yapese believe that the taro plants will "burn up," for they associate cooked food with fire. Both men and women planning to plant are strictly forbidden to have relations with the opposite sex the night before and for a certain period thereafter. A violation of this taboo means, according to the Yapese, that the newly planted corms will fail to develop.

Sizes of taro patches vary from a few square feet to an acre. The larger areas, owned by several families, are divided into individual plots, the ownership of which is well known. Because their boundaries are generally marked by rocks or other landmarks, it is not likely that one can take corms from another's plot "by mistake." Stealing from a neighbor's section is a serious offense, and under the native code a guilty person has forfeited his entire plot.

Clearing swamps for planting taro, and weeding it, are usually done during the early part of the day or late in the evening when it is cool. Women are solely responsible for weeding, gathering, replanting, and fertilizing. They wear special work skirts of strips of banana leaves or palm leaves. The procedures are simple, involving usually only sharpened flattened pieces of iron, used like digging sticks in loosening the tubers or rooting up large weeds. The continuous fertilization of the pits consists of taking a section several yards square, digging out some of the muck, and filling the hole with grass or semidecayed vegetable matter, which rots to become incorporated with the soil. In certain villages only old women are permitted to weed, or harvest a crop. The corm reaches maturity in size and flavor four years after planting.

Women's taro lands, separate from those of the men, are tended exclusively by the women themselves. Their gardening may be done in company with other women or alone, according to an agreement of the moment. A woman who has some weeding or cultivating to do may ask her friend or friends to come along, and they may work, each in her own plot, or all may work the plots in succession. The quantity of taro harvested is governed by the needs of a family, and not more than a week's supply is taken at any one time. Harvesting and planting, therefore, go on concurrently in a patch.

Hawaiian dry-land taro, *Colocasia esculenta*, a better variety than the giant taro, is also raised, but it requires more effort to cultivate and, from the native standpoint, therefore, is less desirable. It is planted by putting a cutting from the top of a *Honolulu* tuber into a little spot of loosened earth and then periodically pulling up the weeds which grow about it. Patches of dry-land taro are small and scattered.

Breadfruit in season is an important food crop needing little attention, for young trees spring from the roots of the old. Suckers also grow from the lower part of the stem of a banana plant. After the sole bunch which a plant bears is taken, the old stem and the suckers, except one, are cut; that one bears a new bunch nine or ten months later.

Yams and sweet potatoes, less important food crops, are generally grown on burned-over land. The Yapese burn the grass and brush off much more land than they need for any crops—just to see it burn! Plains and gentle slopes, set alight each dry season, December to April, are burned bare. The sprouted ends of the yams are planted at the beginning of the rainy season, and as the vines grow they twine around bamboo poles ten feet high, based close to the stem. Since they need good drainage they are set on slopes. The Yapese cultivate six varieties of yams which, maturing in about six months, are left in the ground until people want to eat them, for they soon spoil when dug. Yams are started when the tide is high, since the Yapese believe that, if put in the ground at any other time, they will be retarded in growth and will remain small.

Sweet potatoes and cassava are also planted at the beginning of the rainy season, and sugar cane in small quantities, for the natives boil their own sugar. Children gnaw pieces of stalks of sugar cane like "all-day suckers." Pineapples, introduced by the Spanish, are also favored by the Yapese. Among other introduced crops are oranges and cacao. The Yapese collect the cacao beans, dry them, and infuse them with hot water to make a home variety of bitter chocolate.

Coconuts, the money crop of Yap, as they are in all of Micronesia, have little care. New trees are volunteer growths from ripe nuts, which, fallen on the ground, sprout to lie neglected. When the price of copra is low, natives don't bother to make any.

Although there is a season of rain and one of less rain on Yap, the precipitation is very irregular from month to month and season to season. The same months in successive years often have very different amounts of rain. Water is frequently rationed among the American personnel in Colonia. The Yapese use coconut water regularly to drink, having only a few shallow wells which they generally use for bathing children and washing cooking utensils.

A clean water supply is hard to come by. Water from tree trunks is caught by tying a bit of leaf to a tree and putting the loose end in a barrel or other receptacle. Few people drink from a stream if it can be avoided. In days of dryness, after typhoons have torn away all drinking nuts, the natives dig pits two feet below the normally wet surface of taro pits and drink the foul, salty water that slowly accumulates. When water is needed for cooking or for washing a dish, a Yapese does not hesitate to use taro pit water or some from a stream.

The natives, still largely dependent on their immediate environment for their clothes, agricultural tools, and for utensils for domestic
use, engage in barter rather than in buying and selling. One does not
offer to buy anything from the Yapese. If you do so they will probably
reply it is not for sale, or politely say that they want it themselves.
On the other hand, if you remark, "I should like to have that mat or
wooden bowl," you will probably get it. However, sometime in the
future you will be expected to give something of equivalent value
in return.

The dried arm of a sting ray, the thicker end of which is wrapped
with a leaf tied on with a coconut string—the whole constituting an
abrasive tool to smooth rough surfaces of wood—is exchanged for
food, for a digging stick, or for a hardwood stake.

Yap has been popularly referred to in books and magazines as
"The land of stone money." The large stones, shaped like doughnuts,
brought from Palau before European times in canoes and on rafts,
were later transported on O'Keefe's sailing ships. Some were brought
from Guam. German administrators, recognizing the importance of
these monoliths, ingeniously confiscated them when government
directives were not obeyed. As a consequence of depopulation, these
valuables are now comparatively plentiful, so that even isolated
islands have their form of inflation.

Though stone money is not moved, everyone knows to whom it
belongs. Some of it is strewn along roadsides, under palm trees, near
abandoned stone platforms, along the banks of streams, and leaning
against the foundations of men's clubhouses. Even in poor villages
there is much of it. It is still exchanged ceremonially on important
occasions. Orange-colored shell necklaces—some adorned with
dugong, or whales' teeth—and pearl oyster shells are other types of
"money" used in ceremonial exchanges at marriages, funerals, settlement of legal disputes, and other important rites.

LAND TENURE

The principal types of subsistence areas in Yap are taro grounds,
fishing grounds inside the reef, and stone weirs. In addition to these,
coconut groves and household gardens are considered valuable.
Almost all the land is native owned. Land not only provides sub-

sistence and materials for building, but also determines one's status
and role in native society. A man is a chief or a magician because of
the particular land he holds. Yapese say, "The man is not chief, but
the land is chief." Native systems of tenure and of rights to use and
enjoy the products of the soil are as complicated in Yap as in other
parts of Micronesia, if not more so. The traditional unit of ownership
in Yap is the estate or *tabinaw* (literally, "That which is the land"),
a word synonymous in daily Yapese with that for family or household.
In Yapese eyes the estate consists of all areas belonging to a single
household, which in turn derives its name and social prerogatives
from the land it occupies. Usually such an estate consists of one or
more house platforms of which the most important carries the name
of the estate, together with a number of named land parcels. With
these parcels, as with the name-bearing estate itself, are associated
several taro pits, fishing grounds inside the reef, stone fish weirs,
coconut palms, yam gardens, grassy uplands and woodlots. Yapese
holdings are generally transferred as estate units with traditional rights
and privileges vested in the house site and not in the plots accompanying it. The new owner has a right to social, political, or ceremonial
prerogatives of the former owner of the estate. All house sites and
individual plots, regardless of size or kind, bear proper names.

Although village dance places and community buildings may be
said to be owned severally, there is no land in Yap which may be
truly called common. Estate land is the joint possession of all the
men and unmarried women in a single family group, based on
relationship to the father, and all of them have a voice in the disposal
of the property. Actually, the privilege of distribution and disposal
is vested in the "head" of the estate, who is generally the oldest man.
While he is expected to consult the wishes of the members concerning the disposal of the land, and to yield to their wishes, should they
oppose his, he usually dominates the final decision by virtue of his
seniority in age and presumably greater maturity. He remains, however, trustee rather than sole owner of estate lands, and is expected
to provide plots for subsistence for each adult member of the family
group.

The head of an estate can never completely disinherit a member
of his household, although he can punish a recalcitrant brother or a
nephew by withholding taro lands and gardens which would be his
normal due. He cannot evict him from their ancestral estate nor

deny him access to their ancestral ghosts. Nowadays in Yap, when land is very plentiful, the usual solution of the problem of a trouble-making relative is to give him one of the several estates from the family inheritance, which becomes thereafter the property of his subfamily.

The head of an estate, whose land traditionally entitles him to be director of a particular activity in his village or district—for example, a village or district chief or the chief of ceremonial exchanges—has the right to demand products or services from all members of the estate in his community. If this service is withheld, according to the native code he has the right to destroy trees or other property of the offender. Since ceremonial exchanges are declining and former elaborate agencies of distribution are being curtailed, retaliation of this kind is now rare, and a knowledge of it is kept from the administration for fear of intervention.

Rights to the use of land are further complicated by an obligation as to food products or labor when an unrelated family resides on the land of another family estate. This obligation may be of an informal nature, such as temporary cooperation between relatives, or, under some circumstances, permanent assistance even though no family relationship can be traced.

The idea of payment of rent for land is not clear to Yapese. They feel that if land is used for personal subsistence, no payment should be required. However, if the "tenant" gains a profit in cash by selling products of the land, an appropriate return should be made to the household which is the titular owner.

There is no such thing as "sale" in Yapese land usage, if by sale we mean a transfer of land for payment which completely severs all claims of the former owner of the property. This is because the Yapese purchaser not only receives permanent rights of use for himself and his descendants, but also incurs certain continuing services for the original owner. The Yapese qualify such change of landownership by saying that the purchaser becomes "like a relative" to the seller. And so, like a member of the original owner's family, he is expected to continue to contribute a share of his goods and services to his support. The seller's family group is in turn supposed to concern itself in his behalf. According to custom, failure to maintain these ties, particularly on the part of the purchaser, nullifies the "sale," and the land reverts to the original estate owner. Since the advent of foreigners to the islands, serious misunderstandings have arisen between Yapese and outsiders concerning the status of lands which have been "sold."

At present, as in the past, most of the lands of Yap are acquired or transferred through inheritance within closely related kin groups. Yap custom stresses the continuity of landownership from father to eldest son, minimizing or overlooking possible claims of younger relatives and of women in general. It goes back to a basic Yapese principle that whenever possible an estate should be kept intact through primogeniture and patrilineal inheritance.

The use of fishing grounds within the reef, also an important source of food, is restricted to certain family groups. Among the various kinds of apparatus employed are traps, spears, large "butterfly" nets, hooks and lines, and stone fish weirs visible from the air as huge arrows in the shallow waters of the lagoon. In the deeper waters of the outer reefs, men dive with goggles to spear fish in holes and recesses in the rocks. Sometimes they drive fish into the weirs and stupefy them with a narcotic root. Fishermen go out alone or with friends. Although most fishing within the reef is done alone, fishing in the open sea requires cooperation and relatively large teams. The role of women in collecting seafood is restricted. Occasionally they hunt in ankle-deep water for certain kinds of shellfish, but the take is rarely large.

SOCIAL LIFE

Yapese villages are located mostly along the coast for convenient access to taro swamps and fishing grounds. Each consists of a few scattered houses hidden among coconut palms, nipa palms, breadfruit trees, mangoes or mangroves, and other tropical vegetation. Few villages are visible from an airplane. People live by preference around the perimeter of the island, leaving the whole central region essentially empty. Traditionally the natives erected large houses with hexagonal floor plans. Steep roofs thatched with coconut or nipa palm leaves jutted out from the building at opposite ends. This type of structure, rare today, has been replaced by smaller, flimsier houses, many little more than huts, with corrugated iron or thatched roofs. Some of the places in which the Yap family chooses to live are damp, black "holes" with small door-windows overhung by shutters. Little light can get in, and in bad weather the house is closed tightly.

Balabat, one of the more populous villages in Yap, has 125 people. Numunung has only five households, in huts perched on the side of a hill, above a stream, in the midst of coconut trees and bananas. Some of the Yap houses are modern, constructed of lumber and galvanized iron; but native structures generally predominate, with roofs of nipa thatch if the people have access to nipa palms, or, if not, of coconut thatch. The frame of the structure is bamboo, secured firmly by stout cord made from the fiber of coconut husks. Nipa or coconut thatch is also used for the sides and the floor, which, built up with rocks two or three feet above the ground, is covered with strips of bamboo. In the morning or afternoon, women are generally seen sitting in groups working leisurely at tasks that belong peculiarly to them. In Gilimaan, one was making a grass skirt; another was pounding herbs in an iron mortar to provide medicine for someone who was ill. A third, who was apparently not doing anything, got up to go over to a pepper plant to pick a leaf to chew with betel nut. A mother was feeding her baby a mixture of grated coconut meat and papaya. Few children are seen in Yap villages, in contrast with other islands in the Trust Territory in general where, all the way from the Marshalls in the east to Palau in the west, children are conspicuous by their numbers.

Inside the house, logs, bamboo bundles, and slat floor give little comfort to one who is used to chairs and tables. A house is essentially a sleeping and storage place. Only the most inclement weather drives people inside for entertainment or conversation. Mats of all kinds are used to sit on or sleep on or as shields against wet and wind. They are not hard or tedious to make, and in the evening, tired by heavy work during the day, a woman sometimes relaxes at this light task. Those who can, acquire an old mattress or a cot and, if possible, a mosquito net which is suspended from one corner of the hut. There is little on the floor, even the sleeping mats being leaned in a corner by day. Nearly everything hangs from the rafters, lies on them, or is tied to the wall. Most people who had associations with the Japanese have a strongbox in which they keep a little foreign money and other valuables. A cookhouse near a dwelling varies from a simple sheet of tin leaning against a post to shelter the pot, to a large structure of lumber in which natives both cook and eat. It is necessary to have some shelter to guard against the frequent squalls, but it is not

worth while to make a substantial building, for the first storm
destroys the work. In the cookhouse there are baskets for everything,
the most characteristic being a long, banana-shaped one plaited from
a single coconut leaf. There are technical differences in the many
shapes and varieties, and, in the social sphere, differences in who may
carry what kind.

Yapese villages are accessible only by boats, or by poor roads or
trails. On a rocky, slippery trail, the only route across part of the
main island, a dozen bridges are merely the trunks of trees thrown
across streams. The path leads through dense groves of bamboo of
several varieties which the natives commonly use for rafts to pole
themselves along the coast and up the mouths of rivers.

The most important structure in every village is the men's clubhouse, a sleeping place and social and ceremonial center for the male
members of the village society. It is built on a platform of rocks
about three feet high on which stout posts support a heavy roof
thatched with the leaves of nipa palms. The sides, also of thatch, have
large openings at regular intervals for windows, which are hinged at
the top and propped open by sticks just below the apertures. The floor,
of split bamboo, has two or three small rock-lined depressions in a
row where fires burn to give a flickering light to those who sit around
them. In some of them, fishing nets and fish traps are conspicuous,
as well as headdresses used by the men in their traditional dances. At
various times of day, mornings and afternoons, men frequent these
clubhouses to talk leisurely, to mend nets, or just to sit silently.

The women also have a house in each village exclusively theirs,
where a man may never set foot. These houses, however, are visited
by women only three or four days every month, when the traditional
conventions of the Yapese insist that they go there. They regard
these visits as opportunities to get a rest away from their families
as much as conveniences for physiological reasons.

Near villages on the coast there are generally small copra houses on
the beaches, some of them out in the water, exposed to as much sun
and wind as possible for good drying.

Villages in Yap are classified according to a peculiar caste system,
the origin of which is very obscure. The basic ranking of people comes
from the ranking of the village into which they were born. That is,
a man holds a certain rank because he was born that way and remains that way throughout life. There are some cases of village rank

which allegedly went up or down as the result of loss or triumph in war, and these have led to disputes today among the natives, not all of whom will recognize such changes.

The most striking class distinction is that between the lower four classes, commonly designated as *pimilingai*, and the upper five classes, who maintain a kind of master-serf relationship. The serfs live in certain villages usually not different in appearance from the rest, but on land that is considered to be of the lower grades. Various families in high villages own low-class land in some of the serf villages. Theoretically serfs can be evicted if they fail to perform designated work and ceremonial services for their masters, making roofs, for example, for the houses of people of high-caste villages.

There are actually eight or nine degrees in a social hierarchy which enjoins that people in high-caste villages do not engage in occupations which traditionally belong to those of lowly estate. An old chief stated that the caste system goes back to very early times when Yap was so densely populated that people did not have enough land to raise their food, and those who were hungry hired themselves out to work for those who had food to share.

The social distinction of villages is in part related to their location, the highest being on the coast—Gagil, Tomil, and Rull, for example— and the lowest farthest inland. Gitan, away back in Rull District, is a low-caste village, where the people—poor by Yapese standards— weave roofs of thatch for natives of high-caste villages. In return they generally receive fish and coconuts. Only women of low-caste villages may weave mats, and these they exchange for food with high-class people who have more than they.

People of high caste will not eat with those of low caste, nor take food which has been cooked in the same pot. When a feast is given to welcome a new district administrator, there are sometimes vacant tables, while people of low-caste villages stand outside. The separation of pots and the confusion of grades of society became so embarrassing to the administration of the local hospital that furnishing meals to patients was given up altogether, and now the relatives of patients, who are accommodated in guest houses in the village, cook for those who are ill. A public works official recently dismissed a young man from a high-caste village for unsatisfactory performance on his job. When the youth departed he ordered three low-caste workers to go with him, leaving the staff shorthanded. The people of low villages

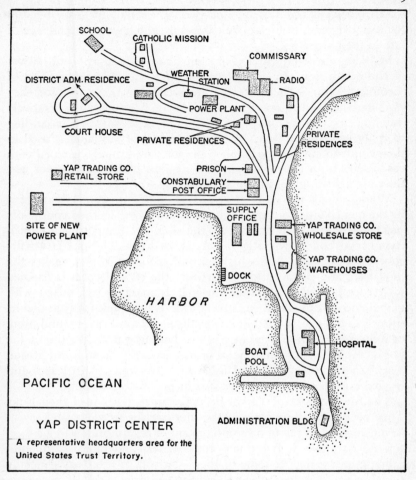

SCHOOL
CATHOLIC MISSION
COMMISSARY
WEATHER
STATION
RADIO
DISTRICT ADM. RESIDENCE
POWER PLANT
COURT HOUSE
PRIVATE RESIDENCES
PRIVATE
RESIDENCES
YAP TRADING CO.
RETAIL STORE
PRISON
CONSTABULARY
POST OFFICE
SUPPLY
OFFICE
SITE OF NEW
POWER PLANT
YAP TRADING CO.
WHOLESALE STORE
YAP TRADING CO.
WAREHOUSES
DOCK
HARBOR
HOSPITAL
BOAT
POOL
PACIFIC OCEAN
YAP DISTRICT CENTER
A representative headquarters area for the
United States Trust Territory.
ADMINISTRATION BLDG.

are generally better workers, but they take orders meekly from their
social and economic superiors.

There is little difference in appearance between low-caste villages
and high-caste, except that the houses of the former are a bit smaller.
However, the people of Yap know well those low in the social scale and
treat them accordingly. One day when passing through the humble
village of Numunung the author observed two men having their
midday meal of grated coconut meat mixed with grated chestnuts in a

wooden bowl. Coconuts are not generally eaten by those high in the social system, for high-caste villages usually have an abundance of taro in their vicinities.

Working cooperatively is characteristic of Yapese as of all natives of the South Seas. In villages groups of women weave sections of coconut thatch. Such gatherings are social occasions, too, for they chat together and review the village gossip. Men work cooperatively building new houses, many of which are erected strictly according to traditional native style. No nails or metal of any kind is used in their construction, for the bamboo supports are securely fastened with cord made from coconut fiber, and sections of thatch for roof and sides are held in place in the same way.

Women cook the daily food and at feasts are generally assisted by the men. Taro is prepared in various ways. One method commonly practiced is to scrape or peel off the skin, cut the corm into small pieces, and boil it in water for about an hour. The pot is usually covered with a taro leaf, which according to the Yapese makes the food taste and smell better. Sometimes the cooked corm is flavored with coconut milk. At other times it is mashed and mixed with grated coconut to which sugar is added. When pork fat is available, thin slices of taro are fried in it. Breadfruit is baked in a ground oven, or more frequently cooked in a pot of boiling water. The top of the pot is covered with several pieces of banana leaf to keep in the steam. The Yapese are very fond of fish which are wrapped in leaves and broiled on top of breadfruit or taro in process of cooking.

The routine tasks of Yapese occupy a small portion of their time. They generally get up early in the morning, between six and seven. Women go off to the taro swamp or yam or potato garden to get food for the day, take it home and cook it. Men go to work to build a house or a canoe. If some of them start off to fish, they generally take food with them so that they can stay away a day, if necessary, to secure a good catch. When they return, the chief of the village distributes the catch among the households, reserving a share for himself. At some of the men's houses are tables on which the catches are piled. Sometimes a low-caste village seems entirely deserted, for the people are away doing work for those higher up in the social scale.

To obtain a canoe, a man who wants one and who can afford to feed and house the canoe maker arranges for the construction. The carpenter, with several other men from the village, goes into the jungle to select a tree of proper size and type. He does whatever magic is necessary, and the tree is cut and roughly worked into shape on the spot. If the canoe is intended for ocean use, the employer deliberates with all concerned and sets a date for its launching. At this time the canoe maker is given the remainder of his fee. During the building he is paid on the installment plan, so that he may have an incentive to continue to work and to work at his best. He is also paid to make the magic requisite for the safety and well-being of the canoe and its occupants on ocean voyages. The launching is a complex performance requiring formal dealings between the canoe owner and the canoe maker, the canoe owner and the assemblage which comes to help the launching, and the canoe owner and the larger assemblage which comes to join in the festivities. The canoe is launched with a traditional ritual, part of which is the placing of a coconut leaf and a banana leaf in the bow. The man who had charge of building the craft walks around it and through it, making occult gestures with his arms and pronouncing an invocation to the spirits to bring good luck to the fisherman.

Making her own clothes takes up some amount of a woman's time. She uses native materials entirely. Cord forms the base-work at the top of the skirt, and from it she wraps and suspends grasses or shredded leaves of various species, textures, and lengths until she has a long, full-bodied garment with a shorter, thicker fringe at the top. Hanging from the branches in sunny spots near her house, the raw material is dried and bleached. Before it is dried, she twists, crushes, and bruises the fiber to make it limp. A woman generally has a shorter work skirt, a couple of partially worn regular ones, and a new skirt in process of formation. There is no hurry or rush, for grass and leaves are gathered when convenient, and work progresses a bit at a time, so that the exact length of the process varies. New skirts have a pungent, hay odor and are greenish and clean. After a rainstorm or two, and a couple of weeks' wear, however, they become dirty, ragged, and full of insects. Ordinary skirts have little color, but at dances or other celebrations color is conspicuous. Years ago the natives made their own dyes, but they were supplanted by Japanese products which were easy to apply. A black cord hanging about the neck of a girl who has reached womanhood may be anything from a dyed strip of coconut fiber to an old typewriter ribbon. The cord, however, is essential for her full dress.

Nowadays men wear loincloths of cotton from a store. There is a basic cloth and another more concealing one worn outside, the color of which is socially significant. Beyond a certain stage of development a mass of bleached pandanus hangs loosely between the legs, suspended from the loincloth front and rear. When a man is dressed for an occasion, it is a fluffy white cluster of fiber.

The recreation of Yapese is largely in restful attitudes, for any diversion which involves physical exercise is not generally popular with natives who live near the equator. They like their traditional dances for their entertainment value as well as for their ceremonial etiquette. Village children swing from hibiscus fiber with a seat formed from the thick part of the stem of a coconut leaf. Women weave balls for children from strips of very young coconut leaves. A similar ball made from pandanus leaf would last longer, but the pandanus would have to be treated with salt water and dried, a longer process, not worth while from the maker's standpoint, since the child would probably lose the toy in a few days.

Native dancing in Yap is a highly developed art in which both men and women engage and in which the people take great pride. The two principal types of classical dances are the "sitting" dance and the "stick" dance. In the sitting dance, where movement of body and hands and fluttering fingers tell a story, the motions of the hands are very important. To the onlooker such a dance may at first seem monotonous, but close observation reveals that subtlety and economy of motion replace extravagant activity. In the stick dance, or *gamel*, the dancers move in intricate patterns to the beat of clashing bamboo sticks. The leaders of the dance, older people, are usually placed in the middle of the group, for age plays an important part in determining roles. The participants are successively younger from the middle toward each end of a line of dancers. Motions and sounds do not begin simultaneously, but proceed in wavelike patterns from the center to the ends. Leaders of a stick dance weave an intricate pattern from the center to each end of two lines of dancers, then back to the middle of the group.

Some of the dances describe long canoe voyages and conjure up events from the legendary past—periods of happiness or war and suffering. Others, introduced from distant islands, are accompanied by chants of words which no longer have any meaning.

At formal performances the dancers dress in brightly dyed grass skirts, wear headdresses of feathers, tinfoil, and palm leaves, and powder their bodies and faces thickly with orange-colored turmeric, called *reng* in Yapese. In order to be skillful, they require much practice, and begin two or three months ahead of time. Some dances belong to certain villages and may not be performed by others without permission. If the people of another village or of an island want to learn one of these, they seek permission from the original owners and pay for the privilege, generally in shell money or turmeric powder.

The Yapese observe many social customs which would be "uncivilized" in our way of living and some which apparently have little value for them. Cooking taro and other food is hedged about with ritual and procedures which have to do with the practice of segregating sexes and age groups in Yapese society. Women wear certain skirts only for cooking and cook the taro in special pots for various members of a family. Older women are forbidden to eat with younger members of their own sex. Adults of opposite sexes may not eat together from the same pot. Near some dwellings are several cookhouses or fireplaces, each covered with a thatch roof, where pots of food are prepared for the various members of a family.

When a girl reaches the age of puberty, she must eat only with her older sisters or with other young women and certainly not with her father. When a boy reaches the age of puberty he may no longer take food with his mother. A son may never put his hand into the pot from which his father takes food, but the father may take food from the pot to serve him.

The best-looking girl in a village and the most popular is chosen to have the honor—in her sense of values—of living for a time in the men's house. The girl is called a *mespil*, a term carrying an uncomplimentary connotation. Later on she will marry a distinguished young man with whom she has associated in the men's house.

A woman is at the peak of her beauty and desirability from about eighteen to twenty-three. She looks for a man who will give her things: fish, betel leaf, areca nuts and lime, fermented coconut toddy, and trinkets. If a young man likes a girl, he pays special attention to her and tries to arrange a private meeting. Should she consent, he brings an ample supply of betel leaf, areca nuts and lime and shares these with her while he makes conversation. At later meetings, which he may arrange by sending a child to tell the woman where he is waiting for her, he brings fish, coconut, yam or taro, and fermented coconut toddy, as well as the makings for the betel chew, and as before, shares these with her. There is an elaborate silent etiquette by which it can be known if the girl likes the boy, whether she will or will not consent to further intimacy than conversation, and whether future meetings may be broached or not. Her manner of tearing the betel leaf that is handed her is one sign; her tapping the boy's hand with the lime shaker is another.

The absence of marriage relationships between Japanese men and Yapese women was in part due to the fact that Yapese women were prohibited from marrying any foreigners, including Palauans, Trukese, and even men of the eastern islands with whom their own people had traditional ties. The same restriction has been observed in the case of Americans.

A divorced wife returns to her father's house and stays there a month or so, and then may go to live with another man. It is a recognized convention even if the new man has persuaded her to divorce her husband and come to live with him. If the husband knows that this has been the case, he is morally powerless to act and, if he is interested in retaliation, must find other grounds on which to take revenge. The divorced wife departs with her skirt, her basket, the few areca nuts and pepper leaves which she happens to have with her at the time, her lime shaker, and that is all.

Although there is considerable license between the sexes in Yap before marriage, a man and wife are expected to remain faithful to each other. According to the old Yapese code, a man who had relations with another's wife was punished by death at the hand of the aggrieved husband or his friends. On the other hand, among the natives of this primitive society, divorce is easy and common. The couple merely separate and the girl returns to her home. When they go to live with new partners that is sufficient indication of a new marriage. If a woman leaves her husband for any reason of her own choosing, he has no alternative to looking around for another companion.

Formal marriages are, however, affairs celebrated by feasts—especially weddings in high families. It is an inexorable rule that a young man must get the consent of the girl's parents. If the parents say "no" the courtship must cease. A parent will cut off a disobedient son without a portion of the family lands. A clever young physician in training, an intern in Colonia Hospital, who comes from a rich

Yapese family, fell in love with a nurse in the hospital who comes from a poor, low-caste family. He wants to marry her, but his parents will not let him, for they have chosen a girl from a rich family in his village. However, he is living with his sweetheart and they have a child.

Sometimes two families arrange the marriage of infants which is to take place when they come of age, a custom practiced in other parts of Micronesia. When a boy and girl are betrothed in childhood by arrangement of their parents, after the girl reaches the age of puberty she may not live in her father's house, nor can she be married for one year. At the wedding the girl's father presents the boy's father with some of the great pieces of stone money which helped to make "His Majesty O'Keefe" famous. The boy's father gives shell money to the girl's father.

Feasts signalize not only important marriages, but other significant events also. When the foundation of a house has been laid, there is a feast, and there is another when the house is finished. The completion of a new canoe, as was already mentioned, is similarly observed.

About 75 per cent of the Yapese are nominally Christians, nearly all Catholics. However, the native, animistic religion, with its priest-magicians, ghosts, and sacred places, still functions strongly, even among many of the converts to Christianity.

Rites propitiating spirits are important parts of Yapese religion. One day the author, in crossing a new, well-built stone causeway on the coast at tide level, saw coconut sprouts and betel-nut fronds laid carefully at intervals along each side. They were placed there as a protection for the future, to keep evil spirits from breaking it or causing it to be washed away.

On the way back from the causeway, our party met a native medicine man or priest, a wizened human being well tattooed and wearing a long beard. Medicine men cure illnesses with special herbs and have the power, so the Yapese believe, to invoke evil spirits. A long vine, *Derris trifoliata*, is a remedy for broken bones. It is cut off about four feet above the ground, pounded lightly, and then wrapped around the area of the fracture. For simple rash and swelling, the leaves of *Cassia alata* are bruised till the sap stands out on them. Then the mixture is rubbed on the irritated spot. For a fever with pain in the arms, chest, and legs, one can take the roots of *Premna integrifolia*, pare them, and squeeze them through coconut cloth into a betel-nut bowl. Coconut gratings are added and the mixture is taken internally. An additional medicine can be made by mixing with the above the scrapings from the inner side of the fruit of *Parinarium glaberrinum*. It is possible to cure eel bites by taking an even number of leaves from *Nephrolepis acuta*, pounding them, and squeezing them on the bite. An important circumstance of the cure is the fact that almost always a magical element enters into the treatment, which in the Yap mind is at least as important as the herbal applications, if not more so. Standard practice is to consult first a man who knows how to make the proper divining magic, and then to appeal to a magical being for a medicinal remedy.

There are a good many witch doctors in Yap who still have great influence over the people, inculcating and reinforcing superstitions and beliefs in good spirits and evil spirits. A strong belief in the supernatural makes the people adhere to old rites and rituals, and in part fear of punishment by evil spirits holds them in subjection to their chiefs. The medicine men cooperate closely with the chiefs, by whose favor they also enjoy considerable prestige and material goods.

Belief in evil spirits has helped to instill good moral practices—the prevention of stealing, for example. A thief knows that the loser will pray to the *monier* ghost or spirit to kill him, and fear of it is a good preventive. Stealing among the Yapese is considered a great crime against society, and fear of punishment by evil spirits is always a deterrent. People dare not enter an open door if they know a house is not occupied. Sometimes an occult sign, like the frond of a coconut twisted into a certain shape, is placed at or near a breadfruit tree or other valuable possession to warn a prospective thief of the evil spirit.

There is apparently no fear of evil spirits attached to excessive drinking of fermented liquid from the cut stem of the flower of the coconut. A visitor is offered *achif* at every native home. It has a sour taste, a bit like fermented apple cider. Eighteen hours after being drawn from the coconut palm, the liquid has undergone sufficient fermentation to acquire appreciable alcoholic strength. Because the bottles or coconut cups in which it is collected are not washed, they contain a quantity of the fermenting bacteria, which increase rapidly when the fresh sap is drawn into the container. Some of it is distilled to make a liqueur. The men say *achif* loosens their tongues at parties —like cocktails in America. Women serve it in moderate quantities at their social gatherings.

However, it is interesting and important to note that the Yapese
themselves have become conscious of the abuse of *achif*, for political
leaders have recently been candidates for office on "dry" or "wet"
platforms. Nearly all those with political ambitions have to commit
themselves on whether or not they favor Western clothes. Not long
ago a chief of Rumung District, who was a candidate for magistrate,
had his shaggy hair trimmed, and put on shorts and a shirt for his
campaign, but was defeated by a conservative vote. However, some
outstanding natives, like Fanechoor, men of ability, and personally
"progressive" (for Western clothes) and "dry," have won in conservative and "wet" municipalities.

GOVERNMENT

The natives have elected many of their hereditary chiefs as
magistrates, either because they like them or because their traditional
rulers are still so powerful that they are afraid to elect anyone else.
The Yap islands are divided into ten municipalities where magistrates are elected annually. The head of the administration meets
with the Council of Magistrates biweekly to discuss problems and
other matters concerning the welfare of the natives and to make
official announcements. In the eastern islands of the district, where
at present the superimposition of a similar type of municipal organization would be meaningless, hereditary chiefs are still recognized as
official representatives of their respective islands, and the welfare of
the people is taken up through them.

Sometimes the administration finds it difficult to get the cooperation of magistrates in work which is clearly in the native welfare.
Ranganibay, an influential chief in the Council of Magistrates, pre-
tends to be interested in Western manners. However, he is really a
conservative and in his district pushes very enthusiastically ceremonial
exchanges of the great circular stones and shell "money," and the
performance from time to time of the traditional dances of his
village. One of the more interesting cases of native backsliding is that
of Yilubuan of Taalaguw Village, who worked for years with the
Japanese administration and was married in a Roman Catholic
church. He is now an active magician who would prefer remaining
away from Colonia to wearing Western clothes.

For the government of Yap, the successful practice of medicine and proper deference for native customs and feelings constitute a delicate problem. The Japanese emphasized good medicine at the expense of custom but made little progress. The difficulty of the administration is to find the middle of the road. Native medicines, sometimes effective, are often nullified by magic and superstition. Promiscuity at an early age and abnormal sex practices thereafter have contributed to making men impotent and women sterile. Habits are irregular, drinking water is sometimes infected and, as was already mentioned, living quarters are unsanitary. Though considerable numbers of pregnant women come to the hospital for delivery for free service, many are still held back by tradition or prejudice. Infant mortality was as high as 80 per cent in Spanish times. In 1929 it was down to 39 per cent and in the thirties it fell to 15 per cent. At present it is 11 per cent. A survey has shown that about 97 per cent of the population has two or more species of worms, including hookworm (*Ancylostoma*). The increasing numbers of sick women and children who come to the hospital in Colonia indicate that the shrewd natives are beginning to accept modern medicine. If we are to summarize the historical picture of Yap medicine, it appears that, after the introduction of foreign diseases, the island probably suffered from the usual epidemics and from more chronic ailments, and experienced a far higher death rate. The history of the medical accomplishments by the Germans, Japanese, and Americans is one of gradually trying to gain the confidence of the majority of the people, and of alleviating the worst effects of these diseases.

In the field of medical research, as an aid to the correct evaluation of methods of improving the health of the natives, the continued need for caution and deference to Yap custom is a primary factor. Although native habits of living are unsanitary and the people do not always seek treatment which might help them, it is essential to make progress slowly.

The poor health of the Yapese in general does not apply to their teeth. An American dentist in the Trust Territory stated that the natives of Yap, the most conservative of the Micronesians, have the best teeth, in large part because they live chiefly on taro and fish which have a high calcium content. Both young and old are fond of chewing betel nut, which acts as a preservative, though the constant chewing with calcinated coral loosens the teeth after about fifteen years. Children of three or four years chew the nuts. Old people whose teeth are poor pound nuts to soften the fibers before stuffing them into their mouths. The natives take small pieces of coral and burn them to get the lime residue, which when crushed to the consistency of grains of salt is poured into a coconut shell made into a shaker. A chewer splits a betel nut in two, sprinkles a little powdered lime on it, then places it with a piece of betel-nut leaf inside his cheek, moving it from time to time between his teeth.

The Government of Yap has made most progress in matters of health and sanitation. The major causes of death among the Yapese are typical of those found among Pacific Islanders in general and include both chronic and epidemic infections. Tuberculosis has been and still is an important cause of death. Other chronic diseases are leprosy and intestinal parasites. An increase in birth rate in recent years is related to improvements in health, morale, and the Yapese way of life. Under the American administration the death rate has fallen by about 50 per cent. The crude birth rate has doubled. Health has improved and several social and cultural changes seem to have helped to raise fertility. The loosening of native etiquette at meal-times is encouraging women to have larger families. Mothers have been reluctant to have large families because of the extra work involved in feeding the children according to their custom of rank, social separations, and separation of the sexes. Their burdens of gardening and cooking are considerably increased as children grow older and belong to more than one age grade.

OUTLYING ATOLLS

The people of Yap or, more accurately speaking, the people of the Gagil District of Yap, traditionally have had complex economic, political, and religious relationships with the inhabitants of Ulithi atoll and a number of other atolls which are scattered eastward for eight hundred miles to islands near Truk. They are called by the Yapese "the East"—in their language Ngek—Islands. The chain of relationship extends from Gagil to Ulithi and on to Woleai. The lands of the Ngek Islands have been "owned" from time immemorial by certain families in three villages in the Gagil District. The affiliation with Yap is a sort of "parent-child, landlord-tenant" relationship, with the Yapese in the parent-landlord position. Although no rent is paid by the tenants of the atolls, substantial presents of food and other goods are exchanged with their landlords at regular intervals in a kind of formalized friendship. Before the more exacting requirements of this relationship weakened, large fleets of canoes made annual trips to Yap bearing tribute to the overlords, receiving in return even larger quantities of foods and other materials. Yapese load taro, chestnuts, bananas, and bamboo on the field-trip ship in Colonia as part of this exchange. In return they obtain from the outer islands pandanus sails, ceremonial loincloths, and other things. There are also conventions of reciprocal hospitality and other social observances between them and their neighboring islanders. The islanders share with the Yapese the worship of ancestral spirits and send regular offerings to the shrines of their "parent" lineages. The people of both Yap and Ulithi have a kind of ancestor worship in which ghosts play a large part in human affairs.

The early history of all the islands in this district is obscure. Yap and Ulithi were probably discovered by a Portuguese captain, Diego da Rocha, in 1526, and subsequently visited by Spaniards, English, and Germans. There is no information on how the whole system of relationships started. One theory is that the Yapese intruded upon the East Islands where they organized the natives and their land in such a way as to reflect their own caste system. The absence of lagoons on a few of the islands makes landing difficult during heavy surf. All of them are now visited on field trips about once every two months. Ulithi Atoll, one of the more important, was a staging center for the United States fleet during World War II. Some fifty miles southeast of Ulithi is Fais, where phosphate was at one time mined by the Japanese. All these islands together have a population of a little over two thousand.

Ulithians and Woleaians are in general lighter skinned and about the same height as the Yapese. They look more Polynesian than the latter. Many men wear loincloths made wholly from hibiscus or banana fiber. Girls, like the Yapese, wear short grass skirts until they reach womanhood, then change to longer hibiscus and banana "wrap arounds."

Ulithi's proximity to Yap accounts for its closeness politically, for its affinities in culture, language, and descent are with the atolls east of it and not with Yap. An annual voyage to the chief of Gagil is expected of the paramount chief of Ulithi to arrange about tribute, which consists principally of fine fiber textiles, mats, rope, and food.

Yap has maintained its influence over its satellites in part by the magic it wields. For instance, there are three special locations on Ulithi to which the chief of Gagil sends his magicians when he wishes to reward or punish the people there. The threat of typhoons, among other evils which Yap magicians were believed to wreak upon their enemies, was one means whereby the Yapese maintained control over the Ngek Islands, and many of the islanders still consider their traditional overlords endowed with such power. The author talked with a chief on Yap who was fined by the other chiefs in the islands for bringing on a typhoon! The relationship between Yap and the Ngek Islands permits visitors from them to receive certain benefits and hospitality as long as they remain on Yap. Many of them have relatives whom they wish to see, while others go because they want to get timber to make canoes and other things to take home. However, the people of Yap place such visitors under restriction by threatening that if they break certain taboos they will be punished by influenza, asthma, yaws, and other diseases.

The advent of the great powers has considerably altered the character of contact and transportation between Yap and Ulithi and the other islands of the native world. The greatest change took place in the second decade of this century, when long voyages in canoes were banned. The Japanese, alarmed at the downward trend in population and the great expense incurred in repatriating men lost at sea, forbade travel between islands distant from one another.

When opportunities for schooling were first made available to the natives of the Ngek Islands, the Yapese were annoyed, for, anxious to retain their superior position, they have viewed with displeasure the growing alienation of the Ulithians, and even now would like to hinder their advancement toward democratic ideas.

Christianity has been a powerful influence in freeing some of the satellites from fear of supernatural reprisals by the Yapese, for it has shorn them of the magic-religious influence formerly associated with these. Nearly all the Ulithians are Roman Catholics. But the natives of Satawal in the extreme east of these far-flung islands still adhere to their old religion. Unlike Yap, these outer islands have no sharp class distinctions. Chieftainships, however, are hereditary and held in well defined matrilineal lineages.

Since there are no Americans resident in the Ngek Islands, the people there are dependent on the bimonthly field trips for medical assistance and trading and communication with the outside world.

FUTURE

As for the future of Yap, it is in health and sanitation that the need for continuing Government assistance is greatest. Tuberculosis, leprosy, parasitic infestation, and skin diseases are major health problems. In the Tinian leprosarium, Yapese patients outnumber those of other ethnic groups in Micronesia. Even after sixty years of foreign government, few sanitary practices have become part of the native way of living. However, as was already indicated, there are some hopeful responses to the efforts of the present administration.

The future offers no food problems to the underpopulated islands. According to a nutrition specialist who visited Yap recently, the natives are eating a balanced diet which they have arrived at over many years of experience.

Copra and sometimes a little trochus shell will probably continue to be the only exports. Unlike the Palau Islands, Yap has been fortunate in remaining free of infestation by the ravaging rhinoceros beetle and the giant African snail. Close quarantine inspections will be necessary to maintain this freedom. The Yapese are well aware of the danger to their coconuts from the rhinoceros beetle and are thankful to the administration for whatever precautions are taken to prevent its entrance to the islands.

It is anticipated that with the increasing urbanization of Colonia and the further development of markets there, the problem of temporary land usufruct will be brought into sharp focus. At present almost no one pays cash rent, but as long as copra sales continue, and house sites at Colonia are at a premium, there will be increasing pressure for a clearer definition of landownership and tenant's rights than has been provided heretofore by undocumented custom.

The copra trade has led to abuses of the traditional usufruct privilege in regard to using land for subsistence. Individuals make and market copra from lands which technically are not their own, without giving the traditional owner any cash compensation. It generally occurs when the landlord and tenant are in some way related, since, according to the native code, kinsmen are expected to aid one another without strict regard to immediate repayment. Comparatively few instances of such abuses have been brought to the attention of the administration, partly because no legal precedent has been established, partly because of family pressure for loyalty, and partly because the exploited owner of the land still feels assured of his ultimate lien on the resources of the "lessee." However, this issue will probably arise with increasing frequency as long as there is a copra market.

A considerable amount of land near Colonia is leased by Kanif families where they have built temporary houses without any gardens or other productive land attached. These are the homes of individuals working in Colonia or of people with relatives in the hospital or in the intermediate school. They go back at intervals from their "town" houses to their villages to get food. Less than half of the population lives regularly in the home district. This pattern of town living is evolving slowly among people in nearly all districts in Yap. Government employment affords work for about 175 Yapese, mainly with Public Works and Public Health. Most of the employees live in villages near Colonia; the rest commute from a distance by boat or truck.

The system of landownership in Yap is well suited to the subsistence economy which prevails. Since through it the members of an "estate," working cooperatively if need be, take care of their own needs for food, clothes, and shelter, the institution makes for security. However, if smoother administration of land matters is to be achieved, a land registry is necessary which may be kept up to date without major overhaul. Ultimately a complete survey and registry of all land in Yap is desirable. Such a task, however, would take a long time and be very expensive. Until land disputes become a greater problem for local courts than they are at present, the solution of the program can be postponed without working serious hardship.

The registration and regulated recording of property holdings in Yap are bound to unearth "family skeletons" and unresolved land disputes. Most of these can be settled by local courts in line with native custom. Where native property concepts differ from those of American laws regarding property, there is need for the establishment of legal definitions and precedent.

Another source of conflict to be anticipated concerns the ownership of certain small plots of land in every village and district which are the possessions of chiefs, and which entitle the possessor to the hereditary position of chieftainship. As long as the Administration maintains the policy of recognizing, whenever possible, existing customary law, it must be sufficiently familiar with inheritance usages to be able to cope with disputes the settlement of which carries political implications. Ultimately the legal department of the Government will have to decide to what extent traditional rights and customs regarding land are to be respected. Since acculturation is inevitable, the Government will have to render the transition as painless and ordered as possible. This acculturation must evolve slowly, for a forced change would probably lead to a noncooperative negativism and the setting up of two systems of law in opposition to each other. A planned program, however, in which an effort is made to incorporate basic native usages into a functioning system would have the advantage of consistency and continuity in contrast to a policy of "muddling through."

Political aspects of the ties of the Yap people with those of Ngek are gradually ceasing to have any bearing on relationships between the two. Social distinctions have been increasingly relaxed, for visitors from Ngek commonly break food taboos without criticism from the Yapese. Since the sanctions invoked by such breaches are supernatural, and not social, the attitude of the Yapese is that the risk lies with the individual concerned. Christians of both groups now ignore such traditional food distinctions.

It would be best to let present trends follow their course with as little Government interference as possible. A slow break has many advantages, for it would permit new economic patterns to be worked out while schools and missions gradually alter values and beliefs. Notwithstanding the traditional ties that have been established between the Yapese and the Ngek people, it is the duty of the administration to see that the latter are not exploited by a few chiefs of Gagil for their own aggrandizement. No obstacles should interpose between the traditional nonmonetary exchanges of goods which, constituting needed products in both groups, are mutually profitable. Surveillance in this respect can be best accomplished only in the Gagil District and in Ulithi, the atoll most affected, since the people involved are not above altering their stories for their own profit.

Students from the Ngek Islands who want education at higher grade levels have to go to Koror in the Palau Islands where there is social discrimination against the "outlanders" by the sophisticated

Palauans. Both Yapese and Ulithians are acutely aware of the amused contempt of their neighbors in the west toward their less advanced culture. This, of course, irks the strangers. They also miss food which they were accustomed to eating in their own islands. It is easier for Ngek Islanders to procure native foodstuffs gratuitously in Colonia, and other districts in Yap, than to buy them in Koror. Colonia offers Ngek Islanders freedom of movement without the embarrassment of mixing with people whose language, customs, and social behavior are unfamiliar. As in Palau, the schools and churches of Colonia are centers for the dissemination of democratic ideas. It is thus possible for a young Ulithian in Colonia to absorb modern ideas, unfettered by traditional usages, and without feeling altogether isolated.

The process of acculturation will go on slowly in Yap as new ideas gradually evolve. At a recent ceremony attended by district chiefs and their retainers, as well as a representative body of the young people, a ceremonious exchange of shell "money" was made to seal a pact between two factions, one conservative, the other progressive. The agreement provided for such modifications in local custom and practice as the abolishment of numerous cooking pots for each age and sex group within a family unit; and abolition of the menstrual hut and of taboos forbidding girls to attend school under certain circumstances.

One of the changes stemming from American rule seems to be an emancipation of the young people. The elders complain that the young people will not pay attention to their counsel, and that drinking, thieving, and general lawbreaking are increasing. There is no doubt that the heads of families and chiefs are losing some of their former authority. That loss will be greater as the people progress toward self-government. Through the leadership of the younger generation, a program of political and social reform is taking shape on Yap. While Americans observe neutrality, the Yap people themselves are adopting new ideas and abandoning some of the old customs. The fact that the young men seem to be impatient with magical healing methods only indicates the extent to which native magic still predominates after years of the foreigner's religion. Its relation to that religion—to all intents and purposes Catholicism—is interesting. There are relatively few real conversions as yet, and only a few sophisticated natives fully understand the major points at issue. In an emergency, most people will revert to Yap magical practices. At

Christian funerals the rites of the Church performed by the priest are followed by the Yap funeral ceremony.

Native women will change their habits more slowly than the men, in part because men will discourage it. The Yapese woman, still a lady in her grass skirt, will go about her duties leisurely, sometimes thoughtfully, now and then haunted by the fear that someday Western civilization will catch up with her.

REFERENCES

Churchill, William, "The Peopling of Yap," *Bull. Amer. Geog. Soc.*, Vol. 43, No. 7, 1911, pp. 510-518.

Duncan, D. D., "Yap meets the Yanks," *Nat. Geog.*, Vol. 89, No. 3, March, 1946, pp. 364-372.

Hunt, E. E., N. R. Kidder, and D. M. Schneider, "The Depopulation of Yap," *Human Biology*, Vol. 26, No. 1, February, 1954, pp. 21-51.

Kim, D. Y., "Taro Culture as Practised by the Yapese," 14 pp., mimeographed (library of J. W. Coulter).

Klingman, L., and G. Green, *His Majesty O'Keefe* (New York: Scribner, 1950).

Lessa, W. A., "Ulithi and the Outer Native World," *American Anthropologist*, 52:1, 1950.

———, "The Place of Ulithi in the Yap Empire," *Human Organization*, 9:1, 1950.

Mahoney, Francis, "Present Relations Between Yap and Ngek Islands," 13 pp., mimeographed (library of J. W. Coulter).

———, "Yapese Land Ownership and Inheritance Customs," 25 pp., mimeographed (library of J. W. Coulter).

Price, Willard, "Hypodermics for a Dying Race," *Asia*, Vol. 36, No. 8, August, 1936, pp. 523-526.

———, "Mysterious Micronesia: Yap, Map, and Other Islands Under Japanese Mandate Are Museums of Primitive Man," *Nat. Geog.*, Vol. 69, No. 4, April, 1936, pp. 481-510.

Schneider, David M., et al., *The Micronesians of Yap and Their Depopulation*, Final Report of Peabody Museum Expedition, Harvard Univ., 1947-1949, CIMA Report No. 24.

United States Department of Commerce, Weather Bureau, "Local Climatological Data, Yap Island, Pacific, 1953."

United States Department of the Interior, "Trust Territory of the Pacific Islands, Yap District Statistical Report, 1954."

XI

Truk

DURING World War II the newspaper-reading public became very familiar with Truk, for it was the main Japanese naval and air base in the western Pacific, guarding against Allied approaches from the south to the mainland of Japan. The great lagoon constitutes the best fleet anchorage in that general area of the Pacific. About the busy little port of Moen today, broken cannons mounted on wheels are still seen; floating cranes rust offshore near the remains of wrecks sticking up out of the water with names in Japanese characters; cracked-up planes lie on abandoned runways partially covered with grass and weeds; electric generators, unused for years, stand in water dripping from the roofs of huge caverns hewn out of hillsides of solid rock. The Japanese had army and navy air bases on Dublon, Eten, Moen, Param, Satawan, and Puluwat, and troops and munitions on other islands as well. They had radio stations on Moen, Ulalu, and Uman; and military installations on all of them.

THE NATURAL SCENE

Truk, a group of high islands, 1,200 miles west of the Marshalls, includes the main islands administratively of Truk District, which also embraces a large number of low coral atolls within easy sailing distance of the principal island group.

The Truk Islands, about seven degrees north of the equator and approximately 151 degrees east of Greenwich, lie in a lagoon surrounded by a great barrier reef, 114 miles long. The reef, roughly triangular, protrudes above the water in about fifty places to form low islets. Some fourteen high volcanic islands and many more low coral-and-sand islets lie in the lagoon, and together have a total land area of about forty square miles.

Of the fourteen high volcanic islands, six range in area from one to thirteen square miles; the remainder are less than one square mile. The four largest are also the four highest. Winiipwot Peak on Tol is 1,480 feet, Tonachaw Peak on Moen, 1,233; Tolomen on Dublon, 1,163 feet; and Chukuchap Peak on Fefan, 1,026 feet. Of the many passes through the barrier reef—some of them narrow, shallow, and dangerous—Northeast Pass is the one most used today.

All of the larger islands have fringing reefs and nearly all of them have swamps between their sandy beaches and the high volcanic uplands. The swamps, belts of various widths parallel to the shores, are of great economic importance, for they are used for raising *cyrtosperma*, or giant taro, a valuable food crop.

Temperatures in the Truk Islands vary only slightly from season to season, somewhat more in the course of the day; it is generally 75° F in the early morning and 85° in the afternoon. Rainfall varies from island to island; Moen has 125 inches; lower islands, forty to fifty. As in all the islands in the tropics, the rainfall differs markedly from year to year. Even the drier season, January to March, is much drier in one year than in another.

Seasons are more identified with differences in rainfall and winds than with changes in temperature. The trades, from the northeast, are strongest from January to June; for the rest of the year, principally in the wetter months, winds are variable. During the season of heavy trade winds, fishing in the open sea is at a minimum.

Because of the hot, damp climate, clothing, books, and furniture become moldy very quickly. Fresh food spoils within a few days. Americans in the islands must put things out in the sunshine nearly every day to keep them dry. Hundred-watt electric bulbs are generally kept burning in clothes closets. The indigenous population, however, has very few possessions requiring such care.

Truk really consists of the deeply eroded summits of a group of volcanoes rising above the submarine Caroline plateau. The parent rock of the larger islands consists chiefly of basalt, volcanic agglomerates, and considerable ash. Terraces, cut by wave action during intermittent periods of submergence, and forming excellent level places for agriculture, were good runways for Japanese airplanes.

Vegetation reflects variations in topography, parent rock, soils, rainfall, and drainage. The high islands were once richly forested but most of the original cover has been destroyed by native agricultural practices. Small remnants of primeval stands are found on steep slopes above six hundred feet; below that, coconut palms and breadfruit trees are the dominant species. Patches of land, burned over intermittently for crops, are covered with tall grasses, shrubs, and weeds.

The low, outlying islands in the Truk District are representative coral atolls. Of those in the north, Namonuito, with almost the area of the Truk group, has only five small ones which are habitable. Four of the Hall atolls have people on them. Of the Mortlock group, southeast, and some others in that direction nearer Truk, eleven are inhabited. The natives of all of these islands have much in common with the Trukese.

THE PEOPLE AND THEIR HISTORY

The people of Truk District, approximately 16,500 in 1954, have a relatively homogeneous culture. Their total number is nearly a quarter of that in the Trust Territory; 70 per cent of them live in the Truk Islands. Their rapid increase in population in recent years is shown in the following table:

TABLE XIX

POPULATION OF TRUK DISTRICT, 1946–1954

YEAR	NUMBER
1946	14,032
1953	15,908
1954	16,500

Those in the high islands live in villages on low terraces, three to six feet above tidewater. On those islands village lands extend from

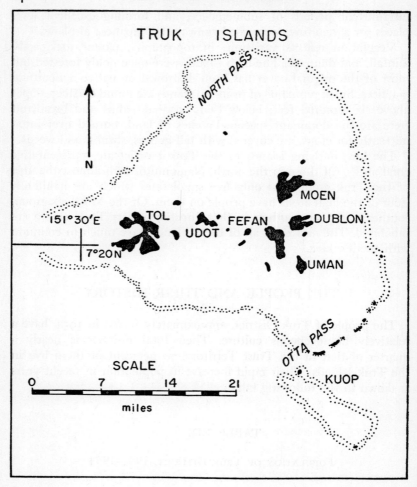

the sea up to the crest of the mountain, where they touch the lands of the village lying on the opposite coast. Villages in the coral atolls are generally on the lagoons, from which their lands stretch across the island to the ocean side. Some of the coral islands, Nama for example, are seriously overpopulated.

The contacts of the Trukese with foreigners over a period of many years, especially with the Japanese, have influenced them only to a small extent to assume modern ways of living. Men wear shirts and shorts, while women dress in cotton "Mother Hubbards." Shoes are not commonly worn, except for walking on the reefs. The people like rice and canned foods. Their traditional thatched houses have been abandoned for modern huts with galvanized-iron roofs.

Although discovered as early as 1565, Truk had no intimate contacts with Europeans until visited by whalers and explorers in the early nineteenth century. The first Christian mission was established in 1879. Spanish sovereignty over the islands, recognized in 1886, did not mean a great deal, for the natives were left much to themselves. Spain had other parts of her empire to think about. Actual administration by a foreign power did not begin until the Germans came, in 1899. They urged the indigenous population to produce copra, fish, and lumber for sale. They ordered each family to plant one hundred coconut palms; many laid out several times that number, and coconut trees became the dominant species for about two-thirds of the way up the slopes of the mountains.

During the Japanese régime, thousands of Okinawans and Koreans came to the larger islands, many of whom brought their families. Japanese also came from the main islands of Japan. Among the horde of newcomers were soldiers and sailors, farmers, fishermen, carpenters, teachers, government officials, and businessmen.

The Orientals encouraged the natives to produce more and more copra and fish and as much of their own food products as possible, for the Japanese also ate sweet potatoes and cassava. Some Trukese operated small stores; others had jobs with the administration. A small number were selected for training as teachers, health aides, carpenters, electricians, and mechanics. All important positions, however, were held by Japanese. Island chiefs and their councils, traditionally in charge of the government of the islands, had little power, except on the low coral islands, for, offering little opportunity for exploitation, they attracted few Japanese settlers.

World War II greatly affected the economy of the islands, but since Truk was by-passed by the American forces there was no great devastation. After the occupation of Saipan and Guam by the United States, the Japanese Navy was no longer able to supply the garrison on Truk; consequently, the 40,000 men stationed there had to become part-time farmers in order to stave off starvation. Japanese commanders, realizing that sweet potatoes and cassava yielded more food per acre than breadfruit and coconuts, ordered the destruction of large stands of those trees in order that the land might be used for the native products. These, raised successively in the same places, completely wore out the soil. Cattle and hogs were nearly all killed, and most of the chickens. The extensive destruction of coconut plantations caused the most serious damage to the economy, since, for years to come, it reduced the copra production to a fraction of what it was before the war. This great setback is still severe, inasmuch as copra is the only agricultural export commodity of importance.

Now, a decade after the war, other effects of the Japanese occupation have ceased to be significant except perhaps for three. First, the natives acquired a taste for rice, and though they will not do the exacting work required to raise it they buy it when they can. Second, on some islands they earn appreciable sums of money by collecting and selling scrap metal from military installations. Third, a very large number of natives are part-Japanese and, having more energy and initiative than the average pure blood, they tend to acquire the more important positions in business and government.

AGRICULTURE

The Trukese still carry on their agriculture in much the same way as missionaries tell us they did when they first came to the islands. The long bush knife and the digging stick are the usual farm implements. In spite of administrative pressure, most ground is cleared by burning. Although much is lost from the soil, there is plenty of land to rotate since the Japanese were taken off to their homeland.

People rely on the perennial breadfruit, which, though producing less food per acre than sweet potatoes and cassava, requires neither cultivation nor rotation; its fall of leaves enriches the soil to some extent and it also grows satisfactorily on steep slopes. Not the least of its virtues is that it keeps well stored in pits for times of food scarcity. There are scores of varieties of breadfruit in Truk.

The time of ripening, related to the seasons, is divided into three periods during each of which a group of varieties matures. The first is from the beginning of May to the middle of July, the second from the middle of May to the middle of August, and the third from the beginning of June to the middle of September. An interesting feature of many trees is that they again produce small crops in December and January. Even some of the heavily loaded trees bear buds which fruit in the "small" season.

As well as on the weather, the yield of breadfruit depends in part on elevation, location of the tree with reference to sunshine and shade, the soil, and the clearing of weeds from the ground underneath the tree and in its vicinity. The tree propagates itself by suckers which spring from the roots, beginning to bear at five years and continuing until it is fifty or sixty; the natives don't know just how long.

The author noted that everywhere on Uman Island men, women, and children were busy preserving their surplus breadfruit for the off season. The fruit is harvested with a pole of hibiscus wood ten feet long, to the small end of which is fastened at a sharp angle a small six- or seven-inch crosspiece. The V-shaped notch is pressed into the stem of the fruit and twisted to break it off to fall to the ground.

Pits of three sizes are dug with mangrove digging sticks or modern spades. The *nas*, the most common, is four feet in diameter and from three to four feet deep; the *choecho*, deep enough to stand a banana leaf in, is five to six feet deep and seven feet in diameter; the *nasenom*, "very big," is twelve feet in diameter and seven feet deep. The pits are lined with grass and then with banana leaves.

The fruit, scraped and cut up, is thrown in until the pit is filled nearly to the top. The top of the pile is covered with a thick layer of banana leaves and then with rocks to form a mound. The top layer of leaves is removed after three months and a new one substituted.

Breadfruit in pits will keep for one to two years. When the pit is opened, the objectionable odor of the fermented fruit becomes dissipated. When pieces of it, washed well with ocean water and then with fresh, are cooked, they are very palatable.

The Trukese recognize two qualities of breadfruit for preserving. The *marakach*, of lesser quality, is saved by the poorer class, who have few trees from which to pick. The *maredip* is good ripe breadfruit chosen from the many trees of wealthier families.

While not unimportant, coconuts play a less prominent role in native diet than they do on the coral atolls, where crops are much more restricted than on the basalt soils of high islands. Coconut milk, pressed out of the grated nut, is usually poured over cooked breadfruit and taro. Because the sale of copra enables Truk islanders to purchase rice, canned fish, and other imported goods, the coconut is of supreme importance. Bananas and giant taro are adjuncts to the main food supply. Wild arrowroot is sometimes dug in October when the plant has dried up. Cleaned, grated, and cooked, it is a delicacy for babies and sick people. In small gardens near their homes the Trukese raise sugar cane, pineapples, red peppers, and a few other vegetables, some of them introduced by the Japanese.

Since the land resources of the low coral islands are meager, and the practice of field rotation or shifting cultivation is not feasible, every square foot of land has to be utilized continuously. Plant refuse, returned to the soil, is applied especially to taro fields, located in natural depressions in or near the centers of the islands. On some, the natives have enlarged and deepened these depressions. Such expenditure of energy is, of course, not necessary on the volcanic islands.

Because little actual labor is involved either in getting food or in providing shelter for families, Trukese, like all the people of the Caroline Islands, have a good deal of leisure, and no inclination whatever to engage in continuous hard toil. Indeed, in the case of some shiftless and lazy members of their society, the chiefs occasionally have to insist on the cultivation of gardens and other lands so that families will be properly supported.

Natives tend to work in spurts and then loaf for several days. It is a very unusual young Trukese who, when hired by the Government or any other agency, will appear at duty regularly week after week. From time to time he is "ill," has some family business, or must take a day off to play baseball. Even for his food he often tends to rely on sharing that of a clan relative before he will work to obtain it for himself.

LAND TENURE

The native system of land tenure is very complex, as complex as that in American Samoa. A distinction is made between the right to cultivate soil and the right to partake of what grows on it. Titles to these rights differ in seniority as well as in type. By native traditional rights, a district chief had paramount claim to all the areas held by lineages or clans subject to him, a claim generally acquired by conquest. He collects tribute in the form of periodic gifts and first fruits. He formally opens and closes the all-important breadfruit season. Nowadays in Truk, the lands are identified as belonging to clans into which the Trukese are divided, but there are no records as to what tracts belong to which clan. Since the war only a few Japanese military maps have been found on which were marked grounds which their military forces planned to acquire. It is believed that all other maps and records were destroyed during the bombing of the atoll. The problem of the Government is to identify and return to the clans land taken from them by the Japanese without due compensation. There was never any division between chiefs and people as there was in Hawaii during the Great Mahele and on the island of Ponape during the German administration. Land which belonged to the Japanese Government is now, of course, the property of the American Government.

The inheritance of real property in Truk is traditionally matrilineal in principle, coming down on the mother's side of the house instead of the father's. The German administration attempted to make inheritance patrilineal as in their own country, the Japanese following suit. The natives, greatly resenting this violation of ancient custom, found various ways of evading the new laws. Americans now want to go back to the old native customary rights. The memory of the people, however, for their old property rights has been dimmed by a long period of foreign rule and there is considerable difference of opinion as to just what is the custom as it affects inheritance of land. The chiefs are the judges under the present administration, and a controversial piece of property may be owned by one man if one chief is the judge, and by another if another chief is to have the authority. The decision can be appealed to American justice, but there is no basis on which an American judge can give a ruling.

On the Polynesian islands of Nukuoro and Kapingamarangi, the native structure in regard to land tenure is different from that of the rest of the Eastern Carolines. There the title to land and property traditionally belongs to the "extended" family, as in the old days in Hawaii, and at present in American Samoa.

FISHING

While there are a great many fishing techniques among the Trukese most of which are known only to the men, the main contribution to this part of the diet comes from the women who fish mainly with hand nets in the offshore shallows and along the reefs. The author watched a large group of women of Tol Island fish with nets, forming a circle and then decreasing its size, sweeping the water with their nets until they came near together. The group cooperates to the extent of sharing the proceeds if one or several women make a large catch while the others in the circle are unsuccessful. Reef flats have many different kinds of shellfish, including clams, lobsters, and crabs, and also sea slugs, all of which are relatively easy for women to take.

Men fish with spears, throw nets, and seines in the lagoons, and occasionally, when the weather is calm, troll outside the barrier reef for bonito, barracuda, and mackerel.

SOCIAL LIFE AND INSTITUTIONS

Traditional ways still persist to a remarkable degree in Truk, especially the clan system, which pervades many aspects of life. It regulates marriage, channels hospitality, and is an insurance for its members against want. The chief of a clan administers its land, designating plots to be cultivated by its members, and supervises the economic activities of the group.

The members of two clans in a village are sometimes unfriendly toward each other, in some cases over a piece of land claimed by each; in others because a man in one clan stole the wife of a man in another; and not infrequently because their ancestors were bitter enemies and fought often.

The clans have totems, generally of different kinds of fish. The Fesilim clan has the *seui*, a fish which may not be eaten by members of the clan; the Sawr clan, a flat fish which may be eaten only under certain circumstances.

In the villages the houses of members of the same clan are generally grouped together. A Japanese type of house, somewhat smaller than the aboriginal dwelling, has supplanted the old thatched structures. The author measured the dimensions of Takeo's house in Lepol Village on Uman Island, a representative native home for Truk. It was a one-floor frame structure on posts two and a half feet high, with a galvanized-iron roof and no gutters. It measured nineteen feet long, seventeen wide, and eleven feet from the floor to the ridgepole. A veranda in front, under the same roof, was about twelve feet long and four feet wide, the entrance a sliding door at one end of the veranda. Inside was just one room with sliding windows at each end, five feet by five feet, protected by galvanized-iron awnings. In one corner of the room, two and a half feet from the floor, a recess six feet by three held pots, pans, and cups. There was no furniture, as we know it, only two small chests in one corner and a small roll of floor mats in another. There Takeo, his wife, and five children lived on the board floor in representative Trukese fashion.

A cookhouse, adjoining the cabin, was shared by a neighboring family, belonging to the same clan, the Fesilim. It was a lean-to with a roof of coconut thatch and a dirt floor where an open wood fire was burning between flat rocks arranged to hold the boiling pots on top. The ground oven is going out of use in Truk. The outhouse at the back stood on posts over tidewater.

At better houses rain water, caught from the roof in gutters, is carried to cisterns or barrels for drinking and washing. Much rain water, however, is caught from slanting tree trunks, at the bottoms of which just above the ground, pieces of bent tin or of banana leaves are placed around the trunk to channel the flow into a pot, pan, or other vessel.

The standard of living of the Trukese family is something like that in high islands in Micronesia in general: two meals a day, of breadfruit, sweet potatoes, taro and fish, depending in part on the season; occasionally coconuts, bananas, tapioca root, and pineapples to furnish variety.

Members of a clan share in joint enterprises like cutting copra, and sometimes share what in our society would be personal property like clothing and food. Sometimes a clan chief takes the wages earned from Americans and applies it for the common benefit, to help build a community house or a boat. Occasionally mandatory sharing imposes considerable strain upon the donor's goodwill, but refusals are rare and may precipitate crises, for they threaten the all-important solidarity of Trukese society.

One of the striking features of the mutual obligations of lineage or clan members is the widespread custom of adopting children, whether born in wedlock or out of wedlock, a common practice in many parts of Micronesia and in other parts of the Pacific.

The extent of time available for anything and everything has led to habits of tardiness common among natives in all parts of the

South Seas. If a meeting of chiefs is called for nine, some will come at ten, and if all are there by ten-thirty business will begin. Of course, no one has a watch; time is judged approximately by the position of the sun in the sky. If the subject for discussion is unpopular, early comers may become bored and go home before the meeting has begun. School meets when the teacher arrives, and if he is there first, pupils come in at a convenient break in their game.

Although all the people in Truk District are members of Christian churches, various activities are still surrounded by ancient religious customs and rituals. Ceremonial feasts during a harvest are founded on the belief that they safeguard future production and food supply.

The essential difference in dogma between Protestant and Catholic beliefs is little understood, and natives change readily from one church to the other. A Catholic who wants a divorce becomes a Protestant, or a Protestant marries a Catholic and joins his church. However, many do not go through the formalities of any proceedings of that nature. If a young woman becomes very dissatisfied with her husband, she goes home to her parents.

Like the natives of many other islands in the Pacific, the Trukese allow their adolescents considerable freedom in sexual matters, for they recognize that young people are preoccupied with sex. There is no stigma attached to young men and women who have sexual relations before marriage. Girls vie with each other for the attention of boys, wear combs in their hair, necklaces and bracelets and use much perfume. Both older women and girls like bright colored dresses. Many men on outer islands, away from district centers, allow their hair to grow four or five inches long and comb it to make it bushy. Most of the people of Truk have never worn a pair of shoes. After marriage, a couple is supposed to give up experimental amours and remain faithful. Adultery is then censured. In the Marshall Islands, where similar freedom is allowed among young people, older people who are church members sometimes fall from grace. In that case the elders meet and strike their names off the rolls. However, if they join the Christian Endeavor and are faithful for a year, they are received back again into the fold. "Otherwise," a missionary said to the author, "we would have no church members."

Truk is a center of "higher learning" in the Trust Territory. Besides its elementary schools, Truk has an intermediate school on Moen which selects the better students from the lower grades in the district.

It is a boarding-school for boys and girls, who are supported by parcels of breadfruit, taro, bananas, dried and salted tuna and barracuda sent at intervals by the parents of the students. The teachers are paid in part from a poll tax of two dollars a year on all men between eighteen and sixty years of age, and in part from an import tax on goods coming into the Trust Territory.

The Pacific Islands Central School, the highest educational institution in the Trust Territory, is also located in Truk, on Moen Island. It chooses the better students from the intermediate schools in the Territory to give them a general education. The manager of PICS generally buys rice, bread, and canned food for the students, since they come from a distance outside the practicable range of sending parcels.

The ages of children at elementary schools in the Trust Territory range from eight to fifteen, at intermediate schools from fifteen to seventeen, and at the Pacific Islands Central School from seventeen to nineteen. Graduates of PICS, with about the equivalent of a junior high-school education in the United States, are usually selected as teachers, nurses, clerks in district administrations, or in other capacities for the government. Nurses are given additional training in district hospitals.

The author visited a summer school of sanitation at Moen held for the first time in 1954. Some twenty teachers and sanitary inspectors from the various districts of the Trust Territory were taught principles of bacteriology, general sanitation, and something about communicable diseases and first aid. Today, tuberculosis is the most serious disease in the Truk District; other common ailments include influenza, skin diseases, and eye diseases. Almost no success has as yet been achieved in education about disease-carrying bacteria.

It is by island standards impracticable to keep flies off anything edible. The height of the breadfruit season is also the height of the fly season. Ripe fruit, fallen from the trees and decaying on the ground, attracts hordes of them. At every stop on a trail, the flies swarmed around the author and companions, alighting on bare arms, legs, and face. When a native chopped open the top of a coconut for a drink of the water, flies were on the opening of the nut first. As the author was a guest of a chief, the latter's daughter generally fanned away some of the insects during the meal.

GOVERNMENT

The Government of Truk is in a transition stage between traditional rule by chiefs and a semblance of democratic forms introduced by the American administration. On Uman, where there is an old and enlightened chief, an island congress had been instituted which at the time of the author's visit was one year old. Traditionally on that island there were the island chief, the village chiefs appointed by him, and a group of advisers to the high chief, including priests and other important people. The congress consists of the chief of the island, an elected congressman from each village, and one from each village appointed by the island chief. There is also a group of advisers to the chief of the island. This congress passes laws to be observed on that island. These are aside from laws which the highest chief is required to enforce for the American authorities. The hierarchical organization of Truk of preforeign rule days had become very autocratic because of the powers placed in the hands of chiefs under indirect rule. Among changes introduced by German and Japanese administrators was that of increasing the judicial authority of certain chiefs, empowering them to render summary decisions for offenses committed by members of villages other than their own. The people had little voice in governmental affairs, and, in part because of the language barrier, the situation has been more or less beyond the control of American administrators, who have had to depend on the higher native officials as interpreters.

Successive administrations—Spanish, German, Japanese, military, and civilian—each with its own policy and objectives, have given the chiefs much experience in dealing with foreign rulers. This experience the chiefs, even though somewhat confused by it all, can turn to their own advantage. Furthermore, now that the very large amount of land on Truk at their disposal gives them almost everything they really need, both chiefs and people can look with some objectivity on rules and regulations made by foreigners who know little of native life and institutions. Chief Tufele in American Samoa once said to the author that his greatest problem was to give a semblance of observance to Government regulations which the native way of living made it impossible to carry out.

In an attempt to let the Trukese commoners have some control over their government, secret elections have been introduced and supported as much as possible by the administration. However, so great is the traditional respect for native higher authorities, and so firmly established is the idea of hereditary succession, that the people find it difficult to vote for anyone but an incumbent chief, even if they admit privately that he is not a good man, or to offend him by voting against him, even if the ballot is secret. Village chiefs on Uman Island are always elected from the Fesilim clan, provided that a member of that clan lives in the village. The prestige of that organization, traditionally the bravest on the battlefield, has been accepted for so long that the people would not want to elect anyone from another clan. The Trukese cannot understand how the highest "chief" in the United States can have a humble origin, because, as they say, "That would not be possible on Truk." Sapota Village on Uman includes adult members of seven clans. Fesilim, however, is not represented, for it died out. However, the chief of Sapota, from the Mawch clan, is a traditional friend and ally of the Fesilim chief. The chief of Lebonolong Village is from the Sawr clan, traditionally the next bravest clan after the Fesilim. Regard for native authority, inculcated by chiefs, native priests, and medicine men from time immemorial, is difficult for Americans to understand; dealing with it requires background, study, and special experience.

On the various islands in Truk, local laws are made by the chiefs. When a new chief succeeds to power, new laws may be enforced. These, however, vary from one island to another. Someday the laws of the islands will have to be made uniform and codified.

The officials of each municipality or district in Truk are a magistrate, a secretary-treasurer, schoolteachers, and health aides. The magistrate is elected by the people or appointed by the Government or, if he is a chief, inherits his title. Of thirty-nine, twenty-seven are elected by the formality of a secret ballot.

One of the more important duties of a magistrate is to see that individual taxes are paid. Other taxes or fees imposed in Truk are for the privilege of operating stores, bakeries, restaurants, fishing boats and passenger boats between islands. A special tax on cigarettes is used in part to pay public elementary schoolteachers.

The American administration of the Truk District has an advisory committee of chiefs which discusses, among other things, ways to spend available funds in the best interest of Trukese, a valuable aid to the administration.

On Moen island, the site of District Administration Headquarters and the place of residence for nearly all the Americans, the natives are sophisticated and, more than those of other islands, have taken over a semblance of Western ways. The largest department store in the Trust Territory, at the port of Moen, is owned by the Trukese but has an American manager. It stocks very many of the things found in a similar store in continental United States. Near it are a motion-picture theater, a bakery, and a soft-drinks counter, backed by a row of quonset warehouses. At the wharf, Trukese arrive and depart in large Diesel-powered boats or native sailboats. Not far from a concrete mixer and a large scoop shovel, groups of men and women are sorting shell cases, cables, lead pipes, and various other kinds of military scrap metal.

THE FUTURE

The economic future of Truk lies largely in the improvement of subsistence agriculture, since there is a large amount of vacant land which can be used profitably for crops. At least 1,000 acres of land in Truk Atoll were overcropped during the war to get food for 30,000 Japanese soldiers, sailors, and civilians, as well as for the natives themselves. The worn-out lands will need careful treatment to restore them to prewar standards of production. The introduction of chemical fertilizer would be of assistance if the government can afford it. More taro could be raised on land which is suitable for it but is now neglected. Much vigilance will be necessary on the part of the Government agriculturists as well as by the Trukese themselves to check immediately any parasite or insect which might harm the breadfruit tree. The extension of coconut planting from seed selected by the agriculturists will help, if due regard is given to spacing the trees properly. More and better fishing is needed by the men, and improved methods by the women of salting and drying the catch from the reefs.

The main problem on the low coral islands is that of relieving the pressure of population, a problem which has arisen on various islands in Micronesia and in other parts of the Pacific. The natives of the

Pacific Islands take the Bible literally in regard to population as well as in other things. They believe they are "blessed" in having many children regardless of food problems. A Lutheran missionary on Truk came to the outlying Mortlock Islands as a bachelor, and sometime after went home to Germany to bring back a bride. When they did not have a child for two years, during that interval they were the subject of continual concern by the native congregation, who prayed aloud in church for their procreative efforts. Since the missionary's wife had not yet learned the language, she was spared embarrassment.

Overpopulation problems in the small coral atolls can be alleviated, temporarily at least, by colonizing the high volcanic islands with people from Nama and other low ones. However, those people are very loath to leave not only the spots that mean home to them but above all a group of people on whom they can depend in time of need. The land there belongs to their clans and to them only. They cannot conceive of any other lands which do not belong to people, whose permission they would need even to settle temporarily. The idea of land belonging to a government and available for "homesteading" is entirely alien. Furthermore, the way of living on low coral land is somewhat different from that in high islands, the main foods being different. The layout of the area also is not the same. These factors have to be taken into consideration in any solution of the problem. Laying out homesteads as in the United States would only complicate the problem. If the low islanders can be induced to move, they themselves will have to choose from available land and take the responsibility of using it as best they know how. They will have to be allowed to take their own social organization with them and establish a village and village life in the traditional manner.

The American administration will have to feel its way carefully and very intelligently in leading the Trukese to assume some kind of place in a modern world which as yet is far from their ken. The natives still await the day when Americans will come to their islands in the same force as the Japanese. They expect to be told what to do by a power at the top. A democracy in our sense of the word is at present inconceivable to them. They feel insecure under a policy which is trying to educate them to choose democratic ways of governmental procedures. The most notable element introduced by the

administration of the United States is the attempted replacement
of the old, hereditary chiefs by elected chiefs.

REFERENCES

Bridge, Josiah, "A Restudy of the Reported Occurrence of Schist on
Truk, Eastern Caroline Islands," *Pacific Science*, 2 (3): 216-222,
July, 1948.

Fisher, Ann, "The Role of the Trukese Mother and Its Effect on Child
Training," 1950, mimeographed.

Gladwin, Thomas, and S. B. Sarason, *Truk: Man in Paradise*, Viking
Fund Publications in Anthropology (New York: Wenner-Gren
Foundation for Anthropological Research, Inc., 1954), 655 pp.

Goodenough, W. H., "Premarital Freedom on Truk: Theory and
Practice," *American Anthropology*, 51 (4): 615-620 (1949).

———, *Property, Kin and Community on Truk* (New Haven: Yale
University Publications in Anthropology No. 46, 1951).

Gulliver, Louis J., "Truk in the Carolines," *U.S. Naval Institute Proceedings*, 69: 1557-1558 (1943).

Murdoch, G. P., and W. H. Goodenough, "Social Organization of
Truk," *Southwestern Journal of Anthropology*, 3 (4), 1947.

Pelzer, K. J., "Agriculture in the Truk Islands," *Foreign Agriculture*,
11 (6): 74-81 (1947).

———, and E. T. Hall, Economic and Human Resources—Truk
Islands, U.S. Commercial Co., Economic Survey of Micronesia, 1947
(typescript).

Taylor, J. L., "The Truk District," Dept. Educ. Truk District, 90 pp.,
mimeographed.

United States Department of Commerce, Weather Bureau, "Local
Climatological Data, Truk, Eastern Caroline Islands, 1953."

XII

Ponape

Ponape appears in the distance from an airplane first as a high mass of land with an outlying smaller piece to the south. Nearer, the smaller area takes the general shape of a coral atoll, the Ant Islands. Close to the main island an islet is conspicuous where coconut palms are laid out in regular rows. Inside the barrier reef which surrounds the fringe of water about Ponape little islands of various dimensions are scattered irregularly. The main island is indented by deep bays and smaller inlets. Close up, the mountains are rugged, and a settlement on Jokaj Island comes into view. The pontoons emerge from their nests as the plane circles for a lower approach to make a water landing. There is a great splash and forward motion and then the waves surge above the windows. When the wheels are lowered into the water, the plane wades ashore like a giant bird and, on reaching the beach, turns around to disembark the passengers. A boat takes them to Colonia (Ponape), the most important settlement on the island.

Ponape, the highest island in the Carolines, roundish and 145 square miles in extent, is the third largest land area in Micronesia. Discovered in 1595 by the Spanish Admiral Álvaro de Mendaña, it lies at 7 degrees north latitude and 158 degrees east longitude. West and south of Honolulu by 3,700 miles, it is on the other side of the international date line.

The island rises from the Pacific Ocean to an elevation of 2,579 feet, which is one of the higher elevations in the Carolines. The topography is a complicated system of ridges and valleys, interlaced with small rivers and intermittent streams, and covered with tall

261

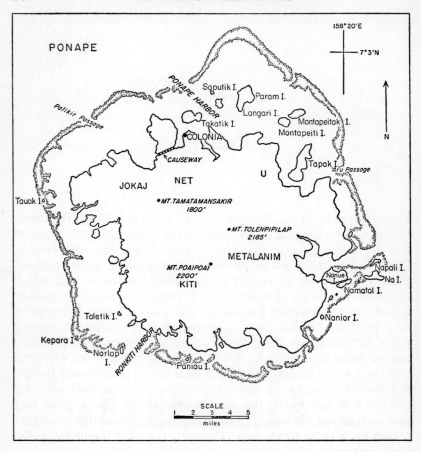

grasses, tropical trees, flowers, and coconut palms which are the backbone of the island's one-crop economy.

The rocks consist of basalt, andesite, and other dark, volcanic materials, with smaller amounts of coarse volcanic breccia, fine tuff, and consolidated fragments produced by explosive eruptions. Many peaks are 200 feet or more, Mount Ninani, 2,595 feet, the highest. There are bold cliffs of columnar traprock, particularly on Jokaj in the north. The lower slopes and level areas consist largely of sand and gravel of water-worn volcanic fragments. Of some twenty-five small islands nearby, half are volcanic. Ponape and the atolls of Ant and Pakin have been called the Senyavin Islands, and are still so marked on some maps.

Climate records show an annual average temperature of 80° F, a humidity of 86 per cent, and rainfall near the coast of about 180 inches a year. The interior of the island, where an estimated 350 inches of rain fall annually, is forest covered. The heavy rainfall on

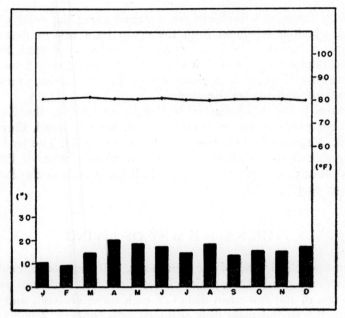

Rainfall and temperature in Ponape

Ponape is an outstanding characteristic of its climate. As well as convectional rains of the usual tropical type, there are rains when the winds blowing from the ocean up over the mountain are cooled and the moisture in them condenses. Usually heavy showers fall in the morning before daybreak, and again in the early afternoon, but frequently it rains most of the day. The humidity is especially high during the early hours of the morning, when the chill resulting from radiation condenses the water vapor in the air into a heavy fog. At that time, with heavy showers besides, the atmosphere reaches the point of maximum saturation, and sleepers wake to find their clothes and bedding damp.

The natives are conveniently divided into two main types: pure Ponapeans—that is to say, those whose ancestry shows no mixture; and mixed, the great majority of whom are part Ponapean and part Japanese. As well as their native language, today many Ponapeans speak Japanese; only a few older people remember German or Spanish.

Native farms and dwellings are scattered along the coast of the island, which is separated from the ocean by a belt of mangrove swamps, a narrow lagoon and encircling reef. The rugged, mountainous interior, uninhabited, is visited by Ponapeans only from time to time for wild foods to supplement their diet. Breadfruit, yams, and a variety of seafoods are the staples.

Ponape is the headquarters of Ponape District in the Eastern Carolines which comprises Ponape Island, Kusaie, Mokil, Pingelap, Ngatik, Nukuoro, and Greenwich (Kapingamarangi). The land area of the district is 216 square miles. The total population of Ponape Island in 1954 was 7,885, and that of all the islands in the Ponape District, 12,327.

THE NATIVE WAY OF LIVING

The traditional food of the Ponapeans, still the most important, can be grouped into three major classes: breadfruit and yams, which form one of the two main dishes of each meal; coconut, and chili pepper, the second main dish, seasoned with turmeric, lemons, and certain leaves and vines; and wild and cultivated fruits and nuts, which are eaten in small amounts and only occasionally.

Breadfruit and yams, the chief starches, need abundant fertile soil. Coconuts, taro, arrowroot, pandanus, and other staples of coral atolls have been relegated to secondary or minor positions. Breadfruit, also important on the little neighboring islands, is generally associated with the rainiest seasons, and is most plentiful in July and August; yams, associated with the trade winds, are harvested in greatest numbers in December and January. However, yams and breadfruit are eaten at the same time during a large part of the year.

Indeed, Ponapeans eat fresh breadfruit and yams, particularly the latter, meal after meal, day after day.

These islanders have seldom experienced serious shortages of food, for preserved breadfruit and yams, neither of which are destroyed by the tropical storms of the Pacific, constitute effective insurance against famine. Typhoons, which wipe out a year's crop of growing bread-fruit, bringing starvation to neighboring atolls, have little effect on the food supply of Ponape; there the traditional famine fare of the Pacific is relatively unimportant.

The pre-European type of government of the island also functions today. Ponape is divided into five districts: U, Kiti, Net, Jokaj, and Metalanim. The main town, Colonia, located in Net, is the seat of the District Civil Administration headquarters. The five districts, called "municipalities" in American administrative procedures, have 120 *kousapw*, or sections. There are approximately 1,000 *pehensapw*, homesteads or farming units, on the island. Each of the five districts of Ponape has two ranking chiefs, *nanmarki* and *naniken*; the sections within the districts are similarly organized politically.

The *nanmarki* (*nahnmwarki*) is the hereditary chief, the Number One man of each district. Material benefits accrue to him as well as the prestige attached to his office, for the people of his district are obliged to take him tribute of the "first fruits" of the land.

The *naniken* (*nahnken*) might be thought of as the "talking chief" —to borrow a term used in Samoa. A man of high ability and con-siderable prestige and authority, in some ways he may be compared to the old Hebrew prophet who could talk up to the king. The *naniken* makes most of the practical decisions and promotions, theoretically in consultation with the *nanmarki*. Sometimes if they cannot reach an understanding, the priests are called in and they render judgment according to omens and oracles. Taboos, or prohibitions, are imposed by the higher chiefs in cooperation with the priests.

In addition to the royal *nanmarki* and the *naniken*, there are many other titles: priestly, titles of address, titles for women, and honor-ific forms. They relate to genealogy, to the prowess of ancestors in battle, to prowess of ancestors in their district, to village, to occupa-tions as fishermen, boat builders, and what not.

Titles created and still create a kind of governmental organization of a high political and social nature. A system of graded positions evolved during the period when Ponape was governed by chiefs who lived at Nan Madol, the old Capital. Sometimes the hereditary right of a man with a title to assume the highest rank, *nanmarki*, is disputed by another who believes that he should succeed instead. Considerable ill feeling is aroused and the case has to be finally decided by the native code of tradition and hereditary precedence in a court presided over by an American judge who works hard to understand the native mind.

Under aboriginal conditions, the political structure of Ponape, closely integrated with the native system of land tenure and the prevalent form of social organization, was very complex. The political boundaries cut the island like a pie, so that each district today includes sections of the forest and mountains, the foreland, and the shore. The residents of a district belong to different matrilineal clans, and, generally speaking, each of the clans of Ponape is represented in each district. Traditionally in a sharp class differentiation, at the bottom were the commoners who did all the manual labor and tilled the soil, and at the top the aristocrats who owned the land and managed its use. Within each district the members of two particular clans always constituted the aristocracy. In the Metalanim district, for example, the upper class was composed of the members of the Tip en pan and Tip en nai clans, while the lower class comprised the members of all the other clans represented in the district. The prestige enjoyed by the two dominant clans in Metalanim, however, did not extend to members of the same clans living in other districts; there they were commoners, and the aristocracy were members of different clans.

A very high degree of architectural skill was exhibited by the ancient chiefs of Ponape in Nan Madol, in Metalanim, a group of over one hundred semiartificial islands off the southeast corner of Ponape. Here are some of the more famous examples of aboriginal architecture in that part of the world, unusual in that the walls are constructed of long pieces of columnar basalt. Though undoubtedly built before European ships reached Ponape, these ruins do not seem to date from great antiquity, but rather appear to be the work of the not too remote ancestors of the current inhabitants who, in a period of power and glory, took advantage of the building materials to exercise their imagination within the local tradition of architecture, politics, and religion.

Today the native community house, with none of the splendor of the past, is an unimposing thatched structure with platforms on three sides, the rear left open. The central ground-level area is where the kava is pounded for the ceremonial drink and where stone ovens are set up. The main, front platform, where the chiefs and people with high titles sit, is higher than the two side platforms and in some community houses is stepped.

Within relatively recent times, the chiefs reorganized the government of the island, subdividing Ponape into a number of small, independent political units. They preserved an ancient pattern of intermarrying lineages through which they retained within their immediate families their prerogatives as chiefs and their attendant wealth. The ultimate title to all land was originally vested in district chiefs who received from the commoners, in return for its use, tribute in the form of first fruits, feasts, and free labor. Political power generally passed from father to son and on to grandson. Inheritance was, however, matrilineal, and a man inherited only the right to work for a high title. Actual appointment to it often did not come until after long years of service and loyalty to the ruling chief.

Traditionally there were about forty clans on Ponape each with its war chief as well as a high chief by lineage. When the missionaries arrived there were about twenty. Blood feuds between clans, socially approved, were permitted to continue until the chiefs decided that the guilty had been punished. Clans were, in fact, allowed by society to act as an instrument of justice. They were generally formed into federations by districts to fight against the tribes of other districts with slings, wooden swords, and clubs. Intermarriage has now scattered members of the various clans about the coast, the only part of the island which is inhabited. But the people still know the names of their ancestral clans and who are their relatives in it. As on Truk, the clans had fish totems, and it was forbidden for a clan member to catch a species which represented his clan. At Metalanim eels are still neither taken nor eaten, for an eel was the totem of an important clan there.

The chiefs more highly respected today are those who know accurately the genealogy of their own families. The nephew of the high chief of Metalanim District told the author his genealogy as far back as ten ancestors. "I had to learn it when a boy," he said. Chiefs keep their family lineage secret in their families. No one, for example, knows the Ponapean name of Paul, the first chief converted to Christianity. This bent toward secrecy may be partly responsible for the fact that Ponapeans even now believe that the man who tells everything he knows will die!

An outstanding feature of the Ponapean way of living is the cult of yams, still carried on in an important way. Besides being a major source of food, the yam is raised traditionally for prestige, for the man who grows the biggest and best yam in a season is socially "king" in his village. There are one hundred varieties of yams, long and thin, or short and thick. Some commonly attain six feet in length and six to eight inches in diameter.

A careful farmer, by selecting the proper proportions of early and late varieties and choosing the time for planting, can have yams for feasts at any time, although it may be necessary to use some before they have grown to full size. Only the best yams are saved for feasts. Their social importance is reflected in the skill and care used in growing them, and also in the interest in their varieties and their characteristics and histories. Most of the current varieties date from the pre-Spanish rule. Ponapeans were eager to experiment with new species from other Pacific islands and from South America which they obtained from early whaling and trading vessels, and especially with those brought back by Ponapeans who visited New Guinea. The best and largest yams are grown in concealed areas, some of them far away from the house of the owner, and heavily overgrown with bush.

In Wiapil Valley far in the interior of the island the vines of yams can sometimes be seen up and over breadfruit trees. The natives do all they can to prevent a foreigner from knowing how to plant, fertilize, and cultivate them. Whereas fertilizer is used for taro throughout most of Micronesia, on Ponape it is used solely in growing yams. Very large yams, such as are desired in competition, can be produced only by selecting a good variety, good soil in a favorable location, the correct time for planting and harvesting, and in addition by digging very large holes, preparing them correctly with alternating layers of earth and leaves or grass, using large enough cuttings, trimming and training the vines properly, and protecting them effectively from pigs, cows, and other animals.

A piece of the tuber with an eye in it, the seed to be propagated, is made ready for planting at the top of a hole dug in the ground with a digging stick, now a crowbar-like piece of Japanese scrap metal. Shaped to fit the variety to be grown, the excavation is about three feet in diameter and five or six feet deep. Three or four holes are sometimes made around a breadfruit tree, and the excavated soil is piled up alongside. After the slip has been planted approximately on a level with the ground, the soil, from which the rocks have been removed, is scooped back to refill the hole. A low wall, echeloned toward the center, is built around the hole to protect the plant from pigs, chickens, and snails. Sticks are placed near together on the top of the wall. When the yam starts to come through, some of the sticks are removed to give the leaves and vine more room. Cultivation is shrouded in secrecy, each man tending his individual plants before sunrise. The yam grows up the breadfruit tree, twining around it. Although it reaches maturity in eight or nine months, some plants, allowed to grow for several seasons, attain weights of from 200 to 250 pounds. The biggest yam a man raises is saved for the great annual festival at which it is presented with great ceremony to the chief, who keeps it for his own use. The man who contributes the most yams for a feast is also greatly respected, a regard which is, of course, encouraged by the chiefs.

"What do the Ponapeans do for the man who raises the biggest yam?" the author asked a chief's son. "He is just famous," was the reply. Each district section chief watches to see which men consistently bring the largest yams, and chooses them to fill titles which are vacant, or, if they already have a title, promotes them to a higher one. It is the size of an individual yam, and not the quantity of yams, that is the more important. A man cannot win much prestige by bringing a large number of small yams to a feast. Each yam, furthermore, must have only a single vine, even if it grew from only a single cutting; otherwise it is regarded as several yams.

The high point of the feast comes when the chief makes a speech eulogizing the man who presented the biggest yam. If he is a man with a low title, the higher one is conferred upon him, called in a loud voice, a distinction which he prizes more than anything else.

Success in prestige competition is regarded as evidence not only of a man's ability, industry, and generosity, but also of his love and respect for his superiors. The latter, in the eyes of the high chiefs who appoint and promote those beneath them, is very important as a qualification for holding a title. Devotion to the chiefs may be shown in other ways as well, but the accepted pattern through which it is formally expressed is by giving feasts in honor of the chiefs and by contributing large yams and sometimes preserved breadfruit. Each head of a household contributes a yam, in addition to other food, when a feast is held. All who are present examine and compare the yams as they are brought into the feast house, and praise the largest yam for its size and quality. They go up to the man who, in their estimation, brought the biggest and best yam to tell him that he is "Number One," and to commend him for his skill and ability as a farmer; finally the chief praises him for his generosity.

Contributions of prestige foods to feasts are arbitrary as measures of generosity, in terms of which they are judged by the chiefs. They are, however, related to an individual's skill in farming, to his industry, and to his ability to produce more food than he requires for subsistence.

No large feast can be celebrated without kava and one or more pigs. The prestige earned by the host through giving a feast is related to the number of pigs and kava plants which he provides, the size of the pigs, and the length of their tusks. Preserved breadfruit, an important contribution, is not as commonly presented at feasts as yams, which are always the basis of active and continuing prestige competition.

THE SPANISH OCCUPATION

Ponape's commercial economy relates to the commodities produced for export and sold to obtain money with which to purchase clothing, hardware, and a variety of imported goods for which Ponape has become dependent upon the outside world since contact. The island has had many contacts with foreigners, for as early as 1826 to 1886 American whaling ships visited it, especially in the 1850's. By the 1870's there were on Ponape trading stations of three German firms, which were combined in 1887 to form the Jaluit Company. Copra, first sold to German trading vessels in the 1860's, remained Ponape's principal export until the outbreak of World War II. Ponape, like most of Micronesia, has experienced the vicissitudes of four foreign rules. On July 27, 1886, the Spanish flag was raised on Ponape when a warship called to claim the island. On March 13, 1887, Spanish officials, fifty Philippine soldiers, twenty-five convict laborers, and six Capuchin priests arrived to set up an administration. Within five days the Spanish priests established a Catholic mission in Kiti District, then a stronghold of American Protestants. The work of building the town of Colonia (Colony) was begun, for which American mission property in this area was taken by the Spanish Government as a site for the administrative settlement.

The Spanish period was marked by Catholic-Protestant rivalry, which broke out into serious wars between Ponapeans and Government troops and ended with the expulsion of the American missionaries in 1890.

On July 1, 1887, less than four months after the arrival of the Spaniards, the people of Net and Sokas (Jokaj) districts massacred a detachment of soldiers. They captured Colonia and slaughtered fifty-eight of its defenders, including the Spanish governor.

Two years of peace followed, during which the Spaniards built and fortified Colonia, began roads to Kiti, Metalanim, and U districts, and established Catholic missions alongside the Protestant mission headquarters.

THE GERMANS

The short-lived régime of Germany was marked by a period of economic improvement in the island, including extensive road building. The Germans accomplished a great deal in view of the fact that there were only five on the island, by securing the cooperation of the chiefs in supreme power to make the people work. Much of their business was done with the *naniken*. They introduced new and better varieties of coconuts from other islands in the Pacific, also cacao, rubber, Manila hemp, varieties of limes, and many other plants both for food and for ornament. A German district governor, Fritz, imported ducks and geese and guinea fowl, providing a new source of meat and eggs for the natives. In their great program of road building, including a road to Metalanim, to Kiti, and around Jokaj, they placed the routes on good sites, up above the ocean and commanding an extensive view; and they built bridges and constructed piers at Colonia. But their harsh methods of forced labor caused considerable dissatisfaction which gathered momentum. Ponapeans, encouraged by Japanese smugglers, did not want to finish the road from Ronkiti south of Jokaj, but the Germans were bent on pushing a strategic route from Colonia to and around Jokaj Island, the high top of which commanded Colonia Harbor. The man in charge of the construction of the causeway to Jokaj Island was from Urundi, former German East Africa, where the natives were very harshly treated. He had a Ponapean flogged almost to death for not working satisfactorily. His companions thereupon shot the German overseer, and, when the German governor arrived on the scene, they shot him also.

The guilty native may have been lying down, or perhaps did not show up for work. The gun may not have been fired with intent to kill, or perhaps a small incident resulted in the murder. At any rate the murder was the starting point for a clan war. In their open resistance to foreigners, this Ponapean outbreak of violence followed the pattern of clan vengeance. Ponapeans, taught not only to love their clan members but also to come to their aid in time of need, rallied to revenge the victim of the beating. Members of traditionally hostile clans sided with the German Government. Warships arrived to land marines who drove the natives from one place to another along the coast, and finally to Mant Island, where the last of them surrendered. The tree in Colonia under which half a dozen of the rebels were publicly shot still stands. Others indicted for any connection with the uprising were banished to the Palau Islands, the most westerly group in Micronesia. Some of them were returned later by the Japanese. Natives from Mokil, Pingelap, Ngatik, and other islands were settled on the lands of the banished Ponapeans to which they were given registered titles.

The year 1912 was the beginning of a new epoch in landholdings for the Ponapeans. The Germans and the high chiefs, after many conferences, decided that the land on the island should be divided between the chiefs and the people and that each family should have a piece of property registered in its name. The chiefs, of course, got the larger shares, but everyone had enough to live comfortably by native standards. The area in the mountains, little used by anyone, was also given to the chiefs, and the boundaries between districts, from the shore to the tops of the mountains, were carefully marked. Thus the Ponapeans passed from a feudal landholding system, by which from time immemorial the chiefs were the sole owners, to a system of private ownership.

In return for receiving titles to their lands, it was stipulated, by a written agreement, that the people were to continue to raise yams and other produce to do honor to the chiefs at the annual feasts of homage. This agreement is still observed today. However, the number of required feasts for the chiefs was restricted by the Government to one a year; but the intermediate feasts, which were voluntary and the most common occasions of prestige competition, were not restricted.

The Germans were very punctual in the arrivals and departures of what few ships they had in the Pacific, often arriving to load copra a day before the scheduled date, for they had to be back at Hong Kong and other Pacific ports on time, to tranship it to larger vessels taking it to Europe. Traders complain of the undependable schedule of freight ships today.

Although Ponape was the last stop before Rabaul, the capital of the largest German colony in the Pacific, few Germans ever lived on the island. The five members of their Government, permanently in residence, were there because of the business in copra.

The economic life during the Spanish and German periods was dominated by the Jaluit Company, which handled three-fourths of the copra exports from the Eastern Carolines. The free feasts which they gave from time to time when a German warship visited Colonia Harbor are still talked about by Ponapeans who remember the régime. On the Kaiser's birthday there was generally a three-day feast for the natives at the expense of the Germans.

The Germans had ambitious plans for Ponape; among others they wanted to make it a vacation resort for people from the disease-infested islands of the southwest Pacific which they governed. They had a good hospital in Colonia. Those who remember this administration say that it is difficult to find anything that the Germans did that can be criticized.

JAPANESE RULE

The Ponapeans at the beginning of the Japanese occupation, in 1914, were largely carrying on the same customs and traditions observed from time immemorial. Japanese companies had operated on Ponape as early as 1893, and, after having been barred by the German

Government in 1901 for selling firearms and liquor to the natives, two Japanese companies reappeared in 1905. In 1906 these two companies amalgamated to form "Nambo," or the South Seas Trading Company (Nanyo Boeki Kaisha), which offered increasingly serious competition to the Jaluit Company until the end of the German rule.

For ten years after they assumed charge in Ponape as in the rest of Micronesia, the Japanese left the natives much to themselves. But with Japan's plan for military expansion, there arose a direct interest in the islands—in developing them economically, colonizing them, and arming them. The Japanese then purposefully encouraged a part-Japanese native population. Part-native children went to Japanese schools and they could own land. All four daughters of the chief of Kiti married Japanese.

By 1939 the 5,905 native inhabitants were outnumbered by the Japanese, and by 1945, at the time when all the Japanese were evacuated by the American Navy, there were 14,066 Japanese on Ponape, of whom nearly 8,000 were military personnel. The combined policies of colonization and militarization saw the native population decline from 90 per cent of the total to 30 per cent within fifteen years, 1930 to 1945.

Five of the six varieties of cassava on Ponape were introduced during the Japanese period. During the war large quantities of both sweet potatoes and cassava were grown by the Japanese, as a result of which the popularity of these foods increased. Low flat lands were used to produce large quantities of rice.

All unoccupied areas which had originally belonged to the chiefs and had been made district property under German law were declared the property of the Japanese administration. The Japanese called in the deeds issued by the Germans and struck out the article which provided that all land for which no titles had been issued belonged to the district, and which also stated that any Ponapean who wished to take part of it as his own could do so with the consent of the district chief and the governor. The amount of land the Japanese seized on Ponape was restricted only by the fact that they did not dare to confiscate an area for which the owner could show a registered title.

Under the Japanese native feasts were encouraged and all forms of feasting seem to have flourished until the war.

Following the evacuation of all Germans by the Japanese, the Protestant Mission was taken over by Japanese Congregationalists of the South Seas Mission (Nanyo Dendo Dan) in 1920, and Spanish Jesuits were made responsible for the Roman Catholic inhabitants in 1921. The Catholic Germans were repatriated. A Japanese Christian minister was brought in for the Protestant Church and Spanish priests for the Catholic Mission. Most of the Spanish priests are still in the mission.

All German traders, interned in 1914 and later evacuated with the German missionaries, and other foreign concerns were effectively discouraged by the Japanese. Trade was completely dominated by Nambo until the appearance of "Kohatsu," or the South Seas Development Company (Nanyo Kohatsu Kabushiki Kaisha), which controlled the sugar industry on Saipan. One of Kohatsu's subsidiaries established bonito fishing and ice production, and smaller Japanese companies exported lumber, fibers, tannin, and drugs, and operated a hydroelectric plant, sawmills, a paper factory, bonito fisheries, and other enterprises.

Japanese colonists, Japanese enterprises, and Japanese plantations required land. In 1931 the regulations were revised to permit the sale, lease, and mortgage of native lands, which had formerly been prohibited; but at least at first such transactions were few, and carefully supervised.

Few Ponapeans saw clearly the course which events were taking on Ponape with the compulsory teaching of Japanese, the alienation of native land, the rapidly expanding Japanese population, and the large number of children of mixed blood born to Ponapean women. Had the trend continued, the Ponapeans as a distinct people would have soon disappeared through interbreeding and the loss of their culture and their lands.

The Japanese, on Ponape for thirty years, 1914 to 1944, exerted a marked influence on the native culture, in food, clothing, shelter, and social and political institutions. Thousands of them, living on the island at one time, could not help leaving a heavy impress. Many more Ponapeans acquired a taste for rice than during Spanish and German days. They began to like sukiyaki beans, tomatoes, cucumbers, and onions. Onions they still want to serve as a savory with native foods.

The Japanese introduced charcoal stoves to replace native earth ovens, and Ponapean women followed the example of the Japanese women who cooked. The business of making charcoal from mangrove wood became important. Within the memory of many Ponapeans cooking was done in earth ovens and by men only.

Men and boys began to wear shirts and shorts like the Japanese, while women and girls wore dresses from cloth manufactured in Japan. The Japanese introduced *geta*, or sandals, and encouraged Ponapeans to wear them, thus decreasing the hookworm infection through the soles of the feet. Ponapeans in Japanese communities commonly wore them. *Geta* are difficult to get now, and Ponapeans have reverted to their old barefoot fashion, with consequent higher infection. It is estimated that about 90 per cent of the native population is infested with hookworms.

Native houses began to be patterned on Japanese styles, with sliding partitions, doors and windows, and decorated fronts. Japanese lanterns hung inside, and large china flower pots painted in Japanese motifs adorned porches. Three styles of houses are now found on Ponape: native with coconut or pandanus thatch, part native, and Japanese style.

Actors of the *no* drama came from Japan to give performances which Ponapeans attended. They listened to the samisen, saw Japanese movies, and sang Japanese songs. Ponapean children still play Japanese games, using words in the Japanese version of hopscotch of which they don't know the meaning. They also play singing games with Japanese tunes.

Young men and women from twenty to forty now commonly speak Japanese which they learned in school. Children of chiefs who were sent to Japan for part of their education speak it fluently. They acquired Japanese *politesse*, taking off their shoes or sandals at the door, bowing politely, and holding things in both hands when offering them. The Japanese took natives in groups, district by district, for inexpensive tours in Japan. In remote parts of the island Japanese songs are still heard on victrolas. One of the more popular records played is *Hito no kimo siranaide nayami wo* (Wishing). "Let Me Call You Sweetheart" is just beginning to be hummed now and then by Ponapean members of the Trust Territory Headquarters staff. In a decade or two it, and "Home on the Range," which is also heard, will have supplanted the Japanese melodies.

Many of the Japanese who came to Ponape were pioneers whose

steamer fares were in part subsidized by the Japanese Government. Japanese single men lived with native families, for there was nowhere else for them to stay. Natives were glad to have them, for they could bring a little *sake* or beer to a native feast, which the Japanese were forbidden to sell to Micronesians. Many a man came to Colonia with his possessions in a *furoshike*, or large scarf. He worked to buy a few fishhooks, hairbrushes and combs, toothbrushes and especially bottles of well perfumed hair oil, and started down the coast on foot peddling his wares. When he could afford it, he added shirts and shorts to his stock, then women's dresses. After a while he set up a little store in a room twelve feet by six, sent home for a picture bride or married a Ponapean. At least one such immigrant finally opened a large store in Colonia where his children became clerks.

Others who came fished with rod and line from the reefs, sold part of their catch and bought rice. They purchased a share in a fishing boat and finally climaxed their business career by owning and operating a large boat to become commercial fishermen. Transportation on Ponape and to the neighboring islands was frequent and inexpensive.

The Ponapeans sold the pioneers bananas, breadfruit, taro, yams, and various other agricultural products. Prosperous Japanese meant prosperous Ponapeans also. Most of those who came were Okinawans, hard workers, and especially good fishermen. They and Koreans were laborers at the Kohatsu Company sugar cane plantation. The Japanese businesses on Ponape flourished. Nine fish-processing plants in or near Colonia cured tuna to send back to Japan. At six sawmills on the island, dams were constructed in rivers so that logs could be dumped behind them; then the dams were pulled down, and the logs were swept to the sea whence they were towed to the sawmills. With stores scattered around the island, the Japanese did a big credit business, for they thought that some day the Government would have control of the land and then they could get some from their creditors. While all this work was done exclusively by the Japanese, the Ponapeans gained by supplying them with native foods. The natives, unreliable, worked only intermittently, taking a day off when they felt like it.

The Japanese bought not only all the copra the natives produced, but husks and shells as well, for in their poor country they found good uses for these by-products. More energetic than the Ponapeans, many of them made arrangements with the natives to harvest their copra for a share of the market price. During the Japanese era, the Golden Age economically for the Ponapeans, the natives had a higher standard of living than they have now.

Stores in various parts of Ponape still stock a considerable amount of Japanese goods, which are much cheaper than similar American products. Shelves carry Japanese canned fish, packages of biscuits, soybean sauce, cloth goods, and various other things. Japanese saws, hammers, and other tools come in now too, for native carpenters are accustomed to working with them.

Among various effects of Japanization was a decrease in the cult of the yam. The Japanese tried to inculcate the greatest respect for the Ponapean who did most for his community rather than for the man who raised the biggest yam. In other words they tried to inculcate a respect for the man who worked regularly, did his share of work on the roads and trails, set an example of cleanliness in his home, and produced a good share of copra.

Native community houses decreased in importance during Japanese rule. The one near Colonia is small and hidden in an unattractive area away from the town.

In Japanese times Colonia, with a population of four thousand Orientals, had electric lights, telephones, ice, restaurants, and bakeries, and stores stocked with a wide variety of imported goods to supply the Japanese community. It was burned to ashes by American incendiary bombs between February 10 and 22, 1944. A Japanese specialist on Micronesian land problems who is helping to unravel the land situation in Colonia took the author about the remains of the town one morning, pointing out old Japanese landmarks. Namiki Dohri, or North Street, was the principal Japanese street. On it were Government Headquarters and the chief drygoods, grocery, and hardware stores. On the outskirts was a Japanese rope factory where coconut husks were the raw materials. Beside it were the foundations of the dormitory which housed the workers. This section was the redlight district; the style of architecture of the part of a house still remaining indicates that it was a brothel. Along the sides of the streets here and there were the stumps of telegraph poles which were blown away in the bombardment. The remains of the foundations of many Japanese buildings are covered with a rank growth of tropical grass, weeds, and jungle. There is a considerable area of filled-in land along the waterfront of the town, land which belonged to the Japanese Government. The Protestant church, near it, was built by the Japanese.

Colonia, razed by the war, is now largely a collection of very scattered quonset huts, put up by the Navy, some of which are in a state of dilapidation and decay. They are used as offices for the administration of the Trust Territory, storehouses, and homes for members of the staff. The Ponapeans live in a district of small frame houses with galvanized-iron roofs. The total population of the town is now 750.

Ponapeans had no quarrel with the Japanese until the Orientals realized they were losing the war. Then they became surly and autocratic, organized forced labor gangs, beat the natives for unsatisfactory work, and took all the native food they could find. Ponapeans fled to the mountains, hills, and bush, and built themselves houses of whatever vegetation they could find to eke out an existence until the American forces arrived. The Japanese program of forced labor disrupted agriculture. Ponapeans were required to work on military installations and on farms established to feed the increased Japanese population when Ponape was cut off from Japan in 1943. Liberation, following the Japanese surrender to American troops, meant to the Ponapeans, above all else, the right to return to their lands. Copra production was slow in reviving, but subsistence farming began immediately.

THE AMERICAN RÉGIME

"Under the Americans we do not have so much money, but we are more free. We can come to them like friends." That is what a Ponapean stated in comparing the present régime with the last one. He sized up the situation fairly well. Under American administration the natives are gradually improving their subsistence farming, the most important factor in raising their standard of living. In addition to the traditional indigenous crops, attention is given to new varieties of bananas, to better methods of raising the Hawaiian taro introduced during the German period, and to improving the strains of breadfruit on the island. Attempts are being made to account for variation in the yields of breadfruit from season to season, something which at present is little understood. A problem for all aspects of agriculture is control of pests, especially the African snail. The Ponapeans, more than the natives of other Caroline Islands, are loath to adopt new crops or to try new methods of improving old ones. The Government agriculturist has little influence because he can't show the natives how to raise bigger yams! If, through some method of science in agriculture, he could produce the biggest yam on Ponape, his future would be eternally assured. As yet the people take little interest in cattle, carabao, and goats, all of which are now on the island.

Coconut plantations will continue to supply the money crop for Ponapeans as they do for many thousands of other islanders in the Pacific. Year in, year out, the natives must depend on selling it to buy the few things they now consider necessities of life: rice, flour, tea, sugar, kerosene, and clothes. Because of their acquisition of new tastes, their development of new needs, and the disappearance of traditional handicrafts through the competition of manufactured products, Ponapeans rely upon imported goods, and to pay for these they must be linked with the outside world to find a market for their copra.

Some of the chiefs on the island who own considerable areas of land have enlarged the acreage used for coconut palms. A former Japanese-owned plantation, now the property of the American administration, operated by a graduate of the University of Hawaii, is outstanding for its modernization. Going there from Ponape gives a visitor an opportunity to see parts of the island remote from administrative headquarters. A large coconut plantation at Metalanim on Ponape is also operated by a graduate of the University of Hawaii. At the harbor the *Lucky* from Kapingamarangi Island comes in loaded with natives. This was formerly a Japanese fishing vessel which had been wrecked, but the Kapingamarangi people salvaged it, and repaired it to put into commission for their own use. Only a native, however, would want to take the 500-mile trip in it.

Rain clouds cluster at the rugged center of Ponape as the small boat crosses the open entrances of wide bays indented between steep radial ridges. A school of flying fish skims the surface across the bow. The *Metompkin*, a derelict Pacific Micronesian Line steamer, sister ship to the *Roque*, lies high on the reef to seaward, wrecked by a mistake in navigation. The surface of the inshore water, made choppy by a strong northeast wind, slaps the little flat-bottomed craft between one crest and the next. The voyage is a continual shower of salt spray and rain. At the entrance to Metalanim Harbor the modern home of the high chief of Metalanim District stands next to a large native ceremonial house where kava is served and other ceremonial customs are conducted. At the little wharf the visitor transfers to a jeep to drive along a good Japanese-made road, arriving in a few minutes at the comfortable home of the manager, the headquarters of a modern coconut plantation. His house is one of a group of buildings including a modern copra kiln and drying sheds. The Metalanim coconut plantation comprises 1,100 acres. The administration plans to homestead some 900 more to Ponapeans, to Pingelap people, and to natives of other islands who may acquire land on Ponape. The plantation formerly belonged to the Japanese Kohatsu Company. Long rows of coconut trees, doing well in rocky soil, are set out between roads which lead to all sections of the plantation. In one area a new road, half a mile long, has been recently constructed. Part of the plantation is enclosed by a stout fence inside which a herd of mixed-breed Brahman and European cattle grazes on grass and weeds, keeping the ground between the trees green and helping to fertilize the soil. Ripe nuts which drop from the trees are picked up from time to time and laid in piles. After a copra cutting, about once a month, the meat is taken to the dry-air kiln in sacks on trucks.

Ponapeans harvest their nuts from areas very much smaller than the Metalanim plantation. If a native needs money he climbs trees to knock down those not quite ripe; he also does so when the price of copra is high. Although the coconut stand of a Ponapean family is small, perhaps five to ten acres, the work of making copra is divided up, one young man making it one month, another the next, and so on. If a native lives near a beach, open to sun and wind, he generally has a drying house two stories high where a canoe is kept on the ground floor. The drying area consists of reeds stretched across supports and tied in place with string made from the fiber.

Much of the copra on Ponape is made in small dryers where coconut shells are burned under trays set over old oil drums cut in two, each part providing a kiln. It takes three or four days to dry in sun and wind and half that time in a kiln. A Ponapean generally lights a fire, lets it burn slowly all day, and renews it the next morning. A little smoke merely helps to sterilize it. After the drying, he usually takes from a few days to a week to arrange transportation on a little trading vessel to Colonia, where it is weighed and bought by the Inter-Island Trading Company, which ships it to San Francisco, Yokohama, or wherever it can be sold. Sometimes it goes to Guam to be stored and disposed of from there. When the price is high, part of it goes into a Copra Stabilization Fund to be paid back to Ponapeans when the price is very low.

The money received from copra is beginning to constitute a form of wealth and consequent social prestige a bit like that which comes from producing the biggest yams, for it enables the possessor to obtain large amounts of imported goods at a premium now that the Japanese have gone. This prestige economy is associated with the distribution of goods through which social approval and consequently social status are gained. A native with a large coconut acreage has a form of wealth which is being more and more appreciated. The output of copra from Ponape District approaches 4,000 tons a year. In 1954 the cash income of natives of Ponape district was $52,500.

On Ponape the people earn a little money in arts and handicraft. Besides, women usually make handicrafts for their own uses and their families, too. Men build canoes, houses, boats, and form small things such as rings, combs, and hooks out of sea shells and turtle shells. They also fashion bowls, spoons, and cups from coconut shells.

Ponapeans, when they have enough money, buy all sorts of things, some of which they don't require. Fifteen natives own jeeps! Putting money away for a day of need is not within their comprehension, partly because their friends would insist on sharing it, and partly because the accumulation of a surplus has never been part of their way of living.

Furthermore, the natives have learned by experience that it is not profitable to save money, for when the Germans succeeded the Spanish the florin was no good; when the Japanese succeeded the Germans the mark was worthless; and now there is uncertainty as to whether the yen some of the people hold is worth anything. Since the natives had more money in Japanese times, they bought more clothes and shoes and sandals than they can buy now. It was an inexorable rule that a Ponapean dressed his best when he went to see a Government official. The informality of American conventions has not inculcated deference toward the administration.

Questions of land tenure, awaiting settlement since the end of the war, have to be resolved for the betterment of subsistence agriculture as well as to increase the copra output. A very great area, in fact most of the island, which was expropriated by the Japanese, is now under control of the American administration. Ponapeans hope for its return with certificates of ownership, for so far they have been given only temporary rights on that land.

Most of the court cases concern land, for many Ponapeans are farming areas for which the title can be revoked. They want irrevocable titles, which would give them more encouragement to farm; until titles are assured, they hold sections undeveloped. Like all Micronesians and other South Sea people, the Ponapeans are land-conscious. Neither they nor their ancestors have been able to conceive of living without it, for to have the right to harvest the fruits of the earth from a piece of ground is to them the essence of life itself.

The land problem is the most pressing question for the administration. One hears frequently in conversation, "Did he have it registered? What did the Japanese survey show? Anyway, the Japanese made a rule that if their lands were not registered they did not belong to them." So it goes all through the island. The problem is all the more important because Ponape is a center of colonization by people from Pingelap, Portlock, Losap, Pis, and other low atolls where life is hard compared with that on the high, mountainous island.

Ponape, a relatively large "high island" 175 miles to the west of Pingelap, has affected the situation, for example, on that atoll in several ways. Though Ponape has richer soil and much greater productive possibilities, it is rainier and therefore not so attractive to the Pingelap people. It is, however, much less crowded and has been available at least as a partial solution to the problem of overpopulation on Pingelap. But the major factor that associated the two was an event that took place in 1911—the establishment of Pingelap Village in the Jokaj District of northwestern Ponape. It happened after the people of the Jokaj District who rebelled against the German Government were exiled to the Palau Islands. The German Government then offered the land thus vacated to people from Pingelap and other islands in the vicinity of Ponape.

Under the American régime many traditional customs will continue to be observed into the indefinite future, the system of titles, for example, and the prestige which they represent for the holders. They will bring the incumbents many material benefits, as they do now, and provide for many of the social and economic controls by which

Ponapean society is still organized and maintained. This system has been in part revived and validated by modern American courts. Natives with the higher titles are salaried Government officials. The system, still embracing virtually every adult member of Ponapean society, is a constant factor in almost every social and Government activity. The higher chiefs are ex officio members of the Ponape Island Congress, and their approval is considered necessary in many cases in the selection of other local Government officials.

The Ponape Island Congress consists of a house of five hereditary "nobles," one for each district; and a people's house composed of elected representatives from each municipality based on the population. Like the other district congresses, it has no legislative authority, but advises the district administrator on matters concerning Ponape Island. Among matters taken up in the Congress of 1954 were establishing a closed season for shooting pigeons and an import tax, the latter not very popular.

The natives have heard of the United Nations, though what it stands for is still as far from their comprehension as is the American form of democratic government.

One of the more interesting experiences of the author's stay on Ponape was to accompany a Government official calling on the highest chief in Metalanim District to obtain his signature on a letter to the Trusteeship Council of the United Nations. The letter concerned the return of Japanese husbands who had been separated from their Ponapean wives and families. When the Japanese were sent away from Ponape, some of them took their Ponapean wives and children with them. Others who left without their families wanted to come back from Japan, where there were about thirty husbands of Ponapeans, five from Colonia. In 1952 the Ponapeans requested their return, and the Trusteeship Council replied that it would be arranged if the chiefs of the districts where the Japanese were to live would agree to it. The letter, to the Trusteeship Council, in the form of a statement to be signed by the five highest chiefs on the island giving their permission, was in a thick envelope in the sole custody of a native commoner in the party. Halfway across Metalanim Bay, a drenching shower forced him to push the document into the bow of the little boat, where he squatted over it to keep it dry.

At the home of the high chief, on the edge of the water, half a dozen natives from Metipw on the other side of the ridge were making kava. Nearly every day a few commoners come from some part of the district to show ceremonial token of their respect and deference for the highest position in their society. They squeeze the pounded root of the kava plant through the fibers of *kelen,* or hibiscus, steeped in water, near where the chief sits cross-legged on his porch. At intervals a native brings him a coconut cupful, turning his head away, as is the custom, when he offers it. The chief takes a sip and returns the cup. Sometimes his wife, sitting beside him, partakes of the potion. The head of the Government party, a secretary in the Island Affairs Department of the Government, explained his mission, and showed the statement, written in Ponapean. The chief read it over, made a few comments, and affixed his signature. Then he devoted his attention again to kava drinking and to sociable conversation.

The social life of Ponapeans, like other phases of their way of living, is gradually undergoing change. Colonia has a "pool hall" with one table, salvaged from Japanese equipment. It opens at eight in the mornings and closes at eleven or twelve at night. An inquiry as to why so many Ponapeans have time to spend in a pool hall in the mornings elicits the information that they are visitors from other parts of the island. A motion-picture theatre in Colonia is owned and operated by a native.

The educational system in Ponape, as in the other islands in the Trust Territory, is still struggling to get on its feet. Pehleng section of the Net District illustrates some of the difficulties involved. Those who drew up the code of regulations which govern the Territory, not being familiar with the situation, stated that the municipality (or district) shall provide the land for schools, dispensaries, and other public buildings. But the municipalities do not own any land. However, Chief Tobias of Pehleng was prevailed on to donate some of his land for a school and a dispensary. The author accompanied the chief of the land office to lay down the markers for the site.

On a bright, sunny morning on the way to Pehleng in an outboard-motor boat, George Higgins, a chief from Mokil, grandson of an Irishman, held the tiller. Opposite Jokaj Rock, going full speed ahead, he put the rudder hard to port, turning the boat at right angles. As he turned off the motor, the craft missed a coral head by four feet, for a depth marker in the vicinity had disappeared. Half an hour later he drew alongside some natives also on their way to Pehleng, who were adrift in their canoe in which the outboard motor was stalled. Taking them in tow, the party arrived at the mouth of the Pehleng River, where the boat was pulled through a mangrove swamp into the estuary of the stream. A mile upstream the group came to the chief's house, a native structure, with pigs nosing about on the earth floor. Then in a heavy rain the party started up a rocky, muddy, slippery trail, alongside which carefully tended yams trailed over breadfruit trees. A bridge made by the trunks of two coconut palms afforded a passage across a stream near the site of the new school. Concrete markers were set at the corners of a roughly rectangular area of about two and a half acres, where the building was in process of construction. It replaced a weather-beaten native-style building which was little credit to the district.

Improvements in education will help the population in many ways, not the least of which will be in the field of health and sanitation. Many people, still believing that sickness is caused by ghosts and magic, have no understanding of how bacteria are spread. Medicine men and medicine women still practice their art with leaves, roots, bark, shellfish, and other animals of the sea. The natives think that black magic causes a ghost to enter the body of a personal enemy to cast a spell of sickness on the victim, who will die unless a witch doctor knows a counteragent. However, little by little, progress in medicine is being made, and the district hospital in Colonia is a center of healing in which the population is gaining confidence. In fact, the American doctor there, a New Englander, is often spoken of among the natives of the town as the "Number One" man in the administration. As the years go on, the local reputation of the hospital will spread to distant parts of the main island and to the small islands in the district.

Notwithstanding their belief in ghosts, evil spirits, and black magic, the Ponapeans are nominally Christians: about 60 per cent Roman Catholic and the remainder Protestant. On a Sunday morning small groups of men, women, and children saunter along the road toward the churches, some of them carrying hymnbooks or Bibles or both. At a parting of the ways, they separate into two companies, one going along the side of the hill to the Roman Catholic chapel, the other down the slope to the Protestant Mission. The Mission Church, a large edifice modeled on the pattern of New England Congregational churches, with two galleries the length of the build-ing, one on each side, and one at the back, has seats which are about

two feet high—planks of wood without any backs. Women sit on
the left of the center aisle and men on the right; girls and boys are
similarly placed in the galleries. Women and girls wear light print
dresses; men, short-sleeved shirts and long trousers, mostly blue, all
inexpensive imports from Japan. Small boys wear shirts and shorts.
Almost everyone is barefoot. The oily black heads both of men and
of women are well combed and scented. The church is always filled.
Before the formal part of the service begins, someone starts to sing a
hymn and the congregation joins in one verse, at the end of which
another is started, and so on for four or five. The superintendent of
the Congregational Mission in Micronesia sits behind the pulpit
between the missionary in charge of the local mission and the native
pastor. The service proceeds as church services do in the United
States, but with much more singing, for the natives love to carry
their parts in soprano, alto, tenor, and bass. Hymn tunes are the
same as those in the United States. Tiny tots in the congregation
keep up a continual chirping and occasional whining, but little attention is paid to them, for after a while a good many of them fall asleep.
The lesson is from the New Testament, since the Old has not been
translated into Ponapean. The natives would probably take it too
literally. If a native from a remote island in Micronesia were suddenly
transferred to a church in the United States on a Sunday morning,
he would understand everything that went on, though no one on
his island had ever seen a horse or an automobile. One Sunday a
missionary who had visited the mission in Ponape from time to time
since 1936 gave a short address of greeting in English, which was
translated sentence by sentence. The native pastor then preached a
sermon, after which the head of the mission talked briefly, also in
English which was translated. One of the difficulties in Micronesia is
that the natives of neighboring island groups speak different languages. The lady, from the Marshalls, knew Marshallese, but the
head of the mission, from Truk, spoke Trukese. Neither of these
languages is intelligible to the Ponapeans. After the sermon, members
of the choir stood up in scattered locations in the church, to go to
the front to sing. Finally a deacon read a report and the service was
closed with more singing and the benediction.

What of the changes in the Ponapeans since the Americans came
and what can be said of the future? An important factor since the
United States assumed charge is a change in the spirit of the people.

During the Japanese régime, although they were well off econom- ically, they had everything done for them and had no initiative to think for themselves. Now that they feel that the future will depend largely on their own efforts, there is a tendency to relinquish their former laissez-faire attitude.

As years pass, Japanese culture on Ponape will be more and more diluted and a veneer of American institutions will be substituted. American corned beef and canned salmon will more and more take the place of Japanese sukiyaki. Rice, however, will continue to be a desirable food. Houses will be constructed much the same as they are today. American movies, contributing their quota to the Ponapean way of life, will probably be shown in other parts of the island as well as in Colonia. Ponape will continue to be the melting pot for natives from less favored islands in that part of Micronesia.

From a material standpoint, Ponapeans, dissatisfied with their canoe civilization, are advancing to an outboard-motor era. The lagoons and inshore waters of Ponape Island, protected by the great coral reef, are ideal for outboard-motor boats. A special advantage is that in some places where the water is so shallow that the reef cannot be passed over by large boats, the motor on a small craft can be shut off while the boat is pulled over the shallows. The greatest change since the beginning of the American administration is the general use of outboard motors. "However, they keep the people poor," an old native in the islands stated. Everyone wants to have one, and each wants to have more horsepower than his neighbor. If a chief gets one of five horsepower, the chief of the next district must have one of seven, and the next one of ten. The passion to be better than one's neighbor is so ingrained in Ponapeans, and in other Micronesians too, that it seems impossible to overcome.

On a trip in an outboard-motor boat, a Ponapean times himself to see how fast he can go between one point and another. Perhaps he visits a friend who gives him breadfruit which he piles in the stern to keep the bow high out of the water. When he comes to a large stretch of open water where there are no reefs, he opens the throttle, making the little craft skim along the surface like a speedboat, while he stands in the stern glorying in the experience.

It is estimated that Ponapeans have 250 outboard motors many of which are attached to canoes. Their put-put-put is heard from remote corners of bays and estuaries morning, noon, and night. The ancient and the modern are well combined when one sees at a distance a canoe riding along without any apparent propulsion. Nowadays a Ponapean is commonly seen struggling up the hill from the harbor to his home in Colonia with a carrying stick over his shoulder, a basket of breadfruit hanging from one end and an outboard motor from the other. Although outboard motors require special care regularly when used in ocean water, Ponapeans look after them only for a while and then, unfortunately, neglect them.

As years pass and the natives get more experience, the motors, ceasing to be playthings, will become tools to be treated sensibly. They will materially shorten the time between villages and native farms along the coast and between both of them and Colonia. The laborious paddling, under a tropical sun, of canoes filled with sacks of copra will gradually cease. The Ponapeans will *put-put-put* themselves into a new way of living.

REFERENCES

Bascom, W. R., Ponape: A Pacific Economy in Transition, U.S. Commercial Co. Economic Survey of Micronesia, Vol. 8.
———, "Ponape: The Cycle of Empire," Scientific Monthly, 70 (3), 141-150, March, 1950.
———, "Ponape: The Tradition of Retaliation," Far Eastern Quarterly, 10 (1), 56-62, November, 1950.
———, "Ponapean Prestige Economy," Southwestern Journal of Anthropology, Vol. 4, 1948, pp. 211-221.
———, "Subsistence Farming on Ponape," New Zealand Geographer, (9) (2): 115-129, October, 1949.
Glassman, S. F., The Flora of Ponape, Bernice P. Bishop Museum Bull. 209, 1-152 (1952).
Murrill, Rupert I., "A Blood Pressure Study of the Natives of Ponape Island, Eastern Carolines," Human Biology, 21: 47-57 (1949).
———, "Vital Statistics of Ponape Island, Eastern Carolines," American Journal of Physical Anthropology, 8 (2): 185, June, 1950.
Nan Madol, Education Department, Ponape District, 1954, 18 pp., mimeographed.
United States Department of Commerce, Weather Bureau, "Local Climatological Data, Ponape Island, 1953."
United States Department of the Interior, "Trust Territory, Statistical Requirements, Ponape District, Fiscal year 1954," 32 pp., mimeographed.

XIII

The Marshall Islands

ONE morning on Majuro in the Marshalls, the author called at King Kabua's palace, having heard much about the kings on those islands and their hold on their subjects. The king was not at home, but the queen was there, bent over the family washtub doing the royal washing. The "palace" was a larger and more comfortably apportioned house than those of the commoners, but there was no evidence of splendor or luxury. I went down to the harbor hoping to find him at the royal yacht, a converted United States Navy boat, given to him during the early occupation of the island. It had two sleeping mats which filled the cabin floor, one on each side. Finally the king was found in his office transacting business with the mate of a vessel at the wharf. He is a tall, handsome, intelligent man, capable of carrying out the responsibilities which devolved on him as one of the hierarchy of chiefs of the Marshall Islands, and as a judge. In the course of our conversation I asked him what were the more important resolutions passed by the recent congress of his archipelago. Without any hesitation he replied, "The resolution governing the control of liquor, which gave each atoll the right to decide whether it would be dry or not." Then he added, "The other important resolution was a tax on copra to raise money for teachers' salaries."

The chiefs in the Marshalls still have title to the lands of the islands, and the commoners theoretically farm at their will, but no commoner has been dispossessed since the American administration took over. The people do pay them tribute of agricultural products and fish. Away at the uttermost ends of the earth, the chiefs and people of these far-flung specks of land in a vast expanse of ocean live their lives apart from the modern world.

THE NATURAL ENVIRONMENT

The Marshall Islands can truly be called the ends of the earth, for each day begins at the 180th meridian a little east of them, and they are among the last islands in the world to see its close. Lying between 4° 30′ and 14° 45′ north latitude, and between 160° 50′ and 172° 10′ east longitude, they consist of thirty-four low-lying coral atolls and single islands arranged roughly in two parallel chains running from north-northwest to south-southeast. The easternmost row, called the Radak ("towards the dawn") Chain, comprises fourteen atolls and two single islands. The westernmost row, called the Ralik ("towards the sunset") Chain, is composed of fifteen atolls and three single islands. Two of the northern atolls of the Ralik Chain, Eniwetok and Ujelang, lie somewhat out of line to the westward, and so isolated from the rest that the Japanese used to administer them from Ponape in the Eastern Carolines rather than with the rest of the Marshalls.

The Radak and Ralik chains lie approximately 130 miles apart, while the average distance between atolls of the same chain is about 50 miles. The greatest distance, about 165 miles, separates Eniwetok and Bikini, whereas Knox is only two miles from Mili. Other nearby pairs are Ailinginae and Rongelap, Ailinglapalap and Jabwot, Arno and Majuro, Aur and Maloelap, Erikub and Wotje, and Taka and Utirik.

All of the Northern Marshalls lie in the westward-running North Equatorial Current. The Equatorial Countercurrent flows eastward through the Southern Marshall Islands, and, at least in the months from September to February, the boundary that separates the two is about that between the northern half and the southern islands. This boundary shifts southward during part of the winter and spring months, when the heat equator is in the Southern Hemisphere.

The total sea area occupied by the islands is roughly 375,000 square miles, or about one and one-half times the size of Texas.

In consequence of their position in the low latitudes and their small area of land, the Marshall Islands have a tropical marine climate, with high and remarkably uniform temperatures, deviating no more than one degree in any month from an annual mean of 81° F. The diurnal variation is also slight; the highest temperature of the day, usually registered between 1:00 and 2:00 P.M., normally exceeds the lowest temperature, registered between 5:00 and 6:00 A.M., by only ten to twelve degrees. Humidity, which is very high, also shows little seasonal difference; it varies, however, during the day, when it is highest about 6:00 A.M. and lowest around 2:00 P.M. The daily mean is 83 to 84 per cent.

The Marshall Islands are characterized by heavy precipitation, but the amount and monthly distribution differ considerably with locality

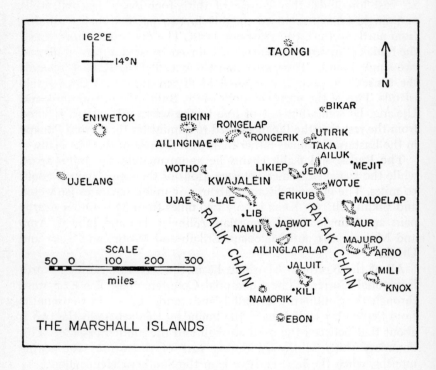

and in the same locality from time to time. The southern atolls, which lie near the southern margin of the belt of the northeast trade winds, receive about 160 inches of rain a year, while the northern atolls, which fall squarely within the trade-wind belt, receive only about half as much. Moreover, whereas the precipitation in the southern islands is distributed fairly uniformly over the year, the northern atolls get very little rain during the cooler months, when the trade winds are often accompanied by long periods of fine weather.

The rainier climate in the south makes for abundant vegetation and more decay of plant life, which helps to form soil. The southern islands, for that reason, are more densely populated than the northern ones.

Occasional droughts, a feature of the weather of all the atolls, mean that during temporary shortages of water food has to be cooked in the salt water of the lagoon. From December to March, the drier season for all the atolls, the natives customarily drink coconut water. A drought kills the banana trees first. In the Northern Marshalls pandanus, coconuts, and arrowroot grow well, but breadfruit, bananas, and taro grow poorly in the dry, sandy soil. Taro there requires meticulous care; leaves are regularly strewn around it to hinder evaporation and to decay into fertilizer. The outstanding feature of all the atolls is the restricted amount of food ordinarily available—a scarcity which means famines in atolls hit by typhoons. The most severe storms are typhoons, which are less common, however, in the Marshalls, especially in the southern atolls, than in the Caroline Islands west of them. Shortly after the Japanese became established in the islands, in 1918, a disastrous hurricane struck Majuro Atoll. Business was ruined, and trading companies withdrew their personnel to Jaluit. A destructive typhoon hit Arno Atoll in the same year, washing out parts of islands and uprooting trees.

All the atolls and single islands of the archipelago are formed exclusively of coral, built upward from submerged mountain peaks which at some time in the geological past rose close to the surface of the sea. There are no volcanic islands as in other parts of Micronesia. The islets of an atoll are, essentially, accumulations of loose calcareous material strewn on the reef surface, or the erosion remnants of higher reef surfaces, or, on many, combinations of these. In general they are partially or almost completely outlined by narrow bands of rock usually sloping away from the islet in all directions. Above them the beaches consist of calcareous sand, gravel, pebbles, cobbles, or even boulders, the slopes of which vary, locally, from gentle to steep.

The constituent islands of an atoll, separated from one another by reefs and passages, vary in size from a few square yards to several square miles; they are normally long, narrow, and curved in conformity with the shape of the atoll. The longest islet, Majuro, on the south side of the atoll of the same name, is approximately twenty-five statute miles but only a few hundred yards wide in most places. The broadest islet in the archipelago, Wotje on the east side of that atoll, is a mile long and three-quarters of a mile in width at its widest point. The highest and widest islets are usually found on the windward, east side. The coral polyps at the edges of the rock to windward, where the ocean piles up, receive more food and build more rapidly. Sand dunes, found most commonly near the beach on the weather side, are usually the higher points on an atoll. The highest of these dunes, on Likiep, rises approximately forty feet above sea level, but on most islets dunes are much lower. Even such small relief as there is varies greatly on different atolls and on islets of the same atoll. Small eminences, and especially depressions, count for much in the native economy because of the ecology of the plants adapted to them. Ebon Island on that atoll, for example, has more natural depressions than islands on the other atolls in general, and so it has more swamps and, therefore, a larger supply of taro. Most of the topographic features of the islets are transitory, or ephemeral, for the normal processes of erosion and deposition work rapidly, and typhoons often alter the topography beyond recognition in a single day, either constructively or destructively.

Normally the surf breaks over the outer reef of an atoll and does not reach the beach of the main island. In stormy weather, however, it often breaks all the way over the lower and narrower parts of the land, and in some instances tidal waves accompanying typhoons have inundated entire islands, destroying the vegetation and drowning the inhabitants.

The soil, generally poor for agriculture, has been enriched on many islands by considerable effort; in some instances earth has been imported from high Caroline Islands or elsewhere. In general, the larger islands afford the less infertile land, but even among them there are differences. Mili and Ebon, with a little more and better soil than other islands, grow yams and limes, and on Majuro there are limes and soursop too.

As a result of their greater humidity, the southern atolls, as we have seen, support a more luxuriant vegetation than those in the north. The most numerous trees in general in the Marshalls are coconut palms, for most of the original vegetation has been replaced by coconut plantations. Only on very small islets are there areas of apparently undisturbed natural vegetation. Coconut plantations vary in density from almost complete cover in the moister south to sparse in the dry, northern atolls. The ground cover under the trees varies from grass and other herbs to a thick tangle of bushes and vines, depending on how diligently the weeds are cleared.

HISTORICAL

The Marshalls were discovered by the Spanish during the sixteenth century, Loyasa in 1526, Saavedra in 1529, but there is no record of their galleons' having made regular stops in these islands on their way to Guam. Indeed, they were entirely neglected by the Spaniards, whose colonization in Micronesia centered in the Marianas.

Germany, eager for colonial expansion in the Pacific, saw an opportunity in the Marshall Islands, to which no other Western power had asserted a substantial claim. A local treaty in 1878 was followed by the formal assumption of a protectorate over the archipelago in 1885, when the commander of a German warship ceremonially raised the German flag on Jaluit, Likiep, and the five southernmost atolls of the Ratak chain, and concluded nineteen separate treaties with local chiefs. This and other German expansion in the Pacific precipitated disputes with both Spain and Great Britain, but by 1886 both nations had formally conceded sovereignty over the Marshalls to Germany.

Even before 1885, however, contact with Westerners was not infrequent, for sailing ships, traders, and missionaries all operated in the Marshalls prior to that date. A few Europeans, Americans, Chinese, and Japanese had settled in the Marshalls and married island women.

German policy with respect to the islands was primarily that of gaining and developing colonies which might prove economically profitable, their possible strategic value in a military sense being definitely of subsidiary importance. This policy was expressed in the strong monopolistic position given to the German Jaluit Company and in the insignificant development of naval and military installations.

In 1914, when the Japanese took military possession of the Marshall Islands, they interned the German Government officers and businessmen and eventually shipped them back to Germany. At first the Japanese Navy administered the islands, but later, in 1922, its rule was replaced by a civil authority. Whereas the Germans controlled largely by indirect rule through the native chiefs, the Japanese shifted to a system of virtual direct rule through a new set of officials. They also greatly expanded their administrative staff. Whereas the Germans attempted to maintain the native political structure and were fairly successful in so doing, the Japanese, although they protested to the League of Nations that they had a similar policy of indirect rule, actually conducted their régime in a manner designed to undermine the native political institutions. A new set of traders, all Japanese, arrived in the atolls. Two Japanese companies started at Majuro, the Nanyo Boeki Kaisha with its main station at Jaluit Island, and a small store at Majuro village, and a smaller company, Nanyo Kabushiki Kaisha, its main station at Roguron Island, and small stores at other places.

Since the Marshalls comprise, for the most part, small islands with poor soil, there was little opportunity for the Japanese there to make a living at farming as on Ponape and other large volcanic islands.

During World War II the Marshalls formed the outer ramparts of the Japanese mandate in the Pacific. In the wake of a terrific bombardment by ships and aircraft, American marines landed on the beaches of Kwajalein in January of 1944, initiating the campaign to secure bases in the islands. The islands were governed by the United States Navy until 1949, when a civilian administration was installed.

THE NATIVES

The Marshallese, somewhat like Polynesians in racial characteristics, in general have brown skins slightly darker than those of the Samoans. Most of them have straight black hair; the hair of the others ranges from wavy to curly. Their total population in 1954 was 11,878, but they were probably never much more numerous than at present, for wars, typhoons, and losses at sea as well as customary abortion and infanticide contributed to keeping the numbers to the maximum that the islands could support. At present they are increasing and, with modern health measures, this increase will probably become more rapid, whether or not to the point of overpopulation will depend in part on unpredictable factors.

One hundred and thirty years of exposure to European and

American ships, a hundred years of missionary effort, and three successive foreign administrations, German, Japanese, and American, dating from 1886, have considerably changed the ancient pattern of life. In place of their former complete self-reliance and dependence on the resources of their own environment, the Marshallese have become entangled in a commercial economy, dependent on the vicissitudes of a world market for a single product, and accustomed to relying on the direction of outside authorities.

Their material culture has become a curious mixture of indigenous and foreign elements, with the latter becoming more and more important. This is equally true of the social side of their culture; for example, they have long been accustomed to wearing Western clothes. They buy in their own stores the yard goods from which the women make their own dresses as well as shirts and trousers for men and boys. Ninety-nine per cent of them are literate in their own language, 20 per cent are literate in English, and 50 per cent in Japanese. The dialect of the eastern chain of islands is slightly different from that in the west.

Many islands have a small number of people of mixed-blood derived from unions between Marshallese and Europeans, Americans, Japanese, Koreans, and Chinese. Japanese took common-law Marshallese wives and raised families. All the mixed-bloods are essentially Marshallese in language and way of living, though some of them show certain variations in attitudes and behavior.

The population of an atoll is usually resident in a single village on the lagoon side of the largest islet, in one-room or two-room shacks, ranged in a double row along each side of a sand and gravel street which parallels the shore of the lagoon. Windows, openings in the sides which swing out, are propped by sticks. Empty petroleum drums to collect rain water stand at the corners. The natives have no furniture in our sense of the word. A family sits on undecorated pandanus mats on the floor by day, and sleeps there at night, after unrolling sleeping mats.

Until the war thatched houses predominated, but since then many families have changed to frame houses with sawed lumber sides, galvanized-iron roofs, and board floors, salvaged in a great variety of shapes and sizes; consequently, many of the houses are ugly, unpainted shanties. Although thatched roofs are cooler than corrugated iron, the natives do not wish to return to thatch, for this covering, made from pandanus leaves, must be replaced every three years in the humid southern Marshalls and every six or seven years in the dry north.

In isolated atolls, however, especially in the far north, pandanus leaves are still used for the sides and roofs of houses. Sections of thatch, made by sewing the leaves together with coconut fiber and an awl-needle formed from a rib of a leaf, are fastened in place with native cord. Sand is the only material on the floor.

Many houses in the islands in general have arrowroot, bananas, and a few papayas planted nearby, some have small sweet-potato gardens in the rear. Toward the back or near one side of a house are usually small wire enclosures for chickens, though villages were stripped of pigs and chickens by the Japanese during the war and there are few today. Pigs, also scarce though increasing, are kept in small pens a short distance away from the houses.

There are few roads except those constructed under the German administration, and those built by the Japanese on Kwajalein and other fortified islands.

On inhabited islands, visitors are struck by straight, hardpacked paths, neatly lined with flat stones, weathered and mossy, set on edge, usually running the length of the principal islets, and crisscrossed with shorter trails. They also date from German times.

NATIVE ECONOMY

Primitive Marshallese agriculture was largely of two sorts, both still practiced: the occasional planting of coconuts, breadfruit, pandanus and other plants, which are then allowed to grow without further tending, and the excavation and care of taro swamps. The general scarcity of provisions in the islands is evidenced by the foods the natives eat regularly—coconuts and pandanus fruit. Taro occupies a secondary role, for on many islands there is none at all. Bananas, usually saved for special occasions, are given to visitors, particularly American administrative personnel. Papayas are fairly common, but, since the Marshallese have not cultivated a taste for them, they are eaten infrequently, and principally by children.

Canned meat, canned fish, flour, rice, sugar, biscuits, tea, and coffee are purchased at village stores. These articles, obtainable only in restricted quantities, supplement the native diet. In the case of imported foods, the important factor is the quantity available, for the villagers' appetite for them far exceeds what they can get. At the end of the Japanese period, just before the war, the Marshallese were buying more and more food in Japanese stores scattered throughout the islands, obtaining the necessary money primarily through the sale of copra.

Lijka farm, a representative one, on the side of Long Island farthest from administration headquarters, comprises three dwelling houses, a cookhouse, and a copra kiln. Nearby are three pigsties. Breadfruit trees are scattered among the coconut palms in the immediate vicinity of the houses, and two banana plants, and a lime tree. It takes thirteen months for the banana plant to bear a bunch of bananas as compared with nine in American Samoa. The sides of two dwellings are of galvanized iron with roofs of coconut thatch; the third has thatched sides and a galvanized-iron roof.

The principal changes in agriculture in the Marshalls during the last fifty or sixty years are the great increase in the proportion of coconuts, the adoption of the practice of cleaning out, periodically, the weedy undergrowth in the plantations, and the destructive burning of vegetable refuse, leaves, husks, and cleared brush rather than allowing them to rot and enrich the naturally sterile soil. The new habit of planting coconuts in rows, rather than at random, is of little consequence other than in identifying German influence. Well before the beginning of "German times," traders made copra a commodity of value; under German and, later, Japanese administrations, people were encouraged, even forced, to increase continually the area of coconuts.

The economic position of the chiefs improved with the development of the copra trade, for as the acreage devoted to coconut palms increased, and richer and richer harvests ensued, more cash flowed into their coffers. It was therefore in their best interests to cooperate with the governing authorities in promoting the great business of the archipelago. Ultimately the extension of coconut plantations eliminated most of the native forest that once covered the unused lands, and reduced the number of breadfruit and pandanus.

A number of species of pandanus, or screw pine, are indigenous to the Marshall Islands, of which *Pandanus odoratissimus*, called *bob* by the natives, is the most common. Its leaves provided the sole material for roofs and sides of the traditional house. Cultivated trees are propagated from root shoots, since plants growing from the fruit revert to the wild form. The fruit consists of separate rounded sections enclosed in a hard green rind. To eat it raw, the natives pull off a section, bite through the fibrous rind and holding it with twisting motions of the hand, chew the end to remove the sweet aromatic juice from the woody threads in which it is embedded. The pandanus, growing satisfactorily on sandy soil where there is not much rain, is, therefore, a dependable food in the northern Marshalls. Sections of baked or boiled fruit are rubbed on a *beka*, or extractor, which scrapes off the pulp, the edible part. If it is to be preserved for a season of food shortage, the pulp is spread on *marbele* leaves to be dried on a grating over a fire. It is then packed tightly in pandanus leaves, and tied up strongly until it is to be used. It is eaten mixed with fresh water to the consistency of soup. Sometimes arrowroot is mixed with it. Although the Marshallese possess the techniques for drying and preserving food—principally breadfruit, pandanus, and arrowroot—their usual practice is to procure fresh vegetables and fish just before they eat them. The pandanus season follows upon that of the breadfruit.

Arrowroot, called *mokemok* by the natives, grows wild in both stony and sandy soil. Its cultivation is largely confined to the northern atolls, whence it is traded to the south. A semidomesticated plant, it flourishes with little care wherever the ground is salt-free and only moderately shaded. When other vegetation in coconut groves is slashed, it is spared, and it benefits from the cutting of the other growth. On land cleared by burning, arrowroot is not killed, for the roots are a foot or more beneath the surface. If the ground is even moderately moist, it will come up again soon after. Although it is planted on the same spot year after year, it does not wear out the soil quickly. The principal centers of production are Ailinglapalap, Aur, Bikini, Kwajalein, Majuro, Maloelap, Namorik, and Ujae.

FISHING

Much of the fish of the primitive Marshallese came from the lagoon, the reef, and the open sea. The native, a good swimmer and diver, used his excellent canoes for fishing. Women and children gathered shellfish on the reef. Contact with Western civilization has changed this only by introducing more effective fishing equipment and by making it less necessary to fish. Fishing has decreased in importance, for canned fish is bought with the proceeds of the sale of copra. A hundred and thirty years of contact with Western civilization has made emulation of that way of living a desirable thing in the eyes of the natives. Civilized people eat canned food—therefore, to appear civilized one should eat canned food. Fishing, however, still provides an important part of the food supply. Large shellfish: giant clams, helmet, and conchs, are secured by diving in the lagoon. The reef and shallow water provide spiny lobsters, and small fish which are speared or caught with throw nets. Reef fishing with rods and lines goes on at all times. In the sea, however, outside the reefs, tuna in abundance, *ulua* (jack), and other species that generally haunt the vicinity of the islands are not utilized to great extent by the natives, as the men lack the equipment and incentive to fish for them. Since, in the cool season, strong, constant winds flow from the northeast, even the lagoon is sometimes so rough that canoe fishing temporarily ceases, especially in the northern islands.

Shellfish and herring are frequently eaten uncooked, and bonito and flying fish are preferred raw. The natives dry in the sun, salt, and smoke fish that they cannot use immediately. Some is saved for times of scarcity. Drying fish is a very old custom, but salting is an art learned from foreigners. It is usual to send a box of dried or salted fish to the mission school where a child is a boarder.

The Northern Ratak atolls of Bikar, Taongi, Taka, the island of Jemo, and the islands of Erik and Luij in Erikub Atolls, have been used by the Marshallese from time immemorial as bird reserves, and the natives visit them only at certain seasons to procure birds and their eggs, as well as turtles and turtle eggs. Although the Germans seized the atolls of Bikar and Bokak as Government property, and the Japanese took them over with all the other German assets, they were not exploited by either, and the Marshallese continue to utilize their resources.

The Marshallese, isolated from the world, still have to depend on local materials for many of the things that they need. They weave fans from coconut leaves and pandanus leaves; they construct fish traps and crab traps by binding hardwoods together in the form of a cage with cord twisted from the fiber of the husk of coconuts; from hardwood, also, they make coconut husking sticks, *kone*; they have pandanus fruit extractors; they carve wooden bailers for taking water from canoes, and wooden bowls for food. They fashion their own canoes from local woods. Marshallese workmanship is excellent, and during the first few years after the war various articles plaited from pandanus and coconut leaves, turtle-shell ornaments, shell necklaces, model canoes, and other such things, mainly in demand as curios, were of some commercial importance. Now, however, such demand is slight outside the Trust Territory. At present, mats and hats of pandanus and coconut leaves, rope braided from coir (coconut husk fiber), some coconut oil, and temporary coconut leaf baskets, all strictly for home use, are about the only items "manufactured" in the archipelago.

Women are hard workers, often doing heavy labor, carrying sacks of husks of coconuts for fuel on their backs. They wash clothes much of the time, and iron them with charcoal irons, making the charcoal themselves from coconut shells. They make starch with arrowroot flour. From native materials they weave floor mats and sails for canoes. They pound pandanus leaves to render them pliable for cutting and weaving into hats. They do the "housekeeping" and carry baskets of coral gravel to spread about their homes. They draw the domestic water and often cut copra with the men. They do most of the cooking, although men cook sometimes. An old chief still brags about his ability with arrowroot and pandanus puddings. The men, as is customary in all Micronesia, do the carpentry and construction work, make boats and canoes, fish, and go on excursions to other islands to get breadfruit and taro.

Although native economy in the Marshalls is still largely indigenous, the material goods from the West to which the people have been introduced over a period of three-quarters of a century have had a profound effect on their way of living. They are very desirous of having more of them, but the amount they can afford is very restricted. Their copra exports, all of which went to Japan in 1954, totaled only four thousand tons. The trochus shell collected in the islands is almost negligible in their economy. Copra production could be substantially increased, but it depends in part on the natives' willingness to work.

LAND TENURE

Landownership and tenure, and political and social life in the Marshalls, are so interrelated as to be inseparable. Traditionally government in the islands was by the *iroij*, "kings" or highest chiefs. These with the *iroij-erik*, "dukes" and "duchesses" related to the kings and queens, formed the ruling class. The commoners were the *dri-jerbal*, also called *kajur*, or subjects or "power" of the king. The *alab*, a group in between, were overseers of the lands of the commoners, which belonged to the "kings." They collected the share of the produce due the chiefs—were the bailiffs so to speak—and, of course, got a commission on their collections.

Of the class of nobles, the paramount chief himself was accorded the greatest respect, his position involving the hereditary acquisition of magical power. The commoners were the workers of the land, the fishermen, the sailors, and the ordinary fighting men. With the possible exception of the *alab*—the head of the commoner lineages,— they were the lower class in every sense of the word. Their tribute supported the nobility; their houses were built in less favorable parts of an island; they were not permitted the distinctive tattoo nor the finer dress of the upper class.

In the old days "first fruits" and a share of the food taken from land and sea were presented to the *iroij*, formally and informally— the first breadfruit, the best taro. A tuna was given to the king, and molefish (*Siganus rostratus*) were reserved for him. All turtles caught were the property of the chiefs. These old practices have been largely discontinued, except occasionally for certain choice parts of some fish. Nowadays when a Marshallese catches a tuna, he gives the *iroij* only a portion of it, or none at all if he so wishes.

The testimony of old natives indicates that under pre-European conditions, the authority of the paramount chief was very great. He had power to dispossess commoners of their land rights at will, and he also controlled the allocation of rights among the lesser chiefs. The commoners worked the land and collected the produce under the eyes of the *alab*, who was supervised by the lesser chiefs, who in turn were responsible to the paramount chief, for the primary rights both to the land itself and to its fruits were held by him.

Subjects of the paramount chief, however, could not be evicted from the land without good reason—mainly for offenses against him, personally, and their rights were, as a rule, respected. The more commoners he had in his realm, the more power he possessed—a larger reservoir of human beings to draw upon for labor and warfare. It was therefore manifestly incumbent upon the *iroij* to treat his subjects with consideration in order to retain their loyalty. The system of land tenure was and is still somewhat analogous to the feudal system of medieval Europe—a stratification of individuals with reciprocal duties and obligations as well as privileges.

In the latter part of the nineteenth century, with the development of copra as the cash crop, the shares of the *iroij* and of the people who produced the copra were established. The paramount chief receives a percentage of the money paid for each pound of copra produced on land in which his suzerainty is recognized. This share varies, ranging from 1½ mills in part of Ralik to 1 cent in the Ratak chain, depending upon the copra potential of the atoll or island and the attitude of the people toward their *iroij*.

Copra is sold by the individual producers to a buyer on the atoll or island or more often to a local general store, which is usually a cooperative enterprise owned by all or by a large segment of the atoll population. After the chief's share has been withheld by the *alab*, the latter's share is retained, and the remainder turned over to the workers. On Majuro Atoll, while the author was there, the buyers of copra in the village were withholding 1 per cent as the "king's" share. In at least one instance which came to my notice, the *alab* was an employee of the village store who took 2 per cent of the sale as his share. Kikimar one day at his farm told the author that the *alab* who gets part of the proceeds of his crop is employed in the public works department of the Government.

The typical Marshallese landholding, or *wato*, consists of a strip of land stretching from lagoon to ocean and varying in size from about one to five acres. Each *wato* has its own name and a history of ownership known to everyone in the atoll. There are different kinds of rights to a holding—through descent, intermarriage, and other clan relationships. Members and associated members of a related social group—the *bwij*, or lineage—work the *wato* under an *alab*, clearing it of underbrush and performing other tasks necessary for the simple type of agriculture practiced in these low-lying coral atolls with their restricted resources. In some instances people are allowed to work land not belonging to their lineage when lineage members do not require its use, that is, when they have more than enough land for their own needs or want to help some less fortunate person.

Many usufruct rights in land are acquired by marriage, for Marshallese have been marrying into other clans and atoll groups for centuries, more and more with recently improved transportation and communication. Today many Marshallese possess land rights in widely separated atolls, something which has done a great deal to break down the old cohesion of atoll life.

As well as rights in land, there were traditional rights in the reef claimed by the chief as his personal property. From time to time, he instituted a taboo during which no one else was permitted to fish a particular reef on penalty of death or expulsion from his land. According to custom, the property rights extended out to where people could stand waist deep, in order to fish with a pole. Since 1934, when the Japanese authorities broke the taboo by declaring reefs open to everyone, anyone who so desired has utilized these once forbidden fishing grounds.

With few exceptions, the pattern of land usage in the Marshalls remains as it was before the advent of foreigners except, of course, that the large villages have added stores, council houses, dispensaries, and church buildings. The system of land tenure and usufruct has changed but slightly despite the acculturative influence of three different régimes.

By the end of the Japanese régime, the authority of the paramount chief had been modified to the extent that he was no longer an autocrat who could move commoners off their land at his will. This modification of the old régime has, of course, been continued by the American administration. The chiefs are naturally intent on holding title to the land in the islands, and they are supported in this attitude by the *alab*, who collect the chiefs' share and their own too, for the middle men fear that otherwise they may lose some or all of their income.

Today, however, the old concepts regarding the nature of land rights are in a state of flux, some natives maintaining that the people themselves are not sure of the extent of the rights of chiefs and commoners. The chiefs argue that they are the only ones who know! Land in Majuro is divided between King Isaiah and a group of people who are taking the place of another king, recently deceased.

Already knowing the implications of democracy, this group does not want a new "king."

There is a good deal of Government land in the Marshalls, some of it in small pieces on various atolls formerly held by the Germans and later by the Japanese Government. The chiefs are objecting to the idea of turning it over to the people, fearing a general distribution which they do not at present want; hence it will be difficult to settle some of the land problems without friction. A possible solution is to make such sections homestead areas for the people of the atoll or island where they are located.

The following breakdown of land ownership in the archipelago is estimated:

TABLE XX

LANDOWNERSHIP IN THE MARSHALLS, 1954

	ACRES
Indigenous Inhabitants	37,194
U.S. Govt. & Trust Territory Public domain	2,572
Homesteaded by Micronesians	659
Total	40,425

There are small land holdings by religious missions, largely worked by indigenous people for their own benefit, the acreage of which is not available.

Trusteeship Government land at present is being leased to the people to work rather than to the chiefs, for the Government would like to divide the land between the chiefs and the people as was done in the Great Mahele in Hawaii. But satisfactory ways and means of doing so have not yet been reached, and no feasible policy has been laid down. The problem is especially difficult since the code of government for the Trust Territory states that things should not be done which are contrary to the customs of the people. No basic system of landholdings has been formulated by the Marshallese to help the administration form a policy. Wotie and Taroa in

Maloelap have considerable Government areas which it is planned to homestead to the original owners, for it would create much dissatisfaction to take people from one island and settle them on another where neither they nor their relatives hold any land.

A land board for the islands consists of ten Marshallese, five from the Upper House of Congress and five from the Lower House, and considerable discussion has taken place between them. The "kings" and other titled people maintain, as in the case of rights, that they and they alone know the system of tenure and that the commoners or their representatives should not be consulted. Because no well defined policy exists, land problems are solved temporarily as far as possible by various expeditious methods.

A few deviations from the general pattern of landownership may be cited. Likiep Atoll is owned in fee simple by the descendants of two European adventurers who purchased the entire atoll from the paramount chief of Northern Ratak (Jurtaka) in 1877, with all rights and privileges appertaining thereto. The land is used by "mixed-blood" descendants and a larger group composed of pure descendants of the original inhabitants of the atoll, all of whom produce copra on a share-crop basis.

Ebeye Village in Kwajalein Atoll is essentially a labor camp whose inhabitants, most of them from other atolls, derive their income either directly or indirectly from employment by the military establishment on Kwajalein Island. The "town" has eight wholesale-retail stores, five bakeries, and a restaurant. All the goods consumed are imported: mainly rice, sardines, and canned beef. Marshallese will continue to crowd into Ebeye as long as the economic attractions of wages remain there. The fact that the owners of the land in the village have not yet been paid any rent for the use of it is a cause of discontent and complaint.

An alienation of property occurred during the period after World War II when the inhabitants of the atolls of Eniwetok and Bikini were required to leave their atolls, which became testing grounds for atomic warfare. The Eniwetok people, transplanted to the uninhabited but smaller atoll of Ujelang, have been able to make a fairly successful adjustment to the new environment and have modified their traditional tenure system in their new home. Some 160 Bikinians who were removed to Rongerik and later to Kwajalein are now on Kili in the southern Marshalls. There is some difference of opinion as to when Bikini will again be sufficiently free from radio-activity to be safe for reoccupation. The atomic bomb tests at Eni-wetok and Bikini and the prospects of peace and war are matters that concern only a few of the more sophisticated natives.

Land disputes have been and still are the cause of almost all family schisms in the Marshalls, for people are continually plotting to obtain more land by marriage, and by "black magic" as in the past. Land is regarded as sacred, something as formerly to fight for and die for; it has been sold or given away to outsiders only because of fear of either physical or moral force. The individual Marshallese is fully aware of the particular categories into which his lineage lands fall and what rights he possesses in them. Genealogies, both royal and common, are traced back in some cases ten or more generations, and many of them, now written down, are carefully preserved by their owners, and used as evidence to support claims in land disputes.

TRANSPORTATION

The complicated titles to land in the islands, the network of rela-tionship of intermarriage with consequent rights to land, the gen-eral scattering of the membership of clans throughout the archipelago, and interisland trade and commerce are all facilitated by a good system of ocean transportation in which the natives prove themselves able seamen.

The Marshallese travel extensively, trading and visiting with their relatives and friends on neighboring atolls. The inhabitants of some of the more isolated islands, Ailuk, for example, used to migrate to some other atoll to visit and trade for a month or two once each year.

Some atolls have one or two twenty-six-foot whaleboats, decked over and fitted with a mast and fore-and-aft-rigged sails. They go from atoll to atoll in calm weather. The hulls were procured from the United States Navy, and the work in decking and fitting them was done by Marshallese boat builders, of which there are two establish-ments, one at Likiep, the other at Majuro, in the Southern Marshalls. There are in the archipelago a number of native-owned schooners about forty feet long, two-masted, equipped with Diesel motors. They are used in hauling copra to Kwajalein or Majuro, and in various other small commercial enterprises, as well as for a considerable passenger service.

In addition to the locally owned boats plying between the atolls, the *Roque*, a Diesel freight ship of some 250 tons belonging to the Pacific Micronesian Line, makes quarterly "field trips," visiting all of the atolls and carrying Trust Territory officials and copra buyers. It also carries a large amount of copra and trade goods. This ship, although expensive to maintain and operate, is indispensable for the good government of the islands.

The favorite months for native travel are July, August, September, and October, when the weather is most suitable for sailing. Native chiefs on the outlying atolls commonly maintain a residence at Jabor, where they visit from time to time during those months.

There is a good deal of cooperation between the atolls, for, with their restricted food supply, the people feel a dependence upon one another. When an atoll or island is struck by a typhoon, natives from other islands hurry to relieve the consequent famine.

GOVERNMENT

Having exercised leadership and authority in the past, the paramount chiefs and the more able of the nobility are still looked to for leadership in the present. This is not an invariable rule, but a tendency—a result of the continuing force of tradition. Since the paramount chief and his nobles were the leaders in war and in sailing expeditions, since they controlled the land and the fruits thereof, provided the primary leadership of the community, and in turn enjoyed the privilege of being fed and supported by the commoners, their traditional position in both government and social life cannot be readily overlooked even with the democratic-like form of government of today.

It is no coincidence, for example, that the present magistrate at Majuro, the most important of all village and atoll officials, although elected by the people, is also the sister's son and heir apparent of a paramount chief. At Majuro he is the principal representative of the village in official dealings with the American Government.

The old Government structure still exists, albeit in the restricted and modified form which evolved during the German and Japanese régimes. Ever since the over-all assumption of political control, first by Germany, then by Japan, and finally by the United States, the political influence of the paramount and lesser chiefs has steadily lessened. During the American administration especially, the commoners have greatly strengthened their relative position, for they are no longer obliged to send a continuous stream of food to nobles and paramount chief, nor can they now be dispossessed by the "king." Concurrently the position of nobles and paramount chiefs has been correspondingly weakened, though the paramount chief is still regarded as having the primary claim to the land itself.

Today the outward distinctions of the old class system are disappearing, for nobility and commoners dress alike and eat much the same food, although, on nearly all the atolls, the hereditary chief has been voted in as magistrate. In the few cases where he has not been elected magistrate, he has only one vote in a meeting to decide questions, just like the commoner. Each atoll has an elected council which discusses economic, political, and social matters pertaining to the local community. In some atolls the council votes what per cent of the proceeds of copra shall go to the chief.

The Congress of the Marshall Islands, an advisory body to the administration, is composed of two houses: the House of Iroij and the House of Assembly. The House of Iroij includes all persons holding the position of paramount chief "in accordance with the traditions, usages, and customs of the Marshallese people." The House of Assembly is composed of representatives of the municipalities of the islands elected by the people. There are some forty members in the Upper House and sixty members in the Lower. The Upper House, composed of those who formerly had supreme power, looks askance at the commoners newly acquiring prestige; the Lower House, on the other hand, examines very critically any measures being discussed by the chiefs. So far, whatever laws have been enacted have been passed by both houses temporarily sitting together.

The *iroij*, viewing the Congress with mixed feelings, do not want to lose their power and are somewhat confused about the situation. They see the usefulness of such a body, but would like to retain at least some of their old authority, and especially to have more share in the government than the bicameral Congress gives them. They still exercise a hold on the people, stronger in the northern, poorer islands than in the more productive south. But the Congress, a factor of unity in the Marshalls which the people did not have before, after four years is making its influence felt. In 1953, for example, when the question of keeping the intermediate school came up, the Congress voted to continue it, and imposed a tax on copra to pay the teachers. The subjects discussed by the Fifth Marshallese Congress, which ended shortly before the author's visit, resembled those taken up by any State legislature in the United States: taxes, plant and animal quarantine, new varieties and strains of stock, rentals for land, and reef and lagoon rights.

The tax on copra for the elementary schoolteachers' salary, $0.001 on every pound of copra produced, is levied on all copra sellers in the Marshalls District. The funds collected, averaging $7,000 a year, are paid through the district administrator. The head tax charged to all males, ages eight to sixty, varies in one atoll to another from about six to ten dollars a year.

It was resolved at the Fifth Congress that the district administrator and the High Commissioner of the Trust Territory be asked to hasten the time of payment of rent to the owners of all lands retained for the use of the United States Navy and Trust Territory.

In accordance with the general policy of the administering authority stated in the Trusteeship Agreement, and by proclamation of the Chief Administrator of the Trust Territory, native customs are recognized by the courts in all instances except where such customs might lead to a serious miscarriage of justice, to a violation of the basic rights of individuals or of the Trusteeship Agreement, to an infringement upon the laws of the Trust Territory, or to a situation endangering public health or morals. The courts may inflict punishment for violation of unwritten but generally recognized local customary law. Sentences are carried out in the same manner as those given for violation of written law.

The position of public defender and counselor was established in September, 1950, under the administrative supervision of the director of internal affairs. An experienced lawyer has been appointed to the post with headquarters at Truk. He protects the legal rights of all inhabitants of the Trust Territory, defending the accused in criminal actions involving serious punishments by preparing their defenses and representing their interests at trials. As counselor, he advises the inhabitants in civil matters of a legal nature, rendering the necessary legal aid and representing them in civil actions. His services have been eagerly accepted and utilized by the Micronesians in all parts of the Trust Territory.

During both the German and the Japanese régimes, the administrative seat of government for the Marshalls was located at Jabor on Jaluit Atoll. Since Jabor was completely destroyed during the war, Majuro Atoll has taken its place as the Capital where Government headquarters are now on the island of Aliga. The natives favor returning to Jabor in Jaluit as the meeting place of the Congress, for it was the seat of the Government under the Germans and the Japanese and, therefore, has the tradition of a Capital. Furthermore, boats can get in and out of the atoll through several passes, whereas Majuro has only one pass. Finally, Jaluit has a greater population than Majuro.

Approximately 200 Marshallese were employees of the administration in 1954. In addition to the salaries paid them, $121,000 was paid in that year in wages to native employees of stores and trading companies, domestic servants, and, perhaps the larger part, to workers for the Navy. More and more the people of these remote islands are assuming a semblance of Western political economy.

SOCIAL DEVELOPMENT

The evolution in the economic and political sphere of Marshallese life has been paralleled by a new social development. Of course, the old social structure based on hereditary distinctions is recognized, for membership in any given class is still determined by birth on the mother's side. A man is *iroij* if his mother was *iroij*, regardless of the rank of the father. There are still the two main divisions in village society—nobility and commoners—membership in which is hereditary and follows the maternal line, but the two classes today do not form a rigid caste system, although it was formerly customary for at least the paramount chiefs to marry within their own class.

The population of an atoll is a well defined social unit because the vast stretches of surrounding sea separate it from other atolls. Contacts with the outside world are restricted, although, as was already stated, interisland communications from time immemorial have led to many blood and clan relationships throughout the whole archipelago. When visitors from a distance arrive they are immediately taken care of by members of their clans; but except for this social relationship, clans mean little nowadays as compared with ancient times when they made war upon one another.

The paramount chief was in former days entirely responsible for the social welfare and safety of the people of his lands. With the coming of foreign governments and the development of the copra trade he paid their doctors' bills and dentists' bills. As more and more medical and dental services were given, the expense correspondingly increased and the chiefs began to find it a burden. The United States Navy, when it was governing, gave a sum to some chiefs to defray these costs. In a few atolls the people with their newly acquired democracy voted money to the chiefs to meet the bills; in the rest they have refused any such subsidy. Therefore the situation is in a transition stage, like other situations in the islands where the people are emerging from paternalistic administration to a new order.

An important factor historically in the social evolution of the Marshallese has been the Protestant Church. In 1852 the Boston Mission Society (American Board of Commissioners for Foreign Missions) extended its activities from Hawaii to Micronesia by sending into the area four people, one of them a doctor. Although they visited the Marshalls at this time, they did not remain, but went on to establish stations at Kusaie and Ponape in the Carolines. In 1857, however, the Reverend Doane, with his wife, returned to Ebon, where he built a church and began his labors. From the first station at Ebon, the missionaries made periodic trips through the southern atolls. A station was started in Majuro in 1869, when a native Hawaiian and his wife took up residence on that atoll. Protestant evangelists reduced the Marshallese language to writing; gave the people schools, medicines, and a new religion; and brought conflicting clans to peace. One of the earlier warrior chiefs to espouse the missionary cause was Kabua of Ailinglapalap who held control over the Ralik chain. It was he who, years ago, made the treaty with the Germans at Jaluit that led to their occupation.

Jesuits of the order of the Most Sacred Heart of Jesus came to the Marshalls in 1899 and built a church on Jaluit. By 1907 additional mission stations had been established on Arno and Likiep, and elementary instruction was being given in German to 117 pupils in the mission schools.

An important aspect of the Protestant Church is that it has been a factor for a hundred years in the gradual Westernization of the Marshallese. It was the strongest influence in the abandonment of useless customs and traditions associated with the native religion. Few very old customs survive, and those that have survived have been modified. The election of deacons by vote year in and year out made it easy for the natives to accept the idea of electing Government officials. Indeed, the Church is still a strong social and political institution in the islands, where it has been careful not to conflict too abruptly with some well maintained native institutions.

Because of traditional premarital sex freedom, a relatively brittle marriage tie in early adult years, and a considerable amount of leeway in regard to postmarital chastity, there is a fairly continuous flow of members ousted from the Church for adultery. They are readmitted, however, after a proper period of repentance.

Although missions have had a strong hold in the Marshalls for many years, "magic" still survives, and occasionally black magic or casting a spell is suspected in cases of peculiar illnesses. Traditional Marshallese "doctors" still disperse herbs for stomach-aches, for headaches, and for love sickness and all other complaints.

THE FUTURE

For a long time into the foreseeable future, the situation in the Marshalls will not be significantly different from what it is today. The changes which have already begun—some of them many years ago—will go on slowly, and a gradual evolution is in the best interests of the people. A well educated native remarked that some of the forward-looking people in the Marshalls feel that even now things may be going a bit too fast, and that certain stabilizing influences in their society may be taken away, leaving nothing in their places and, hence, resulting in a social vacuum which may create unrest among the people.

As was pointed out, agriculture in the islands has two aspects: subsistence and export. Subsistence agriculture is dependent upon the original food plants and on traditional cultural methods and uses of native vegetation. Papayas, limes, and other introduced plants have had little effect on subsistence agriculture and diet. Agriculture and fishing, originally complementary subsistence activities, are still so to a large extent. The relatively small contribution of introduced animals to the diet is due to their restricted number rather than to local acceptance. The changes that have occurred in the past half-century or so will remain: a great increase in the area devoted to coconuts and consequent elimination of original vegetation, greater dependence on imported goods, and the beginnings of substitution of imported for local foods. The pattern of landholding does not always favor fullest use of the land, particularly for subsistence crops. None the less, subsistence agriculture is largely adequate and capable of expanding to support an increase in population.

Such considerations lead to the question of producing other export crops in order to increase the total income of the area, and minimize the risks inherent in a single-crop agriculture. Unfortunately, the prospect of any considerable gains by such means is exceedingly dim. In the entire Marshalls the total area of land suitable for such crops is small and is scattered here and there piecemeal, precluding any large single development or mechanization, and complicating problems of production and shipment. Even in islands with plenty of rainfall, the inherent productivity of the soils for most crops is very low. The calcareous soils rule out some crops and, without measures for maintaining or increasing fertility, the success of others would be foredoomed. Finally, were a new crop that looked hopeful decided upon, the discovery of varieties and cultural methods adapted to the area, the almost certain necessity of pest control measures, fertility problems, and the considerable task of adapting the people's "folkways" to the new crop would together require sustained skilled effort and supervision, with the outcome very doubtful.

It is difficult, then, to suggest lines of improvement for the economic situation, since the future of agriculture is not likely to be much different from that at present. The Marshallese, through many centuries of experience, are using their land in general to best advantage. A research study into the ecology of the breadfruit tree by a qualified tropical agriculturist would probably bring to light reasons for shortages from time to time of that valuable food, and perhaps suggest means of expanding its production. Bananas might be cultivated a little more extensively by digging small depressions, say about two feet, filling them with leaves and other vegetable debris, letting it decay to form a compost, and planting the trees in this— a practice successfully carried out in other islands in the Pacific.

The meager natural resources of the relatively dry Northern Marshalls are adequate to support the population, but on a standard that most Westerners would regard as very low. However, before being educated to be dissatisfied, the Marshallese got along well. They had evolved excellent adjustments to the atoll environment and utilized wisely indeed the resources provided. In the north, the sea, and especially the lagoon, still provide a large share of their nutrition. Their few material needs they wrest by considerable ingenuity, in one way or another, from their difficult surroundings.

Little, if anything, can be done directly by man to lessen, much less prevent, loss of land or soil by typhoon damage either in the Marshalls or elsewhere in the Trust Territory. This fact must be kept in mind if attempts are made to increase soil fertility. Furthermore, greater soil productivity leads, not necessarily to higher or better standards of living, but to larger populations. Well intentioned attempts to improve the lot of the native inhabitants of atolls thus might well jeopardize more lives than ever when the inevitable typhoon sweeps in, and lead to appalling drops in population and lower living standards.

The inclusion of Kusaie in the Carolines in the Marshalls District would be good administration, for it is a high, volcanic island, and has Hawaiian taro, oranges, bananas, and breadfruit to sell in atolls where these do not grow well. Furthermore, Kusaie is nearer to the Marshalls than some of the Marshall Islands are to the headquarters of the administration.

Former Japanese Government lands should be leased or rented to the earlier Marshallese owners or their relatives against the day when further changes in land tenure come about, and payment of claims against the United States Government for occupation and damage to land should be expedited. The land of course should never be allowed to pass into non-Marshallese hands. This, perhaps the most explicit desire of the Marshallese people, was voiced in a joint, unanimous resolution at a meeting of the Second Marshallese Congress. Incidentally, the Marshallese feel that they can settle many of their own problems through the Congress. Nonalienation of land is all the more important now that the American medical program, with its superior facilities, has almost entirely eradicated venereal and other diseases which have prevented a large population increase in the past. There is no serious pressure at present, but the growth in population is steady, and the time may come when every piece of land must be utilized to the maximum extent, as is done in the Gilbert Islands where overpopulation has been a problem for many years. An eventuality of this kind in the Marshalls should be anticipated.

More and more disagreements over land rights will be brought before the district court if, as is probable, the disputants themselves fail to reach amicable settlements. Thus far, however, these cases have been relatively few. Apparently the Marshallese, wary of legal processes that are outside the local culture pattern, are reluctant to bring such highly important problems before outsiders. Instances have arisen in which such disputes have been settled by the traditional authorities rather than through alien American procedure. The administration will have to handle land disputes, carefully and forcefully, through interested, informed, and sympathetic judges. This, a question of personnel, obviously will require a great deal of tact, but it is absolutely necessary if the governing authorities are to have the continued confidence of everyone and at the same time accomplish their mission. The Marshallese are watching every move that the administration makes regarding these matters. Wise moves by the administration will cause any who may be uncertain and wavering in their attitudes to follow the administration's lead. It is, therefore, necessary for the Government to treat all situations involving land rights with great discretion. Problems can be worked out in large part by the Marshallese people themselves with a minimum of American intervention.

Land tenure is one of the more complicated aspects of Marshallese culture. The traditional system itself is greatly involved, but the complexity has increased as concepts regarding it have changed during contact with foreign civilizations. This is the principal reason why a future intensive study of land tenure, covering a number of atolls, is one of the more promising approaches to a fuller understanding of modern change in Marshallese social and economic organization. It would be an excellent guide to any American judge of such disputes.

Since new criteria of social status are evolving, the gradual decline of the old class structure of Marshallese society will continue. The basis for this trend lies in the changing roles of commoners and nobility and in the breakdown of reciprocal obligations between the two classes, as well as in the over-all assumption of political power by a succession of outside nations. The nobles and paramount chiefs, the former leaders of the community, were at least theoretically possessed of superior knowledge, backed by sacred, magical power.

On the other hand, in the recently formed groups of business and professional people—medical aides, teachers, interpreters, storekeepers —leadership does not gravitate to the nobility. A different type of society is evolving on the basis of skills and knowledge introduced by the Western nations and Japan. In the distant future this new society will probably supplant the hereditary class structure, and political leadership will be exercised by persons with a superior position in the new system rather than by the nobility. However, the natives are in no sense a disorganized group with a broken culture. The course of contact has been gradual enough so that adjustments and improvements have been made without the imposition of violent and permanently disruptive factors.

The American administration, with an active program for training Marshallese youth interested in progress, is strengthening these new criteria of status. At present, the bright young men of a village are being attracted primarily to teachers' training schools and to the school for medical practitioners. Other young people are advancing their technical knowledge. Recently half a dozen studying how to survey land quickly acquired the skill necessary to operate the instruments and to calculate the data obtained.

The procession of governments experienced by older people in the islands has made them more phlegmatic toward change than their children. Many of the young people are eager for improvement, especially those who have been to Guam or to the mainland of the United States. A native teacher in the schools stated: "When young people complain about some attitude of the American administration which is opposed to their suggestion, the older folk say to them, 'Well, we've seen them come and we'll see them go. You know that that has been our experience in the Marshalls during the last fifty years.'"

REFERENCES

Cross-Cultural Survey (Institute of Human Relations, Yale University): *Meteorology of the Marshall Islands*, Strategic Bulletins of Oceania No. 2, 1943; *Meteorology of the Marshall Islands*, No. 7, March 5, 1943.

De Laubenfels, M. V., "Ocean Currents in the Marshall Islands," *Geog. Rev.*, 40 (2), 234-259 (1950).

Fosberg, F. R., "Soils of the Northern Marshall Atolls, with Special Reference to the Jemo Series," *Soil Science*, Vol. 78, No. 2, August, 1954, pp. 99-107.

Ittel, W. H., "Sailing Canoes of the Marshall Islands," *U.S. Naval Instit. Proceedings*, 75 (5): 589, May, 1949.

Jenkins, W. S., "Wartime Canoe Building in the Marshall Islands," *American Neptune*, 6 (1): 71-72, Jan., 1946.

Kirtley, Edwin L., "The Liberation of the Marshall Island People," *The Friend*, October, 1944, 5-7.

Markwith, Carl, "Farewell to Bikini," *National Geographic Magazine*, 90 (1): 97-116, July, 1946.

Mason, Leonard, The Economic Organization of the Marshall Islands. U.S. Commercial Co. Economic Survey of Micronesia, Report No. 9, 1946 (typescript microfilm in the Library of Congress).

———, "The Bikinians: A Transplanted Population," *Human Organization*, 9 (1): 5-15, Spring, 1950.

Moore, W. Robert, "Our New Military Wards, the Marshalls," *National Geog. Magazine*, 88 (3): 325-360, September, 1945.

Morison, Samuel Eliot, "Historical Notes on the Gilbert and Marshall Islands," *American Neptune*, 4 (2), 1-32 (1944).

Murdock, G. P., *Food and Water Supply in the Marshall Islands* (Cross-Cultural Survey, Institute of Human Relations, Yale Univ. Strategic Bulletins of Oceania No. 5, 1943), 24 pp.

Nugent, L. E., Jr., "Coral Reefs in the Gilbert, Marshall, and Caroline Islands," *Geol. Soc. Amer. Bulletin*, 57 (8): 735-780 (1946).

Pomeroy, Earl S., "American Policy Respecting the Marshalls, Carolines and Marianas, 1898-1941," *Pacific Historical Review*, 17 (1): 43-53 (February, 1948).

Spoehr, Alexander, "The Marshall Islands and Transpacific Aviation," *Geog. Review*, 36 (3): 447-451 (July, 1946).

———, *Majuro: A Village in the Marshall Islands* (Chicago Natural History Museum, Fieldiana, Anthropology Series 39, 1949), 266 pp.

Steinbach, E., "The Marshall Islands," *Geographical Journal*, 7: 296-297, March, 1896.

Taylor, W. R., *Plants of Bikini and Other Northern Marshall Islands* (Ann Arbor: University of Michigan Press, 1950), 227 pp.

Tobin, J. E., "Ebeye Village: An Atypical Marshallese Community," mimeographed, 1954.

Tracey, J. I., Jr., H. S. Ladd and J. E. Hoffmeister. "Reefs of Bikini, Marshall Islands," *Geol. Soc. of America*. Bull. 59, 861-878 (1948).

United States Hydrographic Office Gazetteer No. 6, *Caroline, Marianas,*

Marshall and Gilbert Islands (H.O. Pub. No. 886, 2nd edit., July, 1944).

United States Navy Military Government Handbook, *Marshall Islands*, OPNAV 500-1, Aug. 17, 1943.

United States Trust Territory of the Pacific Islands, "Annual Report for the Marshall Islands, 1954," mimeographed.

————, "Marshalls District, Statistical Requirements, Fiscal Year, 1954."

Wedgwood, Camilla H., "Notes on the Marshall Islands," *Oceania*, 13 (1): 1-23, September, 1942.

Weitzell, E. C., "The Marianas, Caroline and Marshall Islands," *Scientific Monthly*, 63 (3): 218-226, September, 1946.

Wright, C. H., "Sailing Canoes of the Marshall Islands," *U. S. Naval Inst. Proceedings*, 74 (350): 1529-1531, December, 1948.

ATOLL RESEARCH BULLETINS

Anderson, Donald, *The Plants of Arno Atoll, Marshall Islands*, Atoll Research Bull. No. 7, 1951.

Arno, T., *The Hydrology of the Northern Marshall Islands*, Atoll Research Bull. No. 30, 1954.

Cox, D. C., *The Hydrology of Arno Atoll, Marshall Islands*, Atoll Research Bull. No. 8, 1951.

Fosberg, F. R., *Northern Marshall Islands Expedition, 1951-1952*, Atoll Research Bull. No. 38, 1955.

————, *Northern Marshall Islands Expedition, 1951-1952: Land Biota; Vascular Plants*, Atoll Research Bull. No. 39, 1955.

Hatheway, W. H., *The Land Vegetation of Arno Atoll, Marshall Islands*, Atoll Research Bull. No. 16, 1953.

Hiatt, R. W., and Conald Strasburg, *Marine Zoology Study of Arno Atoll, Marshall Islands*, Atoll Research Bull. No. 4, 1951.

Marshall, J. T., *Vertebrate Ecology of Arno Atoll, Marshall Islands*, Atoll Research Bull. No. 3, 1950.

Mason, Leonard, *Anthropology-Geography Study of Arno Atoll, Marshall Islands*, Atoll Research Bull. No. 10, 1951.

Miller, H. A., *Bryophytes Collected by F. R. Fosberg in the Marshall Islands*, Atoll Research Bull. No. 40, 1955.

Stone, E. L., Jr., *The Soils of Arno Atoll, Marshall Islands*, Atoll Research Bull. No. 5, 1951.

Tobin, J. E., *Land Tenure in the Marshall Islands*, Atoll Research Bull. No. 11, 1952.

Usinger, R. L., and Ira La Rivers, *The Insect Life of Arno*, Atoll Research Bull. No. 15, 1953.

Wells, J. W., *The Coral Reefs of Arno Atoll, Marshall Islands*, Atoll Research Bull. No. 9, 1951.

XIV

Pingelap and Mokil

In this chapter on Pingelap and Mokil, the author begs the reader's indulgence to diverge from the objective nature of the previous discussions and relate personal experiences on a small island in the Pacific where he went to study the problem of overpopulation. Overpopulation problems in Pacific islands are not new, for they have been faced by the indigenous inhabitants from time immemorial. However, they were solved by the aborigines in ways which are entirely contrary to the dictates of modern, civilized people. At the time of the discovery of many islands in the Pacific, or at least when the first missionaries arrived, abortion was a common practice, induced through various means by the local medicine men or witch doctors. Furthermore, what few authoritative records are available indicate that two infants out of three were killed at birth. Malnutrition took a quota from those that were allowed to survive, and casualties in wars between clans were of some consequence. Children who were subnormal or crippled were also put out of the way, and old people were quietly allowed to die.

The birth of twins was considered an ill omen, and one of the two was always killed. The author knew in Fiji one of twins who had been exposed at birth. Exposure by leaving the child for three or four days in the brush or forest was one of the ways of getting rid of it. In the case of the Fijian, when some women going to bury the remains found the infant still alive womanly compassion induced one of them to take him home to bring him up. Turning out to be more intelligent than the average boy, when the author knew him he was a student at the Suva Medical School, preparing to be a native physician among his people. During my visit to Pingelap one of twins "died" under conditions with regard to which I could not get a satisfactory explanation.

Christian teachings, backed up by promulgations of the various governments concerned, have resulted in the lessening or partial abandonment of the practices which kept the population of an island down to the number that could be fed at a subsistence level. However, during the last one hundred years, the greatest factors not only in restricting the increase, but in causing very serious decreases in what might be considered the normal populations of the islands, were the infections and diseases introduced by whalers, castaways, and various other foreigners who visited the archipelagoes, some of whom stayed permanently. Tuberculosis and other respiratory diseases still take a heavy toll.

During the last few decades modern health measures and discoveries such as penicillin have tended to keep down mortality, so that now, in nearly all parts of the central and eastern Pacific, births exceed deaths and the population is gaining. In American Samoa, where, as was already pointed out, the situation is serious, current trends suggest that the indigenous population will double within the next twenty years. The Samoans of Western Samoa are increasing almost as rapidly. In the Gilbert Islands the problem of subsistence became very serious in the middle 1930's. There the Government had successfully prohibited all controls except abortion, which it discouraged but was unable to prevent. The extreme poverty among certain families with insufficient land demanded that some measures be taken to relieve the situation. After careful planning, two thousand Gilbertese were taken off that archipelago to colonize three islands in the Phoenix group. Unfortunately, the settlement scheme on one of them, Sydney Island, proved a failure because of the small annual rainfall there.

Another factor which aggravates the situation now as compared with the pre-European era is that since the advent of missions and modern government, the native can no longer consume the entire product of his lands. He must have a surplus to pay his Government tax and subscriptions to the church, to buy clothing for himself and his family, as well as to provide many other necessities of modern life. With what we regard as a higher standard of living, the islands can support smaller numbers than before foreigners came.

Pingelap has had an increase in population of appreciably more than the atoll can support, and the pinch of hunger is beginning to make itself felt among natives there who have only small scraps of land from which to try to gain subsistence. Like thousands of islands in the Pacific, it has no radio communications, and its only contact with the outside world is the field-trip ship which calls every two or three months. During my stay I was the only Caucasian on the island, and my impressions of the atoll and the circumstances of the natives are representative of those which one still gets in many parts of the Pacific.

My first impression of Pingelap, on a rainy afternoon in July from a stormy ocean, was a dark-green, elongated forest which, on nearer approach, appeared to be separated into two islands by a distinct gap edged with a white line of surf stretching out along the reef. As our field-trip ship, the *Roque*, came closer, another island came into view at the rear, near the south end of which the bright gray roof of a steepled church contrasted with the dark background. Then other small shiny roofs, in line with the church, glistened northward along the coast among the coconut palms.

Fourteen whaleboats filled with natives, all men, put out to meet us, while the remainder of the village population stood in groups on the beach. As the boats drew alongside, nimble brown bodies climbed up ropes and halyards to clamber on board.

I was introduced to Chief Dicksolomon, who wore a straw, stove-pipe hat painted blue to match his denim trousers rolled up to the knees. His first words, spoken in halting English, were "Have—you—a—match?" I learned the significance of his request a little later. Nine native boys, each carrying part of my luggage, prepared to help me off the ship. "Too much rain. We wait," said one of them, so I took refuge in my cabin; but it was not worth while, for a little later, after I had transferred to a small boat, we shipped a wave which drenched all of us. When we reached shallow water a husky native took me on his back to wade ashore, where, in my new quarters in the village, the boys watched me undress to put on dry clothes in a house which, by native standards, was very comfortable. It was the new, half finished Japanese-style house of the chief. I was to live on the second floor; the ground floor, still rocky, was spread with mats of drying copra. Ambilos, who was to be "my man Friday" on the island, unpacked the oil stove, but searched the village in vain for a match; mine were stowed in the bottom of a case which had not yet come ashore.

Pingelap is a representative small coral atoll, a group of three islets, seven or eight feet above high-tide level, enclosing the lagoon, 6°14′35″ north and 158°21′45″ east. A brief account of it in records of the Thilenius expedition (see references chapter XV) states that it was "sighted" in 1793 by Captain Musgrave in the *Sugar Cane*, and that it was discovered by Captain MacAskil in 1809. Captain Moore of the mission ship *Morning Star* also sighted the atoll in 1857. Pingelap, the largest islet, is on the southeast; Tugulu and Takai are on the northwest.

The following are approximately its dimensions, measured on a map with a planimeter:

TABLE XXI
Area of Pingelap

	ACRES	SQ. MILES
Pingelap Islet	275.4	0.43
Tugulu "	140.5	0.22
Takai "	16.9	0.026
	432.8	0.676
Area of Lagoon	298	0.466

The lagoon, entirely enclosed, contains coral heads and inward extensions of the reef, which at the village is shelving and extends far out, but at high tide is sufficiently submerged to permit a canoe to float to the sandy beach. The material of which the reef and islands are composed is wholly coral limestone and its derivatives: boulders, cobbles, pebbles, and sand. There are no climatic records for Pingelap, but the data available for sea level at Ponape, in almost the same latitude, indicate temperatures in the shade between 80° and 85° F for every month, and rainfall approximating 100 inches annually. Trade winds prevail most of the year, strongest in January and February, which is the period of least rain. The last recorded typhoon occurred in 1905. The island lies in the North Equatorial Current, in that part of the Pacific where the direct sunshine keeps the surface-water temperature close to 100° F the year round.

There is no runoff from the island, for at the most the water trickles a few feet on the packed coral of the main trails. There is little real soil, the surface material almost everywhere being stony. Most of the rainfall seeps very quickly into the highly permeable surface, where an hour after a heavy rain there is no water. Artificial catchment of precipitation, very important, furnishes the entire supply of water for cooking and drinking and by far the major supply for domestic purposes in general. It is collected in drums either from houses with galvanized-iron roofs or at the bases of inclined coconut trees, the trunks of which are scored to channel the flow.

The village, strung out along each side of a single straight street starting from the church at the south end and running northward parallel to the beach, consists mostly of frame structures, with a few thatch—all set up two or three feet above the ground. Papayas, bananas, and ornamental shrubs and herbs grow sparsely about the houses, and also a few stalks of sugar cane. In the early part of the day and in the evening children appear in swarms to lie or play in the main thoroughfare.

The morning after I arrived, I asked Ambilos to tell the chief that I wanted to have a meeting of the principal people in the village to tell them why I came. Saying that I wanted to give a present to the chief, I asked, "Shall I give him cigarettes?" Ambilos said slowly, "No; he is a Christian."

Nine leaders of the village assembled at the Government house: Chief Davidsolomon; his son secretary Dickenson; Judge Dikery, Sheriff; Kisio; "Doctor" Kulion; Peter, chief Medical Aid; Dengke; Alden; and Aidel. Chief Dicksolomon was absent.

"What is the greatest problem on Pingelap?" I asked.

"Food," one replied. "When we have some coconut and pandanus, we often call it supper." I told them the reason for my coming: that the administration was interested in their problems, especially their population problem, and hoped to take some of the people to Ponape. They listened very attentively and at the end asked questions: "Who will be chosen to go? When will the emigration take place? The government told us four years ago it was going to take off some people and it has not done anything yet." I said that I thought that the people themselves would choose who should go. Questions about the

number of people who lived on the island in the past elicited the
information that in 1905 there were 900 people,* but that a typhoon
had wiped most of them out.

In 1940, according to their information, an epidemic of "cowpox"
killed many, and at intervals in the history of the island famines occurred because of storms which destroyed their food plants or because

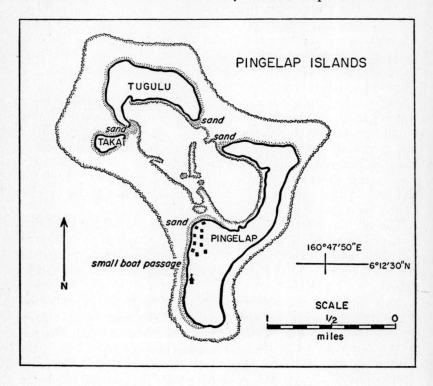

of winds which blew ocean water into their swamp, killing the taro.
Their current food shortage was due to a breadfruit blight and also
to the wearing out of the land. The yield of breadfruit was very small
that season. I did not see one breadfruit on a tree on the southern
third of the main island; however, it was near the end of the regular

---

* Inquiring closely about this figure I came to the conclusion that it is not to
be relied on. There may have been only five or six hundred, for there are no
"records" except for the memory of older people.

season. The yield from bananas and other crops was also less than it used to be.

When I asked the sizes of the larger families in the village, they discussed the question for a minute or two among themselves and then one of them answered, "Ten children"; the smaller ones had "two or three." Why did some have only two or three and others ten? They replied, "We try to have as many as we can and that is the way nature works!" Later I gave Chief Dicksolomon at his house a present of a yard and a half of cloth, a piece of soap, and candy.

After a few days I said to Ambilos, "Tell your sister to ask some women to come to her house, for I would like to know how women live in Pingelap."

"No," said Ambilos, picking his words, "I will not ask my sister. I will ask the second chief's wife, and she will command the women to come." He added: "In America, the women can say something about things. In Pingelap, no."

Sixteen women, all married, and a few children gathered in the village community house, where the second chief himself, Aidel, was sitting, though I told him it was just to be a women's meeting. He smiled, saying, "I want to listen." Three other men also came, to stay for a while. The first question I asked was, "What is the most important thing the women of Pingelap do?" They tossed the question about among themselves for a minute or two. Then one of them, apparently the oldest in the group, said: "Weave mats and make hats, cook, wash, and look after the children. If there is any time left, we help our husbands get taro, or fertilize it or do some other work for them." They agreed with the men that the larger families had about ten children. A girl generally goes to school until she is about fifteen, when, usually, she is married; if not, she starts to help her family. "Although the first child does not come sometimes for four or five years," they said, amused, "we start trying right away." When I asked, "Who wants a big family, the men or the women?" they replied, "Each wants it about the same." If babies come when the people are not married, what happens? "If the man wants it, he can take it into his family. If not, the woman must take it into hers."

My next question, "What do the women of Pingelap like to do best?" caused considerable discussion among them before an older woman who was generally their spokesman said, "We get together in a group of fifteen or sixteen, and each day we do all the things that each woman in turn wants to have done."

All but two of the women had been to Ponape and had seen an automobile, but only six had ever seen a horse, also at Ponape, during Japanese times. They told me the animal was taken out each day in order that people might ride on its back. When I asked about food I found that they used a little rice and sugar in German times, and much more after the Japanese came.

The main evidences of the Japanese occupation of the atoll are the remains of naval and weather stations, heavily built of concrete, the ruins of which still stand, shattered by shells and riddled with bullet holes. The natives told me that the maximum number of Japanese on the island at any one time was fifteen, and that all of them had been taken away in a submarine near the end of the war.

The land of Pingelap, wooded with trees, shrubs, and herbs similar to those on other islands, may be divided into two categories as far as agriculture is concerned: coconut jungle and taro land. The former consists of a dense stand of coconut palms, some pandanus, and bananas, with papayas and giant taro scattered thinly here and there; underneath them grass and various species of ferns grow profusely. The ground, strewn with dead leaves, rotting coconut husks in piles, fallen coconut trunks, and large coral rocks overgrown with moss, is marked by trails leading through the jungle in various directions, most of them to the taro swamp. That area, the heart of village agriculture, comprises about two acres six feet below the general level of the island. There *mwang*, or giant taro, and four other varieties of their staple food grow. It was evident that the swamp land had been extended recently by pick and shovel, for small taro pits had been excavated near it by hard digging through the coral down to permanent ground-water level.

One day I asked: "Why not extend the taro land indefinitely by digging? Then everyone would have enough food."

Ambilos replied: "That would be to take the land from people who don't want to give it up for taro, for they have enough taro land in the swamp. They want the area next to the taro land for coconuts or breadfruit." Fractionalization of land on Pingelap had gone so far that nobody wanted to give up any land for anything.

In the morning on weekdays, men, women and children were continually going to or coming from the taro swamp, some of them to fertilize their rows by placing cut grass and weeds at the roots and covering them over with dirt, others to take back coconut baskets full of taro to their homes in the village. On Saturday a supply is laid in and cooked for Sunday, for, like the natives on most islands, the Pingelapese are strict Sabbatarians.

The morning I talked with the heads of the village, they complained that not only was the soil wearing out, but a disease had attacked the breadfruit trees. While fear of a breadfruit famine probably caused the people to exaggerate the situation, it was evident that all was not well with that species of vegetation. In a space of about fifty yards each way I counted six breadfruit trees, four of which had been felled, because, according to Ambilos, they had the disease.* The leaves of the two still standing were slightly yellowish. Ten minutes' walk from this count, I saw two trees with leaves turning yellow, a small one entirely killed, and a fourth recently felled. It is probable that there were still some trees bearing in the northern part of the main island and perhaps on the other two islands, for I was served baked breadfruit several times. Breadfruit trees, pandanus, and bananas form less and less a part of the coconut jungle as one goes northward from the village, since these food trees are raised, for convenient access to them, mostly on the lands near where the people live.

Copra is the money crop of Pingelap, and much work in making it was carried on between the first call and the second call of the *Roque*, five days apart. The vessel went to Kusaie, the end of its run, before returning to Pingelap, Mokil, and Ponape.

One morning I watched a man and a boy husking coconuts from a pile under the trees near the shore, each of them standing beside a hardwood stake of mangrove stuck firmly in the ground, about three feet high and sharpened at the top. Grasping a coconut in both hands to raise it above his head as he bent over the stake, a husker would bring it down firmly and quickly on the sharpened end, with the nut off center so that he would not break the inner shell. As the top of the stake cut through the outer covering, he would twist the nut to wrench off a piece of the husk, and repeat his work until all the husk was removed. Then he would throw the husked nut aside, pick up another, and go through the same process.

Husked coconuts are carried to the village and placed in a heap

* I doubt if they were felled because they had any disease. Their trunks were very large and probably they were old trees past their best bearing age, cut down to make canoes.

under or close to the owner's house, where a man or woman with a
bush knife, at one blow of the blade splits a nut in two. With a
copra knife another worker scoops out the meat into a box or on a
mat which is then placed in the village street. Each evening, or at
any time before showers, these boxes and mats are moved for shelter
under the houses. In two or three sunny days the product is ready to
be sacked.

Pingelap vegetable foods in order of importance are taro, breadfruit, coconuts, arrowroot, and pandanus, occasionally papayas and
wild yams. Rice, for which the natives acquired a taste during
German times, became a habitual food during the Japanese régime.
Flour, sugar, beans, and onions were also introduced by the Japanese.
Pingelap people still like to flavor some boiled food with dried onions,
and I had brought onions with me for exchange. Among the goods I
observed in the village store were rice, flour, tea, sugar, canned
mackerel, and sardines.

What did I have for food on Pingelap after my bag of rice "disappeared"? For breakfast, taro cakes fried in coconut oil, breadfruit,
boiled fish, and papayas. At dinner and supper I ate fish, two kinds
of baked breadfruit, and taro. Once I had a whole baked young
chicken, but was never offered any rice. Those who brought me meals
asked several times to make sure that I would exchange shares of
rice for the meals if and when the sack of rice were found. But it
never turned up!

Natives catch tuna and swordfish in the open ocean, and, with
spears and nets, take reef fish, keeping some of them alive in two
fish ponds in the lagoon, built at the insistence of the Government
and finished early in 1954, in hopes that fish from them could be
marketed. Doubts of any market discouraged the practice of stocking
them, although the Pingelapese could make them function impor-
tantly in their economy.

I learned through the resentment of two young men not very adept
with boats that the village council had ruled that all the men in the
village must fish. The would-be fishermen set out early one morning
while I was there, were nearly blown out to sea, and returned in the
late afternoon, exhausted by paddling, without catching anything.

After fish, pork is the most important and almost the only meat
on a South Sea island. On Pingelap it seemed that there were
almost as many pigs as children in and about the village: small pigs,

medium-sized pigs, large pigs, poking here and there under houses, between houses, at the backs of houses, and on the beach, picking up pieces of coconut, rinds of breadfruit, and anything else that was edible. Some were white, some black, others spotted. I heard their grunting day and night. Mother pigs with litters licked the sides of troughs where they had just been fed ground coconut meat. A few ducks and chickens mixed among them, picking from the same source. The swine, apparently all those on the atoll, increased the problem of keeping the village clean.

The tasks of Pingelap people are nearly all associated with procuring food. Men going fishing were up at five in the morning to have their canoes ready to start out at the streak of dawn. After fishing four or five hours, they were back by eleven, when the catch was immediately cleaned by the women. After the noon meal nearly all the natives lounged on mats on the floors of their homes or underneath the houses until four or five in the afternoon. Then they went for a swim, had supper, and visited one another for the rest of the day. The women told me they got up at six, did not often eat any breakfast, but started to cook food in the ground oven for the noon meal.

One early afternoon I watched activities on the beach, a hundred yards from the village street. Half a dozen little boys were swimming and another one was fishing with rod and line near a man who was overhauling his canoe. A little girl filled two coconut cups with ocean water to take back to the village. Two women standing in shallow water were washing the entrails of pigs and fish, while three others on the beach were preparing to put two pigs in a ground oven. They were the only natives out of doors at that time, the hotter part of the day.

Grating coconut meat for various uses is a chore generally relegated to children. Little girls sit cross-legged on pieces of logs into the ends of which small-toothed scrapers are fastened. Grasping half a coconut in both hands they grate the meat firmly against the scrapers, from which the particles drop into dishes to be squeezed later to extract the "milk" which is a favorite sauce for many kinds of food.

Village economy on Pingelap centers around the fragmentation of landholdings, which has gone so far as to reduce the amount for some families below the subsistence level. The chiefs and a few others are still sufficiently well off to give feasts. The pattern of land division on the island is that of parallel strips across the atoll, a reasonable manner in which to divide predominantly elongated land forms. The boundaries of holdings are marked by standing coconut trees, coconut branches, or the trunks and branches of coconut palms or other trees laid along them; in some cases low "walls" of coconut husks formed the dividing lines. It is difficult to make quantitative comparisons of taro rows and coconut land belonging to various families, for there seemed to be no standard length of taro row and no unit of area for the coconut land. The people know that some taro rows are longer than others and that some pieces of coconut land are large and others small, for over the years both have been divided and sub-divided until the present pattern has resulted.

A man's wealth is basically measured by his rows of taro, a row, I was told, being considered as fifty feet. However, many people have some considerably shorter. In trying to find out what a representative landholding might be, I elicited the information that an average man had three rows of taro about fifty feet long, and, in addition, a piece of land about ninety yards long and twenty yards wide on which there grew about fifty coconut palms, five pandanus, one or two breadfruit trees, and twenty banana plants. It was evident that ba-nanas could not be raised on much of the land where other trees were growing.

Dikery told me that his father, moderately well-to-do, had holdings in different parts of the main island with the following dimensions: four pieces of taro land with four rows in each piece, all, of course, in the swamp; four pieces of coconut land: the Willes piece, fifty yards by twenty-five yards; Namal, fifty yards by fifty yards; Matiap, fifty yards by eleven yards; and Sigor, fifty yards by eleven yards. His father had given him two rows of taro and the Matiap and Sigor pieces of coconut land. There was nothing written, of course; he had just his father's word. He had one brother and one sister with whom his father planned to share the remainder of his holdings when they were married.

Dison, a wealthy man who had thirty rows of taro and a piece of coconut land about seventy yards long and twenty yards wide, divided his holding among eight children. Another, who had four sons, divided his small plots between two of them, for it was no use to give away pieces any smaller. The other two went to Ponape to look for jobs. A less wealthy native owned five small pieces of land scattered over an area of half a square mile, the smallest unit, approximately thirty yards by four yards, having two bearing coconut palms and five immature trees just beginning to bear nuts.

Scattered holdings apparently imposed no operational handicaps, for only hand tools are used, and whaleboats and canoes give ready access to all parts of the atoll. The problem of overpopulation arises from the fact that the amount of land available for some families is insufficient to support them even at native subsistence standards. A consolidation of the little, scattered bits into one holding by exchange is out of the question, for, everyone knowing how many coconut trees, breadfruit, and pandanus there are in each piece, it would be impossible to exchange all of them for pieces with a like number.

Occasionally there is considerable altercation and argument over trees and boundaries. In some cases if a man has given a friend the right to harvest coconuts from one tree on his land, and if the friend dies, his son claims the right, saying his father told him it was his tree and the son would have it when he died. But the original owner argues, "I gave that tree to your father and not to you." Argument as to ownership arises also if a coconut tree growing near or on the boundary between two parcels of land shifts its position slightly during growth or in a high wind.

A fruitful source of trouble is the sprouting of a new breadfruit tree from the root of an older one. If the right to pick breadfruit has been given to someone besides the owner, does he also have the right to pick breadfruit from the younger tree when it grows up? When a shoot sprouts from a root on a piece of land adjoining the one where the tree is growing, the consensus of opinion seems to assign it to the adjoining owner.

Sometimes trouble stems from absentee ownership when a man goes to Ponape or elsewhere for an indefinite stay. According to the traditional native code, he does not lose his rights to his land, but custom decrees that he must assign his property to someone, generally a brother, to care for until he returns. Perhaps the owner after years of absence dies in Ponape, and his son comes back to claim his inheritance, but in the meanwhile the brother and his family have held the land so long that they have come to regard it as their own. In some cases the brother has died, and his son, becoming owner, refuses to recognize the claim of the returned stranger. The problem of absentee ownership was one of the more important subjects of discussion of the village council, most of whose members felt that a time limit should be placed for the return of the native owner. After that date, if he did not come, he would lose title to his land.

The village government seemed to be divided among the council, the hereditary chief, and the church, the last making itself responsible for the moral behavior of the people. A council, first elected in April of 1954 with one member from each of eight units into which the village is divided, meets twice a month to discuss problems of the village, and of land on the atoll. It also arranges certain village social occasions, such as welcomes for Government officials.

The main events of social life on Pingelap are village feasts, which among the indigenous peoples of the South Sea Islands are held regardless of general shortages of food, for they are an essential part of their way of living. There are always feasts, though the quantity and quality of the food varies. Often given after the arrival of a vessel which brings rice, flour, sugar, and other imported food, they are then bigger and better. The more impressive are the events with which they are associated, the finer are the feasts. On Pingelap they celebrate the birth of a first son, a death, a farewell, the renovation of a church, and other occasions. Men and women united in saying that the greatest festival of the year on their atoll is Christmas, but that it is celebrated only in their homes by families. At the time of my visit they were preparing for a great festival to celebrate the completion of an addition to their church. One of the congregation, commenting on the quality of the woodwork, said proudly, "We have a carpenter who was trained in Japan."

I was a guest at a feast which celebrated an unusual circumstance, the drowning of a chief's son. In January of 1954 when Kulion's son and a younger man went fishing in a sailing canoe on a stormy day, the boat capsized in the open sea beyond the reef. After both men had tried in vain to right it, the older asked the younger to swim ashore and wave his *lava lava* (wrap-around) above his head to attract help. He said he would stay with the canoe in an effort to save it. When the young man, after reaching the shore of Takai Islet, turned to look, neither the canoe nor his companion could be seen. It was now mid-July and Kulion decided to give a feast in memory of his son. As preparations for the event were going on, groups of women were at work, one steaming rice, another boiling taro, a third baking it in a large ground oven, and so on. No breadfruit was prepared because of the scarcity. Half a dozen men and women were preparing to put two full-grown pigs and a young one in another ground oven, where a pile of coral rocks were heated over burning wood. When hot they were raked apart, breadfruit leaves spread over the center, the pigs laid on, covered with more breadfruit leaves, and then the hot rocks from the sides raked up over the whole.

One group of women boiled water in six huge basins set on coral rocks under burning wood, using some for tea and some for coffee. To each they added plenty of sugar. Six or seven women came to the feast carrying loaves of bread of various sizes and shapes, which they piled up on mats at the side of the house.

Preparations went along slowly, for time means nothing to the natives of the South Seas. Men cut coconut fronds and breadfruit leaves to spread on the floor of the house where the feast was to be given. Women gossiped as they sat about, some of them remarking on the possible age of that American who was always taking pictures! A woman near me, employing her time making a coconut-leaf basket to carry away food from the feast, said she was fifty-four. When I told her she was as good looking as a schoolgirl, she replied, "I am good looking," and added, "because my grandfather was a German." Large groups of children hung about amusing themselves in various ways, one little boy blowing up, like a balloon, a fresh piece of a pig's intestine.

At last the rice was ready, near where eighty-nine dishes, pots, pans, and baskets were placed in rows to receive it. Portioned carefully from the many containers in which it was cooked, large lumps of it were put in each receptacle and a little more a second or third time to divide the whole amount as evenly as possible. Kulion seemed to be feeding half the village population. The women, taking their containers with the rice, filed past one end of the house to have pieces of taro, bread, and pork placed on top of it. When I commented to Ambilos on the skill of the carver, in serving the partially cooked pigs, asking if he was specially employed for the feast, Ambilos said indignantly, "He is one of Kulion's friends, but everybody in Pingelap knows how to carve a pig!" High chiefs who attended the feast were served first, sitting on mats on a raised platform at one side of the house.

Kulion made a speech before the rice was served, saying that the feast was in memory of his son. He told me afterward that he did not want him to go fishing that day because of the rough sea, but people urged him to go for they wanted food. He said the feast cost him two sacks of rice, each one hundred pounds, five fifty-pound sacks of flour, and two sixty-pound sacks of sugar, besides cans of shortening, packages of candy for the children, and other materials. Eighty large taro plants were baked. The next day three more pigs were killed and cooked as part of the feast. So in the midst of poverty on Pingelap there is occasionally a scene of seeming plenty. At the feast only fingers were used, the flies came in swarms to share it, and the general conditions of cleanliness were poor.

Some feasts, of course, celebrate weddings. Courtship and marriage are simple affairs in a village on a small island in the Pacific, for the boys and girls know each other well from the time they have been small children. Ambilos described it this way: "The boy speaks to the girl and they agree to marry. Then they tell their parents." Sometimes the marriage is arranged by the parents, a boy's father giving a feast if he is a favorite son. Occasionally the parents on both sides combine their resources to give the feast. A boy marries from eighteen up and a girl from fifteen; usually the couple live at the home of the boy's father and the boy has a little piece of land which his father has presented to him as an inheritance, but sometimes there is not any to give because the plots have been so subdivided. Those who are church members and other churchgoers are married in the church, but a few are married by the chief in his house. Sometimes when there are strong objections to the marriage, the lovers elope in a canoe and flee to Ponape, as two did about five months before my visit. The journey of 175 miles is not very hazardous in good weather, for the regular trade wind blows in that direction much of the year.

Wind, rain, and sunshine on Pingelap are important factors in sanitation, an outstanding problem which the natives don't appreciate. Leaves and other vegetable trash lie about the village, and only heavy drenching tropical showers with a run-off from the hard-surfaced street keep things tolerable. I noticed that the children had a good many scars on their bodies, and in some cases open sores, and that many of them and a number of adults were suffering from an eye disease which made them squint all the time. On asking about one small boy thus affected I got the reply, "He was born that way." Kulion said that the most serious afflictions of the people were "sores, tuberculosis, and leprosy." There were twenty lepers in the village, ten of them returned convalescent patients from the leprosarium on Saipan. A man and his wife were pointed out to me walking down the street, returned patients from Tinian, apparently cured. Three of the lepers were children. The people of Pingelap are beginning to be sensitive about the high incidence of leprosy in their village and it is possible that some kind of campaign among them might make them ashamed to the point of cleaning up the place. On the *Roque* the Officer for Island Affairs introduced me to several natives of the island, calling me "Doctor," whereupon one of them whispered, "Is he going to Pingelap to study leprosy?"

Kulion's experiences are representative of those of higher families in many islands. On graduation from school in Ponape at the age of twenty-one, he remained there for fourteen years and a half—as a teacher for four years and a half, and as a policeman for a decade. After a visit to Pingelap he continued to live at Ponape for three more years, during which time he received hospital training from the Japanese. Then his father died, and he came back to live in the atoll. In 1940, however, when the epidemic of "cowpox" was at its height, the people in the village united to urge him to return to Ponape for more training to help their sick. Accordingly, he stayed there for three and a half additional years. He has been "doctor" in Pingelap since 1943.

Early in the morning after I arrived on the atoll, I heard a commotion beside the house and looked out to see four young men carrying what looked like a tall, heavy chicken coop. After placing it at the back, one of them, Tigkery, came to me to say slowly, "This is your toilet." It was the only one on Pingelap. The seat was almost waist high, and I had to climb up to sit down. The hole was heart-shaped with a rusted can below. In view of the unsanitary state of the village I had considerable satisfaction in knowing I was the only one who used it. Men and women squat at different locations on the reef at low tide or wade out a little into the water when the tide is full, the customary procedures in most islands. On islands occupied by our Navy during the war, tiny backhouses were erected along the shores over the water at regular intervals. I was told that, in some places, Marines did sentry duty to make the natives use them. They stand now, dilapidated and abandoned monuments to the sanitary zeal of the ocean branch of our armed services.

Missionaries, traders, and Government people have been the three types of agents in Pingelap, as in hundreds of other islands in the Pacific, who have made the natives aware of the outside world. The atoll is about halfway between Ponape and Kusaie—two high volcanic islands, and for a hundred and fifty years missionaries and traders traveling between them have stopped off at Pingelap. One of the early traders who came from time to time was an Irishman called Higgins who had headquarters on Mokil Island. His grandson, a chief three-quarters Micronesian, was our helmsman on the Ponape boat trip. He told me that his grandfather had been murdered by a Gilbertese in a drunken brawl.

The church seems to be the strongest social and religious institution in the atoll. There are five services every Sunday: Sunday school, regular church, and Christian Endeavor in the morning, and church and prayer meeting in the afternoon. The people cannot afford lights in the building for evening worship. On weekdays there are two services, six to seven in the morning and five to six in the afternoon, and on Wednesday afternoon there is an extra one, prayer meeting. Two "prayer houses" in addition to the church, one near each end of the village, were for the convenience of people who said it was too far for them to go to prayer meeting in the main building. Some of them would have to walk five hundred yards! A more important reason is that the people of the Pacific Islands, under the influence of missionaries since the middle or early nineteenth century, have developed into fundamentalist communities where they vie with one another in the size and decoration of their churches and in building other places of worship. A native of Mokil Island, showing me the place of worship there, asked: "How are the people of Pingelap getting along with their new church? Will it be as nice as this one?" Incidentally, Mokil also has two prayer houses in addition to the church. On Pingelap each morning, at five-thirty and again at six o'clock, the sound of a horn summoned people to prayers. Children's voices singing hymns rose above the deeper tones. The horn blew again at five in the early evening when once more the singing was conducted.

When I asked the Pingelapese if they performed any native dances, held ceremonies like drinking kava, preserved traditional chants, or carried on other customs handed down from old times, they said they did not, except for a stick dance which the men performed occasionally. It seems that missionary influence and decimations of the population on the atoll from time to time by hurricanes have obliterated almost all aboriginal customs and ceremonies. Perhaps also conquering peoples from other islands may have helped to blot them out.

Pastor Leopold, trained by the Japanese at a "church training station" at Oa on Ponape, received a salary during their régime, but since they left he said he had not received anything. "However," he added, "I was born on Pingelap and my father left me a small piece of land, so we have enough to eat." Later on, I saw his son working in the taro swamp.

The lack of a substantial soil on Pingelap sets one of the more severe limits to agriculture as it does in atolls in general, and is, therefore, the most restricting factor in the number of people the atoll can support. The population of Pingelap was about 500 at the end of the war, in 1945; in 1953 there were 639 people in the village; in mid-1954 the number was estimated at 700. The population problem is specially related to the American administration, with its emphasis on health and sanitation. Many times in answer to questions, I got the reply: "During Japanese times many babies die. With American medicine, all babies live." The problem will probably increase as the children grow older and eat more food and as more keep coming. It is paradoxical on Pingelap, as in the Gilberts and elsewhere in the Pacific, that the work of missionaries and governments which rightly maintain that cleanliness is next to Godliness, should indirectly result in a serious overpopulation problem.

The problem of sanitation in aboriginal times in the Pacific was kept within bounds by witch doctors backed up by the chiefs, all of whom worked together to their mutual advantage. A belief in black magic strongly inculcated the idea that if human excrement, hair, pieces of cast-off paper bark, and other personal coverings were not buried under the soil, an enemy could cast a spell on them which was instantly conveyed to the person responsible. It is not unlikely that the association with witchcraft was developed as a method of dealing with a human problem. The Christianization of the people, not providing any observable penalty for filth, has resulted in a difficult situation now universal in the Pacific among all natives who have partially abandoned their old animistic cult.

A practical way of at least temporarily relieving the population problem on Pingelap is to take several hundred people to colonize part of Ponape, the island with most available land in the Carolines, and a "New World" for people living in impoverished atolls. Sixty-three families totalling 216, or 35 per cent of the population in 1953, want to leave Pingelap to establish homes on other islands. Their first choice is Ujelang, second Kusaie, and third Ponape. The attraction of Ujelang lies in the fact that the greater part of the atoll was planted in coconut trees by Pingelap people taken there during the Japanese régime. It was inspected by chiefs from Pingelap and Mokil in 1947 as a possible outlet for the growing population of these islands. However, soon after the survey Ujelang was placed under the jurisdiction of the administration of the Marshall Islands, which circumstance would now entail considerable red tape to arrange an emigration. The preference of Kusaie over Ponape is due to the lingering memory of very kind hospitality by the Kusaians when the native surveyors visited that island. Ponape, however, has much more land available for colonization than both of those two islands together.

It must be remembered that not only is there overcrowding on Pingelap so far as the taro land is concerned, but that the people have advanced from the days when a mere subsistence on taro and breadfruit was enough. They have now become accustomed to flour and rice and sugar, and to various articles of clothing from the store, to get which they must sell copra. But part of their income from copra goes for taxes, and the increasing population means an ever decreasing amount of coconut land per person. One man told me he had only enough coconut palms to produce one bag of copra for each field-trip ship, that is, every two months. At five cents a pound, this amount brings him thirty dollars a year for clothes, fishing equipment, taxes, and certain foods which he and his family now regard as necessaries.

The day the *Roque* called for copra on the return trip to Mokil and Ponape, an animated scene took place in the village. At six o'clock in the morning people were out on the street, asking if the ship had been sighted. Yes! Someone saw the funnel away out on the horizon. Men began to carry sacks of copra from underneath their homes to be weighed at the community house, a roof of coconut thatch on stout posts in the center of the village. Considerable argument arose over a decision that those who had made their copra during the last three days would get five cents a pound and those who had prepared it before that time would get five and a half cents. Presumably, the former hurried up when they knew the ship was coming and their product was of lesser quality. I noticed that people had climbed trees to get the unripe coconuts for copra. The fact that the price had fallen as of July 2nd from five and a half cents to five cents a pound brought up the question, Who had dried their copra before July 2nd and who after that date?

At Government headquarters, a wooden shack just across the street from the community house, names and amounts were recorded. Then began a parade of natives each with a sack on his shoulder, through shallow water to the canal blasted through the reef to afford nearer access to the shore. My baggage was placed on top of a pile of sacks in a boat loaded to the gunwales. We couldn't have made it in a rough sea, but the rowers pulled slowly to reach the *Roque*, and my things were on deck in a moment. Then began the hoisting and dumping of sacks into the hold. Pingelap copra was off to the world market.

MOKIL VISIT

On the way back, the *Roque* called at Mokil, another small atoll, to load copra. The approach to Mokil is the most difficult one I know in the Pacific, for when we got over the side of the trading vessel and were being rowed toward the reef, the ebbing tide left the water too shallow for the loaded boat. So we all got out to wade about half a mile while the empty whaleboat was dragged across. We embarked again near the outer margin of the lagoon, but after a short distance three of the heavier passengers had to climb out once more to walk through the water. Although the *Roque* was off Mokil reef at seven in the morning, copra loading did not begin until high tide—about three in the afternoon, and even at that time our boat had to be pulled and dragged over two parts of the reef.

Mokil Village, called Kalap by the natives, is the prettiest and cleanest I have seen in the South Seas—a great contrast to Pingelap. A graveled road, raised about six inches above the general level of the ground, and bordered with curbstones, runs the length of the village—about a mile and a half. The street is well shadowed by interlacing branches of coconut palms and pandanus trees growing along each side.

The homes, lined up far apart on the landward side, are painted frame buildings, on posts three or four feet above the ground, with the usual galvanized-iron roofs. Underneath, the earth was hollowed out and the depression filled with a thick layer of coral gravel. Covered concrete cisterns at the back caught the runoff from the roofs. On the lagoon side of the village was a long row of large native boathouses, with gabled roofs of coconut or pandanus thatch, set on stout breadfruit posts, six feet high. One or two canoes were inside each. At the back, similar small roofs protected native ground ovens. Neat stone wharves projected into the ocean between the boathouses, where ramps sloping down to the water were covered with palm leaves, husks of coconuts, and other vegetable debris so that whaleboats and canoes could be dragged over them without scraping their keels. Pigs are kept in pens or tethered to trees, and fowl are kept in chicken houses at the backs of the homes—an arrangement which promotes sanitation.

As I walked along the village street hoping to meet a native who spoke English, Leben approached and introduced himself—a graduate of the Intermediate School in Ponape. He offered to show me around.

The villagers were, as usual on boat day, getting their copra ready to ship. In the village church, one of the nicer ones I have seen in the South Sea Islands, the pews had back supports, well carpentered; the two "prayer meeting houses" in the village were also neat and well constructed. I was struck by the quality of the carpentry work all through Micronesia, where the Japanese chose capable men from the islands each year to send to a carpentry school in Koror in the Palau Islands or to Japan. This interest in vocational training seems more practical than the emphasis which the present régime places on academic subjects. Mokil school was clean-looking, and its children have ambitions to go to the Intermediate School in Ponape. However, if they graduate in Ponape they are not likely to be much better off after they return to Mokil, where only a few of them will get government jobs, teaching or working up copra records. At least one educated boy there was thoroughly dissatisfied with his lot and wanted to go back to Ponape to look for different work.

The children of Mokil were clean, apparently none afflicted with sores or eye diseases. Three groups of youngsters played marbles, another hopscotch. Two little girls sitting on the ground with a squared, native pandanus mat between them were playing on it with pebbles. Boys were wrestling on the piles of copra sacks at the wharves. I was not astonished when the village pharmacist said, in reply to a question, "We don't have many sick people in Mokil."

Leben, nineteen years old, was engaged to be married to Mely, sixteen, and wanted to go to Ponape to get a job as a sailor. He told me that the oldest son in a family on Mokil always marries a daughter of the father's sister. For younger boys in the family, when they are still small, the father arranges later marriages with girls from other families in the village.

A girl has to take her chance that some man will want to marry her. When the parents involved offer strong objections to an engagement, the young couple, like the Pingelapese, put off at night in a canoe. The parents, much concerned, and making diligent inquiries when the next boat arrives from Ponape, generally find that they have gone there. The hundred-mile trip, shorter and therefore less hazardous than that from Pingelap, is accomplished with the same prevailingly favorable winds. After a while the young people usually return to their village and are reconciled with their parents.

Leben had been married twice already, and in the English words commonly used by natives, he had "trowed his wives away," meaning that they had returned to their parents' families. Relations between young men and women in Micronesia, as elsewhere in the Pacific Islands, are very casual. Boys take the girls out under the coconut trees or crawl into the girls' rooms at night.

"What would you do if her father caught you?" one of my American friends asked a boy on Mokil who was bragging about his "affairs" with girls.

"I would just jump out of the window," he said.

"But what about your clothes?"

"Oh, we just wear *lava lava* [wrap-arounds] when we call on girls."

"But what would the girl say to her father?"

"She would say that a boy was trying to come in and she did not know who he was."

Although High Chief August of Pingelap has a curfew rung every evening at nine o'clock, it is interpreted liberally, for young men and women keep the letter of the law by staying off the main street after that time, going to their homes the back way.

It is difficult for an American to imagine the difficulties in the way of courting a girl where the movements of everyone in the village are watched, where privacy is all but impossible, and especially where there may be a rival in the picture. Everyone knows what everyone else is doing. The fact that the women as well as the men do most of their work in groups makes it difficult for a lover to find his sweetheart alone. The young man must be constantly alert so as not to miss the rare opportunity which may occur to arrange a rendezvous. Go-betweens, indispensable for both the boy and the girl, must familiarize themselves with elaborate signals. Even after a time and place have been arranged, perhaps someone else has got to know about it, so the tryst may not be prolonged. What is to be done must be done quickly.

The man who is at least partly responsible for the upkeep of Mokil Village is August, the highest hereditary chief, the elected chief magistrate of the island, and the biggest landowner. He is both respected and feared. The day before our boat arrived he had fined a man five dollars for beating his wife.

The Mokilese had only thirty tons of copra to ship, not as much as usual, because they had been making more boats for the expanding market in Ponape and other islands. The people of Mokil, expert whaleboat and canoe builders, use the excellent hardwood timber of the breadfruit tree. Their whaleboats, about twenty-five feet long, are bow-shaped fore and aft, so that they can be rowed either way without being turned around. The men saw the wood for the boats from squared logs with handsaws, working in groups of five or six. After the thickness of a piece is carefully measured, a man saws until he gets tired, when another takes it up, and so on for each one in the group. When it was suggested to Chief August that he buy a small kerosene-fired saw to cut boards for making boats and canoes, he threw up his hands in remonstrance. "What!" he exclaimed. "Get a sawmill to let the people have all the extra time on their hands to get into mischief?"

The boats, caulked and painted, are promptly repainted when the first coat begins to wear off, and are thus kept in good condition. A spick-and-span one may be twenty years old. The Mokilese made forty boats for the Navy during its régime, to send to Guam, the Navy furnishing the lumber and the nails. Both boys and girls learn to manage boats at an early age, rowing and steering as well as the men. A boy of six held the helm of our whaleboat, loaded with copra, all the way from the village to the *Roque*.

Examples of the industry of the Mokilese in agriculture were large hollows, excavated in the stubborn ground near the backs of houses, into which had been piled banana leaves, rotting coconut husks, and other leafy plants. These, left to decay, provided a good compost bed in which banana plants were growing, although beneath the compost was hard coral where nothing could subsist. Mokil has had a fish pond as part of its economy for many years.

Our day at Mokil was drawing to a close when all the sacks of copra were stacked in the hold of the *Roque*, and the decks piled with baskets of taro, bananas, rolls of pandanus floor mats, boxes and cartons of dried fish, two whaleboats and three canoes. Forty-three native passengers, men, women and children—the total allowed —with their small lockers, packages, and parcels, found room on the deck among the cargo. A girl of eighteen carrying a baby of eight months squeezed past me at the rail, while three live ducks found standing room on the afterdeck. Children chased one another up and down the companionway to the forward deck, called over the rail to their friends in the boats below, and talked excitedly about their first trip to Ponape. Four of the friends, seemingly under seven, rowed off after an orange, dropped accidentally into the water and quickly carried away by the tide.

Twenty-four whaleboats and two canoes were hugging the sides of our little vessel or moored to one another near it when, at ten minutes past six, the *Roque* blew a blast on her siren. A brisk breeze had arisen, and amid great splashing, rowing, and towing the flotilla got clear. Eight of the craft were towed in close to the reef against the wind before we turned around to head out to sea. The captain and the Government Officer for Island Affairs kept calling to those in the boats to take off more people because there were more on board than had bought tickets! I heard the Government officer going about after dusk looking for stowaways. At eight o'clock Mokil was a thin gray line far behind on the eastern horizon.

REFERENCES

Maude, H. E., "The Colonization of the Phoenix Islands," *Jour. Pol. Soc.*, New Zealand, Vol. 61, Nos. 1, 2, 1952.

Murphy, Raymond E., "Land Ownership on a Micronesian Atoll," *Geog. Rev.*, 38 (4): 598-614, October, 1948.

————, "The Economic Geography of a Micronesian Atoll," *Annals Assoc. Amer. Geog.*, 40 (1): 58-83, March, 1950.

————, "Adoption on Mokil," *American Anthropologist*, 55 (4): 555-568 (1953).

St. John, Harold, "Report on the Flora of Pingelap Atoll, Caroline Islands, Micronesia, and Observations on the Vocabulary of the Native Inhabitants," Pacific Plant Studies 7, *Pacific Science*, 2 (2): 96-113, April, 1948.

Weckler, J. E., *Land and Livelihood on Mokil, an Atoll in the Eastern Carolines*. CIMA Report No. 11, 1949, 147 pp.

XV

Retrospect and Prospect

THE unusual circumstance that available land exists on the larger islands in the Trust Territory for expansion is an important factor in the present happiness and cooperation of the native population. Everywhere there is friendliness, an appreciation of American efforts, and an apparently ready response to the new vistas being opened up. Above all, the natives have faith in the good intentions of the Americans. The indigenous people of the islands, in general, *judged by the standards of their own culture*, are today well fed and well housed. Their material needs are being cared for. In view of the short time since the Trust Territory was taken over by a civil government (July 1, 1951), the administration has accomplished much. It took the Japanese civilian government about ten years to get organized after nine years of Navy government.

Life for most of these attractive, brown-skinned Micronesian peoples is simple and primitive. They have no literature since few of them have any but the most elementary education. For centuries before foreigners came, they maintained a happy existence, developing a culture admirably adapted to the conditions under which they lived. A strongly developed communal family or clan system removed the fear of individual want or incapacity, and promised care in time of sickness or old age. Few natives today seek a change which involves any particular effort on their part, for, free from individual poverty or want, they prefer the idle, happy life which they have always known. They do not wish increased economic returns at the price of hard work. They regard their way of living as superior to ours.

But whether happily or unhappily for them, the old days are gone beyond recall. The simple seventeenth and eighteenth century cultures of Micronesia cannot withstand the intense pressures and aggressive inroads of twentieth century Western civilization. In Hawaii today, the Polynesian way of living has disappeared. In every South Sea area invaded by the West there has come the slow disintegration of native cultures and the adoption of some of the best and much of the worst of alien ways. Problems have to be solved, and not the least of them is the approaching overpopulation.

Most of the vital statistics available for the Japanese rule in the islands are confusing. It is true, however, that, under the Japanese, the native (*'kanaka*) population increased for the whole area, the rise between 1921 and 1938 being about 7 per cent. Undoubtedly during that period general medical and sanitary practices were considerably improved. During that time the mandated area became progressively more cut off from the outside world, as the Japanese did not desire any nationals except their own in the islands. Inter-island migrations of natives occurred to some extent, but there were no large-scale native migrations into or out of the area.

It has been difficult to determine the exact population. However, under United States administration, vital statistics for the most part are being kept by the natives, and the figures, some of them estimates, have to be revised constantly. Density of population does not present a serious problem at present, except on a few small islands, where the shortage of arable land is particularly acute, for example, on atolls of the Eastern Carolines. As was already pointed out, Pingelap has 700 people on a land area of little over two-thirds (0.676) of a square mile. Kapingamarangi has 511 people on one-half (0.521) square mile. The importance of the coming population problem is intensified by the fact that, traditionally and by force of present circumstances, the inhabitants are dependent to a great extent upon local agricultural products. Shortage of land on some islands will have to be faced in the immediate future by the administration, especially in view of the high survival and birth rate.

Other problems derive from isolation. The total area contained within the perimeter of the islands is approximately the area of the United States—nearly three million square miles, of which, however, only 687 square miles are land, the rest being the extensive stretches of the Pacific Ocean separating the ninety-six atolls and island units. Sixty-four of these are inhabited; most of the rest are too small or lacking in resources to support a permanent population, though neighbors from surrounding islands visit them to gather coconuts, to fish, or to catch birds.

The negligible natural resources, the cultural and linguistic differences of the population, and the fact that the Japanese gave the Micronesians no training whatsoever in self-government, constitute problems in the economic, political, and social adjustment of the people of the Trust Territory to the conditions of the modern world. Furthermore, since the inhabitants of each island group are proud of their own language, history, and culture, they resist being integrated politically and socially with the members of other groups. The solution of all these problems will be the more difficult because of the lack of background and experience in native administration on the part of American personnel.

AGRICULTURE AND FISHING

Since most of the agricultural operations in the Territory to date have been carried out to alleviate immediate needs, the situation has now reached the point where it is necessary to make long-range plans.

It would be better if the administration of the Trust Territory, to improve the standard of living, put more emphasis on raising the agricultural subsistence level of the people rather than on raising crops for export. One of the more valuable contributions to the subsistence agriculture of the Micronesians would be a detailed study of the varieties of breadfruit in the Territory, including their relationship to the climate, soil, and other aspects of the natural environment where they grow. It would have to be done by specialists in tropical agriculture. Such a study would undoubtedly result in the introduction of new varieties into coral atolls to prolong the breadfruit season and relieve food shortages there.

Some of the difficulties of introducing anything new in agricultural extension work are similar to those in American Samoa. For example, a man from a village in Truk begged a bull carabao which had been imported at considerable expense by the Government. It was sold to him at a nominal sum to breed with young cattle. After keeping it for a while, he gave in to social pressure to kill the animal and provide a feast for the village.

In 1949, 375 cattle and 800 hogs were taken from the Com Marianas Ranch on Tinian for distribution to the natives. About half of the total of each were sold to farmers on Saipan, the rest being distributed among the remaining districts of the Trust Territory to be used as nuclei for breeding herds. The cattle were sold to the natives at a fraction of their worth in order to impose no financial burden on the purchasers, and restrictions were drawn up regarding their slaughter. However, since no efforts to enforce the restriction orders were made by the district administrations, as soon as the natives discovered there would be no penalty for disregarding them, a great slaughtering for festivals took place. After a few weeks nearly all the breeding herd had disappeared. Better luck was had with a Brahman herd imported in 1949, of which some descendants of part European stock are distributed on several islands. Continued importation and distribution of cattle like these on islands where they can subsist will help the diet of the inhabitants.

Extension activities constantly must take into account the great diversity of conditions in this island region. The extension worker must know thoroughly the various types of authority in any community: heads of households, kin elders, foremost religious men, native officials exercising powers bestowed by the Government, and so on, for the success of his efforts will largely depend on his ability to get along with, and use, such leaders. Understanding and interest in the people as well as in the problems in the field are basic to the success of any agricultural program put forward. Some of the greater successes of the extension worker may come if he is able to harness to his program the important cooperative institutions existing in all these little intimate island communities in greater or lesser degree, for the native peoples are accustomed to working in groups rather than as individuals.

Replanting of hardwood forests on some islands, of mangrove trees in Truk and others, and of coconut trees wherever they can grow well, should form part of the economic and conservation program. The future of the Trust Territory economically will depend more than anything else on the copra trade. However, that business fluctuates with world economy and with international agreements. The small part the Micronesian output plays in world commerce is shown by the fact that prior to World War II the total annual amount for the world averaged 2,130,000 tons, of which Micronesia produced less than half of 1 per cent. Incidentally, the Philippine Islands are contenders for the largest percentage.

Before 1954, most of the Trust Territory output of copra had been sold to Japan. She was pleased to have it, for it was of better quality than the product from the Philippine Islands. In 1954, however, she entered into an agreement with Indonesia for an increased reciprocal trade on an exchange basis—Indonesia to furnish raw materials for Japan's manufactured goods. That agreement took away half the former market for Trust Territory copra. The Trust Territory is now dependent on a market in the United States, where, in Cincinnati, its quality is valued by Procter & Gamble Co. Plans have been made to have all the Trust Territory copra, estimated at 3,000 tons a quarter, taken to Majuro in the Marshall Islands, there to be transshipped to a large United States cargo steamer which will call once every three months. Approximately 12,372 short tons of copra were produced during the year 1955 and sold in Japan and the United States. These copra sales returned to the natives of the Trust Territory a total of $1,334,414.

The problem of increasing the copra output is related to controversial problems of land tenure. All public domain is held by the Government of the Trust Territory for the benefit and use of the Micronesians. While a large proportion of the land is still designated as public domain, none of the Trust Territory land taken over from the Japanese is withheld from the Micronesians, if the area is suitable for agriculture or for residence. An example of the intricate questions which arise is that of a tract of land in Ponape which was sold to a Japanese who married a Ponapean. Upon the repatriation of the Japanese national to Japan at the end of hostilities, his son took over the land and continued to farm it. The son, considered a Ponapean, is accorded locally all the Ponapean privileges and rights. But the question has not yet been settled as to whether or not the land is alien property, although there is a tacit understanding on the Micronesian status of children of Japanese-Micronesian marriages. On the other hand the Trust Territory Code states that if the son was a Japanese national at birth, he is not a citizen of the Trust Territory, and there is no provision in it for the naturalization of Japanese aliens.

Many records of landownership, on Rota Island and elsewhere, have been lost or destroyed—perhaps some quite conveniently! Although older people remember fairly well what areas belonged to whom, others assert doubtful claims to tracts they want. It will probably be a long time before all land claims on Rota are settled, but meanwhile there is more than enough homestead area in the thirty square miles of that island for its 850 people. Several bombed villages in the Territory have been rebuilt without regard to the old private ownership lines, and the problem of title in those cases is now difficult to solve. A landownership study of Mokil listed in the references was intended chiefly as a type study.* To the anthropologist it may suggest the value of mapping as a basis for investigating social organization. For the administrators of the islands, such a study is recommended as a practicable method of attacking one of the greater problems facing the United States throughout Micronesia—landownership. The hundred-odd islands and island groups of the United States Trust Territory of Micronesia could be divided into relatively few classes within each of which the customs of landownership and land inheritance would be essentially similar. Such a classification would greatly simplify the problems of island government. The project would require extensive field work in addition to the utilization of all information now available or being made available by studies that are under way. Much could be done through conferences with representatives of various island units at Government bases. Ideally, the work, joint enterprise of geographer and anthropologist, would be of unquestionable scientific value, and at the same time have the virtue of being of immediate and direct use in the administration of the islands.

Fish from the seas surrounding the islands provide a potentially important industry but as yet little more than subsistence fishing is carried on. Since reef and lagoon fish can, in most localities, supply all local requirements, a long-term objective of the administering authority is to develop a commercial fishing industry, based primarily on the tuna resources of the area. Shortly before the war the Japanese were rapidly expanding their tuna fishery in the islands. In 1939 they had at least five ocean-going research vessels in the Mandated Islands working on the problems of expanding the tuna catch alone. It is significant that in 1937 the tuna caught by the Japanese in their Mandated Islands was equal to the production of our California

* See references on Pingelap and Mokil.

tuna fishery, and that the latter was the second most valuable resource of that kind in our nation.

The Trust Territory does not form a part of a customs union with the United States, nor have any formal customs or trade agreements been negotiated with other countries. Products of the territory except copra are at present subject to the same United States customs duties as products of other foreign countries, but exports from all countries to the Territory are free of import controls. Measures to facilitate reciprocal free trade between the Trust Territory and Japan, the Trust Territory and Guam, and the Trust Territory and the United States would be advantageous. There is a port charge on Trust Territory

TABLE XXII

Exports from Mandated Islands to Japan, 1940*

RANK	ITEM	VALUE MILLION YEN
1	Sugar	20.7
2	Minerals and miscellaneous	9.1
3	Dried bonito	8.8
4	Copra	2.1
5	Rope, cord, and twine	1.3
6	Drugs and chemicals	1.0
7	Cassava starch	.7
8	Bone, horn, shell, and hides	.6
9	Alcohol	.5
10	Metal products	.5
11	Machinery, boats, and vehicles	.5

* This represents pre-World War II trade between what are now the Trusteeship Islands and Japan.

goods imported into Guam and an import duty on all goods except copra imported into the United States. Yet in postal matters the Trust Territory is considered a part of the United States with the same airmail and surface mail rates. This difference is confusing. The outlook for the islands from the commercial viewpoint is not promising. Uncertain marketing opportunities, increasing competition from synthetics, and the breaking in of new areas of production point to difficult conditions for such an isolated area as Micronesia. As was already stated, therefore, the welfare of the island peoples would be better served by our encouraging them to fall back as far as possible on subsistence economics, and to become, so to speak, an island peasantry rather than to expose themselves to the vagaries of world markets.

EMIGRATION AND COLONIZATION

Homesteading projects in the area might well be studied carefully, for natives with a coastal way of living will not want to use land in the interior of a large island. Surveying lots of ten or fifteen acres, as for a farm for Europeans or Americans, would merely confuse the Micronesians. Areas available will have to be given in large blocks to groups of natives selected by themselves, who will decide how it should be divided, which part of the area is good for breadfruit, which for taro, for coconuts, and so on. They know very much more about the soil and what can be raised on it than any Americans in the islands.

For example, to transfer a large company of Pingelap people successfully and happily to Ponape needs careful and systematic planning over a considerable period of time, under the leadership of a capable member of the administration.* The people of Pingelap should be allowed to choose the families who would emigrate; and, if they want to, to transfer their own village social organization to the new colony. They must have at their head a native who has good qualities of leadership and a pioneering spirit. The land should be given to them in a block and the apportioning of it left up to them as a community project. Some places will be chosen for dry-land taro, others for wet-land taro, still others for breadfruit trees. The Hawaiian *ohana*, or kinship feeling, will dominate any colonization project in the Trust Territory.

---

* Since this was written, a migration of Pingelapese to Ponape has begun.

TRANSPORT

Problems of freight and communication assume a unique importance in the islands, for upon assured means of carrying imports of necessities for living and exports of copra and other products, standards of living directly depend. Without assured means of communication, schools cannot be established or coordinated education programs maintained; adequate sanitary standards cannot be enforced or disease successfully fought; social progress will be imperiled and emergency needs cannot properly be met. In other words, political, economic, educational, and social progress in this vast domain of scattered and far-flung islands is dependent upon adequate means of getting about. Furthermore, an increase in travel between the various islands in each district and between districts will achieve two things. It will relieve population pressures in some islands by encouraging the families concerned to get land on others where there is room to expand. For example, from the airplane windows one day we saw Oroluk Atoll, at present uninhabited, but used as fishing grounds by Kapingamarangi people. They have also planted taro on one of the islands in that group, for, foreseeing a future overpopulation problem, they plan to relieve it by frequent communication with Oroluk. More travel would also have educational value for the natives, for they would see islands new to them, learn about the problems of their neighbors, and perhaps begin to think about future political cohesion.

SOCIAL AND RELIGIOUS MATTERS

Problems of health in the Trust Territory are those which affect many other islands in the Pacific. In all of them the common diseases include hookworm, filariasis, and respiratory infections like tuberculosis. A leprosarium was built on Tinian, where those afflicted with leprosy are gathered from various parts of the Trust Territory.* Since leprosy is not a highly contagious disease, noninfected adult members of a family sometimes accompany the patient to the leprosarium and

* As mentioned in an earlier footnote, this leprosarium was discontinued in 1955.

remain with him during treatment. Most of the patients live in attractive little family cabins built for them by the Government, the more advanced and active cases being cared for in hospital wards.

Medicine has done its part well in the Trust Territory. Now the need is for emphasis on "health" and "sanitation," the problem being not so much to cure diseases, as to prevent their further spread. The health program, the best organized in the Trust Territory, is appreciated both by the Americans and by the natives; as a result, it receives good cooperation and it will confer increasing benefits as years pass. The natives appreciate the hospitals and the little dispensaries that have been established in remote districts. The employment of native midwives is gradually being replaced by maternity care in hospitals.

At each of the six district hospitals there are qualified American or European doctors and nurses. The doctors make regular field trips to outlying islands, where there are native Micronesian medical practitioners who have been trained on Guam or at the Central Medical School in Fiji. There are also trained Micronesian nurses at the district hospitals. No sick person in the Trust Territory is refused medical treatment because of inability to pay.

Sanitation is a problem more of education than of drainage. School children in many islands are required to pick up coconut husks lying on the ground and to put them in piles. The husks are excellent water containers for breeding mosquitoes which carry the active agent of filariasis, very prevalent in some places. The Navy Medical Department, after painstaking research over four or five years, identified the mosquito as culex, but the species has still to be determined.

Campaigns to eradicate rats are under way on various islands, both as an economic measure and as an aid in sanitation. The rodents not only eat the copra prepared by the natives, but they climb coconut trees to gnaw off young nuts, and then come down to chew through the husk and shell. Natives are encouraged to have cats to keep down the rats, and in some villages there are many of them; however, on the atolls in times of food shortage the cats are killed and eaten.

Primarily the social welfare of the people is assured by the system of relationship which exists within their society. Ties of family, clan, neighborhood, and tradition link the people in complex relationships in which every individual is assured of assistance when it is needed. The care of widows, orphans, and abandoned children, the poor, the ill, and all unfortunates is the accepted responsibility of the indigenous society. Such a social system has removed fear of individual want or incapacity. To this indigenous pattern of security, and always within the bounds of native custom, the administration is adding the knowledge and facilities of modern science.

Under existing conditions in the Trust Territory, Americans are required for professional services in positions of major responsibility. But the most enduring benefits of the public health effort will result from good technical training of selected Micronesians for health services to their own people within the limitations of their own resources to support such services. Since training of this sort has been given increasing priority, and selected Micronesians, both male and female, have shown aptitude, interest, and ability in this field, they have permitted a reduction of American public health personnel.

American medical and public health personnel whose occupation or position brings them into close association with the native population can probably develop more satisfactory relationships, and give more effective service, if they are more sensitive to the implications of cultural differences and know something of the specific culture of the group with whom they are working and of the possible range of differences within the group. A knowledge of the folk medical notions of Yapese-speaking patients, for example, could be an invaluable asset for an American physician, nurse, and social worker. Such a knowledge would make them aware of the areas where the ideas of the patient about a given disease or its cure might differ significantly from theirs and should provide some guides as to how the physician's ideas might be made meaningful to the patient. In addition, there is much in the folk medical knowledge that can be utilized to obtain the cooperation of patients in some procedures which, when presented in American terms, are not acceptable.

In the field of education vocational training is of paramount importance. A good knowledge of the carpenter's trade would contribute much to the economy of the islands, the more so because native traditional ways of house building and canoe making and fishing are being lost. Public works officials in the Territory have a responsibility in helping to train young men to be carpenters, mechanics, welders, and electricians. All through the islands it is difficult to get natives to take care of their tools, to oil and clean them properly, and not to leave them lying in the places where they were last used.

In the elementary schools children are provided with opportunities to learn some skills in vocational activities. Boys acquire skills in agriculture, woodworking, fiber handicrafts, fishing, and handling tools. Girls learn how to sew, to cook, to make household handicrafts, and, in some districts, learn something about agriculture and fishing. A knowledge of stonemasonry would be excellent for the Ponapeans and Trukese, for they have so much material on which to expend it in their islands. The Palauans and the Yapese had to have such knowledge to make Yap stone money, although there is little good building stone in their islands.

Agriculture and animal husbandry should form a more important part of school instruction. Students should not only learn about them from books, but be given more opportunities in school hours to plant and tend some of the crops and look after animals about which they learn.

Positions for mechanics who can repair outboard motors, for electricians, and in other vocational lines are developing in the Trust Territory. A few exceptional students should be sent to Guam or Honolulu each year, but while there their education should be carefully supervised so that when they return to Micronesia they will fit into positions as mechanics, as interpreters for the administration, as assistant agriculturists, clerks, bookkeepers, or into other places for which they have been trained. Certainly students with outstanding traits of leadership or ability should be sent from each district every year for advanced training in accredited agricultural schools.

Roman Catholic missions in some districts have the reputation of fulfilling the needs of boys and girls better than their Protestant contemporaries and the public schools. It is generally agreed that they are better than the public schools of the Trust Territory. Thus when a girl leaves the elementary grades in a Roman Catholic mission, she can make all her own clothes and children's clothes too. For boys the emphasis is on taking care of cows, goats, pigs, and chickens. In the Catholic mission manual training starts with instruction in the use of hammer, saw, and chisel, and how to keep the saw clean and the chisel sharp, instead of training in an electrically operated "Smith-shop" which was imported for a public school, but to which, of course, students have no access when they go back to their home villages. It must be pointed out, however, that on Ponape, for example, the Catholic missions, including many nuns, have a much larger staff than do the Protestant. On Koror, on the other hand, the Liebenzeller Protestant mission has the reputation of providing the best vocational training in the Trust Territory, laying great emphasis on agriculture. The Protestant Mission on Roguron in the Marshalls also has good vocational training. The local reputation of a school in the Trust Territory depends on how well it carries out a program of vocational education.

In general, island parents today feel a strong duality of need in educational matters. On the one hand, they continue to maintain the traditional forms of cultural transmission to carry on their local ways of life. On the other, all but the very conservative want their children to gain better knowledge and mastery of the larger world about which they are hearing more and more.

On many islands young people are being blamed for a restiveness toward the status quo which is due to their sympathy with movements to change the old social and political order and advance to some kind of régime more in step with the modern world. In the old days all the people unhesitatingly obeyed the chiefs, but now, gradually feeling the influence of a democracy beginning to be introduced by the American administration, the young people chafe at a discipline still imposed by traditional authority.

The problem of language is a difficult obstacle to overcome in education. As was already mentioned, languages spoken in the Territory may be classified generally into nine distinct groupings, some of which may be in turn subdivided into local dialects. None is Territory-wide in usage. Language studies and attempts at standardization made by various foreign groups since the time of early Western exploration and settlement in the area have not proved satisfactory. During World War II the United States made a systematic attempt to survey the field from a practical standpoint, and published a Civil Affairs Study entitled the *Languages of the Japanese Mandated Islands.**

Although the Christian religion has been taken over by the Micronesians, it is for them incomplete and inconsistent with some old beliefs to which they still cling. Christian ideas are superimposed on traditional ideas and the natives are not conscious of a conflict until an issue arises. They are as well intentioned and as reasonably con-

* See references.

scientious as American Christians, but they all, like the Palauans, still believe in ghosts. The feelings of the Trukese in this respect are representative. Ghosts in old times on Truk, associated with certain clans and villages, were visions of dead chiefs who, appearing under certain circumstances, were supplicated in times of crisis, like a war against an enemy clan. People will give something they prize to a chief if he asks for it because they are afraid of the spirits of his ancestors. The Trukese, astonished that an American man or woman will stay alone in a house from time to time, often refer to it, never daring to do such a thing themselves.

Trukese will not give a child the name of a deceased person. A missionary there told the author of an incident that had happened recently in his church when during a baptismal service he asked what the child would be called. The father replied, "We haven't any name." After some hesitation the members of the congregation were asked for suggestions, but for every one that was proposed someone remembered a deceased person on the island who had been so called. The missionary finally suggested the German word *Gottlob*, meaning "worship." Someone remembered a Lob, but not a Gottlob, and so the baby was called Gottlob. In some cases on Truk, a child's name has combined a syllable of his father's name with a syllable of his mother's. Trukese will not prepare for an expected baby by having any garment ready or mosquito net or small sleeping mat, for they say that the spirits would be warned, and that they like to take infants.

The Trukese believe there is a special place in heaven for the chiefs and another place for the common people. They believe that deceased chiefs still share the life of an island, and that although the body dies the ghost or spirit still lives. If a native is asked his father's name and his father is dead, he will not mention his name, but will say, "My father is dead." To mention his name would mean for him to call on his ghost.

A problem of missionaries is to reconcile the natives to the modern concepts of Christianity. The Christian of the Trust Territory is the Christian of America one hundred years ago with his Puritanical repression of dancing and smoking. He is confused by the apparently un-Christian conduct of soldiers and sailors who, he learns, belong to churches back home. This psychological attitude will have to be learned before Micronesians can be made to realize what modern

Christianity means. The Old Testament is easier for them to understand than the New, for it lays down the law of Moses in unequivocal terms.

Another problem of missions is to reconcile the different points of view of Catholics and Protestants, for the natives shift their allegiance from one church to another for small reasons. A Protestant pastor recently reproved a chief for something of doubtful morality. The chief retaliated by ordering several people in his village who were Protestants to join the Catholic church, and they did. When the missionary asked them about it they said, "The chief told us to do it and we had to obey him."

Moral problems chiefly concern sex relations, drinking, and stealing. Moral standards differ the world over. Since Micronesians are amoral rather than immoral, many adultery cases come into court. Sex relations between unmarried people do not constitute a delinquency in Micronesian eyes. The question is, What disciplinary measure should be used to try to prevent them? An American judge, long resident in the Trust Territory, maintains that Americans are too strict in prosecuting some sex offenses which should be left to the families concerned to settle.

Few Americans realize that in Micronesia the lineage obligation is stronger than the marriage obligation, and that a marriage vow in Micronesia is much less binding than in the United States.

The question of alcoholic beverages is also difficult to handle. In one district there is virtually prohibition because of the order of a highly respected chief, a man of great ability. On the other hand, in the same district there is considerable distillation of liquor from sugar and yeast, juice from coconut buds, and other raw materials. In another district the natives import beer, and thus have little incentive to make moonshine. Nearly all the serious crimes in the Territory have been committed by natives drunk with home-brew.

The problem of stealing, already referred to for Samoa and Yap, is related to old and new religions. In the old religions of Micronesia there was a *taboo* on stealing. Another person's property was inviolate because of the spirit which was associated with it. A man believed—and the belief was firmly inculcated by priests and witch doctors—that if he took what belonged to another an evil spirit would torment him and bring him ill luck. The spirit of the devil or an equally evil ghost was the guard of property left unattended. This was especially the case in regard to the property of foreigners who, because of their own superior abilities, were thought to have special protection for their belongings. The missionaries with the Bible taught the natives that they must not fear the devil, for he and all evil spirits had been conquered and could not harm them. The natives tried this theory out a little and it worked, then some more and it still worked, until now thievery is omnipresent. A missionary told the author he has seen this problem grow and develop during the quarter of a century he has served among the people. When he first arrived at a port near his post, he left his baggage, including cartons and some small pack-ages, unguarded at the wharf for five days before taking a small boat out to the island where he was going to work. When he was ready to put his belongings on the small boat, everything was exactly where he had put it. He said, however, that such security of private property under similar circumstances now is impossible. This is true through-out Micronesia. The question of how to deal with the situation is still far from an answer. The laws regarding it are not adequate. There must be two witnesses to a theft according to the bylaws of the Code of the islands, something which is often, of course, very difficult to get. The same missionary told me that one time two chickens were stolen from his flock. He suspected the thief, went to him, recovered his chickens, and threatened dire penalties if such a thing should occur again. The thief promised faithfully that hence-forth he would obey the law of Moses and that it would never happen again. Although the missionary was willing to forget the incident, the local native chief of police, on hearing of it, pressed the mission-ary to file a suit. When he did, reluctantly, the case came to court, and the prisoner, pleading "not guilty," was acquitted because there were no witnesses.

Natives do not regard taking things from the Government as steal-ing. They were spoiled in the earlier days of American administration by a very generous Government, and by soldiers and sailors who shared food and all kinds of things. Now they think that all Govern-ment employees should share with them. The tremendous amount of Japanese war materials still lying around and being salvaged prompts them to annex unguarded Government materials which they can use. At some ports pilfering is a problem during the unloading of ships.

GOVERNMENT

Training for self-government in the Trust Territory, as was already discussed, has been started in districts where attempts are being made to inculcate fundamental principles. The next attempts are to take some form of self-government or part self-government to the island level. There it should remain for a long time. Island district congresses have been organized, and perhaps, after many years, a territorial government will take form.

In regard to native progress towards self-government, several things have to be kept in mind. The Japanese never gave the Micronesians any training in that way, for Japanese police masters, in charge in all districts in the islands, stood over the people, making them conform to all rules and regulations. They worked a good deal, of course, through Micronesian chiefs. However, the administration today might well borrow some of this policy, for in addition to learning their rights under democracy the natives should also be made acutely aware of their responsibilities. It must be remembered, too, that the changes which seem to have come have taken place under the urging of a conquering people who drove out the Japanese at the point of the sword. If the natives were suddenly left to themselves, they would very soon revert to their old way of living.

In some districts in the islands there is a Government "headquarters" in a rain-soaked, wind-swept hut, where records are blotted out, and money is stolen. Formerly a Japanese police master sat all day long in a place which was then kept spick and span in a landscaped plot with Japanese shrubbery along the driveways. Under his supervision Micronesians assisted in keeping the books.

Nowadays the natives are told that they must keep their own records, elect officials, support an educational program, maintain their schools, and learn the principles of self-government. They have as yet an imperfect idea of what it all means!* For example, the members of a council do not want to accept responsibility for a decision in which eight vote "yes" and two persist in voting "no." They have never had such a responsibility and would like to pass it on to some-

---

* A district administrator in the Trusteeship Islands who read this wrote that this sentence "is a masterpiece of understatement."

one else, for it is only after many years of training and experience that they can face up to that element of democracy.

The most important factor in the administrative situation is that the American idea of democracy, a Western concept, is not understood by the Micronesian. He as yet has not been able to think it through in terms of his obligations toward the social organization to which he belongs. He cannot see how the individualism of democracy can advance his self-interest within the concept of his own society and community, a concept which the administration also on its part is yet too inexperienced to understand.

It must be realized that the natives may not be pushed into self-government, but that the process of evolution, always slow, and at times painful, must go on largely by their own efforts. It will be at least thirty years before the Micronesians themselves will be able to operate a homestead program. They may be competent enough, but they will not consider it wrong to give a chief any homestead land he asks for, whether or not he fulfills the qualifications laid down. A hopeful trend among young men is setting in, in that they would like individual ownership of land. The older people in general still want clan ownership.

There will be no such thing as informed public opinion in Micronesia for a long time into the future. Even if a native is well trained, he will slip back into indifference if supervision is removed at a too early date. A German who has lived continuously for seventeen years in Micronesia maintains there is little change in native ways of thinking during that time. It will be at least thirty years—a whole generation—before there is any noticeable change in native attitude.

The Department of the Interior is at a disadvantage in governing the Trust Territory in that the United States has never laid down any policy in regard to governing native people. It is commonly said in the Trust Territory that the farther away from district headquarters, the less confusion there is about the policy of the Government, for, of course, the farther away from headquarters, the less upset are the traditional ways of living of the natives. What is needed is a policy at a high level which is adapted to the social organization of the people. After all, the islands are some six thousand miles away from the "interior." With an untrained staff, poor equipment, and insufficient transportation, the officers of the Trust Territory are struggling to ascertain just what they should know to do a good job.

They are so busy trying to master their office jobs that they have not the time to get out to make the close contacts with the natives and to give them the direct supervision which is essential in applying any policy at this stage of their development. Few members of the Ponape Administration, for example, have ever visited Kiti, an important district on that island. On the other hand, there is enough work in that district for two officers of Island Affairs. If, as in the British South Pacific Territories, the officials were required to tour their areas annually, this problem would be partially solved. The lack of continuous administrative policies has also a poor influence on their morale.

There have been five district administrators, two interim administrators, and nine Island Affairs officers in the Ponape District since the war. Continuity of policy is therefore difficult, unless it is laid down at the highest level. The High Commissioner of the Trust Territory must be one who has come up through the ranks, who has served in the administration of the Trust Territory, and who, therefore, knows from actual contacts with the islands what the problems are.

Sometime in the future it is hoped that there will be developed a decentralized organization for the Trust Territory in which specially trained field representatives will be distributed in the more important atolls and other islands to engage in various activities, not as specialists, but as advisers to work with the Micronesians in education, economics, agriculture, practical craftsmanship, and other fields in which their advice and assistance will be of value.

In this connection several departments of the Government could be effectively combined—Island Affairs, Agriculture, and Education, for example. They deal with three things basically related. The knowledge required in each for good work is elementary compared with American standards, and a staff member in any one of these could become familiar with what is required in the other two. It should be possible for the agriculturist or the educator to rise to be head of Island Affairs, which, with Health and Sanitation, is one of the more important departments of the Government. Another reason for such a combination is the small population of the Territory.

In regard to political changes in Micronesia, to urge haste and strive for a violent, cataclysmic or dramatic coup would be fraught with great unhappiness for the natives. There has long been an extended family form of control in the islands—a form of self-government—with a happy people living under it. The way of political advance involves careful study and observance of the needs and factors underlying the existing situation. Over long generations the natives themselves have worked out systems to meet conditions imposed by their environment. Continuity of good government depends on a general evolutionary change of existing controls in the present extended family setup, worked out by the people themselves, assisted by the administration.

A problem in the Trust Territory is finding the best natives to train in the various branches of the Government service. Some of them hold their jobs merely on the basis of knowing a little English, but they have neither the respect nor the confidence of the people at large because they come from obscure families who have no social or political standing in the community. All through the Trust Territory, particularly on Koror, Ponape, and Yap, the natives respect rank and family.

In connection with government, it must be kept in mind that the islands of Micronesia are of paramount importance to the people of the United States as outposts of defense. They were acquired at the sacrifice of thousands of Americans in our fight to preserve the standards of liberty in a free and unfettered world. Measures for defense must continue and will continue. They can be reconciled with the interests of the natives in their slow advance economically, socially, and politically, and in their present more rapid advance toward better health and sanitation. The United States is in the Trust Territory of the Pacific to stay for a long time, judging by world events. It follows, then, that the islands should be governed in such a way as to secure friendliness, loyalty, and cooperation throughout the indigenous populations. The lives and destinies of the people are strictly a civil matter; the tactical military problems are matters for the Pentagon. The Trusteeship of the Pacific Islands differs from all others in that it is called a strategic Trusteeship, which means that in the administration of the islands the authorities have the double obligation not only to take care of the interests of the people, but to govern the Territory in such a way as to contribute to the peace of the world. The United States, committed with conviction to a long-term partnership in Pacific security, must retain certain areas under military control.

The nature of the Micronesians themselves presents difficulties and hinders progress in our sense of the word. Secretiveness is a common characteristic not only on Ponape, but throughout Micronesia. The Palauans want the administration to enact a law that no one may go around at night without a light. According to their old customs no one went about unannounced. In all the islands, people spy so that they can gossip about one another.

It is difficult to ascertain how things are going among the natives not only because of their secretiveness but also because of the language barrier. Among those who speak English, some will tell one story, and others a very different version of the same circumstance. Knowing that Americans have difficulty in understanding what is taking place, some of the people, with ulterior motives, misrepresent the situation. Here again the lack of tenure for Government employees militates strongly against good government of the natives. After many years of foreign rule, techniques for manipulating foreign administrators are now well developed and very practical. An American is just beginning to learn something about the natives when he has to leave. And knowing his term of office will be up in two years, he cannot be expected to take a deep interest in them anyway. He will have to study native ways for some time before he realizes that the main reason an individual does not save is that there are so many ways for the members of his clan, his extended family, his brothers or his parents to get his money away from him.

But because of the lack of a desire to save money, we must not get the impression that the Micronesians are very different human beings from ourselves. They do accumulate material goods that they think are worth saving. As has already been pointed out, they save breadfruit in pits for future use. The coconut tree is their bank. Some of them save money to buy bags of cement to make the foundations of new houses. Generally a man can buy only a few at a time and he mixes and pours that amount. When he can buy more, work on the foundation progresses and in two or three years the house is finished. Their skills in boat building and native house building, handed down as capital from father to son, would not have lessened if they had not been disparaged by foreigners.

The Micronesians are very conscientious about some things—carrying letters, for example, in islands where there is no mail delivery at all. If a note is given to a native for someone on a distant island, it always gets to him though weeks may elapse in the process of delivering it. A missionary who was stationed for many years in the Mortlock Islands told the author a story of mail-carrying associated with the natives' ardent love of smoking. Letters came to him at intervals from Truk—a long distance in point of time and travel in small boats. The Mortlock people roll their own cigarettes with tobacco purchased in Truk, and sometimes are very short of paper. Occasionally the letter addressed to him was taken from its envelope and the envelope was used for cigarette paper. On one occasion when the writing left a wide margin, the margin was carefully torn off and used also. But the written part was delivered to him intact. People in Truk, after getting to know these difficulties about cigarette paper, formed the habit, when giving a letter to a native, of giving him also some extra paper for his cigarettes. A roll of newspaper is a valued present on some islands, though the natives will not read it.

The natives of mixed blood, different from pure Micronesians, must be regarded in a different light. It has to be kept in mind that many leading chiefs and "native" businessmen have foreign blood in their veins: Spanish, German, Japanese, American, or British. Some of the more outstanding had Irish grandfathers or great-grandfathers who forsook the "ould sod" for a piece of coral. The great majority of part-Micronesians are Japanese mixtures. Most of these people are in mental development above the average pure-blooded Micronesian commoners. The chiefs, however, throughout the South Seas, are superior to all others both in physical development and in mental power.

The basic weakness in the administrators, lack of training and experience, is being very gradually overcome. Members of the staff from the top down have never before had any occasion to acquire or utilize the kind of training and experience necessary in the Trust Territory. It is to the credit of the personnel that they have made much progress in the short period they have been operating. However, a sound and comprehensive solution of local problems is too much to expect of a temporary staff with men whose experience in civil administration is in many cases slight and whose careers are not closely bound up with the future of the islands. A permanent administration, defined and guided by organic legislation and making full use of the steadily increasing knowledge of Trusteeship problems, has a far greater chance of success.

There is an evident inconsistency between American administrative policy and its actual implementation in the field. There appears to be an ambivalence in our whole approach to the problems of administering dependent peoples. On the one hand, we profess to respect and to preserve tradition and custom, while on the other we attempt to bring to the natives that which we judge to be best in our own culture, and which, therefore, we think must be best for them. This frequently leads to embarrassing situations, especially among members of a staff who have had little or no previous experience with native populations. Before a native does away with his traditional way of living and throws away his good customs, he had better make certain that he has something of value to replace them.

The Department of the Interior could well follow the excellent precedent set by the Navy when it was charged with the administration of the Trust Territory. It had a special school where its officers were trained in anthropology, geography, administration, and other social sciences before they were sent to the islands. Such training, of course, would be expensive, but it would lead to a better selection of personnel, and that, in turn, would be a partial solution. Another possibility would be to make the appointment of the officer for Island Affairs a three-year appointment with the privilege of taking one-quarter in training at Stanford University where the Navy officers were indoctrinated. So long as the present lack of tenure holds, promising young people cannot be induced to enter the service. As was already stated, they are recruited for the Trust Territory for only a two-year period, at the end of which, when they are just beginning to be oriented toward the natives and their problems, they go home. Tenure for Government employees is a real problem in the Trust Territory; as one administrator there expressed it, "From the employment point of view it is terrible."

Unanticipated difficulties of living in the tropics militate against morale. Few Americans find in the islands the South Sea paradise they have dreamed of. Coral rocks, sharp and dangerous, skirt the shores; natives die of tetanus from cuts made by them. There is little swimming for there are very few beaches with sand. After one is in the water, tridacna clams, sting rays, and "Portuguese men of war" are hazards. Indoors, flour soon spoils, powdered eggs are used for frying, sugar and salt must be kept in hot-boxes, and clothes must be hung in closets where electric bulbs are continually burning to prevent mildew. Under these conditions, the maintenance of morale among members of the administration and their families is an important factor in general welfare.

The establishment of the headquarters of the administration of the Trust Territory in Guam is important from the point of view of shopping for women. At Agana they have rest and relaxation and can temporarily forget the trials of housekeeping in the tropics.

The presence of Guam in the heart of the Territory may affect the outlook of the Micronesians too, enabling them to broaden their horizon in every way. The High Commissioner of the Trust Territory has his headquarters there; the Bank of Guam serves the small needs of the islands; and until recently Micronesians went to Guam for all their professional training.

Most buildings in the Trust Territory are of wartime construction —old quonsets, wooden shacks, and the like. They are wearing out, as is equipment of all sorts. There is no money for permanent roads; and jeeps, pickup trucks, and heavier vehicles bounce and rattle over roads that cause abnormal depreciation of rolling stock.

There is one problem the solution of which must guide all forms of planned development in the Trust Territory: the transition from one form of culture to a new way of living. A basic difficulty lies in the disappearance of the old customs, for the administration has gone far enough now—perhaps a bit too far—in encouraging their disappearance. The present situation should be allowed to crystallize, and further changes should develop slowly while the situation is observed very carefully. The task is, therefore, one of easing the adjustment and ensuring that the best features of Western civilization are disseminated without disrupting local social organization.

What should be the attitude of the administration of the Trust Territory toward the native people? They should respect their beliefs, institutions, social organization, and culture. They should avoid interfering with institutions which do not militate against the best interests of the indigenous population. For example, they should allow a yam cult to continue where there is no question of sufficient food for the population, for, if and when it becomes useless to the natives, it will gradually disappear of its own accord.

The basis for a sound administration of the Trust Territory can be stated in two general propositions. The first is indirect rule. The natives are fully capable of running their own internal affairs. The second is economic rehabilitation in which the islanders can become self-sufficient by a combination of peasant farming and copra production. Local institutions must be oriented to local needs. The Micronesians probably will never be completely self-sufficient, but by the granting of aid specifically designed to establish an integrated socioeconomic system, demoralization can be avoided; the natives will be able to contribute a greater share of their own upkeep, and the cost to the United States will be less over the years.

Deep-rooted beliefs, attitudes, and values are easily overlooked by administrators of native peoples, since they are usually unspoken and often unconscious. Prejudices, fears, loves, attachments, kinds of pride, jealousies, magical beliefs, habits of feeling and of symbolizing are all part of Micronesian existence. The administrator should recognize their great significance because such habits are not isolated phenomena but form patterns which are interrelated one with another and which, as a whole, are integrated in the native life.

More studies of native ways of living and particularly native ways of thinking will have to be written in terms of their bearing on administrative problems before much progress can be expected in guiding the Micronesians into improved circumstances. The anthropological studies that have been made to date should be utilized more fully by a wider segment of Trust Territory personnel. Frequently, people working with natives every day are unaware of simple facts of native anthropology and custom.

Since 1947 the Trust Territory research program has involved some 120 scientists drawn from thirty universities and other institutions, principally in the fields of anthropology, entomology, and ecology. These specialists have prepared reports on their investigations and, to date, many of the reports in anthropology, in entomology and conchology, and other fields, particularly biology, have been published by museums or in scientific journals.

Of the scores of studies of various kinds made since the war, few have been made available to the rank and file of the members of the administration in terms which are valuable to them in their work. Though the anthropological studies are excellent academic treatises, they are organized and presented in a way that is of little value to district administrators. For example, a study of "The Role of The Trukese Mother"* is an excellent means for gaining insight into the

* See references on Truk.

culture of the Trukese, but no administrator is going to wade through it. Furthermore, it is a single-spaced mimeographed document. The first thought of the scientists is to have their studies read by their chiefs and colleagues so that their scholarship will be recognized. The author was asked over and over again by junior members of the administration, "Couldn't we see some of the studies and articles people write about these islands?" On the other hand, the situation would profit greatly if the administrators and the officers for island affairs had a little training in anthropology, both for their own work and better to evaluate, from a practical standpoint, the work done by professional anthropologists. Three officials at least should have a good training in anthropology—the agriculturist, the Island Affairs officer, and the educator. A knowledge of agriculture alone is of little use to a man dealing with the yam cult of Ponape.

Applied anthropology is the more important in Micronesia because the natives are broken up into units with diverse customs, institutions, and languages. However, a study of how to apply a modern administration to the people of one district has value in any other. The concepts are the same, though the application is different. Education in anthropology teaches how to cope more readily with any situation.

The United States does not have within its Federal system of employment a colonial service. Broadly speaking it has only the civil service, and the Foreign Service system. Neither of these is suited to the Trust Territory employment situation. The United States is not yet laying the groundwork of training personnel for what must constitute a long-time job. An orientation course was established in September, 1952, at the Honolulu headquarters to acquaint recruits and their dependents with living and working conditions in the Territory. A course of this kind, lasting a few weeks, is of little value.

Less time should be given annually to the collection and compilation of statistics. It is impracticable for members of the administration to go out into the field merely to gather accurately the figures which are called for in annual reports. On the other hand, entire dependency cannot be placed on the figures gathered by the natives. However, progress is necessarily so slow in almost all aspects of native welfare that biennial reports of figures obtained less haphazardly than they are at present would mean more to readers of these reports. Members of the staff would then have more time to get to know the Micronesians of their districts and would be able to include in their reports discussions of progress achieved and, more important still, the methods by which it was achieved. This is, of course, a point for the Trusteeship Council of the United Nations to decide, but from the author's experience on the Secretariat he is convinced that the same suggestion applies to the three other Trusteeships in the Pacific.

A very important consideration in the advance of the people of the Trust Territory is that progress in any one field must be geared to progress in other fields. If the cash income of the population is increased and they are not sufficiently advanced socially to spend the additional income wisely, their last state may be worse than the first. Outboard motors are not necessary for many Ponapeans who have them; it would have been much better for them to spend their money in improving their elementary homes. On the other hand, it is no service to the natives to help them to acquire tastes that they have no means of satisfying with their present or prospective incomes. They would rather eat American corned beef than yams, but where can they get the money to buy it? Furthermore, they are not likely to be politically stable if they are not self-sufficient economically.

Education, especially, must be held to the pace of economic, social, and political development. It must prepare young people to cope with the gradually changing social, economic, and political environment, and help them to assume growing responsibilities which go along with their advancement.

There will be economic, political, and social difficulties as the Micronesians see their old customs and traditions disappear without anything adequate as replacement. The change-over period will have many pains and aches for them as well as for the administration. This, a basic idea important for the administration to grasp and for the natives to understand, will have to be consistently kept in mind over a period of many years.

The question of how far to impose our economic and cultural patterns on the Micronesians is a delicate one, but one thing is sure: there must be only a very slow evolution. The natives will continue to live in their great watery fastness, little disturbed by modern currents of world commerce. The indigenous tempo of life is leisurely and the indigenous way of living involves an amplitude of time. In the long future sequence of island events, the first phase of American administration is less than a ripple on the great blue expanse of ocean that surrounds the islands of the Trust Territory.

REFERENCES

Bailey, K. H., "Dependent Areas of the Pacific," *Foreign Affairs*, 24 (3): 494-512, April, 1946.

Chapman, W. McL., "Tuna in the Mandated Islands," *Far Eastern Survey*, Vol. 15, No. 20, October, 1946.

Clyde, Paul H., *Japan's Pacific Mandate* (New York: Macmillan, 1935), 244 pp.

Converse, Elizabeth, "The United States as Trustee: I, American Trusteeship of Pacific Islands, Security Measures; II, Our Responsibility for Micronesian Welfare Cannot Be Discharged Cheaply or Easily"; *Far Eastern Survey*, 18: 260-263, Nov. 2, 1949; 18: 277-283, Nov. 30, 1949.

Emerson, R., "American Policy Toward Pacific Dependencies," *Pacific Affairs*, 20: 259-275, September, 1947.

Goodenough, W. H., "Native Astronomy in Micronesia: A Rudimentary Science," *Sci. Monthly*, 73 (2): 105-110 (1951).

Gressit, J. L., *Insects of Micronesia*, "Introduction," Vol. 1 (Bernice P. Bishop Museum, 1954).

Mason, Leonard E., "Trusteeship in Micronesia," *Far Eastern Survey*, 17 (9): 105-108, May 5, 1948.

Murdock, George P., *Social Organization and Government in Micronesia*, CIMA Report No. 19.

Nugent, L. E., "Coral Reefs in the Gilbert, Marshall, and Caroline Islands," *Bull. Geol. Soc. Amer.*, Vol. 57, pp. 735-780 (1946).

Oliver, Douglas L. (Ed.), *Planning Micronesia's Future: A Summary of the United States Commercial Company's Economic Survey of Micronesia, 1946* (Cambridge: Harvard University Press, 1951).

Pelzer, K. J., "Micronesia—A Changing Frontier," *World Politics*, 2, Jan., 1950, 251-266.

Reed, W. W., *Climatological Data for the Tropical Islands of the Pacific Ocean (Oceania)* (U.S. Department of Agriculture, Weather Bureau, *Monthly Weather Review*, Supplement 28, 1927).

Robbins, Robert R., "United States Trusteeship for the Territory of the Pacific Islands," *U.S. Department of State Bulletin*, 16 (409): 783-790, May 4, 1947.

Saunders, Lyle, *Cultural Difference and Medical Care* (New York: Russell Sage Foundation, 1954).

Sayre, Francis B. "The Pacific Islands We Hold," *Atlantic*, 185 (7): 70-74, January, 1950.

Thilenius, G. (ed.), *Ergebnisse der Südsee Expedition, 1908-10*

(Hamburg, 1914-1938). Twelve volumes of comprehensive studies in German, by areas.

United Nations, "Report on Pacific Islands Trust Territory, with Summary of Trusteeship Council Debate," *United Nations Weekly Bulletin*, 7: 108-115, illus., Aug. 1, 1949.

United States Department of the Interior, annual reports of the High Commissioner of the Trust Territory of the Pacific Islands to the Secretary of the Interior.

United States Department of State, *Draft Trusteeship Agreement for the Japanese Mandated Islands*, with article-by-article explanatory comments, and statement by President Truman and the U.S. Representatives on the Security Council (Washington, Far Eastern Series Pub. 2784, 1947).

————, "Report on United States Trust Territory," *U.S. Department of State Bulletin*, 21: 47 (1949).

United States Navy Department, *Handbook on the Trust Territory of Pacific Islands* (Washington, D.C., 1948). 311 pp., 20 plates, map. Prepared at School of Naval Administration, Stanford, Calif.

Useem, John, "The American Pattern of Military Government in Micronesia," *American Jour. of Sociology*, 51 (2): 93-102, September, 1945.

————, "Americans as Governors of Natives in the Pacific," *Jour. of Social Issues*, August, 1946.

————, "Social Reconstruction in Micronesia," *Far Eastern Survey*, 15 (2): 21-24, Jan. 30, 1946.

Weitzell, E. C., "Resource Development in the Pacific Mandated Islands," *Jour. Land and Public Utility Economics*, 22 (3): 199-212, August, 1946.

Index

Items in the index are grouped mainly under the respective islands. Cross references for more important topics are added as a further aid.

Abortion, 321, 322
Act of Berlin, 6
Administration of Pac. Dependencies, 11, 352, 354, 359, 362, 364, 370, 373; lack of training, 368, 369; morale of, 370. *See also* Government *under* Guam, Hawaii, Marshall Islands, Mariana Islands, Palau, Ponape, Truk, Yap; and Administration *under* Samoa, American; and Trust Territory of Pacific Islands, United States
Agana, 370. *See also under* Guam
Agriculture, 372; extension, 350; future of in Trust Terr., 349-353. *See also under* various islands
Angaur. *See under* Palau
Animal husbandry, 358
Anthropologist, 352
Anthropolgy, 369, 371, 372
Atolls, 3, 5, 163, 164, 189, 292, 293, 324
August, Chief, 343, 344
Aunuu, 67

Babelthuap. *See under* Palau
Boat making, 344. *See also* Canoe builders, Canoes
Brahman cattle, 350
Breadfruit, 41, 76, 77, 78, 80, 133, 135, 140, 329, 330, 331; famine, 329; study of, necessary, 349. *See also under* Truk
British Samoa. *See* Western Samoa
British South Pacific Territories, 365
Buildings: dilapidation of, 370. *See also* Houses *under* Samoa, American

Cacao, 79, 114-115, 194
California tuna fishery, 352-353
Canoe builders, 344, 357
Canoes, 331, 333, 342, 345
Carabao, 349. *See also under* Guam
Caroline Islands, 162, 187; to Spain, 171
Carpentry, 342, 357
Cats, 356
Cattle, 350, 358. *See also under* Guam, Mariana Islands, Ponape, Samoa, American; Hawaii, Territory of, grazing
Cement, 367
Central Medical School. *See* Suva Medical School
Cereus, night-blooming, 15
Chants, 49, 338
Chickens, 330, 331, 358, 362
Chiefs, 335, 368; in heaven, 360; obedience to, 359. *See also* Administration *under* Samoa, American; and Government
Chinese, 16. *See also under* Hawaii, Guam
Christianity, 361; modern concepts of, 360. *See also* Missionaries
Christmas, 334
Church: members, 336. *See also* Missionaries
Cincinnati, 351
Civil affairs, 359
Civil government, 347
Clans, 321, 347, 356, 360. *See also under* Ponape, Truk
Cleveland, President, 6

377

388   INDEX

Yap—*Continued*
  Exchange, 240; ceremonial, 233, 241
  Food: taboos, 240
  Future of, 238-242
  Government, 233-235
  Grass skirts, 211, 216, 227, 228-
    229, 236, 242
  Herbs: medicinal, 231, 232
  House platforms, 209, 213, 214, 218,
    219, 223
  Infant marriage, 231
  Infant mortality, 214
  Land: burned over, 209, 217; estate
    (*tabinaw*) 239; registry, 239; sale
    of, 220, 221; tenure, 218-221
  Liquor (*achif*), 232-233
  Lizards, 211
  Loincloths, 208, 228
  Magic, 232
  Magistrates, 233; cooperation of,
    233; Council of, 233
  Medicine men, 231, 232
  Medicines: native, 234
  Natural environment, 209, 211
  Rainfall, 210, 211, 217
  Sex practices, 214, 230, 234; sterility,
    234

Yap—*Continued*
  Shell money, 229, 231, 233, 241
  Social life, 221-233
  Stone money, 213, 214, 218, 358
  Taro, 215-216
  Temperature, 210
  Trails, 210
  Villages: accessibility of, 221, 223
Yap, East Islands: Outlying atolls,
    Outlying islands, 235-238
  Ancestor worship, 236
  Bamboo, 236
  Banana: fiber, 236; "wrap around,"
    236
  Chestnuts, 236
  Discovery, 236
  Exchange of goods, 236
  Ghosts, 236
  Hibiscus fiber, 236
  History, 236
  Loincloths, 236; ceremonial, 236
  Pandanus sails, 236
  Taboos, 237
  Trading, 238
  Tribute, 236, 237
  Typhoons, 237